Programming Open Service Gateways with Java Embedded Server™ Technology

The Java™ Series
Lisa Friendly, Series Editor
Tim Lindholm, Technical Editor
Ken Arnold, Technical Editor of The Jini™ Technology Series
Jim Inscore, Technical Editor of The Java™ Series, Enterprise Edition

Ken Arnold, James Gosling, David Holmes
The Java™ Programming Language, Third Edition

Joshua Bloch
Effective Java™ Programming Language Guide

Greg Bollella, James Gosling, Ben Brosgol, Peter Dibble, Steve Furr, David Hardin, Mark Turnbull
The Real-Time Specification for Java™

Mary Campione, Kathy Walrath, Alison Huml
*The Java™ Tutorial, Third Edition:
A Short Course on the Basics*

Mary Campione, Kathy Walrath, Alison Huml, Tutorial Team
*The Java™ Tutorial Continued:
The Rest of the JDK™*

Patrick Chan
The Java™ Developers Almanac 2000

Patrick Chan, Rosanna Lee
*The Java™ Class Libraries, Second Edition, Volume 2:
java.applet, java.awt, java.beans*

Patrick Chan, Rosanna Lee
The Java™ Class Libraries Poster, Sixth Edition, Part 1

Patrick Chan, Rosanna Lee
The Java™ Class Libraries Poster, Sixth Edition, Part 2

Patrick Chan, Rosanna Lee, Doug Kramer
*The Java™ Class Libraries, Second Edition, Volume 1:
java.io, java.lang, java.math, java.net, java.text, java.util*

Patrick Chan, Rosanna Lee, Doug Kramer
*The Java™ Class Libraries, Second Edition, Volume 1:
Supplement for the Java™ 2 Platform,
Standard Edition, v1.2*

Kirk Chen, Li Gong
*Programming Open Service Gateways with Java™
Embedded Server*

Zhiqun Chen
*Java Card™ Technology for Smart Cards:
Architecture and Programmer's Guide*

Li Gong
*Inside Java™ 2 Platform Security:
Architecture, API Design, and Implementation*

James Gosling, Bill Joy, Guy Steele, Gilad Bracha
The Java™ Language Specification, Second Edition

Jonni Kanerva
The Java™ FAQ

Doug Lea
*Concurrent Programming in Java™, Second Edition:
Design Principles and Patterns*

Rosanna Lee, Scott Seligman
*JNDI API Tutorial and Reference:
Building Directory-Enabled Java™ Applications*

Sheng Liang
*The Java™ Native Interface:
Programmer's Guide and Specification*

Tim Lindholm and Frank Yellin
The Java™ Virtual Machine Specification, Second Edition

Vlada Matena and Beth Stearns
*Applying Enterprise JavaBeans™:
Component-Based Development for the J2EE™ Platform*

Roger Riggs, Antero Taivalsaari, Mark VandenBrink
*Programming Wireless Devices with the Java™ 2
Platform, Micro Edition*

Henry Sowizral, Kevin Rushforth, and Michael Deering
The Java 3D™ API Specification, Second Edition

Kathy Walrath, Mary Campione
*The JFC Swing Tutorial:
A Guide to Constructing GUIs*

Seth White, Maydene Fisher, Rick Cattell, Graham Hamilton, and Mark Hapner
*JDBC™ API Tutorial and Reference, Second Edition:
Universal Data Access for the Java™ 2 Platform*

Steve Wilson, Jeff Kesselman
*Java™ Platform Performance:
Strategies and Tactics*

The Jini™ Technology Series

Eric Freeman, Susanne Hupfer, Ken Arnold
JavaSpaces™ Principles, Patterns, and Practice

Jim Waldo/Jini™ Technology Team
*The Jini™ Specifications, Second Edition,
edited by Ken Arnold*

The Java™ Series, Enterprise Edition

Rick Cattell, Jim Inscore, Enterprise Partners
*J2EE™ Technology in Practice:
Building Business Applications with the Java™ 2 Platform,
Enterprise Edition*

Patrick Chan, Rosanna Lee
*The Java™ Class Libraries Poster, Enterprise Edition,
version 1.2*

Nicholas Kassem, Enterprise Team
*Designing Enterprise Applications with the Java™ 2
Platform, Enterprise Edition*

Bill Shannon, Mark Hapner, Vlada Matena, James Davidson, Eduardo Pelegri-Llopart, Larry Cable, Enterprise Team
*Java™ 2 Platform, Enterprise Edition:
Platform and Component Specifications*

http://www.javaseries.com

Programming Open Service Gateways with Java Embedded Server™ Technology

Kirk Chen
Li Gong

ADDISON–WESLEY

Boston • San Francisco • New York • Toronto • Montreal
London • Munich • Paris • Madrid
Capetown • Sydney • Tokyo • Singapore • Mexico City

Copyright © 2002 Sun Microsystems, Inc.
901 San Antonio Road, Palo Alto, California 94303 U.S.A.
All rights reserved.

Sun Microsystems, Inc., has intellectual property rights relating to implementations of the technology described in this publication. In particular, and without limitation, these intellectual property rights may include one or more U.S. patents, foreign patents, or pending applications. Sun, Sun Microsystems, the Sun Logo, Java Embedded Server, Java, Jini, Solaris, Forte, JDK, PersonalJava, J2ME, JavaBeans, EJB, and JavaMail are trademarks or registered trademarks of Sun Microsystems, Inc., in the United States and other countries. UNIX is a registered trademark in the United States and other countries, exclusively licensed through X/Open Company, Ltd.

THIS PUBLICATION IS PROVIDED "AS IS" WITHOUT WARRANTY OF ANY KIND, EITHER EXPRESS OR IMPLIED, INCLUDING, BUT NOT LIMITED TO, THE IMPLIED WARRANTIES OF MERCHANTABILITY, FITNESS FOR A PARTICULAR PURPOSE, OR NON-INFRINGEMENT.

THIS PUBLICATION COULD INCLUDE TECHNICAL INACCURACIES OR TYPOGRAPHICAL ERRORS. CHANGES ARE PERIODICALLY ADDED TO THE INFORMATION HEREIN; THESE CHANGES WILL BE INCORPORATED IN NEW EDITIONS OF THE PUBLICATION. SUN MICROSYSTEMS, INC., MAY MAKE IMPROVEMENTS AND/OR CHANGES IN THE PRODUCT(S) AND/OR THE PROGRAM(S) DESCRIBED IN THIS PUBLICATION AT ANY TIME.

Copyright information for Appendix B, "OSGi Service Gateway Specification," appears on page 438.

The publisher offers discounts on this book when ordered in quantity for special sales. For more information, please contact:

Pearson Education Corporate Sales Division
One Lake Street
Upper Saddle River, NJ 07458
(800) 382-3419
corpsales@pearsontechgroup.com

Visit AW on the Web: www.awl.com/cseng/

Cataloging-in-Publication Data

Chen, Kirk.
　Programming open service gateways with Java embedded server technology / Kirk Chen, Li Gong.
　　p. cm.
　Includes bibliographical references and index.
　ISBN 0-201-71102-8
　1. Java (Computer program language) 2. Embedded computer systems—Programming.
I. Gong, Li. II. Title.

QA76.73.J38 C4775 2001
005.2'762—dc21   2001033573

All rights reserved. No part of this publication may be reproduced, stored in a retrieval system, or transmitted, in any form, or by any means, electronic, mechanical, photocopying, recording, or otherwise, without the prior consent of the publisher. Printed in the United States of America. Published simultaneously in Canada.

Text printed on recycled paper
1 2 3 4 5 6 7 8 9 10—CRS—0504030201
First printing, August 2001

To Anselm Baird-Smith
—Kirk

To Isabel Cho
—Li

Contents

Preface xiii

Acknowledgments xvii

1 Introduction 1
    1.1 The Internet and the Networked Home 2
    1.2 The Service Gateway 3
    1.3 Challenges 5
        1.3.1 A Multitude of Competing Solutions 5
        1.3.2 A New Application Environment 8
    1.4 Java Embedded Server Technology 9
    1.5 The Open Services Gateway Initiative 11
    1.6 Operational Model 13

2 Getting Started 15
    2.1 Setting Up the Java Embedded Server Software 15
    2.2 The "Home, Sweet Home" Bundle 16
        2.2.1 Create the Directory 16
        2.2.2 Define the Manifest 16
        2.2.3 Write an Activator 17
        2.2.4 Compile the Activator Class 17
        2.2.5 Pack Up 18
    2.3 Running the Bundle 19
        2.3.1 Getting Help 20
        2.3.2 The Cache Directory 21
        2.3.3 The Bundle Base URL 22
        2.3.4 Brief Summary of the Major Commands 22

3 Architecture and Basic Concepts 25
- 3.1 Motivation 25
- 3.2 Architecture 26
- 3.3 Service 27
- 3.4 Bundle 28
  - 3.4.1 A Bundle Is a Packaging Vehicle 28
  - 3.4.2 A Bundle Is a Functional Module 29
  - 3.4.3 The "Hooks" to the Framework 30
- 3.5 The Framework 32
- 3.6 Cooperation among Bundles and Services 33
  - 3.6.1 Exporting and Importing Packages 34
  - 3.6.2 Registering and Obtaining Services 37
  - 3.6.3 Package versus Service Dependency 38
- 3.7 Life within the Framework 39
  - 3.7.1 Installing a Bundle 39
  - 3.7.2 Starting the Bundle 40
  - 3.7.3 Importing Packages and Getting Services 40
  - 3.7.4 Handling the Dynamic Service Dependency 41
  - 3.7.5 Updating a Bundle 42
  - 3.7.6 Stopping and Uninstalling a Bundle 45
- 3.8 The Component-based Model 46
- 3.9 Forget CLASSPATH 49

4 Developing Bundles 51
- 4.1 Writing Service Bundles 51
  - 4.1.1 Design the Service Interface 52
  - 4.1.2 Implement the Service 53
  - 4.1.3 Register the Service in the Activator 54
  - 4.1.4 Define the Manifest Headers 55
  - 4.1.5 Create the Bundle 56
- 4.2 Same Service Interface, Different Implementations 56
- 4.3 Retrieving Resources from within the Bundle 60
- 4.4 Obtaining and Calling Registered Services 61
  - 4.4.1 Interbundle Dependency and Class Loading Issues ... 64
  - 4.4.2 Service Use Count 65
  - 4.4.3 Compiling Client Bundles 65

4.5	Service Factory 66
	4.5.1	Producing a Customized Service for Each Client Bundle .. 66
	4.5.2	Service Cache 69
	4.5.3	Customization for Getting and Releasing Service 70
4.6	Relevant `org.osgi.framework` APIs 73
	4.6.1	`BundleContext` Interface 73
	4.6.2	`ServiceReference` Interface 80
	4.6.3	`ServiceRegistration` Interface 80
4.7	Library Bundles 82
4.8	Advanced Examples 86
	4.8.1	A Mailer 86
	4.8.2	A Line Printer Daemon Print Service 89
4.9	Writing Bundles That Contain Native Code 96
4.10	Common Mistakes 105
	4.10.1	Activator 105
	4.10.2	Manifest 105
	4.10.3	Creating a JAR File 106

5 Cooperation among Service Bundles 107
5.1	Event Handling 107
5.2	Bundle State and Service Registration 111
5.3	Synchronous and Asynchronous Events 112
5.4	Dealing with Service Unregistration 114
	5.4.1	Don't Start without the Service 114
	5.4.2	Discovering Stale Service 115
	5.4.3	Carrying On without the Service 116
	5.4.4	Picking an Alternative 121
	5.4.5	Cascading Service Registration 123
	5.4.6	Refusing Service 125
5.5	Cooperation with Asynchronous Events 128

6 Design Patterns and Pitfalls 131
6.1	Designing the Service 131
	6.1.1	Separating Service Interface and Implementation 131
	6.1.2	Challenges in Designing a Service Interface 132
	6.1.3	Approaching an Interface Design 133
	6.1.4	The Social Aspect 139
6.2	Designing Library Bundles 139
6.3	Delegation and Callback 140

	6.4	Leveraging the Service Registry 143
	6.5	Threading 146
		6.5.1 Preventing Runaway Threads 146
		6.5.2 Writing a Multithread Server Bundle 148
		6.5.3 Using a Thread Pool............................ 152
	6.6	Managing Object Allocation 155
		6.6.1 Nullify References After Use..................... 156
		6.6.2 Managing References among Bundles.............. 157

7 Standard Services 161
7.1 The Log Service 161
7.1.1   Using `LogService` to Write Logs 161
7.1.2   Using `LogReaderService` to Get Logs 163
7.1.3   Performing Persistent Logging 165
7.2 The HTTP Service 168
7.2.1   The Standard `HttpService` API 168
7.2.2   Performing Basic Authentication.................. 181
7.2.3   The Extended HTTP Service 184

8 Device Access 187
8.1 Introduction 187
8.1.1   The Software Stack in Device Access 187
8.1.2   What Device Access Is *Not* 188
8.2 Motivation 189
8.3 Cast of Characters 191
8.3.1   Device Service 191
8.3.2   Driver Services................................... 193
8.3.3   Driver Locator 196
8.3.4   Device Manager................................... 196
8.4 Writing DA Services 198
8.4.1   The Base Driver.................................. 198
8.4.2   Device Detection 200
8.4.3   Device Refinement................................ 205
8.4.4   The Reconfiguration Process...................... 216
8.5 Putting It Together 218

9 Permission-based Security and Administration 225
9.1 Permission-based Security inside the Java 2 Platform 225
9.1.1   Code Source..................................... 226
9.1.2   Permission...................................... 226

	9.1.3	Policy 227
	9.1.4	Granting Permissions to Classes 228
	9.1.5	Security Manager 229
9.2	OSGi Permissions 229
	9.2.1	`AdminPermission` 229
	9.2.2	`ServicePermission` 229
	9.2.3	`PackagePermission` 230
	9.2.4	Permission Required by the Framework APIs 230
9.3	Enabling Security 231
	9.3.1	Setting Up a Policy 232
	9.3.2	Running with Security Enabled 232
9.4	Using Permissions in Your Service 234
	9.4.1	Checking Permissions 235
	9.4.2	Performing Privileged Actions 238
	9.4.3	Creating Your Own Permission Types 245
9.5	Administration 250
	9.5.1	Resolving Bundles Dynamically 251
	9.5.2	Relevant APIs 261

10 Future Directions 265

- 10.1 Removing Phantom Bundles 265
- 10.2 Dynamic Permissions 267
- 10.3 Preferences 268
- 10.4 User Administration 269
- 10.5 Configuration Management 269
- 10.6 What's Next 270

A Code Examples 271

A.1	Chapter 4—Developing Bundles 271
	A.1.1 The LPD Print Service 271
A.2	Chapter 8—Device Access 278
	A.2.1 Serial Service and Driver Locator 278
	A.2.2 Driver Service and Modem Service 284
	A.2.3 Web Interface to the Serial Ports 291
A.3	Chapter 9—Permission-based Security and Administration 297
	A.3.1 Parameter Services 297
	A.3.2 Parameter Configuration Servlet 305
	A.3.3 Facilitator 310

B OSGi Service Gateway Specification 321

    org.osgi.framework 323
        AdminPermission 332
        Bundle 335
        BundleActivator 350
        BundleContext 352
        BundleEvent 369
        BundleException 373
        BundleListener 375
        Configurable 376
        FrameworkEvent 378
        FrameworkListener 381
        InvalidSyntaxException 382
        PackagePermission 384
        ServiceEvent 388
        ServiceFactory 391
        ServiceListener 393
        ServicePermission 395
        ServiceReference 399
        ServiceRegistration 401
    org.osgi.service.device 404
        Device 406
        Driver 408
        DriverLocator 411
    org.osgi.service.http 413
        HttpContext 417
        HttpService 420
        NamespaceException 424
    org.osgi.service.log 426
        LogEntry 429
        LogListener 431
        LogReaderService 432
        LogService 434

Bibliography 439

Index 441

Preface

Technology is invented and advanced by, well, technical people. However, a truly successful technology is marked by its adoption by people in their daily lives. Few ponder radio frequency modulation when they turn on the TV, or the internal combustion engine when they drive around. The technology has disappeared behind the utility.

The last decade saw two new technologies begin to blend into our lives: the computer and the Internet. We only need to launch a browser and the resources of the World Wide Web are at our fingertips, and we are hard pressed to tell the difference between a computer and a game console, a personal digital assistant (such as PalmPilot), or a cell phone. It is now entirely feasible to bring services to smart consumer devices at home and to small businesses through the Internet. Utility providers and network, computer, wireless, consumer electronics, and home appliance companies recognize the tremendous potential and have started to tap into this market. As a result, new horizons are open for application developers.

The Open Services Gateway Initiative (OSGi) was formed to explore these exciting opportunities, and its membership includes such diverse companies as Bell South, Echelon, Electricite de France, IBM, Sun, Ericsson, Nokia, Sony, Maytag, and Whirlpool, to name just a few from a roster of more than 80 organizations. With these combined resources, OSGi stands a good chance to turn this vision into reality.

The OSGi Service Gateway Specification 1.0 defines a Java™ technology-based software architecture for developing and deploying services, which is the topic of this book.

What compels us to write this book, in addition to our enthusiasm for the emerging new applications, is the unique software model involved. We stumbled through a lot of unfamiliar territory ourselves when we worked on the Java Embedded Server™ product, the predecessor to the OSGi Service Gateway Specification, only to find our fellow developers encountering and struggling with the same class of problems. It is our hope to be able to elucidate the model and capture the hard-won solutions in one place.

This book is primarily for programmers interested in writing services for residential gateways in the Java programming language. It should also be useful to anyone who wants to learn about residential gateway technology and the efforts made by the OSGi consortium.

This book may be of interest to those who are involved with component-based software construction in general. Interestingly, nothing in the underlying programming model limits the kinds of applications that can be written. It aims at residential gateway applications at the "small" end of the spectrum in terms of code size and resource consumption, but it is just as viable for developing applications for desktop and enterprise environments. Indeed, the task will be made easier and the end result will be more powerful when fewer constraints on computing resources are imposed.

We assume the readers are well versed in the Java programming language and experienced in software development on the Java platform. However, no experience is needed in embedded systems at the hardware and operating system levels.

Many trade-offs on the contents of the book had to be considered, and these were not easy decisions to make. We wrote this book with the following goals in mind:

- **Practical.** This book is about *programming* service gateways and is primarily for programmers; therefore, a lot of its content is devoted to coding. The book does not dwell on the high-level vision, and it gets down to earth promptly. As a result, the material is best understood by practicing the examples near a computer. Reading it on a beach chair will almost surely ruin your vacation.

- **Software Only.** We are primarily concerned with the software aspect of the residential gateway, and particularly with applications for the Java platform. We don't deal with hardware design and configuration or operating system and system software of the gateway in this book.

- **"Horizontal."** One of the biggest challenges in developing examples for the book is to stay "horizontal" and relevant at the same time. By "horizontal" we mean you do not need to acquire highly specialized hardware and software to learn how to program a gateway. All the examples in this book can be built and run on a familiar personal computer or a workstation. We want to focus our effort on the generic mechanisms that apply to *all* service gateways with the OSGi architecture, rather than diverge into specifics of certain systems that are interesting to some readers but alien to others. For instance, as part of the Java Embedded Server project we have developed code to control a vending machine, a smart coffee maker, an NEC touch-panel golf score keeper, an Ericsson e-box, and an X10 lamp module. From first-hand experience we know that what we present is entirely within the realm of feasibility. However, the aforementioned applications are simply too complicated or have details that are too specialized to be good tutorials.

- **Realistic.** We are *not* going to program a refrigerator, a washing machine, a microwave, a thermostat, or a toaster in this book. It is still not possible to go to Sears and buy a freezer that watches inventory and downloads e-coupons. Our smart espresso machine, for which we programmed a Web interface to monitor its water level and temperature and to control caffeine potency, uses proprietary commands and is not generally available. Many of the similar appliances we've seen are prototypes. This, however, is more an issue of business development than technological know-how. With the application development paradigm presented here, you should be able to develop applications for these smart appliances when they do roll down the production line en masse.

- **Focused Scope.** The technologies applicable to residential gateway applications have mushroomed during the last few years. Each warrants a book of its own to treat the subject thoroughly. Therefore, we do not teach you BlueTooth, USB, or HomePNA here. We are confident that experts in these areas can readily plug implementations of these technologies into the OSGi framework after they have learned how it works and what benefits it brings.

Organization of the Book

You can read this book from cover to cover, or you can select the chapters that address your particular needs. For the impatient, it is possible to jump to Chapter 4 and try out the code in action, because clear step-by-step instructions are given. However, you are strongly encouraged to read Chapter 3, which puts things into context.

Chapter 1 describes the backdrop from which the residential gateway market emerged, and its propellants and challenges, then explains the history of the Java Embedded Server product and the OSGi consortium, and introduces our view of what OSGi is trying to achieve.

Chapter 2 outlines steps to develop your first bundle and familiarizes you with the Java Embedded Server execution environment.

Chapter 3 explains the OSGi architecture and basic concepts, including the interaction of various entities during interbundle class sharing, service registration and retrieval, and bundle life cycle operations.

Chapter 4 teaches you how to develop services, how to write library bundles, and how to include native code in your bundles. Two advanced examples are given in this chapter.

Chapter 5 analyzes the dynamic nature of cooperation with services, and proposes strategies to cope with the situation. Events are also discussed at the beginning of this chapter.

Chapter 6 describes design patterns and pitfalls.

Chapter 7 explains how to use the OSGi standard services: HTTP and Log services.

Chapter 8 explains the OSGi Device Access (DA) and how to develop services to communicate with devices using the DA.

Chapter 9 discusses permission-based security and administration.

Chapter 10 summarizes the issues being worked and our view of the future directions that the OSGi consortium could take.

Appendix A contains the complete source code of the examples in this book. Appendix B is a copy of the OSGi specification. A list of references is included at the end of the book.

Online Resources

A copy of the Java Embedded Server product can be downloaded from Sun Microsystems' Web site at

http://www.sun.com/software/embeddedserver

For updated information about the book, visit the following URL:

http://java.sun.com/docs/books/jes

Full details of the OSGi consortium can be found at

http://www.osgi.org

Acknowledgments

Kirk Chen

Many people have generously contributed their time and ideas to this book, for which I am truly grateful.

Jan Luehe reviewed the book with characteristic thoroughness. His meticulous attention to detail and unwavering insistence on clarity and accuracy greatly improved the quality of this book. David Bowen provided careful and thoughtful review; he made me think harder and be precise on many important topics. They both managed to achieve this despite their hectic schedules of working on the Java Embedded Server product and contributing to OSGi specification development activities. Anselm Baird-Smith, Zhiqun Chen, and Alice Tull provided in-depth comments. I would also like to thank Liang Zhu for his helpful feedback. They prompted me to clarify confusions and flesh out underdeveloped concepts in the early drafts of the book. Paru Somashekar reviewed the device access chapter and gave me good comments.

I am very grateful to the external reviewers, whom I have never met, for their encouragement, constructive criticism, and valuable comments. Barry Busler, Joshua Engel, Mark Kuharich, Lou Mauget, Kevin Ruland, Mike Talley, Daryl Wilding-McBride, and an anonymous reviewer provided detailed feedback for the book. Being too close to the material can be a liability. Their fresh perspective took me back a step to rethink some of my assumptions and to address issues that matter to the reader. Chapters have been restructured and contents added as a result of their suggestions.

Jan Luehe, David Bowen, Zhiqun Chen, and Suzanne Ahmed pointed out errors in the manuscript or brought my attention to them. The discussions I had with Christian Kurzke on device access were very enlightening.

This book benefited from working with other members of the OSGi consortium. Tommy Bohlin, B. J. Hargrave, Peter Kriens, and Ben Reed have made significant contributions to the evolution of the specification to its current state.

Sections 4.2, 6.4, and 9.5.1 cover or expand some of the solutions that they described in discussions.

I also want to thank Li Gong for giving me the opportunity to write this book. Tim Lindholm and Lisa Friendly provided me with helpful reviews; their advice also helped me navigate hurdles in the writing process. Julie DiNicola and Tyrrell Albaugh from Addison-Wesley patiently answered my questions; coordinated reviews, copyediting, and production; advised me on schedules; and undertook many other efforts for a complex book project.

Raj Mata provided me with marketing research materials. Keith Rodgers and Rob Patten both went over part of the book. My managers, Mark Fulks and Harry Burks, allowed me to take time off from a busy project schedule and gave me considerable latitude to work on the book, for which I'm very grateful.

I was privileged to have worked with Anselm Baird-Smith, Ross Dargahi, Pierre Delisle, Yaroslav Faybishenko, and Kevin Kluge on the first Java Embedded Server project, with Bob Mines as our manager. I am also blessed with the opportunity to work with David Bowen, David-John Burrowes, David Connelly, Ulrich Gall, Christian Kurzke, Jan Luehe, Alice Tull—who either worked on the OSGi specifications at one time or are still working on them—and many others comprising the extremely talented and dedicated Java Embedded Server team throughout its history. I owe my professional growth to what I have learned from my colleagues at Sun Microsystems.

ServiceSpace and its programming model are the brain child of Anselm Baird-Smith while he was at Sun Microsystems. He created the first working prototype, which became the basis for the Java Embedded Server product. The concept of bundles and their life cycles, services and the importance of their interface and implementation separation, the essential common hosting framework and service registry, the challenges and benefits of a component-based model, the crucial implementation detail of using class loaders to achieve insulation among bundles, the view of leveraging the underlying Java platform as much as possible (using JAR files for bundles and Java™ 2 Platform security), the design of HTTP service as the control point and user interface to the gateway through the use of servlets, and the relevance of such an application model to intelligent devices were but some of the ideas put forth by him and remain at the core of this software architecture today. It is only fitting for me to dedicate this book to him.

Finally, I am grateful to Michael Fleming, my undergraduate English professor, for having shown me that writing in the English language can be as rewarding as writing in programming languages.

Li Gong

I am grateful to past and current members of the Java Embedded Server team, without whom there would not be a Java Embedded Server product. I also appreciate the collaborative spirit and the technical insights offered by members of OSGi's Java Expert Group. It was my privilege to chair this group until the completion of the Open Service Gateway 1.0 specification. I am indebted to Kirk Chen, my coauthor who did most of the work when my new duties called me far away. I'd like to thank Dick Neiss, my manager during my tenure as head of the Server Products Group at the Consumer and Embedded Division, for his encouragement and support. Finally, I'd like to express my gratitude to Lisa Friendly and Tim Lindholm, editors of the Java series at Sun Microsystems, and Julie DiNicola and Mike Hendrickson from Addison-Wesley for making this book possible. Working with them has been a real pleasure.

CHAPTER 1

Introduction

X*COFFEE* was not what the designers of the Internet had in mind when they connected computers at research sites across the United States under the auspice of DARPA. Nor was it an expected application when the nuclear scientists at CERN invented the Web to facilitate information sharing. *XCoffee* refers to a video frame-grabber, installed in 1991, that is connected to a camera focused on a coffee machine in the Trojan Room at the Computer Laboratory of the University of Cambridge in England. Its installation had a very simple motivation. The Laboratory had a coffee club that shared the use of the coffee machine. Club members often negotiated several flights of stairs only to find the coffee pot empty. Frustrated, a couple of club members rigged up a system—including the camera, the frame-grabber, a client program, and a server program—in a day or two so that, with *XCoffee,* Cambridge students and faculty members could check, from the convenience of their computers, whether there was enough coffee or whether a new pot needed to be brewed. Eventually, everyone with access to the Web, from anywhere in the world, could view the status of the coffee pot (http://www.parkerinfo.com/coffee.htm). At the time, *XCoffee* was viewed with more amusement than understanding, but it served as a good indicator of what was to come.

In this chapter, we briefly trace the trend in Internet technology that led to the vision and opportunity of a networked home. We describe the service gateway as the functional nucleus in such an environment, depict the challenges facing software vendors trying to enter this market, explain the pioneering work of the Java Embedded Server™ product, and introduce the Java™ technology-based solution specified by the Open Services Gateway Initiative (OSGi) for developing and deploying services for the home.

1.1 The Internet and the Networked Home

Since the early 1990s, the Internet has grown tremendously and its impact is now felt in almost every aspect of our lives. It has changed the way we obtain entertainment, communicate, and conduct commerce, and is becoming a household presence like the telephone and the television.

Because of the ubiquity of the Internet and the vast resources it makes available, a computer that is *not* connected to the Internet becomes less useful, and the features available locally become less relevant. In fact, many people own a general-purpose computer solely to access the Internet.

As the Internet matures, *services* are being offered in addition to contents. We shop, trade stocks, plan trips, and get news on the Internet, and we want to do these things not only sitting at a desk, but also on the road. Thanks to hardware that is getting more powerful and less expensive, many smart and connected devices such as mobile phones, pagers, and personal digital assistants have emerged on the market. As a result, a traditional computer cannot meet the requirement of staying connected while at the same time be portable, specialized, and convenient. People have begun to dub this trend the **post-PC era**.

As we bring computing technology to our daily lives, we find our homes full of promising opportunities. On one hand, broadband services such as digital subscriber line (DSL) and cable modem are widely available, a growing number of households own multiple personal computers (PCs), and all forms of home entertainment are becoming digitized. On the other hand, various device control networks, pioneered by CEBus, Echelon, and X10, have already been developed for use inside the home.

Cahners In-Stat reported that the number of cable modem subscribers in North America reached 1.8 million in 1999, and the number of broadband cable data subscribers worldwide will be 9.5 million by 2002. In fact, today more than 110 million homes in North America are within a short distance of a broadband coaxial cable line and 77 million homes have cable TV services. The research firm also predicts that the average number of connected nodes per home network will increase from 2.9 in 1999 to 5.0 by 2003 [1].

Enthusiasts predict fascinating applications: refrigerators ordering groceries automatically, TV programs delivered based on personal interests, merchandise offerings catering to consumer taste, optimally tuned climate control systems for comfort and energy conservation, not to mention microwave ovens that can be turned on from afar.

The market potential is huge. Cahners In-Stat estimates that the revenue for cable broadband services will increase from its current $1 billion to $4 billion (US) by 2002. Alliend Business Intelligence projects that home networking equipment market alone will reach $2.4 billion by 2005, whereas Parks Associates estimates that the total value of the end user market will be more than $4.5 billion by 2004 [1].

Given the market size, it is not surprising that a large number of companies are investing millions of dollars in developing technologies, creating standards, and manufacturing novel products. Numerous field trials are also underway as a necessary step in understanding customer needs. Although the application for service gateways is in the pilot stage, some of the dreams have begun to take shape. For example, the TiVo service allows you to rate TV programs and record your favorites automatically through a recorder connected to the service provider over the phone line. The Echelon LonWorks control network allows you to control light switches, window blinds, and thermostats through a browser over the Internet (`http://demo.echelon.com`).

As another example, in the Danish capital of Copenhagen, a trial began in September 2000 in which each family received a futuristic Electrolux Screenfridge, a Tele Denmark 2-Mbit/second ADSL high-speed data connection, and an Ericsson WAP phone. For the next few months, the families had the opportunity to try out an array of applications—Internet e-mail, intrafamily messaging, Web access, online grocery shopping, weather information, and news—targeted to improving the quality of life at home [1].

Some of us will really enjoy a good successor of *XCoffee,* a coffee maker that not only sends us detailed status information about itself automatically, but also produces personalized coffee at just the time we need it.

1.2 The Service Gateway

Traditional service providers such as utilities, telephone, and cable TV companies all have their own dedicated wires into the home. However, in the envisioned networked home of the future, this configuration will soon become unmanageably complex for a diversified portfolio of services, such as home security, health monitoring, telephony, and audio/video media, each possibly using a different communication technology. It will also miss interesting opportunities for integration. As a result, a centralized device interfacing the external Internet and the internal device and appliance networks has been proposed (Figure 1.1). This device is called a **service gateway**.[1]

---

[1] This term is used interchangeably with **residential gateway** in this book, although it could be argued that a service gateway may operate in settings other than the residence, such as a retail outlet or an information kiosk. They refer to the same type of device in terms of what they do, however.

4 CHAPTER 1 INTRODUCTION

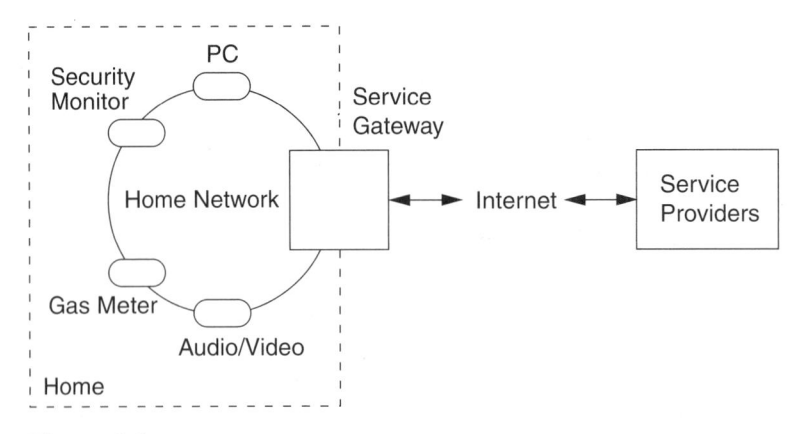

Figure 1.1 The role of a service gateway

A typical native platform of a service gateway consists of

- A processor
- Memory
- Persistent storage (disk or flash RAM)
- TCP/IP networking
- A device network (for example, a serial or parallel port)
- An operating system or real-time operating system

The familiar cable set-top box can be augmented with more "smarts" and transformed into a residential gateway. For example, Motorola's DCT-5000+ set-top is equipped with a 300+-MHz MIPS processor, 14 MB of memory, an integrated cable modem, the Ethernet, Universal Serial Bus (USB), and IEEE 1394 interfaces. Its main application is to provide traditional video services and high-speed Internet access [2].

Other companies have designed service gateways from the ground up. For example, Ericsson's e-box features a 100-MHz 486 CPU, 32 MB of memory, 24 MB of flash memory, a 10BaseT Ethernet interface, and a serial port. Its purpose is to provide e-services: Internet access, alarm and security, remote energy control and management, health care, e-commerce, and entertainment [3].

These are just a few examples of what is being tried out today. As costs decrease, more powerful devices can be expected to emerge on the market.

The residential gateway can participate in a wide range of home-based services:

- Home security, fire alarm, disaster alert, and emergency response
- Home-based health care, patient diagnosis, and child-care monitoring
- Energy management involving heating, ventilation, and air-conditioning

The benefits of delivering services to homes are twofold. For the consumer, her demands are met exactly when and how she needs them inside her home; intermediaries are eliminated so that she can hope for cheaper products and services. For merchants and service providers, they can serve a much more focused market more efficiently and can open new revenue streams with value-added services. The residential gateway can also leverage one service to benefit another. For example, it is possible for the home theater system to send a signal to lower the automated window blinds when a movie starts on a Sunday afternoon. A gateway that can authenticate a user via a cell phone can also let the user remotely open a door when a family member forgets to bring the key.

1.3 Challenges

Although optimism abounds, unique challenges are to be met on this new frontier. Two primary concerns are the large number of competing solutions and an uncharted new environment in which to develop and deploy applications for homes.

1.3.1 A Multitude of Competing Solutions

Although IP over T1 and the Ethernet are the winning formulas for wide area networks and local area networks (LANs), respectively, many solutions are vying to serve the home. Although we do not offer detailed treatment of these alternatives, we feel it is beneficial to present a high-level view of the technological landscape.

For physical media used to network the home, the consensus seems to be that the existing infrastructure should be leveraged and no new wires should be introduced. Consequently, we end up with the promising contenders presented in Table 1.1.

When it comes to connecting devices, there are many interfaces from which to choose. Table 1.2 summarizes some of the common device interfaces and their data rates.

Table 1.1 Physical Media within Homes, Their Data Rates, and Related Consortia

Physical Media	Data Rate	Associated Consortium
Infrared	9,600 bps–115 kbps; up to 4 Mbps	The Infrared Data Association (IrDA) http://www.irda.org
Phone line	1–10 Mbps	Home Phoneline Network Alliance (HomePNA) http://www.homepna.org
Radio frequency	1–2 Mbps	Home Radio Frequency Working Group (HomeRF) http://www.homerf.org
Power line	PowerPacket technology from Intellon at 14 Mbps	Home-Plug Powerline Alliance (HomePlug) http://www.homeplug.org
TV Cables	27 Mbps downstream, 500 Kbps–10 Mbps upstream	Cable Television Laboratories, Inc. (CableLabs) http://www.cablelabs.com

Table 1.2 Device Interfaces and Their Data Rates

Device Interface	Data Rate
Serial port	115 Kbps
Parallel port	115 KBps–3MBps
USB	12 Mbps
IDE	3.3–33 MBps
SCSI	5–160 MBps
IEEE 1394 (Firewire or iLink)	100–400 Mbps

Many comprehensive protocols are also out in the arena. These protocols are generally built on top of physical and data link layers, and focus more on the functionality provided by application layers in the OSI reference model. Some of them address a particular application domain—for instance, LonWorks, CEBus, Blue-Tooth, and Home Audio Video Interoperability (HAVi), whereas others attempt to provide a generic framework for enabling all devices—Jini™ connection technology and Universal Plug and Play (UPnP) are examples; these protocols are catalogued in Table 1.3.

Table 1.3 Other Prevailing Protocols

Protocol	Built On	Applications
LonWorks `http://www.echelon.com`	Power line, twisted pair, and so on.	Control network for devices such as sensors, switches, and instruments
CEBus (Consumer Electronics Bus) `http://www.cebus.org`	Power line, twisted pair, coaxial cable, radio frequency	Communication among residential consumer products
X10 `http://www.x10.org`	Power line	Communication and control among household electronic devices
BlueTooth `http://www.bluetooth.com`	2.4 GHz radio link	Sending and receiving voice and data within 10 m between portable devices wirelessly
HAVi (Home Audio Video Interoperability) `http://www.havi.org`	IEEE 1394	Allowing digital consumer electronics and home appliances to communicate with one another
Jini technology `http://www.sun.com/jini` `http://jini.org`	Java platform	Allowing a Jini technology-enabled device to join a federation and publish its service without prior setup. Others in the community can look up and discover the service, which is defined by a service interface and is represented as an object in the Java runtime environment. The object is exchanged using RMI.
Universal Plug and Play `http://www.upnp.org`	IP networks	Allowing devices and their capabilities to be discovered, utilized, and controlled. Devices are addressed by IP addresses; what services they provide and how they are controlled are described by XML.

1.3.2 A New Application Environment

The potpourri of standards provides pieces to the puzzle, whose completion, however, is anywhere but close. We have little experience creating and managing software applications in the residential market, which is made vividly clear by the following parody [4]:

This article first appeared in Salon.com, at `http://www.salon.com`. *An online version remains in the Salon archives. Reprinted with permission.*

Sunspots: Excerpts from a Diary of a Networked Future

By Mark Gimein

"[Sun Microsystems CEO Scott] McNealy gave several examples of the Net connected future: Light bulbs will be able to warn when they're about to expire, letting the factory automatically deliver a replacement. Vending machines will bill you automatically when you order a Coke with your cell phone. And the TV set-top box will be the nerve center of home networks that tie together dishwashers, thermostats, video cameras and everything else."

—From CNet News.com, Nov. 17

. . . . . .

Jan. 17, 2003

Help! The washing machine has crashed and will not give up my socks. When I try to open the door, the screen flashes "Error in scripting routine, line 18637." I see the socks spinning inside. Apparently I have put in a mismatched pair, and the machine doesn't seem to like that. I think I am not the only one who has had trouble. McNealy was on television last night, saying that we could reduce processor load by investing in clothes that we can "wash once, wear many times."

. . . . . .

June 9, 2003

I spent three hours today trying to get Sprint to reverse the charges for a 45-minute call to Turkey, but have had no success. I tried to explain that I did not call Turkey, but simply bought a Coke from the vending machine using my cell phone. The phone people say they understand, but it was the new Java-enabled bottle cap that actually made the call. The bottle caps report on a random sample of consumer purchasing behavior. But somehow a programming mistake had the bottle cap misdialing. Instead of calling the toll-free customer response number, it dialed into an international network.

. . . . . .

Aug. 24, 2003

Windows 2003 for Set-Top Boxes came out yesterday. I didn't want to spend $595 for an upgrade, but I don't think I really had a choice. It turns out that Windows 2000 was incompatible with my washing machine, and some of my clothes are still trapped inside. The new version promises 100 percent compatibility with major appliances. The trade-off is that it is not fully compatible with the embedded operating system in the toaster, but there might be a workaround. I'm told that in extremes I can control the toaster directly through Sun's Web site. Or maybe I can just do without English muffins for a while. The toaster has a slow microprocessor, and toasted muffins just don't seem all that important when you have to wrestle the computer to get them.

Copyright © 1999 Salon.com. All rights reserved.

Humor aside, the story leaves few doubts that programming for devices of the future should not be taken lightly. Programming for a conventional computer deals with data that seldom have direct physical consequences; data integrity can be protected by means of backups, transactions, and other techniques. However, it becomes a little difficult to recover from a home appliance gone awry.

The setup and configuration of the device should be simple and automatic, whereas complicated appliances and services should be managed remotely by the service providers. It is well known that many people cannot program their VCRs. For them, managing smart appliances must be as simple as turning on the radio. Often, a service such as recording a TV program depends on the presence of another service, such as an electronic programming guide. Thus it must be possible for the residential gateway to detect the need for a service, discover its presence or absence, and ensure that it is available.

The Java Embedded Server product from Sun Microsystems is targeted to the residential gateway market and is designed to meet these challenges. By adding the Java Embedded Server software to a hardware product, device manufacturers can easily transform any broadband termination device, such as a DSL/cable modem or set-top box, into a residential gateway.

1.4 Java Embedded Server Technology

Since their inception, the Java programming language and the Java platform have been widely accepted as the way of programming for the Internet. Because the Java programming language is platform neutral, developers can write and test applications in a desktop environment such as the Solaris™ Operating Environment or Windows, then deploy them to the target device. An application written for one device can be directly deployed on another device as long as the other device provides a Java™ virtual machine. The Java runtime environment has the unique capability of loading code securely at run-time from the network. As a programming platform, the Java programming language protects developers from many well-known programming mistakes that have plagued C programmers. It shortens development cycles and boosts code quality.

Having realized the great potential of applications on smart connected devices, and the strengths of the Java platform in addressing this class of software, Sun Microsystems developed and released the first version of the Java Embedded Server product in October 1998. Its architecture represents a unified software programming interface that allows services to work together. (A more precise definition of service in the context of the OSGi architecture is given in the next chapter. Here it simply means a functional component.) A service, as a component, can be programmed to implement any protocol or perform any function in an insulated or cooperative manner. More specifically, the foundation of the Java Embedded Server product, a framework known as ServiceSpace, deals with the following issues that are important for provisioning services to the residential gateway:

- **Just-in-time service delivery.** The framework allows for a service to be downloaded over the network when the service is needed. The service may be used once and then discarded or it may be kept persistently on the residential gateway for a longer period.

- **Service updates and versioning.** The framework can be used to check quickly the version of a service that is running in a gateway and to update this service dynamically from a remote location. This is very useful for developers of software for embedded devices. These devices have traditionally been loaded with a static application environment. A critical application bug can be expensive to fix. Using the Java Embedded Server product, this is no longer a restriction. A newer version of the software can be loaded into the framework through the network.

- **Service discovery and dependency resolution.** To leverage components that others have developed, the framework provides a service discovery mechanism with which a downloaded component can consult a service registry in the framework to obtain and use an existing service. The framework also resolves dependency relations when one service depends on another to function.

Shortly after version 1.0 of the product was released, the cartoon in Figure 1.2 appeared, to the amazement of the members of the project.

Figure 1.2 A misuse of the Java Embedded Server product. It seems to suggest that the general populace is quite ready to accept the prevalence of technology in their daily lives. (Illustration by Phil Frank.)

The Java Embedded Server product has gone through several revisions, including versions 1.0, 1.1, and 1.2. The current version is 2.0, released in August 2000. To simplify and expedite the development process for services, this version is bundled with a customized version of the Forte™ for Java™ Community Edition, an integrated development environment, as well as a number of prepackaged services. The Java Embedded Server version 2.0 software is an implementation of the Service Gateway Specification 1.0, released in May 2000 by the OSGi.

1.5 The Open Services Gateway Initiative

Sun Microsystems is a founding member of the OSGi consortium (http://www.osgi.org), an independent, nonprofit industry group that has defined an open standard for connecting future generations of networked consumer and small business devices to Internet services. The need for standardization is obvious:

- **Platform independence.** Different types of gateway devices usually have their own native platforms and various combinations of processors and operating systems. Such diversity is much more common for the embedded devices than for desktop computers. It would be infeasible for service developers to write applications and port them to many platforms with drastically different underlying characteristics, let alone have them work with one another seamlessly. This problem can be solved by leveraging the "write-once-run-everywhere" value proposition of the Java technology and by agreeing to a common standard for the gateway software.

- **Vendor independence.** An open specification focuses on defining application programming interfaces (APIs), making it possible for residential gateways manufactured by different vendors to host services written by different service providers that are provisioned by different gateway operators. The roles of various participants are discussed in the next section.

- **Future-Proof.** An open standard coupled with the dynamic upgradability of the Java technology means that a residential gateway hardware box has longer utility. It can remain the same while the user changes service providers or adds new services.

- **Integration.** An open standard enables coexistence and integration with multiple LAN and device access technologies, and can provide a software platform that can accommodate existing technologies so that, for example, a Jini™ technology-enabled printer, a HAVi-compatible audiovisual receiver, and a UPnP camera, can all interoperate via the standard platform.

The specifications that the OSGi consortium produces provide a common foundation for Internet service providers (ISPs), network operators, and equipment manufacturers to deliver a wide range of services via gateway servers running in the home or remote office.

The release of Java Embedded Server software version 1.0 predates and in fact catalyzed the formation of the OSGi. The product attracted several software companies, service gateway hardware vendors, and service providers. Sun Microsystems began working with IBM, Ericsson, and others to standardize the API to ensure interoperability of software solutions in the residential gateway market. In March 1999, 15 companies formed the OSGi consortium. The OSGi Java Expert Group was officially established, and one of the coauthors of this book, Li Gong, was elected by the group members and formally appointed by the OSGi Board of Directors as the first Java Expert Group Chair. Sun Microsystems contributed the specifications of Java Embedded Server software version 1.1 (the latest version of the product at the time) to the OSGi, which became the basis and a starting point for the specification work by the Java Expert Group. The group eventually produced the official OSGi Service Gateway Specification version 1.0, which was approved by the OSGi Board of Directors and released at Connections 2000, an event held in San Diego, California, in May 2000. Although it stemmed from the Java Embedded Server product and its ServiceSpace architecture, the OSGi specification has evolved the APIs and other features. As a result, Sun Microsystems has rebuilt the Java Embedded Server product from the ground up and released the OSGi-based version 2.0 of the product in August 2000.

The OSGi has attracted lots of attention and has been growing fast. As of this writing, more than 80 companies, including many notable device manufacturers, software developers, network operators, and service providers, have joined the OSGi.

1.6 Operational Model

The residential gateway market and the business model associated with it are still in the early stages. Probably the closest resembling practices in existence today are ISP and the cable TV companies. However, the extrapolation depicted in Figure 1.3 seems to be reasonable.

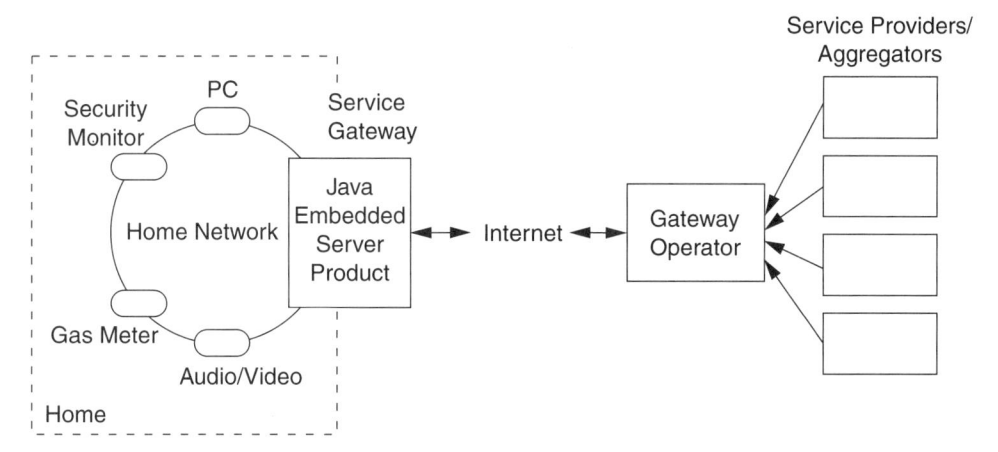

Figure 1.3 Operational model using the service gateway with the Java Embedded Server software.

For example, to avoid costly customer visits by technicians, an energy company may wish to deploy a piece of software that runs on home gateways in residence and reads gas meters remotely. The energy company would be the **service provider**. Additionally, the following players may also be involved:

- A company that manufactures the gateway box hardware
- Another company that supplies basic OSGi-based framework and core service software. (This portion of the software provides a generic infrastructure and services for deployment of other application components. In Figure 1.3, the Java Embedded Server product from Sun Microsystems is an example.)
- A **gateway operator** to install and manage the meter-reading software for its subscribers
- A **service aggregator**, because many services may be in demand at home, to integrate and package services from different service providers, then deliver them to the gateway operator.

One entity can serve multiple roles. A gateway hardware vendor may also supply the framework and other "horizontal" software; a gateway operator may also act as the aggregator.

Unlike a conventional computer, the gateway box usually does not need to have a display or input device such as a keyboard or a mouse. It should be maintenance-free from the home user's point of view, and should be administered through the network by the gateway operator. The box should boot up as soon as it is powered up.

The hardware aspect of the service gateway and its associated business model is not discussed further in this book. Beginning with the next chapter, we focus on the software that runs the service gateways.

CHAPTER 2

Getting Started

YOUR primary task when working with the Java Embedded Server product is to develop software components known as **bundles**. In this chapter we write a simple bundle that can be installed and activated with the Java Embedded Server software. We think it is important to set things up early so that you can run code and see how it works in action as you read along. Hands-on experiments usually provide helpful revelations in understanding a programming paradigm.

2.1 Setting Up the Java Embedded Server Software

We assume you already have the Java runtime environment and development tools installed on your computer. If not, you should install them before proceeding. If you need permission-based security,[1] you must use Java™ 2 SDK versions 1.2 or 1.3. Otherwise, JDK™ version 1.x or its compatibles should work fine.

Install the Java Embedded Server product on your computer. For the rest of this book, we refer to the location of installation as *jes_path*. You should end up with the following directory hierarchy for the distribution:

```
jes_path
   |---- bin
   |---- docs
   |---- lib
   |---- bundles
```

The OSGi framework interfaces and classes, and their implementation, are included in *jes_path*/lib/framework.jar. You need it to build your own bundles as well as to run the Java Embedded Server software.

---

[1] At the time of this writing, the Java Embedded Server software version for download does not support permissions. A version that does will be made available. We discuss permissions in Chapter 9.

The `bundles` directory contains the bundles shipped with the product, including the Log and HTTP bundles. The `docs` directory has the documentation set. Don't worry about other directories for now.

2.2 The "Home, Sweet Home" Bundle

Programming tutorials have traditionally begun with a "Hello, world" example since 1978. We are writing code for residential gateways, so home is the world for us. In this section we develop a bundle that simply displays "Home, sweet home" when it is activated, and "I'll be back" when it is deactivated.

A bundle is packaged as a Java archive (or JAR) file. A JAR file is essentially a ZIP file with a manifest, and it can be created, updated, and examined with the jar tool. More information can be found online (http://java.sun.com/j2se/1.3/docs/guide/jar/index.html).

The steps to develop the example bundle are

1. Create the directory structure for the bundle.
2. Declare the necessary headers in a manifest stub.
3. Write an activator.
4. Compile the activator class.
5. Pack up all classes in a JAR file and apply the manifest stub.

2.2.1 Create the Directory

Create a directory named `home`, change the directory to `home`, and save the files you are about to create there.

2.2.2 Define the Manifest

Use your favorite text editor to create a file named `Manifest` that contains only one line:

```
Bundle-Activator: home.SweetHome
```

This file is a **manifest stub,** because at the time when the bundle JAR file is created, other meta-information will be appended to what we have just defined to form the real manifest as the `META-INF/MANIFEST.MF` entry in the JAR file. For the rest of the book, we just refer to this file as the manifest for the sake of brevity.

2.2.3 Write an Activator

Now create the file SweetHome.java as shown:

```
package home;
import org.osgi.framework.BundleActivator;
import org.osgi.framework.BundleContext;

public class SweetHome implements BundleActivator {
   public void start(BundleContext ctxt) {
      System.out.println("Home, sweet home");
   }

   public void stop(BundleContext ctxt) {
      System.out.println("I'll be back");
   }
}
```

This class implements the BundleActivator interface, whose start and stop methods are called to perform operations when the bundle is started or stopped, respectively. In this case, they display some innocuous messages.

The parameter BundleContext ctxt is passed to the activator by the framework when the bundle is either activated or deactivated. From the bundle's perspective, it serves as the execution context for the bundle to interact with the underlying framework. In our simple example, we have no use for it.

2.2.4 Compile the Activator Class

Set your CLASSPATH environment variable to the JAR file containing the framework class library:

```
setenv CLASSPATH jes_path/lib/framework.jar
```
[2]

---

[2] We show commands in the C shell on the Solaris system. If you work in the Bourne or Korn shell, use the following to set the environment variables:

```
set CLASSPATH=jes_path/lib/framework.jar
export CLASSPATH
```

If you work on Windows platforms, use the backslash as the path separator, and set the environment variables as

```
set CLASSPATH=jes_path\lib\framework.jar
```

Change to the directory a level above home, and compile the activator with

```
javac home/SweetHome.java
```

At this point, you should have the following files in the directory home:

```
home/Manifest
home/SweetHome.java
home/SweetHome.class
```

2.2.5 Pack Up

Finally, it's time to create the bundle JAR file:

```
jar cmf home/Manifest home.jar home/*.class
```

The command option m in cmf indicates that the next argument on the command line is the manifest stub to be applied. home.jar is the bundle generated by the command. You can inspect its contents using

```
jar tf home.jar
```

which should report

```
META-INF/
META-INF/MANIFEST.MF
home/SweetHome.class
```

The META-INF directory and META-INF/MANIFEST.MF entry are standard to JAR files; the latter is the real manifest of the JAR file. Henceforth, we assume the home.jar bundle is placed at /home/joe/bundles/home.jar. Substitute it with the actual path where you save the JAR file.

The package name must correspond exactly to the directory structure, and it must be preserved in the bundle JAR file. In our example, the activator class belongs to the home package, and it is physically saved inside the directory home. This structure is also captured in the JAR file, as shown by the table-of-contents output from the jar tf home.jar command.

2.3 Running the Bundle

We first launch the Java Embedded Server software by setting its classes on the CLASSPATH and loading the main class:

```
setenv CLASSPATH jes_path/lib/framework.jar
java com.sun.jes.impl.framework.Main
```

The following output will appear on your screen:

```
Java Embedded Server 2.0

Copyright 1998, 1999 and 2000 Sun Microsystems, Inc. All rights
    reserved.
Use is subject to license terms.

Type 'h[elp]' for a list of commands.
>
```

The user interface to the framework is an interactive command console. To install our bundle, use the `install` command:

```
> install /home/joe/bundles/home.jar
```

The bundle is installed when the prompt returns. Use the `bundles` command to examine the current status of the installed bundle:

```
> bundles
ID   STATE     LOCATION
--   --------- ------------------------
1    INSTALLED file:/home/joe/bundles/home.jar
>
```

Next, start the bundle:

```
> start 1
Home, sweet home
```

The number 1 is the bundle identification (ID) as reported by the `bundles` command. When the bundle is started, its activator's `start` method is invoked, and we see the expected message displayed. Try issuing the `bundles` command again to see the change of state:

```
> bundles
ID   STATE       LOCATION
--   ---------   ------------------------
1    ACTIVE      file:/home/joe/bundles/home.jar
>
```

Now stop the bundle by issuing the `stop` command:

```
> stop 1
I'll be back
```

The bundle activator's `stop` method is invoked, which produces the expected message. You can start and stop the bundle multiple times, and check how the bundle status changes.

Finally, let's uninstall the bundle, then recheck the bundle status:

```
> uninstall 1
> bundles
>
```

The bundle is gone from the framework. You may use the `shutdown` command to exit the framework:

```
> shutdown
%
```

2.3.1 Getting Help

After launching the framework, type "help" at the prompt to see a list of commands, their abbreviations, and syntaxes:

```
  > help
b[undles]
e[xportedpackages]
debugon      <name> [,<option>,...]
debugoff     <name>
g[et]        <property_name>
h[elp]       [<command>]
i[nstall]    <bundle_url> [, ...]
m[anifest]   <bundle_url | bundle_id>
r[un]        <filename | url>
```

```
se[t]        <property_name>=<property_value>
ser[vices]   [<filter>]
sh[utdown]
sta[rt]      <bundle_url | bundle_id> [, ...]
sto[p]       <bundle_url | bundle_id> [, ...]
tty
un[install]  <bundle_url | bundle_id> [, ...]
up[date]     <bundle_url | bundle_id> [bundle_update_url] [, ...]

    <bundle_url> and <bundle_update_url> must be the URL of a bundle
    or be relative to the bundle base URL.
    .jar suffix will be appended if not specified.

JES cache directory:    /home/joe/jescache
Bundle base URL:        file:/home/joe/jes2.0/bundles
Java 2 security support: No
```

To see a more detailed description of a command, specify the command after typing "help":

```
> help install
Install the specified bundles.
```

The help feature also displays the current settings for the cache directory and the bundle base URL, which we describe next.

2.3.2 The Cache Directory

The Java Embedded Server software caches installed bundles loaded over the network and keeps track of their status, so that after the framework is shut down and restarted, the bundles are reinstalled, and those that used to be active are started again. A cache directory on the local file system is created for this purpose.

You can learn the whereabouts of the cache directory by using the `help` command. For example, the output in Section 2.3.1 shows that the cache directory is at /home/joe/jescache. By default, the cache directory is created in the user's home directory under the name of jescache. You can override that by setting the com.sun.jes.framework.cache.dir system property:

```
java -Dcom.sun.jes.framework.cache.dir=/tmp/mycache com.sun.jes↵
.impl.framework.Main
```

If you want to start from a pristine state, remove the cache directory.

2.3.3 The Bundle Base URL

In the framework, bundles are identified either by an ID number or by a location string. The latter is usually a URL or a path on the local file system. For example,

```
> install c:\mybundles\hello.jar
```

installs a bundle from the local file system, whereas

```
> install http://myhost:8080/bundles/hello.jar
```

fetches the bundle remotely from an HTTP server and installs it in the framework.

If an absolute URL or path is specified, it is used directly to obtain the bundle. If a relative URL or path is specified, it is concatenated with the base URL to retrieve the bundle. By default, the base URL is the current directory.

You can set the `com.sun.jes.framework.bundles.baseurl` system property to point to the location of a pool of bundles. For example,

```
> set com.sun.jes.framework.bundles.baseurl=http://myhost:8080/↵
bundles
> install hello.jar
```

You can find the current setting for the bundle base URL from the `help` command output. For instance, the help display in Section 2.3.1 shows that the current bundle base URL is `file:/home/joe/jes2.0/bundles`.

Unlike the `com.sun.jes.framework.cache.dir` system property, which can only be set when the framework is launched, the `com.sun.jes.framework.bundles.baseurl` property can be modified at any time using the `set` command, and it takes effect immediately.

2.3.4 Brief Summary of the Major Commands

The framework command console allows you to control a bundle's life cycle. The following commands serve this functionality:

- `install` installs a bundle from a URL.
- `start` activates an installed bundle by its ID or location string.
- `stop` deactivates a bundle by its ID or location string.
- `update` updates a bundle to a newer version using its ID or location string.
- `uninstall` uninstalls a bundle by its ID or location string.

The following commands report useful information about bundles and services in the framework:

- `bundles` displays all bundles currently installed in the framework and their states.
- `services` displays all services registered in the framework.
- `manifest` displays headers defined in a bundle's manifest.
- `exportedpackages` displays the exported packages as well as their exporters and importers.

The two following commands allow you to set or retrieve system properties in the Java virtual machine:

- `set` sets a system property.
- `get` displays the value of a system property.

Please consult the documentation located in the *jes_path*/`docs` directory for more details on how to use the framework console. We return to the command console often to see code in action as we delve into the intricacies of bundles and services.

CHAPTER 3

Architecture and Basic Concepts

IN this chapter we explain the OSGi software architecture and concepts. The groundwork is necessary before we dive into coding details because the OSGi Service Gateway Specification does not merely specify another set of APIs. A new programming model is also introduced. It is essential to establish this model in your mind from the outset.

3.1 Motivation

Let's begin by putting forth a few specific goals for residential gateway applications.

First, a gateway customer ought to have the freedom to choose a version of a service from any one of multiple competing vendors. If multiple companies are to develop services, they must program against a consistent model and API. Their services need to cooperate with, *and* be insulated from, one another when existing on the same gateway. For example, a chat service from America Online can use a 3Com modem service on the gateway, but it should never clash with an offering from MSN, accidentally or not.

Second, the relationship between the customer and the service provider should be flexible: The customer can subscribe to services as well as discontinue them at any time. This requires the capability of installing a service, putting it to use, and removing it later. It also requires that the service be packaged in a form that can travel easily across the network.

Third, a service must be developed with enough stability so that variations or changes of its internal implementation do not cause repercussions on other services that depend on it. For example, it is desirable to use a photo-swapping service without worrying about how the images are transferred. Depending on the hardware configuration of the box, one implementation of the service may use USB, another may use the Ethernet.

The OSGi architecture provides a programming model that satisfies these requirements.

3.2 Architecture

The residential gateway software architecture is depicted in Figure 3.1. It usually consists of several layers. The operating system and the Java platform,[1] usually supplied by gateway vendors, make up the foundation of the execution environment. The OSGi software runs on top of the Java runtime environment. It consists of

- The framework,[2] which serves as the underpinning common environment for hosting a set of bundles
- The bundles, which are the software components plugged into the framework. A bundle may provide zero, one, or multiple **services.**
  - The OSGi defines two standard services: the Log service and the HTTP service. It also specifies the DA architecture. Only the Log service is mandatory; the HTTP service and the DA are optional for an OSGi 1.0-based implementation.
  - Service providers are expected to develop bundles to extend the functionality of the gateway.

In this paradigm, new bundles can be developed separately from the framework or any other existing bundles. They can then be deployed to the framework at *runtime*. Consequently, the "purpose" of the gateway is determined by the combined functionality of the active bundles, which can come and go over time. Like a versatile actor, it can be cast into drastically different roles.

Next we explain what a service and a bundle are; then we describe how they interact in the framework.

---

[1] The service gateways are high-end devices, but they are resource-constrained devices nonetheless. The Java Embedded Server product supports two types of the Java platform that target this class of applications: PersonalJava™ and Connected Device Configuration Foundation Profiles; the latter is part of the Java™ 2 Micro Edition (J2ME™) [5–8].

[2] This colorless but agreeable term is *the* term used in the OSGi specification. The counterpart in the Java Embedded Server version 1.x products that predate the OSGi was ServiceSpace. The term is no longer in use in version 2.0 of the product.

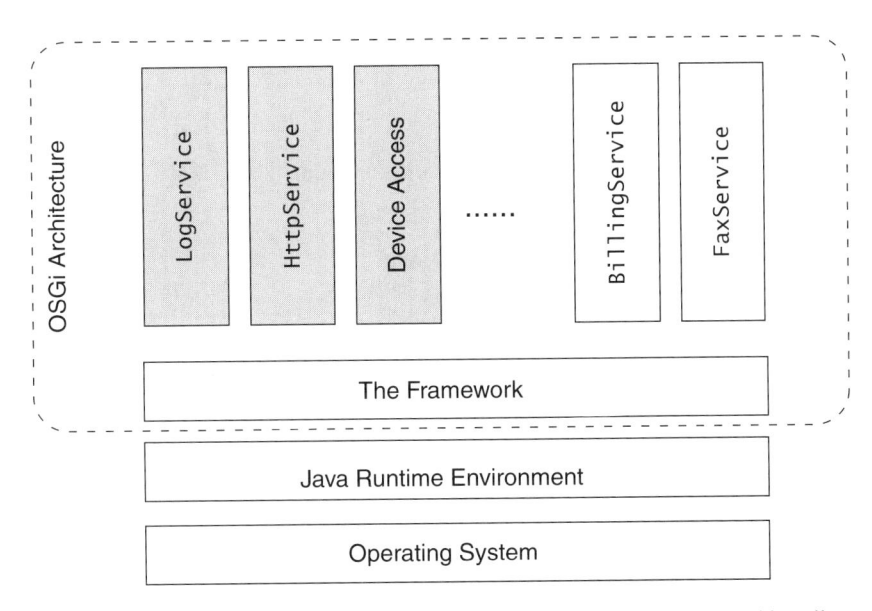

Figure 3.1 The service gateway software architecture. The standard bundles are shaded. The framework and the bundles are software written in a way that is compliant with the OSGi specification.

3.3 Service

A service does something useful and is implemented in the Java programming language. For example, a Web server is a service; so is the program that calculates taxes, the application that reports electricity consumption, and the security software that turns on the lights in an unoccupied home. In a business setting, a service may tell the temperature and merchandise quantity in vending machines; another may page the administrator when a critical connection to a customer's site goes down. The list of possible services can only be bound by one's imagination. It is important for us to demystify this much overloaded term and for you to understand its generality.

To develop a service, you usually define an interface that says *what* the service does, along with corresponding implementation classes that spell out *how* the service is to be performed. For example, the following is a service that plays digital music. First, we show its service interface:

```
package player.service;
// imports
public interface DigitalPlayer {
    /**
     * Plays music read from the stream.
```

```
    */
    public void play(InputStream musicStream);
}
```

The class that implements the interface may look like

```
package player.impl.mp3;
import player.service.DigitalPlayer;
// other imports
public class MP3Player implements DigitalPlayer {

    public void play(InputStream inStream) {
        // Read MP3 encoded bytes from the stream,
        // send to the appropriate codec
        // available in this service implementation.
    }
}
```

The specific code that reads, decodes, and plays MP3 is inconsequential to this discussion and is not shown in the `play` method.

The separation of interface and implementation ensures the service interface to the callers remains stable while the implementation undergoes changes. In our example, the code using the `DigitalPlayer` interface won't be affected if we substitute the `MP3Player` class with a `RealAudioPlayer` class, which would implement the same service interface but decipher the given stream in an entirely different format.

3.4 Bundle

A bundle is a form of packaging for services. It is also a functional unit with life cycle operations and class loading capability. Lastly, it contains well-defined "hooks" that allow it to be plugged into the framework.

3.4.1 A Bundle Is a Packaging Vehicle

A bundle is a JAR file that contains class files and resources such as images, HTML pages, and other data files. Bundles are usually delivery and deployment vehicles for services. For instance, a bundle that contains the music player service may also include a collection of MP3 files to play. Another bundle that contains a lighting control service may also come with a set of HTML pages and images that serve as its user interface. Packaging code together with data makes deployment very convenient. Figure 3.2 presents an internal layout of a bundle JAR file that contains the player service.

```
META-INF/MANIFEST.MF
player/service/DigitalPlayer.class      ──── The service interface
player/impl/mp3/Activator.class
player/impl/mp3/MP3Player.class         ──── The service implementation
player/skin/regular.html                ──── The resources
player/media/mp3/sample.mp3
```

Figure 3.2   An internal structure of a bundle.

The contents of the bundle show that it contains the class files of the interface and implementation for the digital music player service as well as the resources of a sample MP3 tune and a user interface in HTML for the player.

3.4.2   A Bundle Is a Functional Module

A bundle is not just a static archive. It is associated with life cycle operations and it is self-contained with respect to class loading.

3.4.2.1   Bundle Life Cycle

A bundle can be installed, started, updated, stopped, and uninstalled by the framework. A detailed explanation of the life cycle operations is forthcoming in "Life within the Framework," on page 39. Each of these actions moves the bundle to a new state. Figure 3.3 shows the bundle state transition.

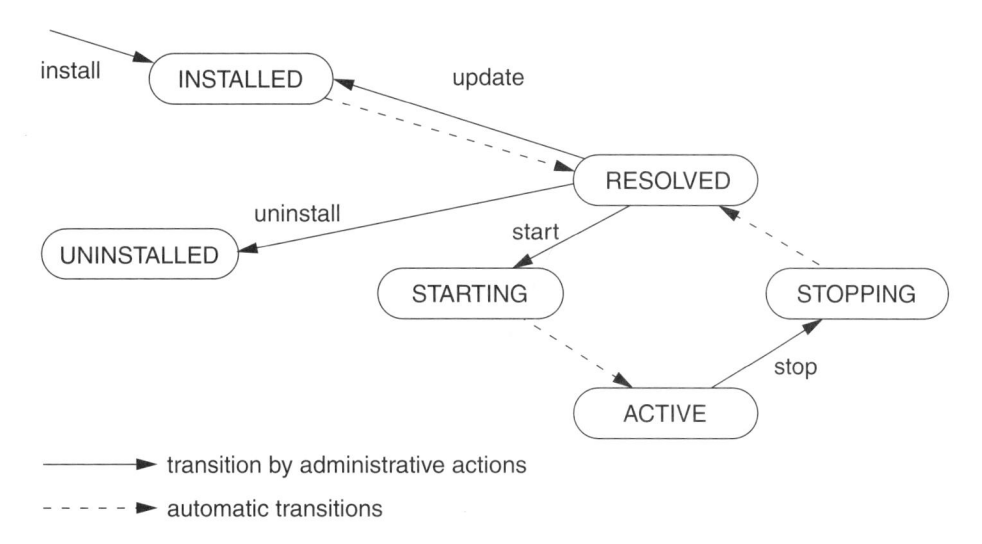

Figure 3.3   Bundle state transition diagram

In the last chapter, we had a taste of the bundle life cycle operations when we installed, started, stopped, and uninstalled the "sweet home" bundle using the command console.

Once a bundle is started, it becomes active, meaning that it works according to the prescription of the design. For instance, after an HTTP bundle is started, it is ready to accept requests from Web browsers.

3.4.2.2 Bundle Class Loading

A bundle is self-contained. Each active bundle has its own class loader that, by default, can load classes only from within the bundle itself. Code within one bundle cannot refer to classes inside another bundle, let alone instantiate them or invoke their methods. This is how bundles achieve insulation from one another. The system classes or the classes on the CLASSPATH are exceptions, of course, and they are always available to all bundles.

This feature protects classes in one bundle from running into conflicts with those in another, and prevents code in one bundle from interacting with that in another in haphazard and potentially dangerous ways. For instance, if one bundle defines a class `foo.Bar` and another bundle happens to define a class with the same name but entirely different semantics, and the package `foo` is not exported and shared (see "Exporting and Importing Packages" on page 34), the two bundles can coexist, and both versions of `foo.Bar` can be loaded and executed without a problem within the Java virtual machine.

3.4.3 The "Hooks" to the Framework

Because bundles are to be installed into the framework, standard interfacing mechanisms are defined within each bundle from which the framework learns how to host the bundle. They are the manifest and the activator of the bundle.

3.4.3.1 The Manifest

The manifest file is a standard entry in a JAR file. It includes meta-information about the archive itself, such as the checksums and signatures of the individual files when the JAR file is digitally signed. An additional set of manifest headers have been defined in the OSGi Service Gateway Specification from which the framework can gain knowledge about the bundle to host it successfully. This file is shown as the META-INF/MANIFEST.MF entry (Figure 3.4) in the music player example presented earlier, and it may declare the following:

```
Bundle-Activator: player.impl.Activator
Export-Package: player.service
Import-Package: http.service
```

This declaration identifies to the framework that this bundle's activator (discussed in the next section) is the `player.impl.Activator` class. The bundle exports classes in the `player.service` package and requires the `http.service` package to be exported by another bundle.

3.4.3.2 The Bundle Activator

The activator is implemented by a bundle to perform customized operations at the time when the bundle is started and stopped. It implements the `start` and `stop` methods of the `org.osgi.framework.BundleActivator` interface, which is defined as follows:

```
public interface BundleActivator {
    public void start(BundleContext context);
    public void stop(BundleContext context);
}
```

In the player example, `player/impl/Activator.class` is the activator included in the JAR file (Figure 3.4).

Recall from the previous chapter that the `SweetHome` class that we wrote is an implementation of a bundle activator.

```
META-INF/MANIFEST.MF                    ——— The manifest
player/service/DigitalPlayer.class
player/impl/mp3/Activator.class         ——— The activator
player/impl/mp3/MP3Player.class
player/skin/regular.html
player/media/mp3/sample.mp3
```

Figure 3.4 The internal structure of the bundle.

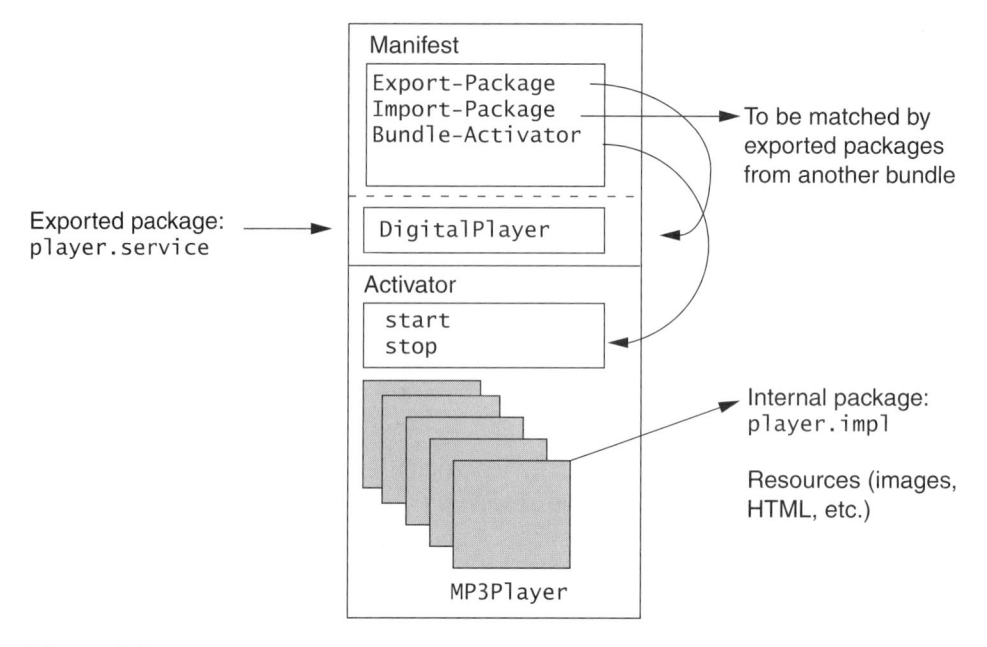

Figure 3.5 The anatomy of a bundle

Having introduced the various pieces, we illustrate the entire internal structure of a bundle in Figure 3.5.

Because the interaction between bundles and the framework is standard, the bundles can be developed outside their hosting environment. The developers can focus on the service that the bundle is to provide, and they can do so off the target device. In principle, once the development work is completed, one can be assured that the resultant JAR file is ready for any OSGi-based framework from any vendor.

3.5 The Framework

The framework provides a hosting environment for bundles. Its responsibilities are

- Managing the life cycle of bundles
- Resolving interdependencies among bundles and making classes and resources available from a bundle
- Maintaining a registry of services

- Firing events and notifying listeners when a bundle's state changes, when a service is registered or unregistered, or when the framework is launched or raises an error

The framework is the common ground where all installed bundles and registered services come to play. It is agnostic to the specific applications of individual bundles, and is only concerned with the generic housekeeping for all bundles. The framework's functionality is best illustrated when we describe how the framework interacts with bundles and services, in Section 3.7.

The framework remains a behind-the-scene character: There is no `org.osgi.framework.Framework` interface or class in the API, and thus no instance of the framework can be obtained. A bundle accesses the functionality of the framework indirectly through the **bundle context**.

As shown in "The Bundle Activator" on page 31, the bundle activator's `start` and `stop` methods are both passed an `org.osgi.framework.BundleContext` object as the sole argument. For classes inside the bundle, this object is the "window" into the framework: It represents the execution environment in which the bundle finds itself.

For human developers, the Java Embedded Server command console provides interactive access to the underlying framework, as we saw in the previous chapter.

3.6 Cooperation among Bundles and Services

We mentioned that bundles are insulated from each other because they have their own class loaders. However, bundles and their services also need to cooperate with one another to achieve some overall functionality. One practice is to build an application using bundles as the building blocks: Common operations are factored out and programmed into a set of basic modules; more sophisticated and high-level bundles then rely on the basic modules to get their work done.

For example, imagine that we want to develop a streaming audio service that may depend on, say, an HTTP service to make MP3 files available for remote players.[3] However it is not desirable to package the HTTP service into the streaming audio bundle because, as it turns out, a remote home appliance diagnostic service may also rely on it. Such an application scenario calls for three bundles activated

---

[3] Incidentally, if you wonder why a residential gateway would want to serve MP3s, Napster-like applications should come to mind.

on the gateway: the remote diagnostic bundle and the streaming audio bundle, both of which require a third HTTP bundle to work properly.

Sharing is realized by exporting and importing packages for bundles and registering and obtaining services.

3.6.1 Exporting and Importing Packages

A bundle can earmark a set of packages within its possession for *export,* which means the bundle informs the framework to make the classes in the exported packages available for any other bundles that need to use them. The bundle can export none, some, or all of its packages.

A bundle expresses its intention to export packages by declaring the packages with the Export-Package header in its manifest. Multiple packages are separated by commas. Each package can be optionally followed by a semicolon and a version specification. For example,

```
Export-Package: com.acme.foo; specification-version=2.0,
    com.acme.bar
```

declares that the bundle wants to export version 2.0 of the com.acme.foo package and version 0.0 of the com.acme.bar package (because no version is given). The version number has the following components:

```
major.minor.micro
```

as defined by the Package Versioning Specification in the Java™ 2 platform [9]. For instance, version 2.0.3 is higher than 1.5.0, but lower than 2.1.0. Version 1.0 is the same as version 1.0.0.

A bundle can also declare to *import* packages, which indicates that the bundle needs to use the specified classes in order to run. The framework does the matchmaking and ensures that the importer finds the exporter before the former can be started. This process is called **resolution**, and a bundle is said to be **resolved** if the packages it needs to import have already been exported by some other bundles present in the framework.

A bundle declares to import packages using the Import-Package header in its manifest. For example,

```
Import-Package: com.acme.foo; specification-version=1.0,
    com.acme.bar
```

indicates that the bundle needs to import *at least* version 1.0 of the com.acme.foo package and any version of the com.acme.bar package.

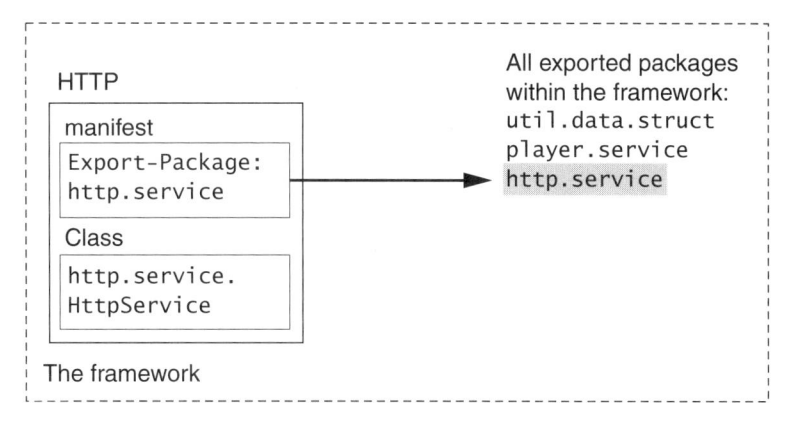

Figure 3.6 The HTTP bundle exports package `http.service` to the framework. `util.data.struct` and `player.service` are examples of packages that have been exported by other bundles (not shown).

You cannot export or import individual classes or interfaces. The package is the smallest unit for this purpose.

When packages are exported by a bundle, they are said to be exported to the framework. They are not exported to individual importers in a peer-to-peer fashion. Figure 3.6 and Figure 3.7 illustrate the package exporting and importing process within the framework respectively.

Internally, the framework interprets the package importing and exporting directives from the bundles' manifests and links up appropriate data structures in their class loaders. Therefore, when the streaming audio bundle tries to access the `http.service.HttpService` interface, the bundle's class loader tries to load the class from the following places, in this order:

1. The system classes and the classes on the CLASSPATH

2. The exported packages that the bundle imports

3. The bundle itself

In this case, it doesn't find the interface in step 1, but it has better luck with step 2, because the HTTP bundle has declared to export the package, and the framework has arranged to add it to the set of the exported packages accordingly.

Suppose two bundles attempt to export the same package. The framework then consults the version specification of the packages offered by the two bundles and

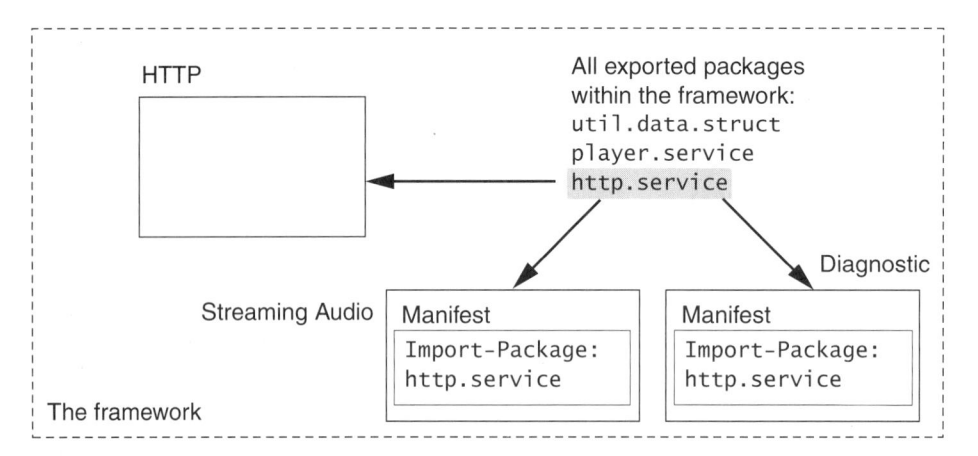

Figure 3.7 Streaming audio and diagnostic bundles import `http.service`. The same package has been automatically imported back by its exporter, the HTTP bundle, at the time of the export.

picks the bundle with the higher version of the package as the exporter. For example, if bundle A has the following declaration:

```
Export-Package: http.service; version-specification=1.0
```

and bundle B has the following declaration:

```
Export-Package: http.service; version-specification=1.1
```

then bundle B is chosen as the exporter for the package `service.http`. If neither A nor B bothers to specify versions, or if both specify the same version, then the framework arbitrarily selects one.

If a package has already been exported, subsequent attempts by other bundles to export the same package are silently ignored by the framework, even if a bundle that arrives later carries a package with a higher version. Thus, if bundle A has exported its `http.service` package for some time before bundle B arrives and tries do the same, B's version will *not* be exported even though it's higher than that exported by A.

For these reasons, a bundle that *declares to export* some packages may not eventually *export* them, because the framework is the decision maker and it may have chosen another bundle as the exporter. Conversely, an active bundle declaring to import packages must have succeeded in importing them from *some* exporter, or it would have failed to be resolved and started by the framework.

3.6.2 Registering and Obtaining Services

If a bundle contains some services, it usually registers the services with the service registry maintained by the framework when the bundle is started. Registering a service makes it obtainable for code in other bundles to use, so it is also known as **publishing** the service. We call the bundle that publishes services the **service-providing bundle.** For example, in its activator's `start` method the HTTP bundle may register its service by calling `registerService` on the `BundleContext` interface:

```
// in the HTTP bundle's activator
public void start(BundleContext bundleContext) {
    Properties props = new Properties();
    props.put("port", new Integer(80));
    HttpService[4] http = new HttpServiceImpl();
    bundleContext.registerService("http.service.HttpService", http,
        props);
}
```

This code registers the `HttpServiceImpl` instance `http` under its interface class name `http.service.HttpService` along with a service property of the port it is going to use.

What does the service registry look like? It is a structure that maps the types and a set of properties of a service to the service object itself.

Bundles are not required to publish services. A bundle can simply export a set of common utility or helper classes as library classes for other bundles to use in its `Export-Package` manifest header; it does not need to have an activator. We call this type of bundle **library bundles**. You may also have bundles that provide neither services nor library classes. For instance, a bundle can act as a server, accepting connections at a well-known socket.

Once a service is registered, another bundle—let's refer to it as the **client bundle** or the **calling bundle**—can look it up with a set of criteria, one of which is the name of the requested service interface. If it finds what it wants, it can obtain the desired service and invoke the service's methods. For example, the diagnostic bundle may get the HTTP service registered earlier by the HTTP bundle in its activator's `start` method as follows:

```
// in the diagnostic bundle's activator
public void start(BundleContext bundleContext) throws Exception {
    ServiceReference ref = bundleContext.getServiceReference(
```

---

[4] This is our fictional HTTP service. The OSGi Http service is not explained until Chapter 7.

```
            "http.service.HttpService");
        HttpService http =
            (HttpService) bundleContext.getService(ref);
        http.post(data);
    }
```

The calling bundle must obtain `org.osgi.framework.ServiceReference` before it can retrieve the service object itself. This indirection gives the bundle a chance to examine the service properties associated with the service before committing to using it.

Chapter 4 provides abundant details on how to develop, register, obtain, and invoke services.

3.6.3 Package versus Service Dependency

The package dependency as expressed by importing and exporting packages is determined at bundle development time.

Package dependency is static. Once a package has been exported, it remains in effect to all its importers, even when the bundle that has originally exported it is either stopped or uninstalled. For example, when you refer back to Figure 3.7, the uninstallation of the HTTP bundle does not prevent the streaming audio and the diagnostic bundles from continuing to use the package `http.service`.

Why is the framework designed to leave packages exported when their bundles are stopped or uninstalled? Classes inside the Java virtual machine are subject to garbage collection when they are no longer in use. Thus, their removal cannot be dictated. Explicitly requiring the classes to be kept around defines a deterministic behavior that is highly desirable for applications developed for and running in the framework.

On the other hand, service dependency is established by a bundle's getting a service registered by another at run-time. It happens *after* the package dependency between the two bundles has already been resolved.

Service dependency is dynamic. While a bundle is active, it can register or unregister its service at any time. When a service is unregistered, we also say it is **withdrawn**. This dynamic characteristic creates unique challenges for the callers of a service: When they try to obtain the service, it may not have been registered yet, so that the callers are left empty-handed. Even if the callers succeed in obtaining a registered service, it may be withdrawn later, leaving the callers with a stale service. In "Handling the Dynamic Service Dependency" on page 41, we sketch a solution using events.

3.7 Life within the Framework

Let's follow a few common scenarios to explore the interplay of various entities in the framework. We avoid covering every detail for fear of obfuscating the discussion. With the basic concepts soundly established, you will be able to complete the picture from the tutorials in later chapters as well as from the official specification itself.

3.7.1 Installing a Bundle

To install a bundle (Figure 3.8), we simply supply the framework with the URL of the bundle's JAR file. The bundle's JAR file may reside on a Web server over the network or on the local file system.

The framework retrieves the contents of the bundle from the given location and installs it on the gateway. Once installed, the bundle is assigned a unique integral ID, and its state becomes INSTALLED. An event is broadcast to notify the listeners that the bundle has been installed.

Bundles with the same location strings are considered identical. Consequently, if the same bundle was moved to a new location, it would be regarded as a different bundle and would get installed twice.

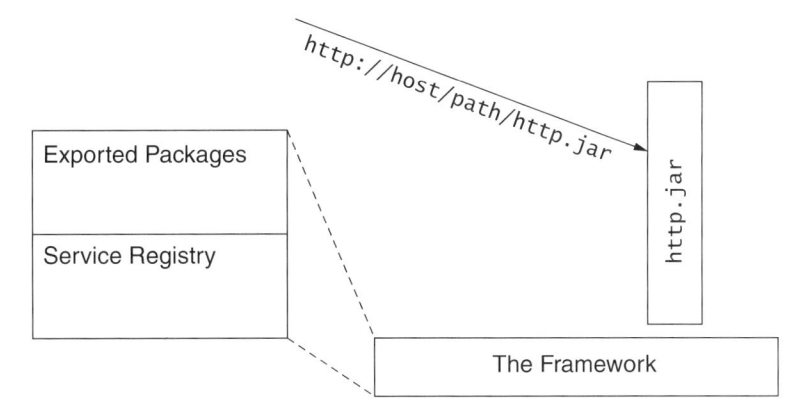

Figure 3.8 Installing a bundle

3.7.2 Starting the Bundle

The framework examines the manifest headers of the bundle, and extracts the following information about the new bundle:

- What packages this bundle offers to export (`Export-Package` header)
- What packages this bundle needs to import (`Import-Package` header)
- Which class is the activator for this bundle (`Bundle-Activator` header)

If the bundle needs to import packages, the framework checks whether any of the resolved bundles have exported those packages. If this succeeds, the bundle is resolved; otherwise, the bundle activation fails.

If the bundle is resolved or does not import any package, the bundle enters the RESOLVED state. It then exports its packages, as declared in the `Export-Package` manifest header, to the framework.

The framework creates a `BundleContext` object for the bundle, calls the `start` method of the bundle's activator, and passes in `BundleContext` as the argument. The bundle should register any services it provides in the `start` method at this time. If it does register a service, an event is broadcast to notify interested listeners that a service has been registered. For the brief period when the `start` method is being executed, the bundle is temporarily in the STARTING state.

On the successful return from the activator, the bundle moves into the ACTIVE state, and another event is broadcast to notify interested listeners that the bundle has been started (Figure 3.9).

3.7.3 Importing Packages and Getting Services

Next, suppose the streaming audio bundle, `mp3.jar`, comes along and gets installed much as `http.jar` depicted in the previous section. When the bundle is to be started, the framework attempts to satisfy its import requirements. `mp3.jar` states that it imports the `http.service` package, which has been exported by `http.jar`. The framework finds the match and marks `mp3.jar` as RESOLVED. Because `mp3.jar`'s dependency on `http.jar` has been resolved, the `mp3.jar` bundle can be started, and it becomes ACTIVE.

During the course of its execution, `mp3.jar` needs to call the `HttpService` API. Knowing what it needs, it asks the framework for a service implementing the `http.service.HttpService` interface from the service registry.

The framework returns a reference to the requested service, represented by a `ServiceReference` object, to the calling bundle (`mp3.jar`, in our case). The caller then proceeds to obtain the service itself and invokes the appropriate API defined by the service (Figure 3.10).

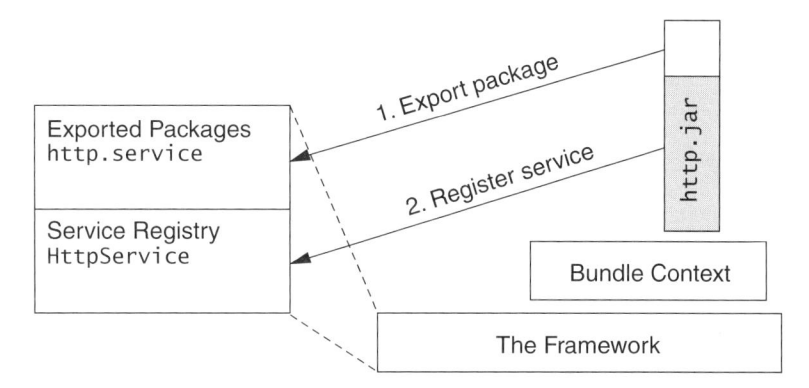

Figure 3.9 Starting a bundle: exporting packages and registering services. The shaded portion of `http.jar` shows the implementation package internal to the bundle, whereas the unshaded portion indicates the exported package to be shared with other bundles.

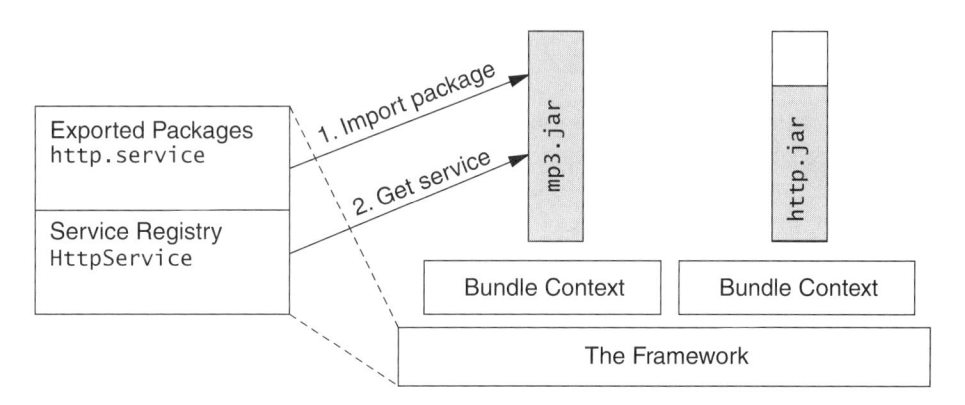

Figure 3.10 Importing packages and getting services

An important aspect of the interaction is that the `HttpService` interface is the coupling contact between the calling bundle `mp3.jar` and the service-providing bundle `http.jar`, and it is the only interface from the `http.service` package exported by the latter (Figure 3.11).

3.7.4 Handling the Dynamic Service Dependency

Within the framework, events are broadcast when bundles go through their life cycle states and when services are published or withdrawn. Let's examine how

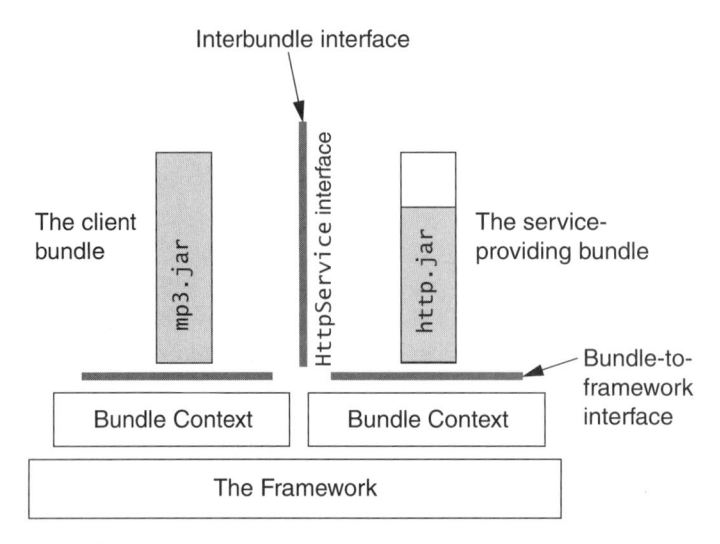

Figure 3.11 Two well-defined interfacing mechanisms. A service interface serves as the interbundle interface and the bundle context serves as the bundle-to-framework interface.

events can be used to cope with the unregistration of a service as a result of its bundle being stopped and uninstalled.

The streaming audio bundle understands that HttpService is registered by another bundle that is outside its control and may disappear (be unregistered) at any time, so it needs to monitor the unregistration events of the service.

Suppose that http.jar has to be uninstalled. As part of the process (see Section 3.7.6), the framework calls the stop method in the http.jar bundle's activator, which unregisters HttpService from the framework registry. The framework then removes http.jar from the gateway.

Bundle mp3.jar, having depended on http.jar for its service, receives the notification that HttpService is being unregistered (HttpService's unregistration is not completed until all interested parties have been notified and they have finished any action in response to the pending event of HttpService being unregistered). The mp3.jar bundle does the proper cleanup to ensure it no longer calls HttpService. It may continue to monitor service registration events, hoping that HttpService may come back, in which case it reobtains HttpService.

3.7.5 Updating a Bundle

One of the most important features of the framework is the capability of updating a bundle at run-time, which allows a newer version of a bundle to take over on the gateway. This is essential for delivering bug fixes and feature enhancements to deployed gateways in the field.

The new bundle should strive to make changes only in the implementation, not the exported packages. This practice minimizes disruption to bundles that depend on the bundle undergoing update. For the Java Embedded Server product, the new versions of the exported packages will not be exported and will not take effect until the next time the framework is restarted.

It is imperative to reaffirm the behavior that the framework refuses to export a package that has already been exported, and the exported package will remain regardless of whether the exporter is stopped or uninstalled. Therefore, it is impossible to have the new package take over by restarting the old bundle or by uninstalling the old and then reinstalling the new bundle. If you modify the classes in the exported package, the only way to use the new version is to shut down the framework, then relaunch it. This is why a stable and minimal interface between bundles is crucial for updates to be effective and successful.

Assume that `http.jar` is updated. Let's follow the procedures of an update. The HTTP bundle is stopped. As a result, `HttpService` is unregistered. Recall that `mp3.jar` is using the service and is monitoring its availability, so `mp3.jar` is able to brace itself for the change.

The new version of the HTTP bundle is fetched from the following sources:

1. If the existing bundle has the manifest header `Bundle-UpdateLocation` defined, then that location is used to fetch the new version. This configuration is useful when the old bundle knows the location of future updates ahead of time.

2. If no `Bundle-UpdateLocation` is defined, then the new version is expected to come from the same location as the old bundle.

The new bundle will be installed. If installation fails, the framework reverts to using the old bundle. Otherwise, the new bundle's state becomes INSTALLED, and an event is broadcast to notify interested listeners that the bundle has been updated. Because the HTTP bundle was active prior to the update, the new bundle is started.

As the new HTTP bundle is started, no package is exported because the `http.service` package exported by the old version remains in effect and is still imported by the `mp3.jar` bundle. `HttpService` is registered again at this time. The service interface remains intact (as part of the `http.service` package), but its implementation surely has changed.

The client bundle, `mp3.jar`, learns that the new service is registered and it should reacquire the service. Once this is achieved, it can go about its own business as before.

This narrative demonstrates how the principle of separating interfaces from implementations works in reality: The HTTP bundle only puts its service interface in one package (`http.service`), and it hides its implementation classes in another package (`http.impl`), which is not exported. In this way the HTTP bundle can update its implementation and ensure that its callers won't break because of binary incompatibility, and they can take advantage of the update right away.

Because a bundle's original location string and bundle ID are usually used to establish its identity, when the bundle is updated in the framework, they remain unchanged.

We can also demonstrate the update process using the bundle created in the previous chapter. Install and start the example bundle as before, then make the following change to the source `SweetHome.java`: Replace the string `I'll be back` to `Bye` in the `stop` method. Recompile and repackage the bundle JAR file as described previously, except that the altered JAR file is named `newhome.jar`. Now do the following:

```
> bundles
ID  STATE       LOCATION
--  ---------   -------------------------
1   ACTIVE      file:/home/joe/bundles/home.jar
```

This shows the original bundle's location and ID.

Next we update `home.jar`, whose ID is 1, with the new bundle `newhome.jar` identified by its URL:

```
> update 1 file:/home/joe/bundles/newhome.jar
I'll be back
Home, sweet home
```

Notice that you must specify a space, not a comma, between the ID and the URL. The old bundle was stopped (we see its activator's `stop` method was called), then the new one was installed and started (thus its activator's `start` method was called). Then we reexamine the bundle status:

```
> bundles
ID  STATE       LOCATION
--  ---------   -------------------------
1   ACTIVE      file:/home/joe/bundles/home.jar
```

It shows that the ID and location of the original bundle are unchanged, despite the fact that the new bundle was fetched from a different URL.

Lastly, we stop the bundle:

```
> stop 1
Bye
>
```

The message displayed testifies that the bundle has indeed been updated to reflect the new behavior.

3.7.6 Stopping and Uninstalling a Bundle

When a bundle is to be stopped, the framework calls the bundle activator's stop method. While the method is being executed, the bundle is briefly in the STOPPING state. The framework then automatically performs the following tasks:

1. Unregisters the service provided by the bundle. During this process, an event is broadcast to notify interested listeners that the service is being unregistered.

2. Releases any services in use by the bundle (details in Chapter 4)

3. Removes any event listeners added by the bundle

4. Moves the bundle back to the RESOLVED state

5. Broadcasts another event to notify listeners that the bundle has been stopped

If http.jar is stopped, HttpService is unregistered in step 1, and nothing needs to be done for steps 2 and 3, because it is not using any service from another bundle and it has not added a listener. On the other hand, if mp3.jar is stopped, nothing needs to be done for step 1 because it has not registered any service. However, HttpService, which it has been using, is released at step 2, and its event listener is removed at step 3. Both, of course, follow through with steps 4 and 5.

When uninstalled, the bundle is removed from the gateway, an event is broadcast to notify the listeners that the bundle has been uninstalled, and its state becomes UNINSTALLED.

Even when a bundle is stopped or uninstalled, the packages it has exported remain in force to ensure that other bundles that have come to depend on those packages still have access to them.

3.8 The Component-based Model

To write applications for an OSGi service framework is to develop bundles. The programming model is component-based, in contrast to the library-based model. Figure 3.12 illustrates the typical structures of the two models.

In a library-based model, we approach an application such as a word processor by designing and developing a collection of classes that are roughly divided into various functional modules or libraries (for example, print, format, utilities, and so on; see Figure 3.12a). Although the modules *could* be designed into components that have well-defined and controlled interfaces, they are not *required* to be that way. Real-world factors such as deadlines, inexperience, and expediency usually intervene and lead to an end product comprising modules that are arbitrarily accessible, tightly coupled, and inflexible.

In the best of times, even if a module is carefully crafted, it must be combined with a larger application to be reused. For example, suppose that the print module is designed to be shared with a diagnostic agent, which also needs the print functionality. We would have to make the print classes a permanent part of the diagnostic application.

After the application has been deployed, bug fixes or new features customarily require a new release. Customers have to bring down their running systems for the upgrade.

The library-based approach also imposes a "take-it-or-leave-it" situation from the user's point of view: Each new release of an application packs in more features, maintains backward compatibility, and consumes more hardware horsepower. Although many of us do not need the new features—we may not even know their existence—we must still pay the price for the added slowdown, incompatibility

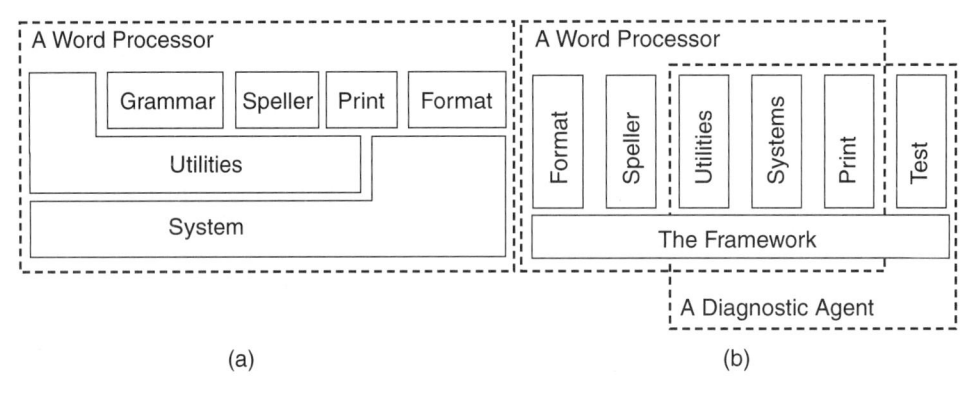

Figure 3.12 The library-based model (a) and the component-based model (b)

problems, and unreliability. We simply cannot rip out the part that we don't need and keep those that we like and know well. For instance, suppose we don't need the grammar checker in Figure 3.12a. Regardless, it is not an option to do without it.

In a component-based model, a run-time hosting framework makes a big difference. Because bundles may go through life cycles, their coupling points must be consciously made minimal and their interaction controlled. In this model, new applications naturally form themselves as bundles are plugged in. For example, in Figure 3.12b, the system, utilities, format, speller, and print bundles form a word processor application, whereas the system, utilities, print, and test bundles form a diagnostic agent application. Depending on whether the grammar checker is needed, its bundle can be installed or removed dynamically.

The envisioned operational environment of residential gateways requires a component-based model because pieces of the software come from multiple vendors and at different points in time. The static library-based approach is clearly inappropriate in this context.

In the component-based model, bundles should be "unbiased" to a wide range of application contexts; otherwise, their usefulness is limited. For example, if the print bundle expects fancy formatting specific only to the word processor, it may not be suitable for the diagnostic agent. This aspect makes design more difficult in the component-based model than the library-based model, because with the library-based mind-set a designer would never anticipate that a word processor and a diagnostic agent—applications that are world apart—may share commonalities.

Many developers do not appreciate this shift of mental models, which can cause much frustration when they start programming for service gateways. This is because we are used to writing monolithic software for which all pieces are present at run-time.

In summary, here are the main distinctions between the two models:

- In a library-based model, multiple layers of software abstractions stack up one *on top of* another, whereas in a component-based model, multiple software components plug in *side by side* with one another.

- In a library-based model, once a module is compiled into the software, it is always available at run-time. In a component-based model, a component can come and go dynamically at run-time.

- In a library-based model, the sum of all libraries must be packaged together for the product to work. In a component-based model, a subset of components can be packaged together and can serve useful functionality as a product.

- In a library-based model, one most likely must rebuild and repackage the entire set of libraries to fix bugs and add features at compile-time. In a component-based model, new components can be added or existing components can be updated in an incremental way at run-time.

- In a library-based model, changes made to public interfaces have less impact because one has to rebuild the software in its entirety. In a component-based model, the cost of redoing public interfaces can be prohibitive because other components may have relied on them at run-time.

- In a library-based model, the flow control of an application usually starts at one entry point (e.g., `public static main(String[] args)`). In a component-based model, components are controlled by a hosting environment and they interact with one another to function.

It is essential to realize that the component-based model requires more discipline on the part of developers during the design stage but provides more stability, extensibility, and flexibility over the library-based model at run-time. Two important issues are the following:

1. In the component-based model, the service on which you depend may not always be there. You must program your bundles in anticipation of this possibility. In the OSGi framework, the main solution is to use the service registration/unregistration events, which you should monitor and handle accordingly. More in-depth treatment of these topics is given in Chapter 5.

2. You must strike a balance between insulation and sharing among bundles. At one extreme, total isolation causes common functionality to be duplicated in many bundles, which increases footprint and reduces maintainability. At the other extreme, sharing everything reverts back to the library-based model with all its stated evils. As a rule, you must follow the principle of separating interfaces from implementations for services, and you must have interbundle coupling embodied in service interfaces only. This way you can achieve the best results. We follow up on more involved design issues in Chapter 6.

Other component-based Java technologies also exist. For example, an applet is a component that has life cycle operations and it is hosted by a Web browser. Its application, however, is mostly limited to a user interface. JavaBeans™ defines reusable components, but they are mainly geared toward manipulability using a visual builder tool during development. Enterprise JavaBeans™ defines a distributed component model, but its complex features such as transactional and distributed processing and persistence are not needed by many applications in resource-constrained environments.

3.9 Forget CLASSPATH

Each paradigm of programming has certain "cardinal sins." With unstructured programming languages such as BASIC, it's probably `goto`, which can easily create incomprehensible spaghetti code. With structured programming languages such as C, it's probably the use of `switch` on types, which tests a fixed set of conditions and does not evolve well with the application.[5] With *library-based* object-oriented programming, it is the inclusion of the entire class library with the application, which creates software bloat.

Veteran programmers know that they can put classes they need to use on the CLASSPATH. When they begin working in a component-based framework such as that used in the Java Embedded Server product, many find it natural simply to put the bundle JAR file they have developed on the CLASSPATH. Some do this because they are frustrated by not being able to understand interbundle class resolution well or how to get it to work.

However, to add bundle JARs to the CLASSPATH is to commit a cardinal sin in this new paradigm. Once a bundle JAR is part of the CLASSPATH, it morphs into the underlying platform and can no longer be used as a component. You cannot control its life cycle, nor can you update it. Moreover, you do not have the benefit of per-bundle insulation provided by the framework: All classes inside the JAR file are made accessible to all bundles in the framework.

It is imperative that you use the `Import-Package` and `Export-Package` headers in bundle manifests to set up interbundle class resolution. The CLASSPATH should only contain classes that make up the framework.

---

[5] "Anytime you find yourself writing code of the form, 'if the object is of type T1, then do something, but if it's of type T2, then do something else,' slap yourself." [10]

CHAPTER 4

Developing Bundles

IN this chapter we describe how to develop bundles. First, we outline the steps to develop a bundle that provides a service, to supply multiple implementations for the same service interface, and to retrieve resources packaged inside the bundle. We then cover how to use services provided by another bundle. Next we discuss how to program service factories and their usefulness. In the section that follows, we explore how to develop library bundles that make class libraries available to be shared by other bundles. Lastly, we explain how to develop bundles that carry native code.

During the process of developing bundles, we introduce you to relevant APIs in the OSGi framework with examples. The complete API specification can be found in Appendix B.

Two more elaborate examples are presented to broaden your understanding of the development of service and library bundles. A section on common mistakes is included to help you avoid many of the errors that frustrate newcomers.

The main goal of this chapter is to familiarize you with the process of developing individual bundles. However, keep in mind that any bundle hardly functions alone in the framework. How to write cooperative bundles is covered in detail in Chapter 5.

4.1 Writing Service Bundles

A service should provide a public interface that specifies what it does and the necessary implementation classes that realize how it is done. The service must be registered with the framework to be useful for other bundles on the gateway.

The general process of developing a service bundle is as follows:

1. Design the service interface.
2. Implement the service.

3. Write a bundle activator that usually registers the service in its `start` method and unregisters the service in its `stop` method.

4. Declare the packages exported by your bundle in the `Export-Package` manifest header; the service interface should belong to the exported packages.

5. Compile the classes and pack everything into a bundle JAR file.

Let's see how this is done with a simple service example.

4.1.1 Design the Service Interface

Suppose we want to develop a dictionary service that returns word definitions.[1] The service interface may be defined as:

```
package com.acme.service.dictionary;
/**
 * This service produces definitions of words.
 */
public interface DictionaryService {
   /**
    * Gets the definition of a word.
    * @param word the word whose definition is sought.
    * @return the definition or null if the word is not found.
    */
   public String getDefinition(String word);

   /**
    * Gets the definitions of the words beginning with the specified
    * letter.
    * @param alpha the first letter of the words.
    * @return an array of definitions, or null if either no
    * definition is found or the letter is invalid.
    */
   public String[] getDefinitions(char alpha);
}
```

The service interface should be placed in a dedicated package, because it is to be exported to and accessible by other bundles. It should be annotated with ample

---

[1] Hopeless spellers may get excited over this service; the rest of us only need to heed the mechanisms of the process.

comments to define unambiguously the semantics of what the methods are supposed to do. Whenever possible, document all parameters, return values, and exceptions of the methods using the appropriate `javadoc` tags. We often call the interface a **contract**, so let's make it detailed enough to read like one.

4.1.2 Implement the Service

The following class provides a trivial implementation of the previous service interface. We return the Devil's definitions authored by Ambrose Bierce (circa 1881–1906) [11].

```
package com.acme.impl.dictionary;
import java.util.*;
import com.acme.service.dictionary.DictionaryService;

class Devil implements DictionaryService {
   private Properties defs;

   Devil() {
      defs = new Properties();
      defs.put("accuse", "To affirm another's guilt or unworth; " +
            "most commonly as a justification of ourselves for " +
            "having wronged him.");
      defs.put("admire", "Our polite recognition of " +
            "another's resemblance to ourselves");
      defs.put("calamity", "Misfortune to ourselves, " +
            "and good fortune to others.");
      defs.put("kill", "To create a vacancy without nominating " +
            "a successor.");
   }

   public String getDefinition(String word) {
      return (String) defs.get(word);
   }

   public String[] getDefinitions(char alpha) {
      Vector v = new Vector();
      for (Enumeration e = defs.keys(); e.hasMoreElements(); ) {
         String w = (String) e.nextElement();
         if (w.length() > 0 && w.charAt(0) == alpha)
            v.addElement(w + ": " + defs.get(w));
```

```
        }
        String[] result = null;
        if (v.size() > 0 ) {
            result = new String[v.size()];
            v.copyInto(result);
        }
        return result;
    }
}
```

The implementation class should reside in a different package from that of the interface and should be made package private. Hiding the implementation leaves the service interface as the only contact point between the service-providing bundle and the service-using bundles, and is critical for successful bundle update. We explore this theme in more depth later.

4.1.3 Register the Service in the Activator

We register the service in the bundle activator's `start` method, so that our service becomes available when the bundle is started. We unregister it in the bundle activator's `stop` method, so that it is withdrawn when the bundle is stopped. The bundle activator is defined as

```
package com.acme.impl.dictionary;
import java.util.Properties;
import org.osgi.framework.BundleActivator;
import org.osgi.framework.BundleContext;
import org.osgi.framework.ServiceRegistration;
import com.acme.service.dictionary.DictionaryService;

public class Activator implements BundleActivator {
    private ServiceRegistration devilReg;

    public void start(BundleContext ctxt) {
        DictionaryService devil = new Devil();
        Properties devilProps = new Properties();
        devilProps.put("author", "Ambrose Bierce");
        devilProps.put("description", "The Devil's Dictionary");
        devilReg = ctxt.registerService(
            "com.acme.service.dictionary.DictionaryService",
            devil, devilProps);
```

```
    }

    public void stop(BundleContext ctxt) {
        if (devilReg != null)
            devilReg.unregister();
    }
}
```

BundleContext ctxt is passed to the start and stop methods by the framework. The bundle interacts with the framework through its bundle context. The start method instantiates an instance of Devil, and registers the service object under the name of its service interface (com.acme.service.dictionary.DictionaryService) with the framework using the registerService method of the BundleContext instance. The service is also registered with the properties of author and description to describe its attributes further. The stop method unregisters the service using the ServiceRegistration object returned at the time of registration.

As a convenience, the framework automatically unregisters any services registered by the bundle when it is stopped. Therefore, the stop method may be equivalently defined as

```
    public void stop(BundleContext ctxt) {
        // nothing needs to be done; the framework will unregister
        // the Devil dictionary service automatically.
    }
```

We always explicitly unregister our services in this chapter, but keep this framework feature in mind.

4.1.4 Define the Manifest Headers

The manifest is defined as follows:

```
Exported-Package: com.acme.service.dictionary;
 specification-version=1.0.0
Bundle-Activator: com.acme.impl.dictionary.Activator
```

We declare here that the service interface in the com.acme.service.dictionary package is to be made available to other bundles using the Export-Package header. We also specify that the version of the exported package is 1.0.0. If the specification-version clause is omitted, the version number is 0.0.0 by default.

4.1.5 Create the Bundle

Compile the code, and package everything in a JAR file, with contents that look like

```
META-INF/
META-INF/MANIFEST.MF
com/acme/service/dictionary/DictionaryService.class
com/acme/impl/dictionary/Devil.class
com/acme/impl/dictionary/Activator.class
```

The bundle is ready. Launch the Java Embedded Server software as described in Chapter 2, and install and activate the bundle. You will see the following output from the `bundles`, `services`, and `exportedpackages` commands:

```
> bundles
ID   STATE     LOCATION
--   --------  -------------------------
1    ACTIVE    file:C:/users/joe/bundles/dictionary.jar
> services
[com.acme.service.dictionary.DictionaryService]
    author=Ambrose Bierce
    description=The Devil's Dictionary
> exportedpackages
Package: com.acme.service.dictionary (1.0.0)
    Exported by: 1 (file:C:/users/joe/bundles/dictionary.jar)
```

This output tells us that the dictionary bundle is active in the framework. It has registered `DictionaryService` with the properties `author` and `description`, and it has exported the package `com.acme.service.dictionary`, version 1.0.0, in which the service interface `DictionaryService` resides.

4.2 Same Service Interface, Different Implementations

An advantage of separation of interface and implementation is that you can provide different implementations to the same interface. Let's see how we can provide another implementation of the `DictionaryService` interface in our dictionary bundle.

The following implementation class returns word definitions from *Webster's* dictionary:

```
package com.acme.impl.dictionary;
import java.util.*;
import com.acme.service.dictionary.DictionaryService;

class Webster implements DictionaryService {
    private Properties defs;

    Webster() {
        defs = new Properties();
        defs.put("accuse", "to charge with a fault or offense");
        defs.put("admire", "to marvel at or esteem highly");
        defs.put("calamity", "a state of deep distress or " +
                "misery caused by major misfortune or loss");
        defs.put("kill", "to deprive of life");
    }

    public String getDefinition(String word) {
        // code is the same as in Devil
    }

    public String[] getDefinitions(char alpha) {
        // code is the same as in Devil
    }
}
```

The following shows the revised activator. Code in bold type signifies what it takes to register another instance of the service:

```
package com.acme.impl.dictionary;
import java.util.Properties;
import org.osgi.framework.BundleActivator;
import org.osgi.framework.BundleContext;
import org.osgi.framework.ServiceRegistration;
import com.acme.service.dictionary.DictionaryService;

public class Activator implements BundleActivator {
    private ServiceRegistration devilReg, websterReg;

    public void start(Bundledevil ctxt) {
```

```
        DictionaryService ds = new Devil();
        Properties devilProps = new Properties();
        devilProps.put("author", "Ambrose Bierce");
        devilProps.put("description", "The Devil's Dictionary");
        devilReg = ctxt.registerService(
            "com.acme.service.dictionary.DictionaryService",
            devil, devilProps);
        Properties websterProps = new Properties();
        websterProps.put("author", "Noah Webster");
        websterProps.put("description", "Webster Dictionary");
        websterReg = ctxt.registerService(
            "com.acme.service.dictionary.DictionaryService",
            new Webster(), websterProps);
    }

    public void stop(BundleContext ctxt) {
        if (devilReg != null)
            devilReg.unregister();
        if (websterReg != null)
            websterReg.unregister();
    }
}
```

Because we have only revised the implementation portion of the dictionary service, we do not need to change anything in the manifest. We are still exporting the same package containing the service interface.

Create the bundle JAR file for the new bundle. Let's call it newdictionary.jar. It should have the following contents:

```
META-INF/
META-INF/MANIFEST.MF
com/acme/service/dictionary/DictionaryService.class
com/acme/impl/dictionary/Devil.class
com/acme/impl/dictionary/Webster.class
com/acme/impl/dictionary/Activator.class
```

Because we have modified the dictionary bundle, we can update the existing version that is active in the framework to the new one.

```
> update 1 file:/C:/users/joe/bundles/newdictionary.jar
> services
[com.acme.service.dictionary.DictionaryService]
    author=Ambrose Bierce
```

```
    description=The Devil's Dictionary
[com.acme.service.dictionary.DictionaryService]
    author=Noah Webster
    description=The Webster Dictionary
```

The `update` command updates the old dictionary bundle with an ID of 1 to the version identified by the URL. After the update, the `services` command shows that there are two services registered in the framework now.

So far we have seen the option of packaging multiple implementations of a service interface into one bundle. The advantage is that the implementations may share common structures or code. In the example of the Devil and Webster dictionary services, it would be silly to duplicate the code that accesses the hash table in the `getDefinition(s)` methods. It can be factored out and shared by both implementations. The disadvantage is that if only one implementation is needed, both must be installed.

A second way of packaging the bundle overcomes this problem: You may split the Devil and Webster implementations into their own bundles, and include the service interface classes in both bundles. With this arrangement, you can install only the needed bundle. The layout of the Devil bundle looks like

```
META-INF/
META-INF/MANIFEST.MF
com/acme/service/dictionary/DictionaryService.class
com/acme/impl/dictionary/Devil.class
com/acme/impl/dictionary/Activator.class
```

and the layout of the Webster bundle looks like

```
META-INF/
META-INF/MANIFEST.MF
com/acme/service/dictionary/DictionaryService.class
com/acme/impl/dictionary/Webster.class
com/acme/impl/dictionary/Activator.class
```

The manifest definitions for both bundles need not be changed. Apparently the activator in either bundle needs to be trivially changed to register only the corresponding implementation of `DictionaryService`. Its code is not shown.

Although the same `com.acme.service.dictionary` package in which the service interface class `DictionaryService` resides appears in both bundles, only one bundle is chosen to export the package, at the framework's discretion. The other bundle, having failed the bid to export the package, imports the package offered by the winner. It is critical that the service interface class, `DictionaryService.class`, be identical in both bundles, so that either one can be used interchangeably. We elaborate on this requirement from the perspective of class loading and type integrity in "Interbundle Dependency and Class Loading Issues" on page 64.

4.3 Retrieving Resources from within the Bundle

A bundle can carry not only code, but also data. Packaging classes and required resources together make the bundle a self-contained deployment unit.

In our dictionary bundle, it is apparent that inserting individual word definition entries into the data structure is awkward. Unless we add tens of thousands of `put` statements to our implementation code, our dictionary service won't be of much use.

Let's create a property file containing the dictionary entries, pack the file into the bundle, and write code to retrieve the entries in the dictionary service.

Here's a segment of the text file `webster.properties`:

```
# The word definitions from Webster's Dictionary
...
accuse=to charge with fault or offense
admire=to marvel at or esteem highly
...
calamity=a state of deep distress or misery caused by major↵
misfortune or loss
kill=to deprive of life
...
```

Save the property file in the directory in which the implementation classes reside and create the bundle JAR file. Its contents will look like this:

```
META-INF/
META-INF/MANIFEST.MF
com/acme/service/dictionary/DictionaryService.class
com/acme/impl/dictionary/Devil.class
com/acme/impl/dictionary/Webster.class
com/acme/impl/dictionary/Activator.class
com/acme/impl/dictionary/webster.properties
```

We modify the constructor of `Webster` class to retrieve the properties:

```
import java.io.*;
class Webster implements DictionaryService {
    private Properties defs;
```

```
    Webster() {
      try {
        String resourceName =
          "/com/acme/impl/dictionary/webster.properties";
        InputStream in =
          this.getClass().getResourceAsStream(resourceName);
        if (in != null)
          defs.load(in);
      } catch (IOException e) {
      }
    }
    ...
}
```

A class loader is created for each bundle for loading classes and resources from the bundle. When you call the `getResourceAsStream` or the `getResource` methods, the class loader associated with the bundle is called to duty to retrieve the resources. That's why you can use any class object inside the bundle and call `getResourceAsStream` on it. The resource name should be the full path to the resource internal to the bundle JAR file. This technique works for any type of data files, be they GIF or JPEG images, HTML pages, or configuration properties.

You may also call `getResource` and get a URL pointing to the desired resource. We discuss the use of the URL in more detail when we discuss the HTTP service in Chapter 7.

4.4 Obtaining and Calling Registered Services

After the dictionary bundle has been installed and activated in the framework, we can witness packages being exported and services being registered using commands in the framework console. However, the service itself is never invoked. Many developers are not comfortable with the notion of activating code that is not run and does nothing. In fact, this is one unique aspect of our programming model: You set up services waiting to be invoked by code from another bundle.

In this section, let's write a caller bundle whose sole purpose is to exercise `DictionaryService` in the dictionary bundle. To get our terminologies straight, recall that we refer to the caller bundle as the **calling bundle,** or the **client bundle**, and we refer to the bundle that registers services as the **service-providing bundle**.

Follow these three steps to obtain and use a service from a different bundle:

1. Declare an `Import-Package` header in the manifest of the client bundle. The value specifies the name of the package that is expected to be exported by the service-providing bundle. The package should contain the service interface needed by the client bundle.
2. Call `BundleContext`'s `getServiceReference` method, specifying the name of the service interface to obtain `ServiceReference` to the service. You may optionally provide a filter to select service references based on service properties.
3. Call `BundleContext`'s `getService` method, passing in `ServiceReference` obtained in step 2, to get the service object itself.

Let's define the manifest of the caller bundle first:

```
Import-Package: com.acme.service.dictionary
Bundle-Activator: com.acme.caller.dictionary.Activator
```

Here is the activator that retrieves `DictionaryService` in its `start` method and prints the definitions for words starting with the letter "a":

```
package com.acme.caller.dictionary;
import org.osgi.framework.BundleActivator;
import org.osgi.framework.BundleContext;
import org.osgi.framework.ServiceReference;
import com.acme.service.dictionary.DictionaryService;

public class Activator implements BundleActivator {

   public void start(BundleContext ctxt) throws Exception {
      ServiceReference[] ref = ctxt.getServiceReferences(
         "com.acme.service.dictionary.DictionaryService",
         "(description=The Devil's Dictionary)");
      if (ref == null) {
         System.out.println("The Devil's Dictionary " +
            "service has not been registered");
         return;
      }
      DictionaryService ds =
         (DictionaryService) ctxt.getService(ref[0]);
      String[] aDefs = ds.getDefinitions('a');
```

```
        if (aDefs != null) {
            for (int i=0; i<aDefs.length; i++)
                System.out.println(aDefs[i]);
        }
        ctxt.ungetService(ref[0]);
    }

    public void stop(BundleContext ctxt) {
    }
}
```

We know that the dictionary bundle registers two versions of `Dictionary-Service`. In this example, we specifically request `DictionaryService` implemented by the Devil's dictionary. Because both versions implement the same service interface, we can only distinguish them using their associated service properties, as spelled out with the condition (`description=The Devil's Dictionary`) in the `getServiceReferences` call. Had we specified the condition (`description=The Webster Dictionary`), we would have gotten Webster's version of `DictionaryService`. The condition is expressed using a filter string. We look at the use of filters in more detail when we explain the `getServiceReferences` API in "BundleContext Interface" on page 75.

If you do not care which version of `DictionaryService` is returned, specify `null` as the condition.

The `getServiceReferences` method returns an array of service references that satisfy the given criterion. We are happy with the first one in the array, and we use that to retrieve the service itself.

After calling on the service to get the meanings of all the words beginning with the letter "a," we signify that we are finished using the service by calling `ungetService`.

Create the caller bundle, install it, and start it in the framework, and you will see the following output:

```
> bundles
ID   STATE      LOCATION
--   ---------  ----------------------------
1    ACTIVE     file:C:/users/joe/bundles/dictionary.jar
2    INSTALLED  file:C:/users/joe/bundles/caller.jar
> start 2
admire: Our polite recognition of another's resemblance to ourselves
accuse: To affirm another's guilt or unworth; most commonly as a
justification of ourselves for having wronged him.
>
```

4.4.1 Interbundle Dependency and Class Loading Issues

In the previous example we saw that the caller bundle depends on the dictionary bundle in two aspects: It imports the package exported by the dictionary, and it obtains the service registered by the dictionary. It is important to understand that importing the packages in which service interfaces/classes are defined is a prerequisite to using the services successfully. For example, the caller bundle must import the package com.acme.service.dictionary, which contains the interface class DictionaryService (a type), before obtain the DictionaryService object (an instance of the type). What will happen if the dictionary bundle neglects to export com.acme.service.dictionary or the caller bundle does not bother to import the package? Well, as soon as[2] the caller bundle tries to cast the service obtained from the registry to the desired DictionaryService at the following statement

```
DictionaryService ds = (DictionaryService) ctxt.getService(ref[0]);
```

NoClassDefFoundException is raised because without the package exporter and importer correctly set up, the caller bundle's class loader is not able to find the class definition needed.

Another issue concerning type integrity is also worth exploring. It comes up when one service interface is included in two or more bundles with different implementations (see the description of packaging options on page 59). Within the Java virtual machine, a type is uniquely defined by two elements:

1. Its fully qualified class name
2. The class loader that has loaded the class

Thus, if two types differ in either of these regards, they are treated as different types by the Java virtual machine.

We explained that although the Devil and the Webster bundles both export the com.acme.service.dictionary package, where the DictionaryService interface resides, only one, say the Devil bundle, prevails. In other words, when the Webster bundle attempts to load DictionaryService, it uses the class loader of the exporter—the Devil bundle—rather than its own. Bear in mind that although the Webster bundle also contains a copy of the DictionaryService class, it is always ignored. As a result, to code inside any bundle, one and only one type is present: com.acme.service.dictionary.DictionaryService class loaded by the Devil bundle's class loader.

---

[2] This exception could happen earlier if the Java virtual machine performs eager class resolution.

What would happen if instead of loading `DictionaryService` from the exporter (Devil), the Webster bundle loaded its own copy of the service interface class? Chaos. Effectively two distinct types are floating around in the Java virtual machine: the $DictionaryService_w$ loaded by the Webster bundle and the $DictionaryService_d$ loaded by the Devil bundle. Both bundles would register their implementations of the dictionary service, but when the caller bundle tries to obtain an instance, it may very well cast a $DictionaryService_d$ instance to the $DictionaryService_w$ type or vice versa, resulting in `ClassCastException` being raised.

Although this hypothetical scenario won't happen with a correctly implemented framework, you can experience a similar problem if the copies of `DictionaryService` classes packaged into the Webster and the Devil bundles differ, which may also lead to class cast problems for the caller bundle. This is why we emphasize earlier that the two copies of the class should be identical.

4.4.2 Service Use Count

A service use count is maintained for each service used by each calling bundle in the framework. Each time the bundle calls `getService`, the count is incremented; each time the bundle calls `ungetService`, the count is decremented. When the count is decreased to zero, it means that the calling bundle has finished using the service. At this point we say that the bundle has *released* the service.

You cannot obtain the service use count directly in your program, but you can check the return value of the `ungetService` API. It returns `false` if the count has become zero, and returns `true` otherwise.

By the time your bundle is stopped, if `ungetService` is not called as many times as `getService` for a given service, the framework automatically sets the service use count of the bundle to zero and forcibly releases the service.

4.4.3 Compiling Client Bundles

To build a client bundle, you must put the service-providing bundle's JAR file on the CLASSPATH at *compile-time*. For instance,

```
setenv CLASSPATH jes_path/lib/framework.jar:/home/joe/bundles/↵
dictionary.jar
javac com/acme/caller/dictionary/*.java
jar cmf com/acme/caller/dictionary/Manifest caller.jar com
```

However, make sure the service-providing bundle's JAR file is *not* on the CLASSPATH at *run-time*. See "Forget CLASSPATH" in Chapter 3 on page 49.

4.5 Service Factory

We have seen that after a bundle registers a service, other bundles can use it. So far, all client bundles are using the same instance of the service. Many applications may find this arrangement lacking under the following circumstances:

- A service-providing bundle may want to provide different instances of a service based on which bundle makes the request. This allows a customized service to be returned for each caller.

- A service-providing bundle may need the opportunity to perform application-specific logic when a client bundle gets or releases the service.

A service factory can address these issues. We illustrate how to write a bundle that registers a service factory through an example.

4.5.1 Producing a Customized Service for Each Client Bundle

We begin by introducing `ParameterService`, motivated by the following requirements: Bundles need to store or access some configurable parameters at run-time. Additionally, parameters pertinent to one bundle should not be accessible and modifiable by another. The service interface is defined as

```
package com.acme.service.param;
/**
 * This service allows a caller to store and retrieve parameters
 * in the form of a key/value pair.
 */
public interface ParameterService {
   /**
    * Stores a parameter.
    * @param key the name of the parameter.
    * @param value the value of the parameter.
    */
   public void set(String key, String value);

   /**
    * Retrieves a parameter.
    */
```

```
   public String get(String key);
}
```

Its implementation is just as straightforward:

```
package com.acme.impl.param;
import java.util.*;
import com.acme.service.param.ParameterService;

class ParameterServiceImpl implements ParameterService {
   Properties props;

   public void set(String key, String value) {
      props.put(key, value);
   }

   public String get(String key) {
      return props.get(key);
   }

   ParameterServiceImpl(Properties initProps) {
      if (initProps != null) // copy initial parameters if any
         props = (Properties) initProps.clone();
      else
         props = new Properties();
   }
}
```

At this stage, we could register this service directly as we did before. However, this would mean that all bundles that require `ParameterService` would share the same `ParameterService` instance. As a result, its data integrity and security would be brittle: Different client bundles would follow only a "gentlemen's agreement" to access their parameters under their own key namespace, but how do you prevent a careless or malicious bundle from messing around with another's data? The performance of `ParameterService` itself is also a concern: How do you synchronize concurrent access from multiple bundles while minimizing performance penalty? To address these issues, we introduce the main character of this section, a `ServiceFactory` implementation:

```
package com.acme.impl.param;
import org.osgi.framework.Bundle;
import org.osgi.framework.ServiceFactory;
import org.osgi.framework.ServiceRegistration;

class ParameterServiceFactory implements ServiceFactory {
    public Object getService(Bundle bundle, ServiceRegistration reg)
    {
        return new ParameterServiceImpl(null);
    }

    public void ungetService(Bundle bundle, ServiceRegistration reg,
                      Object service)
    {
        // does nothing
    }
}
```

In our activator, rather than register an instance of `ParameterService`, we register the service factory:

```
ctxt.registerService("com.acme.service.ParameterService",
     new ParameterServiceFactory(), null);
```

It is important that the service factory be registered under the type of the service it is going to generate. In the previous example, the object being registered is of the type `ParameterServiceFactory`, but the type under which it is registered is `com.acme.service.param.ParameterService`.

Now from the client bundle's perspective, it will use the following sequence to retrieve and use `ParameterService`:

```
ServiceReference ref = ctxt.getServiceReference(
    "com.acme.service.param.ParameterService");
ParameterService myParams =
     (ParameterService) contxt.getService(ref);
```

The same APIs are used as in "Obtaining and Calling Registered Services" on page 61. The fact that the registered service is implemented as a service factory is transparent to the client bundles. However, for each calling bundle, the framework delegates its `getService` call to `ParameterServiceFactory`'s `getService` method instead of returning an instance directly from the service registry. Consequently, each calling bundle gets its own copy of `ParameterService`. They can set or get parameters as they wish, without worrying about potential clashes in key names or values compromised by another bundle accidentally or maliciously, because each copy maintains its own instance of the parameter data structure (`Properties props` of the `ParameterServiceImpl` class). Figure 4.1 illustrates the difference with or without the service factory.

4.5.2 Service Cache

When a bundle calls the `getService` method for the very first time, the framework is required to cache internally the service instance produced by the service factory for the requesting bundle. Subsequently, if the same bundle calls `getService` again, the framework returns the cached service, rather than invokes the service factory's `getService` method to generate new ones repeatedly.

A service use count is maintained for each calling bundle in the same manner described in Section 4.4.2. When the count is decreased to zero, the framework removes the service from its internal cache automatically.

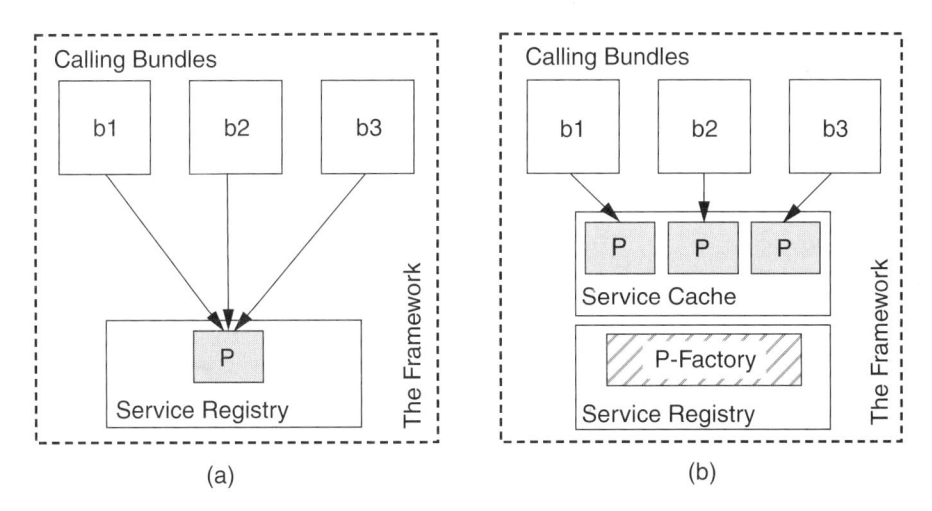

Figure 4.1 Getting service with (a) and without (b) using a service factory. P is an instance of `ParameterService`, P-Factory is an instance of `ParameterServiceFactory`.

4.5.3 Customization for Getting and Releasing Service

In many situations, a service-providing bundle needs to know when a client bundle starts using the service it provides, and it needs to know when the client bundle finishes using the service. A service factory makes this possible by allowing you to customize behaviors in the `getService` and `ungetService` methods, respectively.

In our example, when a client bundle releases the service by calling `ungetService`, the instance of `ParameterService` it has been using is removed from the framework cache. So the next time the same bundle calls `getService`, it gets a brand new `ParameterService`, and loses all its previously stored parameters. To correct this problem, we can save the parameters persistently in the `ungetService` method.

Every bundle has its own private data storage area, accessible as a `java.io.File` object returned by the `BundleContext` method `getDataFile`. Passing in an empty string ("") returns the root `File` to the storage area.

Within the parameter bundle's data storage area, a subdirectory is created for each client bundle to save its parameters as a property file. We use the bundle ID as the directory name because it is guaranteed to be unique within the framework and persistent until the bundle is uninstalled. The directory structure is shown in Figure 4.2

```
Parameter bundle's
    data root
       |
       ├──── 4
       |     └── parameters.properties
       |
       ├──── 1
       |     └── parameters.properties
       |
       ├──── 7
       |     └── parameters.properties
       |
```

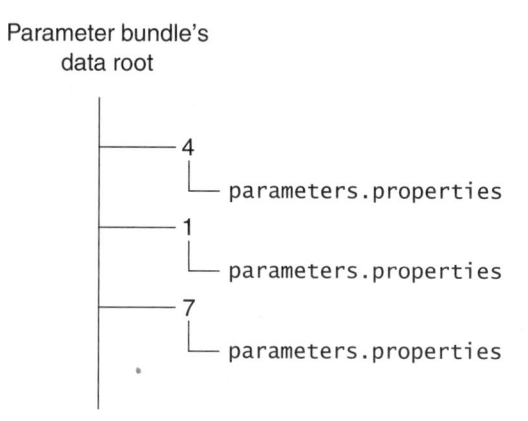

Figure 4.2 In the parameter bundle's data area, we currently maintain parameters for three client bundles, whose IDs are 4, 1, and 7 respectively.

We encapsulate the details of accessing the parameter bundle's data storage in a `ParameterStore` object, whose complete implementation is included in Appendix A, section A.3.1.6. For now, it's sufficient to know that its `load` method retrieves the parameters for a given bundle, whereas its `save` method stores them.

The service factory is changed to accommodate this feature as follows:

```
package com.acme.impl.param;
import org.osgi.framework.Bundle;
import org.osgi.framework.BundleContext;
import org.osgi.framework.ServiceFactory;
import org.osgi.framework.ServiceRegistration;
import java.util.Properties;
import java.io.IOException;

class ParameterServiceFactory implements ServiceFactory {
   private ParameterStore store;

   ParameterServiceFactory(ParameterStore store) {
      this.store = store;
   }

   // A client bundle starts using ParameterService.
   public Object getService(Bundle bundle, ServiceRegistration reg)
   {
      try {
         // retrieve the parameters for the client bundle
         return new ParameterServiceImpl(store.load(bundle));
      } catch (IOException e) {
      }
      return new ParameterServiceImpl(null);
   }

   // The client bundle finishes using ParameterService.
   public void ungetService(Bundle bundle, ServiceRegistration reg,
                    Object service)
   {
      try {
         // save the parameters for the client bundle
         ParameterServiceImpl ps = (ParameterServiceImpl) service;
         store.save(bundle, ps.props);
      } catch (IOException e) {
```

```
            }
        }
    }
```

The `Object service` argument in the `ungetService` method may need explanation. When the calling bundle finishes using the service, the framework passes the cached service instance back to the service factory's `ungetService` method automatically. This is how we know `service` is the expected `ParameterServiceImpl` instance for saving the parameters.

We never make use of the `ServiceRegistration` argument in `ServiceFactory`'s `getService` and `ungetService` methods. It is useful when the same service factory is registered multiple times.

The activator registers the service factory as follows:

```
ParameterStore store = new ParameterStore(ctxt);
ctxt.registerService("com.acme.service.param.ParameterService",
        new ParameterServiceFactory(store), null);
```

When the client bundle signifies that it has finished using `ParameterService` by calling `ungetService`, its parameter set is written to the parameter bundle's persistent storage area. When it calls `getService` again, the saved parameters are restored. What makes this solution more significant are the following two circumstances:

1. When the client bundle is stopped without having called `ungetService`. The framework, as a step in stopping the client bundle, calls `ungetService` automatically. In our example, the framework "ungets" `ParameterService` for the client bundle.

2. When `ParameterService` is unregistered, perhaps because the parameter bundle is being stopped. The framework also calls `ungetService` to "unget" `ParameterService` automatically on behalf of each client bundle.

In either case, the client bundles' parameters get a chance to be properly saved.

A service factory relieves a programmer from keeping track of complicated, dynamic dependency relations. It allows a service-providing bundle to discover the client bundles of its service and to act accordingly.

We have not seen the last of `ParameterService`. When we discuss events in Chapter 5 and permissions in Chapter 9, we revisit and expand this example. For simplicity's sake, we use system properties to configure parameters for services in the examples that follow. Moreover, `ParameterService` cannot perform this duty until permission-based security is explained.

4.6 Relevant `org.osgi.framework` APIs

Until now we've come across a number of OSGi APIs, which are summarized here. We use a few fictional services (for example, `PrintService`) in our examples. Their particular service interfaces and implementations are of little interest to our discussion and are not shown.

The emphasis is on how to use these APIs through examples. The formal and complete API specification can be found in Appendix B.

4.6.1 BundleContext Interface

The `BundleContext` APIs allow you to register services with the framework's service registry, to query registered services, and to retrieve services from the registry. You can also access a per-bundle private, persistent data storage area by using the `BundleContext` API.

An instance of `BundleContext` is created by the framework and is passed to a bundle as an argument in the bundle activator's `start` or `stop` methods. Normally a bundle should keep `BundleContext` received in its activator private, thus any service obtained by calling `getService` on `BundleContext` is attributed to this bundle (that is, its use count of the service is incremented). There is no ambiguity referring to the bundle as the calling bundle, as we do throughout this book.

However, what happens if bundle A is bent on giving out its `BundleContext` to bundle B? When code inside bundle B calls `getService` using bundle A's `BundleContext`, the service is still considered being used by A, not B. In the specification, A is referred to as the **context bundle** (instead of the **calling bundle**) to avoid any confusion regarding to which bundle the service use count should be charged. To keep it simple, do not share `BundleContext` objects across bundles.

public ServiceRegistration registerService(String clazz, Object service, Dictionary props)

The parameter `clazz` is the class name of the service, and `service` is the service object itself. If a service object is an instance of multiple types, it can be registered using the following alternative, which takes an array argument.

public ServiceRegistration registerService(String[] classes, Object service, Dictionary props)

The framework ensures that service is indeed of the type or types specified in the `classes` parameter. The class names must be fully qualified and should specify the service interface names (for example, `com.acme.service.dictionary.DictionaryService`), not the implementation class names (for example, `com.acme.impl.dictionary.Devil`).

Additionally, a set of properties can be registered together with the service. What goes in the properties is entirely application specific, and this parameter can be `null` if there are no properties to register. Properties consist of name/value pairs. The property name must be of type `java.lang.String`; the value can be any object. Let's look at some examples. The following code registers a service under its class name with no property:

```
bundleContext.registerService(
    "com.acme.service.print.PrintService", printService, null);
```

The following code registers a service under its class name, and registers a set of properties that describes its characteristics:

```
Properties props = new Properties();
props.put("location", "first floor");
props.put("laser", Boolean.TRUE);
props.put("capability",
    new String[] {"double-sided", "manual-feed", "color"});
props.put("dpi", new int[] {72, 300, 640, 1024});
props.put("paper", new String[] {"A4", "Letter", "Legal"});
bundleContext.registerService(
    "com.acme.service.print.PrintService", printService, props);
```

The following code registers a service under multiple classes with properties:

```
String[] classes = { "com.acme.service.print.PrintService",
   "com.acme.service.format.FormatService",
   "com.acme.service.speller.SpellingService" };
bundleContext.registerService(classes, printService, props);
```

In this case, `printService` obviously must be an instance of `com.acme.service.print.PrintService`, `com.acme.service.format.FormatService`, and `com.acme.service.speller.SpellingService`. The framework performs a type check and if `printService` is not an instance of any of the said classes, service registration fails.

The following code registers a service factory without properties:

```
bundleContext.registerService("com.acme.service.fax.FaxService",
    new FaxServiceFactory(), null);
```

Unlike service registration, type checking for service factory registration is postponed until the client bundle calls `getService`. Only then does the framework ensure that the service generated by the factory is compatible with the type used at registration.

public ServiceReference getServiceReference(String clazz)

The parameter `clazz` is the interface name of the service to get. The returned service reference is an indirection to the service object. If no service is found, this method returns `null`.

Oftentimes we register multiple instances of services under the same service interface. We have seen that in the dictionary bundle, `Devil` returns definitions of a humourous and cynical flavor, whereas Webster returns the definitions in the canonical sense, but both implement `DictionaryService`.

As another example, a `PrintService` interface allows a caller to make a hardcopy of data, but one implementation may use a local inkjet printer and another may use a laser printer over the network.

In situations like this, certain properties associated with the registered service are used to distinguish one instance from another.

To obtain a service based on certain criteria, use the method described in the next section.

public ServiceReference[] getServiceReferences(String clazz, String filter) throws InvalidSyntaxException

The syntax used for expressing conditions in the filter argument is based on RFC 1960, "A String Representation of LDAP Search Filters" [12]. Each term in the filter expression has the format

    (attribute name *op* value)

where `attribute name` is the name of the property. It must be a string and it is case insensitive in filter evaluations. `value` can be of the following types:

- `String`
- Number: `Byte, Short, Integer, Long, Float, Double, BigInteger, BigDecimal`
- `Character`
- `Boolean`
- `Vector` or array of the previous

- Array of the primitive types (`byte`, `short`, `int`, `long`, `char`, `float`, `double`, `boolean`)
- Nested `Vectors` or arrays to any depth

op is one of the relational operators defined in Table 4.1.

Table 4.1 Relational Operators in LDAP Filters

Operator	Meaning	Applicable Data Type
>=	Greater than or equal	`String`, `Character`, number
<=	Less than or equal	`String`, `Character`, number
=	Equal	All
~=	Approximately equal	`String`
=*	Present	`String`

The expression uses a prefix notation and defines three logical operators: AND (&), OR (|), NOT (!).

Note that we only borrow the LDAP filter *syntax* but otherwise do not involve the directory service itself in any way.

For those who find the formal definitions in the RFC unpalatable, the following examples should give you everything you need to know about syntax. The following code finds any print service that uses a laser printer and can do double-sided printing:

```
refs = bundleContext.getServiceReferences(
    "com.acme.service.print.PrintService",
        "(&(laser=true)(capability=double-sided))");
```

Because the property name is case insensitive in evaluation, you may spell `capability` as `Capability` or `CAPABILITY` without affecting the outcome. Note that you must not enter quotes around `String` or `Character` values. The following code finds all services registered with the framework:

```
refs = bundleContext.getServiceReferences(null, null);
```

The following code finds all print services:

```
refs = bundleContext.getServiceReferences(null,
    "(objectClass=com.acme.service.print.PrintService)");
```

objectClass is a special property that is automatically inserted by the framework at the time of service registration. It has the class names with which the service has been registered. The following statement

```
refs = bundleContext.getServiceReferences(
   "com.acme.service.print.PrintService", null);
```

can be used equivalently.

The following code finds all services from Acme. An asterisk in the value represents a wildcard. It matches zero or more arbitrary characters:

```
refs = bundleContext.getServiceReferences(null,
   "(objectClass=com.acme.service.*)");
```

The following code finds print services that use a laser printer or have resolution in dots per inch (DPI) of at least 300.

```
refs = bundleContext.getServiceReferences(
   "com.acme.service.print.PrintService",
   "(|(laser=true)(dpi>=300))");
```

Notice that the property value dpi is an array with multiple possible resolution values. In this case, each element in the array is checked in turn to see whether the element meets the condition. If any element satisfies the condition, the property is considered to satisfy the condition. If the array value has elements that themselves are arrays, each of them will be checked recursively. The same algorithm is applied if the property value is of type java.util.Vector.

The following code finds the service that can do printing and formatting, and is located on the third floor. Notice that & and | can precede any number of conditions:

```
refs = bundleContext.getServiceReferences(null,
   "(&(objectClass=com.acme.service.print.PrintingService)" +
   "(objectClass=com.acme.service.format.FormatService)" +
   "(location=third floor))");
```

The following code finds print services that do not use a laser printer but that have a DPI of at least 300.

```
refs = bundleContext.getServiceReferences(
   "com.acme.service.print.PrintService",
   "(&(!(laser=true))(dpi>=300))");
```

The following code finds print services that can do any kind of binding at all:

```
refs = bundleContext.getServiceReferences(
   "com.acme.service.print.PrintService",
   "(binding=*)");
```

Notice here that =* represents the presence test operator. If nothing appears to the right of =*, the expression is interpreted to perform the existence test. However, (binding=*foo) is interpreted to match a property named "binding" whose value ends with "foo."

To include characters such as *, (, or) in the value of the filter, "escape" them with a backslash. For example,

```
refs = bundleContext.getServiceReferences(
   "com.acme.service.format.FormatService",
   "(section_separator_char=\\*)");
```

finds all formatting services that use a string of asterisks as the section separator.

RFC 1960 states that the semantics of the approximate equal operator (~=) is implementation specific. The Java Embedded Server framework evaluates (attribute~=value) as follows: Any nonalphanumeric characters are removed from the property and the filter value, and letters are compared in a case-insensitive way. If the filter value still appears in the property, the expression is evaluated to be true. The operator does not implement any "sound like" semantics, however. For example, assume the property vendor has the value "Sun Microsystems, Inc." Then

```
(vendor~=sun)
(vendor~=sunmicro system)
(vendor~=Systems inc)
```

all evaluate to true.

public Object getService(ServiceReference ref)

This method gets the service referenced by the specified ServiceReference object. The call is delegated to a service factory's getService method if ref represents a registered service factory, rather than just returning the registered service itself. The framework increases a service use count for a particular client bundle each time it calls getService.

public boolean ungetService(ServiceReference ref)

This method "ungets" the service referenced by the specified ServiceReference. The framework decreases the service use count for the calling bundle.

ungetService returns `false` if the count has dropped to zero. It returns `true` otherwise. The call is delegated to a service factory's `ungetService` method if the service use count drops to zero, and `ref` represents a registered service factory, rather than the service itself.

For example, the following code gets the fax services from the service factory:

```
ServiceReference ref = bundleContext.getServiceReference(
    "com.acme.service.fax.FaxService");
FaxService fax1 = (FaxService) bundleContext.getService(ref);
FaxService fax2 = (FaxService) bundleContext.getService(ref);
boolean isReleased = bundleContext.ungetService(ref);
```

In this example, we are getting service produced by `FaxServiceFactory`, because that is what we registered earlier. Because the framework caches the service produced for each calling bundle, `fax1` and `fax2` are identical service instances; in other words, `fax1 == fax2`. Additionally, `isReleased` reports `true` because we have two `getService` calls but only one `ungetService`.

As another example, the following ensures that the fax service is truly released:

```
while (ungetService(ref));
```

If `ungetService` is called more times than `getService`, no harm is done. It keeps returning `false`.

Suppose `getService` is invoked again afterward. The service factory will instantiate a new `FaxService`:

```
FaxService fax3 = (FaxService) bundleContext.getService(ref);
```

where `fax3 != fax1` and `fax3 != fax2`. Note that `fax1` and `fax2` are still valid object references, but because the service they reference has been released, you are not supposed to use the service instance through them any more.

public File getDataFile(String path)

This method gets the `File` representing the path to the bundle's data storage area if the gateway supports a local file system. Each bundle is allocated such a data directory, and can use it in an application-specific way. If `path` is assigned an empty string (""), this method returns the root path of the directory. For instance, given

```
File root = myBundleContext.getDataFile("");
File d = myBundleContext.getDataFile("myapp.properties");
```

and if `root.getPath()` returns /home/joe/jescache/bundle1/data, then `d.getPath()` returns /home/joe/jescache/bundle1/data/myapp.properties.

4.6.2 ServiceReference Interface

`ServiceReference` serves as an intermediary so that the client bundle can examine various properties of the service before committing to using it. It is returned by `getServiceReference(s)` APIs on the `BundleContext` interface or by the `getReference` method on the `ServiceRegistration` interface.

public Object getProperty(String key)

This method returns the value of the specified key in the service properties.

public String[] getPropertyKeys()

This method returns all property keys. Together with the `getProperty` method, you can examine the entire property set. See `ServiceRegistration` API `setProperties` for an example of modifying existing service properties.

public Bundle getBundle()

This method returns the bundle that has registered the service. A return value of `null` means that `ServiceReference` is stale—in other words, the service it references has already been unregistered.

4.6.3 ServiceRegistration Interface

The `registerService` API on the `BundleContext` interface returns a `ServiceRegistration` object.

public ServiceReference getReference()

This method returns the service reference for this registration. Service references obtained from different `ServiceRegistration` instances are all different, even for the same service object. For example,

```
FaxService fax = new FaxServiceImpl();
ServiceRegistration reg1 = bundleContext.registerService(
    "com.acme.service.fax.FaxService", fax, null);
```

```
ServiceRegistration reg2 = bundleContext.registerService(
    "com.acme.service.fax.FaxService", fax, null);
```

`reg1.getReference().equals(reg2.getReference())` is evaluated as `false`.

public void unregister()

The service registration object can be kept around by the caller as a token for unregistering the service later using this method. If necessary, the original registering bundle can pass the object to other entities, which will be able to perform service unregistration on behalf of the original registrant. Whoever has the service registration object can unregister the service, so give it out judiciously. For example,

```
ServiceRegistration printReg =
    bundleContext.registerService(classes, printService, props);
...
printReg.unregister();
```

public void setProperties(Dictionary properties)

This method allows a caller to modify the properties associated with the registered service after the registration. For example,

```
ServiceRegistration printReg = bundleContext.registerService(
    classes, printService, initProps);
// get existing properties
Hashtable props = new Hashtable();
ServiceReference printRef = printReg.getReference();
String[] keys = printRef.getPropertyKeys();
for (int i=0; i < keys.length; i++)
    props.put(keys[i], printRef.getProperty(keys[i]));
// modify a property
String features = (String)props.get("features");
features += " transparency double-sided n-up";
props.put("features", features);
printReg.setProperties(props);
```

adds a few descriptions to the print service's `features` property.

4.7 Library Bundles

It is often the case that certain standard class libraries, or utility or helper classes need to be shared by many bundles. Library bundles fill this role.

In a conventional Java runtime environment, you usually add additional class libraries to the CLASSPATH before running an application. However, by packaging them into library bundles, you can gain additional manageability and flexibility: You can choose to install them only when needed and you may be able to update the bundles with a newer version without shutting down the framework.

Generally, library bundles do not register any services or have activators. They can be constructed with these two steps:

1. Define the library classes and interfaces in their appropriate packages. Generally they should be public classes and interfaces.

2. Declare the packages with the Export-Package header in the manifest.

Imagine that Acme has a data structure package that needs to be packaged as a library bundle. The following is a skeleton definition for a linked list:

```
package com.acme.util;

public class LinkedList {

    public LinkedList() {
       // construct an empty linked list
    }

    public void append(Object e) {
       // append an object to the linked list
    }

    public java.util.Enumeration elements() {
       // return an enumeration of all elements in the list
    }

    // Other operations on the LinkedList.
```

```
    class Node {    // an element in the list
       Object data;
       Node next;
    }
}
```

We export the package by declaring it in the manifest:

`Export-Package: com.acme.util`

This tells the framework that the classes from the `com.acme.util` package are to be made accessible to any bundle that chooses to import this package. Use the `jar` command to pack up the bundle, whose contents look like

```
META-INF/
META-INF/MANIFEST.MF
com/acme/util/LinkedList.class
com/acme/util/LinkedList$Node.class
```

You can install and activate this bundle just like any other bundle. Using the Java Embedded Server software, library bundles must be activated before any other bundles can use the exported classes.

To use these data structures from another bundle, declare the manifest in the other bundle like this:

`Import-Package: com.acme.util`

We can then write code similar to the following, directly referencing the `LinkedList` class:

```
import com.acme.util.*;
...
LinkedList list = new LinkedList();
list.append(new String("Some text"));
list.append(new Integer(100));
```

Put the library bundle's JAR file on the CLASSPATH only when you compile the previous code. See "Compiling Client Bundles" on page 65.

A bundle can package other JAR files inside its own bundle JAR file. This mechanism is very convenient when dealing with units of classes that are functionally self-contained. Imagine that you are developing a bundle that depends on some class packages from a third party. It is much cleaner and less error prone to include the JAR file from external sources inside your own bundle than to extract and manipulate classes written by others. The latter may not even be an option if the JAR file has been digitally signed to ensure its authenticity and integrity, or disassembling is forbidden by the license terms.

Suppose a demonstration version of a thesaurus service is packaged as a nested JAR file in the dictionary bundle. We would have the following layout of the dictionary bundle:

```
META-INF/
META-INF/MANIFEST.MF
com/acme/service/DictionaryService.class
com/acme/extra/thesaurus.jar
com/acme/impl/Activator.class
com/acme/impl/Webster.class
com/acme/impl/webster.properties
```

The new kid on the block is the nested JAR, thesaurus.jar. Suppose its contents are as follows:

```
META-INF/
META-INF/MANIFEST.MF
com/acme/demo/service/ThesaurusService.class
com/acme/demo/impl/ThesaurusImpl.class
```

In situations like this, the containing bundle's manifest may declare a new manifest header, Bundle-ClassPath. This header determines the CLASSPATH for the bundle. That is, when Bundle-ClassPath is present, only the packages from the JARs listed in the header are accessible to the bundle itself or to other bundles (if an Export-Package header is also declared). The search order for loading a class from the bundle is also dictated by the order in which the JARs are enumerated in this header. Let's see how this header works for the following three cases:

1. No Bundle-ClassPath is specified in the containing bundle's manifest. In this case, only packages in the containing bundle are accessible. Packages in nested JARs are completely ignored, as if thesaurus.jar didn't exist in the dictionary bundle at all.

2. The Bundle-ClassPath header is defined in the containing bundle's manifest. Only packages in the JARs that are listed are accessible. Packages in nested JARs not listed in Bundle-ClassPath are ignored. Nested JARs are identified by their paths internal to the bundle. A special path, a dot (.), is used to identify the containing bundle itself.

For example, suppose the dictionary bundle has the following declaration in its manifest:

```
Bundle-Classpath: .,com/acme/extra/thesaurus.jar
Export-Package: com.acme.service, com.acme.demo.service
```

If so, then all packages in the dictionary bundle and `thesaurus.jar` are accessible to the bundle itself. They are

```
com.acme.service
com.acme.impl
com.acme.demo.service
com.acme.demo.impl
```

During class loading, the dictionary bundle is searched before the nested `thesaurus.jar`, following the declarative order in the header.

The `Export-Package` declaration in the dictionary bundle then only allows the `com.acme.service` and `com.acme.demo.service` packages to be exported and accessible to other bundles.

Beware that the paths to the nested JARs are relative inside the containing bundle. Had `thesaurus.jar` been packaged at the top level in the dictionary bundle instead of at `com/acme/extra`, `Bundle-ClassPath` would have been defined as

```
Bundle-ClassPath: .;thesaurus.jar
```

3. `Bundle-ClassPath` does not include the dot (.).

    Packages in the containing bundle are skipped. For example, if dictionary bundle's manifest is defined as

    ```
    Bundle-ClassPath: com/acme/extra/thesaurus.jar
    ```

    then only the `com.acme.demo.service` and `com.acme.demo.impl` packages of nested `thesaurus.jar` are accessible.

    The `Bundle-ClassPath` header controls not only the classes but also the resources in the JARs. For example, in the last case, the `webster.properties` resource is inaccessible because it resides in the containing bundle, which is bypassed entirely.

4.8 Advanced Examples

We now present more elaborate examples of how to develop bundles. We also want to point out the idea that this new model does not limit you from leveraging the full power of the Java platform: You can use extensions such as JavaMail™ and Java servlets. You can apply object-oriented abstraction of any complexity in your service implementation.

4.8.1 A Mailer

This bundle mainly demonstrates how to deal with nested library JAR files. It uses the JavaMail API[3] to send out an e-mail message when it is started or stopped.

Although e-mail delivery appears to be an activity performed by humans at desktop computers, it can lend itself to interesting applications on a residential gateway. For example, a home security bundle can notify you if it detects an intruder on the premises by sending an e-mail message to your pager.

To use the JavaMail API in your code, you first obtain the `javax.mail.Session` object, which encapsulates various environment properties for the e-mail application, such as the name of the mail server. With the `Session` object, you can create `javax.mail.internet.MimeMessage`, in which you specify the sender, recipient, subject, and body of the e-mail message. Lastly, use `javax.mail.Transport`'s `send` method to deliver the e-mail message.

The JavaMail API makes use of the JavaBeans™ Activation Framework (JAF), which is concerned with assigning data content handlers to particular data types. The familiar "mailcap" specification (RFC 1524 [13]) is one concrete example of the JAF. For more details on JavaMail and JAF, please consult related white papers and Java documentation [14].

We develop the mail sender bundle first. The code that implements its activator is as follows:

```
package com.acme.mail;
import java.io.*;
import java.net.InetAddress;
import java.util.Properties;
import java.util.Date;
import javax.mail.*;
import javax.mail.internet.*;
import org.osgi.framework.*;
```

---

[3] You can download the JavaMail class library (packaged in `mail.jar`) from http://java.sun.com/products/javamail/index.html. Note that JavaMail requires the JavaBeans™ Activation Framework (packaged in `activation.jar`).

```java
/**
 * This class delivers an email notification
 * when the bundle is started or stopped.
 */
public class Notification implements BundleActivator {
   public void start(BundleContext ctxt) throws Exception {
      send("Home, sweet home!");
   }

   public void stop(BundleContext ctxt) throws Exception {
      send("I'll be back!");
   }

   private void send(String msgBody) throws Exception {
      String to = System.getProperty("com.acme.mail.recipient");
      String subject = "JavaMail library bundle example";
      String from = System.getProperty("com.acme.mail.sender");
      String mailhost =
         System.getProperty("com.acme.mail.server");
      String mailer = "JES Mailer Bundle";
      Properties props = System.getProperties();
      props.put("mail.smtp.host", mailhost);

      // Get a Session object
      Session session = Session.getDefaultInstance(props, null);

      // construct the message
      Message msg = new MimeMessage(session);
      msg.setFrom(new InternetAddress(from));
      msg.setRecipients(Message.RecipientType.TO,
            InternetAddress.parse(to, false));
      msg.setSubject(subject);
      msg.setText(msgBody);
      msg.setHeader("X-Mailer", mailer);
      msg.setSentDate(new Date());

      // send the thing off
      Transport.send(msg);
   }
}
```

This mail sender bundle has the following manifest:

```
Import-Package: javax.mail, javax.mail.internet, javax.activation
Bundle-Activator: com.acme.mail.Notification
```

We do not specify package version numbers in the `Import-Package` header, effectively importing any versions of the packages that have been exported. The bundle contains

```
META-INF/MANIFEST.MF
com/acme/mail/Notification.class
```

We then create the mail library bundle. The JavaMail API and the JAF come in two JAR files: `mail.jar` and `activation.jar`. Conventionally these JAR files are expected to be included in your CLASSPATH, but here we nest them inside a separate mail class library bundle. We could package the library and the code that uses it into a single bundle, but keeping the former self-contained in its own bundle allows it to be shared by other bundles without much overhead. We then define the following manifest file to export the packages:

```
Export-Package: javax.mail; specification-verion=1.1.3,
  javax.mail.internet; specification-version=1.1.3,
  javax.activation; specification-version=1.0.1
Bundle-ClassPath: mail.jar, activation.jar
```

We declare that the library bundle exports three packages from the JavaMail API and the JAF. Furthermore, we also specify the version numbers for these packages so that the framework can pick the appropriate exporters. As a rule, it is recommended that exporters always specify versions of packages to be exported. Importers, on the other hand, don't have to, unless they must import one particular version. We do not include the dot (.) in `Bundle-ClassPath` because there is no other class present in the mail library bundle. For the same reason, we have no `Bundle-Activator` manifest header either.

The contents of the newly created library bundle are simply

```
META-INF/MANIFEST.MF
mail.jar
activation.jar
```

Install and activate the mail library bundle first, then install the mail sender bundle. Set the mailer's parameters using the `set` command from the Java Embedded Server console like this:

```
> set com.acme.mail.recipient=joe@acme.com
> set com.acme.mail.sender=joe@acme.com
> set com.acme.mail.server=mail.acme.com
```

Then you can activate and deactivate the bundle to have the e-mail messages sent.

4.8.2 A Line Printer Daemon Print Service

In this example we develop a print service. The complete source code is located in Appendix A.1.1. Here, we show the part of the code that is instructive to our discussion.

First and foremost, we present the `PrintService` interface:

```
package com.acme.service.print;
import java.io.IOException;
import java.net.URL;

/**
 * PrintService prints contents from a URL or
 * gets status of a print queue.
 */
public interface PrintService {
   /**
    * Prints the contents from the source to the specified printer.
    * @param printer the name of the destination printer
    * @param source the source of the contents to be printed
    * @exception IOException if printing fails
    */

   public void print(String printer, URL source) throws IOException;

   /**
    * Gets the status of the specified printer.
    * @param printer the name of the printer
    * @return the status of the print queue as an array,
    * one element per print job;
```

```
     * null if no entries are present in the queue
     */
    public String[] getStatus(String printer) throws IOException;
}
```

This is a generic interface that specifies two major features pertinent to a printer: printing some contents from a source URL and obtaining the status of the print queue. It is not difficult to propose a multitude of possible implementation scenarios. For example, one implementation may use a proprietary protocol to access a local printer through a printer driver installed in the operating system; another may use a standard network protocol to communicate with a printer on the network.

In this case, let's implement the service interface with the LPD protocol, which interacts with the printer over the TCP/IP network. This protocol has been widely used in many UNIX environments and can be installed and configured on Windows NT platforms as well. The protocol is specified in RFC 1179 [15].

We implement the service as an LPD client that connects to a remote print server on the well-known port of 515. The setup is illustrated in Figure 4.3.

Based on the request/response nature of the protocol, we provide further abstraction in our service implementation. We first initialize a `Printer` object with the name of the printer server. Whenever we want to request a function (such as getting status or printing), we call the `request` method on `Printer`:

```
package com.acme.impl.print;
import java.io.*;
import java.net.*;

class Printer {
    private String printServer;
```

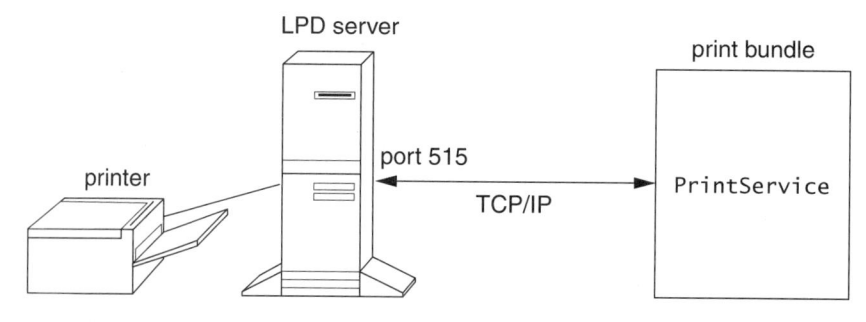

Figure 4.3 The LPD printer

```java
    Printer(String ps) {
       this.printServer = ps;
    }

    /**
     * Send a request to the printer daemon.
     * @param command a number representing a command
     * @param queue the name of the print queue
     * @param operand the operand needed by the command
     * @return a connection to the printer daemon.
     * @exception java.io.IOException if communication to the daemon
     * fails.
     */
    PrintConnection request(int command, String queue,
       String operand) throws IOException
    {
       // Open a socket on the print server at port 515;
       // send the request in the format defined by the RFC;
       // return a PrintConnection object that encapsulates the
       // connection to the print server, so that the required
       // information can be exchanged to complete the request.
    }
}
```

According to the RFC, to get status, send the sequence of protocol elements depicted in Figure 4.4 to the daemon.

A single round-trip is sufficient to retrieve the print queue status. However, a few exchanges are needed to deliver a print job, as shown in Figure 4.5.

```
                    SEND_QUEUE_STATUS SP queue LF
   printer    ◄────────────────────────────────────── printer
   daemon     ──────────────────────────────────────► client
                      status for the print queue
```

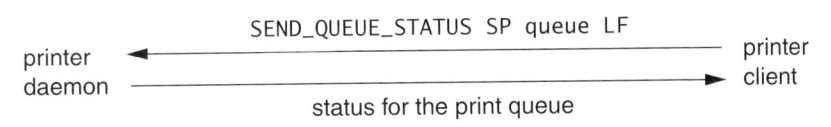

Figure 4.4 Protocol operation for getting print queue status. In the request sequence, the constant symbol SEND_QUEUE_STATUS is 4 in the program, SP is a white space (ASCII 32), queue is the print queue name, and LF is the line feed character (ASCII 10). The status is returned by the daemon as strings.

```
                    RECEIVE_PRINT_JOB SP queue LF
                ◄─────────────────────────────────
                                Ack
                ─────────────────────────────────►
   printer        RECEIVE_CONTROL, control sequence     printer
   daemon       ◄─────────────────────────────────      client
                                Ack
                ─────────────────────────────────►
                    RECEIVE_DATA, source contents
                ◄─────────────────────────────────
                                Ack
                ─────────────────────────────────►
```

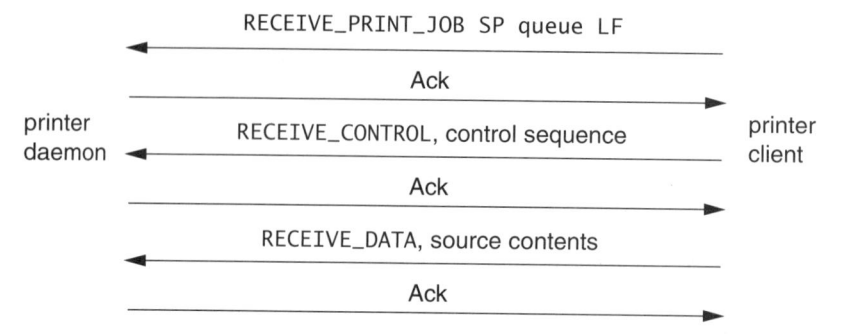

Figure 4.5 Protocol operation for sending a print job to the daemon. The request has a similar format. The constant symbol `RECEIVE_PRINT_JOB` has a value of 2 in the program. This request is followed by a negotiation consisting of subcommands `RECEIVE_CONTROL` and `RECEIVE_DATA`.

`PrintConnection` encapsulates a session between the client and the server during the process of fulfilling a request:

```
package com.acme.impl.print;
import java.net.*;
import java.io.*;

class PrintConnection {
   private static int RECEIVE_CONTROL = 2;
   private static int RECEIVE_DATA = 3;
   private Socket sock;
   private String host;
   private String printQueue;

   PrintConnection(String q, Socket s) throws IOException {
      this.sock = s;
      this.host = InetAddress.getLocalHost().getHostName();
      this.printQueue = q;
   }

   // Get a character stream from the printer daemon.
   Reader getReader() throws IOException {
      InputStream in = sock.getInputStream();
      return new BufferedReader(new InputStreamReader(in));
   }
```

```java
    // Get a byte stream from the printer daemon.
    InputStream getInputStream() throws IOException {
        return sock.getInputStream();
    }

    // Get an acknowledge byte from the daemon. 0 means success.
    int getAck() throws IOException {
        return sock.getInputStream().read();
    }

    // Send control sequences to the daemon. This identifies the data
    // that follow and their size.
    void sendControl(int jobNumber, URL src) throws IOException
    {
        // Construct the control sequence as defined by the RFC.
        // Request to send the control sequence to the printer.
        // Send the contents of the control sequence to the printer.
    }

    // Send data to the daemon. The data source can be a local file
    // or from a URL pointing to a remote location.
    void sendData(int jobNumber, URL src) throws IOException {
        // Read from the specified data source.
        // Request to send data to the printer.
        // Send the data to the printer.
    }

    // Close connection to the daemon.
    void close() throws IOException {
        sock.close();
    }
}
```

With the `Printer` and `PrintConnection` classes defined, we are ready to implement the `PrintService` interface with the `PrintServiceImpl` class. The `getStatus` method implements the protocol operation of getting the print queue status; the `print` method implements the protocol operation of delivering a print job to the printer daemon:

```java
package com.acme.impl.print;
import java.net.*;
import java.io.*;
```

```
import java.util.*;
import com.acme.service.print.PrintService;

class PrintServiceImpl implements PrintService {
   private final static int SEND_QUEUE_STATE = 4;
   private final static int RECEIVE_PRINT_JOB = 2;
   private Printer printer;
   private static int jobNumber = 100;

   PrintServiceImpl() {
      String lpdServer =
         System.getProperty("com.acme.service.print.lpdserver");
      printer = new Printer(lpdServer);
   }

   public String[] getStatus(String printQueue) throws IOException {
      // Request print job status from the printer
      // Process the report from the printer and return the result
   }

   public void print(String printQueue, URL src)
      throws IOException
   {
      // Request to send print job to the printer
      // Send control sequence describing the print job
      // Send the data to be printed.
   }
}
```

At this point we have completed our LPD `PrintService` implementation. The next order of business is to write the bundle activator:

```
package com.acme.impl.print;
import java.util.Properties;
import org.osgi.framework.*;
import com.acme.service.print.PrintService;

public class Activator implements BundleActivator {
   private ServiceRegistration reg;
```

```
    public void start(BundleContext ctxt) {
        PrintService svc = new PrintServiceImpl();
        Properties props = new Properties();
        props.put("description", "A sample print service");
        reg = ctxt.registerService(
            "com.acme.service.print.PrintService", svc, props);
    }

    public void stop(BundleContext ctxt) {
        if (reg != null)
            reg.unregister();
    }
}
```

We then define the manifest as follows:

```
Bundle-Activator: com.acme.impl.print.Activator
Export-Package: com.acme.service.print
```

We now use the jar command to zip the classes into a bundle. The contents of this bundle will look like

```
META-INF/MANIFEST.MF
com/acme/service/print/PrintService.class
com/acme/impl/print/Activator.class
com/acme/impl/print/PrintServiceImpl.class
com/acme/impl/print/Printer.class
com/acme/impl/print/PrintConnection.class
```

The process of implementing the print service is not unlike conventional programming using the Java programming language. It is up to you to decide what types of class hierarchy should be constructed, what kind of data structures must be written, and so on.

Moreover, development of the service implementation is mostly confined in a particular application domain. In other words, you are free to program whatever is necessary to bring about the desired functionality. The OSGi framework itself and its programming paradigm do not restrict what can be done in one particular application domain. You only need to follow some simple rules to make your code an accepted "citizen" in the OSGi world.

4.9 Writing Bundles That Contain Native Code

Because one of the intended uses of the residential gateway is to control low-level devices, in many circumstances we need to resort to native code to achieve certain functionality unavailable in the Java platform.

The framework allows a bundle to carry several dynamically linked native libraries for different operating system and processor environments, and at installation time attempts to match the appropriate native library with the underlying platform. If the framework succeeds in finding such a match, the native library will be linked into the Java virtual machine.

The framework learns the characteristics of the native platform from the OSGi environment properties established when the framework is started (Table 4.2).

Table 4.2 OSGi Environment Properties

Environment Property	Meaning	Example Value
org.osgi.framework.processor	The processor of the gateway	sparc
org.osgi.framework.os.name	The operating system running on the gateway	Solaris
org.osgi.framework.os.version	The operating system version	2.6
org.osgi.framework.language	The language used in the operating system	en

Each bundle that carries native libraries must define a `Bundle-NativeCode` header in its manifest, which tells the framework which library to pick. For example, imagine a bundle that provides a service that returns the free space on a file system, a function implemented in native code. It may have the following declaration in its manifest:

```
Bundle-NativeCode: com/acme/impl/filesys/libfilesysinfo.so;
   osname=Solaris; processor=sparc; osversion=2.5,
   com/acme/impl/filesys/libfilesysinfo.so; osname=SunOS;
    processor=sparc; osversion=5.5,
   com/acme/impl/filesys/filesysinfo.dll; osname=Windows NT;
      processor=x86; osversion=4.0
```

This header contains three clauses separated by commas. It says that the bundle contains two native libraries: `libfilesysinfo.so` for the Solaris/SunOS system and `filesysinfo.dll` for Windows NT. Notice for some Sun's platforms, the operating system value is Solaris 2.x, whereas for others it reports SunOS 5.x. They effectively refer to the same environment, and we supply both as a precaution. Such situations are expected to be common in other operating environments as well, and this technique can be quite useful.

The following are more examples of how to define the Bundle-NativeCode header:

```
Bundle-NativeCode: libX; libY; libZ; processor=x86; osname=Linux,
 libA; libB; processor=x86; osname=Windows NT
```

This code says install libX, libY, and libZ on an x86 machine running Linux, but install libA and libB if the machine runs Windows NT. If you want a group of libraries to be installed on one particular platform, separate them with semicolons and place them at the beginning of the same clause.

The following code causes either libX or libY, but not both, to be installed on an x86 machine running Linux.

```
Bundle-NativeCode: libX; osname=Linux; processor=x86,
 libY; processor=x86; osname=Linux
```

The framework picks one arbitrarily between the two. If you want them both to be installed, declare libY in the same clause with libX. Note that the order in which the attribute specifications appear (osname or processor) in a clause does not matter.

The following code says install libX on an x86 machine with Linux version 6.0 or 6.1, but pick libY on an x86 machine running any of the three Windows variants.

```
Bundle-NativeCode: libX; osname=Linux; processor=x86;
 osversion=6.0; osversion=6.1,
 libY; processor=x86; osname=Windows NT; osname=Windows95;
 osname=Windows98
```

Note that if the same attribute specification (osversion and osname) is repeated in a clause, their values are OR'ed together during the matching process.

Now consider the following code:

```
Bundle-NativeCode: libX; osname=Linux; processor=x86;
 osversion=6.0,
 libY; processor=x86; osname=Linux; osversion=5.2,
 libZ; processor=x86; osname=Linux; lang=en
```

If an x86 machine runs Linux 6.0, libX will be chosen as the exact match. If it runs Linux 6.1, however, all three are valid candidates, because 6.0, 5.2, and no version number are considered backward compatible with (because they are less than) version 6.1: At this point, the next criterion we can use is the language setting. If the operating system language locale is set to English (en), libZ is the only winner. However, if the operating system language setting is Japanese (ja), then the framework will pick either libX or libY, because they have no specific requirement for the language.

If the machine runs Linux 5.0, then only libZ can be selected, because libX and libY require an operating system with incompatible version numbers, whereas libZ has no specific requirement on the operating system version number.

To summarize, the framework uses the algorithm presented in Figure 4.6 to find the "best" matching native code clause.

Now let's look closer at the native code example, which implements a service that reports free disk space. Just like any other services, we begin by defining the service interface:

```
package com.acme.service.filesys;
/**
 * This service returns information about a given file system.
 */
public interface FilesystemInfoService {
   /**
    * Gets free space on the given file system.
    *
    * @param path the path indicates which file system to query; if
    * null is specified, the current directory is used.
    * @return the free space in bytes.
    * @exception java.io.IOException if low-level operations fail to
    * get the value of free space.
    */
   public long getFreeSpace(String path) throws java.io.IOException;
}
```

Next we provide the implementation class, defined as

```
package com.acme.impl.filesys;
import java.io.IOException;
import com.acme.service.filesys.FilesystemInfoService;

class FilesystemInfoServiceImpl implements FilesystemInfoService {
```

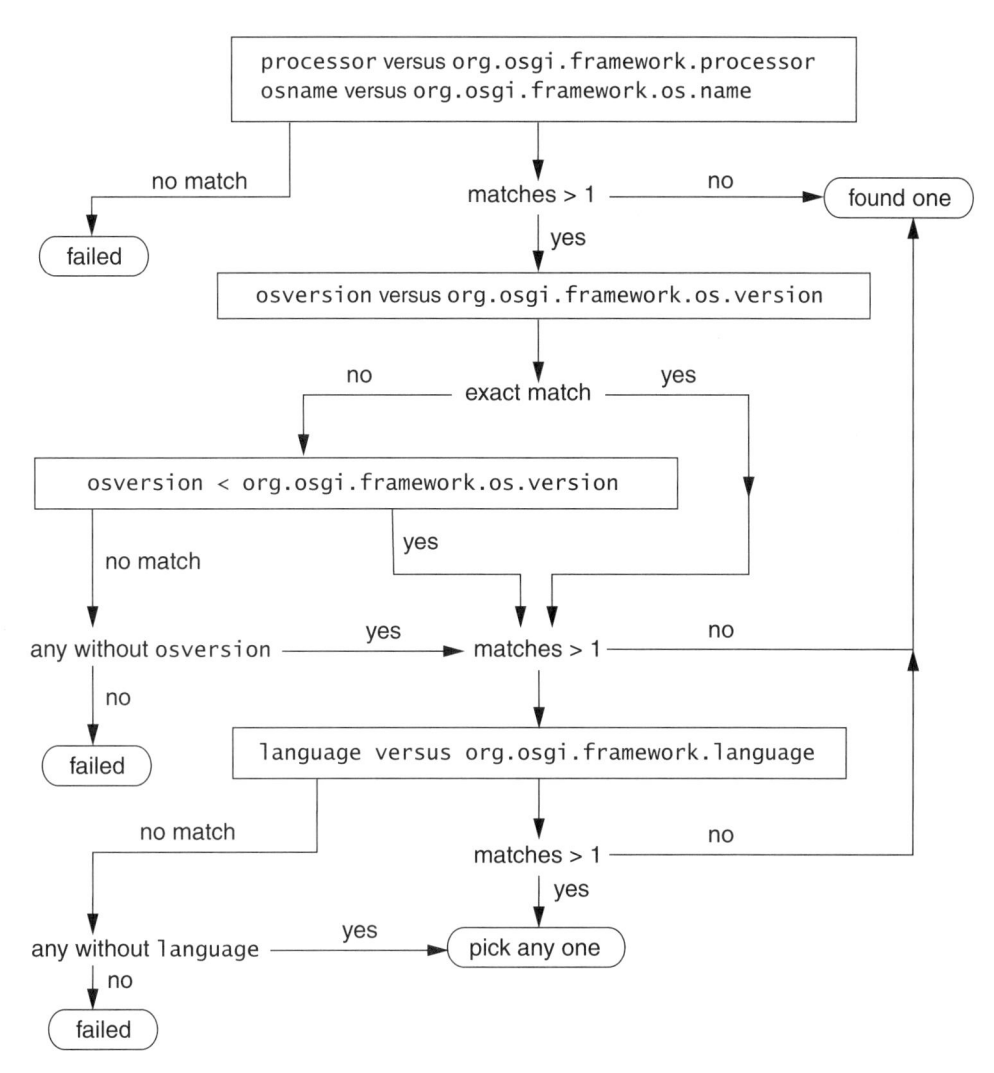

Figure 4.6 The algorithm that matches a clause in the `Bundle-NativeCode` header with the underlying native platform

```
public native long getFreeSpace(String path) throws IOException;

static {
   System.loadLibrary("filesysinfo");
```

          }
    }

The `getFreeSpace` method is declared to be native without an implementation body, and the native library is to be loaded and linked when the service implementation class is loaded.

The following code shows the C implementation on Solaris systems, which invokes the system call `statvfs` to obtain the free disk space information:

```
/*
 * The native implementation of the following method in class
 * com.acme.impl.filesys.FilesystemInfoServiceImpl:
 *     public native long getFreeSpace(String path)
 *         throws java.io.IOException;
 * The free disk space is obtained by calling statvfs system call on
 * Solaris systems. Refer to man pages for more details.
 */

#include <sys/types.h>
#include <sys/statvfs.h>   /* for statvfs system call */
#include <unistd.h>        /* for getcwd system call */
#include "utils.h"         /* for throw_exception */
#include "com_acme_impl_filesys_FilesystemInfoServiceImpl.h"

JNIEXPORT jlong JNICALL
Java_com_acme_impl_filesys_FilesystemInfoServiceImpl_getFreeSpace
(JNIEnv *env, jobject obj, jstring path)
{
    struct statvfs buf;  /* for saving the result of statvfs call */
    long availspace;
    const char *pathstr;

    if (path == NULL) {
      /* use the path to the current directory
        * if path is not specified
        */
      if ((pathstr = getcwd(NULL, 64)) == NULL) {
            /* throw java.io.IOException if getcwd fails */
            throw_exception(env, "java/io/IOException",
            "cannot get path to current directory");
            return -1;
      }
```

```
      } else {
        /* convert path from jstring to C string */
        pathstr = (*env)->GetStringUTFChars(env, path, NULL);
        if (pathstr == NULL) {
            /* OutOfMemory error has been raised */
            return -1;
        }
      }
      /* get the file system status */
      if (statvfs(pathstr, &buf) == 0) {
        /*
         * calculate free disk space: # of free blocks available to
         * non-super-user times block size in bytes
         */
        availspace = buf.f_frsize * buf.f_bavail;
      } else {
        /* throw java.io.IOException if statvfs fails */
        throw_exception(env, "java/io/IOException",
           "cannot get file system status");
        availspace = -1;
      }
      (*env)->ReleaseStringUTFChars(env, path, pathstr);
      return availspace;
}
```

The `com_acme_impl_filesys_FilesystemInfoServiceImpl.h` header file is generated by the `javah` command:

```
javah -jni com.acme.impl.filesys.FilesystemInfoServiceImpl
```

It declares the function prototype for the `getFreeSpace` method, which by now is a little beyond recognition:

```
/* DO NOT EDIT THIS FILE - it is machine generated */
#include <jni.h>
/* Header for class com_acme_impl_filesys_FilesystemInfoServiceImpl
   */

#ifndef _Included_com_acme_impl_filesys_FilesystemInfoServiceImpl
#define _Included_com_acme_impl_filesys_FilesystemInfoServiceImpl
#ifdef __cplusplus
extern "C" {
#endif
```

```
/*
 * Class:      com_acme_impl_filesys_FilesystemInfoServiceImpl
 * Method:     getFreeSpace
 * Signature:  (Ljava/lang/String;)J
 */
JNIEXPORT jlong JNICALL
Java_com_acme_impl_filesys_FilesystemInfoServiceImpl_getFreeSpace
(JNIEnv *, jobject, jstring);

#ifdef __cplusplus
}
#endif
#endif
```

We add a utility function, throw_exception, into our utils.h header file so that its definition can be shared by the C implementation for both Solaris systems and Windows NT during compilation. Here is the contents of the header file:

```
#ifndef _utils
#define _utils

/*
 * Throw an exception.
 * param name: the name of the exception class; e.g.,
 * java/io/IOException
 * param msg: the message associated with the exception
 */
void throw_exception(JNIEnv *env, const char *name, const char *msg)
{
    jclass cls = (*env)->FindClass(env, name);
    if (cls != NULL) {
        (*env)->ThrowNew(env, cls, msg);
    }
    (*env)->DeleteLocalRef(env, cls);
}
#endif
```

The shared library can be created with the following command line, assuming the JDK software is installed at /jdk:

```
cc -G -I/jdk/include -I/jdk/include/solaris filesysinfo.c -o ↵
libfilesysinfo.so
```

WRITING BUNDLES THAT CONTAIN NATIVE CODE

Now we complete the picture with the Windows version, implemented by invoking the Win32 API GetDiskFreeSpace:

```
/*
 * The native implementation of the following method in class
 * com.acme.impl.filesys.FilesystemInfoServiceImpl:
 *     public native long getFreeSpace(String path)
 *         throws java.io.IOException;
 * The free disk space is obtained by calling WIN32 API
 * GetDiskFreeSpace. Refer to documentation for more details.
 */

#include <wtypes.h>   /* for DWORD */
#include <winbase.h>  /* for GetDiskFreeSpace */
#include "utils.h"    /* for throw_exception */
#include "com_acme_impl_filesys_FilesystemInfoServiceImpl.h"

JNIEXPORT jlong JNICALL
Java_com_acme_impl_filesys_FilesystemInfoServiceImpl_getFreeSpace
(JNIEnv *env, jobject obj, jstring path)
{
    DWORD sectorsPerCluster;
    DWORD bytesPerSector;
    DWORD numOfFreeClusters;
    DWORD totalClusters;
    const char *pathstr;
    long availspace;

    if (path == NULL) {
       /* NULL path name means current directory */
       pathstr = NULL;
    } else {
       /* convert path from jstring to C string */
       pathstr = (*env)->GetStringUTFChars(env, path, NULL);
       if (pathstr == NULL) {
            /* OutOfMemory error has been raised */
            return -1;
       }
    }
    /* get free disk space */
    if (GetDiskFreeSpace(pathstr, &sectorsPerCluster,
```

```
                &bytesPerSector, &numOfFreeClusters, &totalClusters)) {
         /* calculate free disk space */
         availspace = sectorsPerCluster * bytesPerSector *
            numOfFreeClusters;
      } else {
         /* throw java.io.IOException if GetDiskFreeSpace fails */
         throw_exception(env, "java/io/IOException",
            "cannot get free disk space");
         availspace = -1;
      }
      if (pathstr != NULL)
         (*env)->ReleaseStringUTFChars(env, path, pathstr);
      return availspace;
   }
```

The Windows Dynamic Linked Library can be created with Microsoft Visual C++ development tools like this:

```
cl -Ic:\jdk\include -Ic:\jdk\include\win32 -MD -LD filesysinfo.c↵
   -Fefilesysinfo.dll
```

where c:\jdk is assumed to be the location where the JDK software is installed.

The bundle has the following layout:

```
META-INF/MANIFEST.MF
com/acme/impl/filesys/FilesystemInfoServiceImpl.class
com/acme/impl/filesys/filesysinfo.dll
com/acme/impl/filesys/libfilesysinfo.so
com/acme/impl/filesys/Activator.class
com/acme/service/filesys/FilesystemInfoService.class
```

Finally, we must set the native library search path for the operating system. If you are using a Java™ 2 Runtime Environment, you can specify the java.library.path system property at the startup of the Java Embedded Server software:

```
java -Djava.library.path=jes_cache_dir/libraries↵
     com.sun.jes.impl.framework.Main
```

where *jes_cache_dir* is the cache directory on your system.

If, however, you are using a JDK version 1.x the Java runtime environment, set the `LD_LIBRARY_PATH` environment variable for the Solaris system (and most of UNIX):

`setenv LD_LIBRARY_PATH ${LD_LIBRARY_PATH}:`*`jes_cache_dir`*`/libraries`

or set PATH for Windows NT:

`path %PATH%;`*`jes_cache_dir`*`\libraries`

We do not explain the C code in any depth because the Java™ Native Interface (JNI), UNIX system calls, and WIN32 programming are all beyond the scope of this book. However, we do want to present a not very trivial example to describe the entire process of developing service bundles with native code.

For details on JNI, please consult *The Java™ Native Interface: Programmer's Guide and Specification* by Sheng Liang [16].

4.10 Common Mistakes

It is surprisingly easy to trip up on the journey to your first working bundle. Some of the most common logistical and syntactical mistakes are summarized in this section. More complex programmatic and design issues are addressed in Chapter 6.

4.10.1 Activator

- The activator must be defined as a public class because it is to be accessed by the framework. Do not make it package private.

- The activator must have a public default no-arg constructor. Not defining any constructor is fine, because the default constructor will be automatically provided. However, if you explicitly define a constructor other than the no-arg constructor, no default constructor will be provided. This causes a failure when the framework tries to instantiate your activator.

4.10.2 Manifest

- The `Bundle-Activator` manifest header must correctly point to the path to the class implementing the activator inside the bundle JAR file.

- Check whether your manifest header definitions comply with the manifest specification (available at `http://java.sun.com/products/jdk/1.2/docs/guide/jar/manifest.html`). Starting from Java 2 SDK, the syntax is more strictly enforced:
  - The same header cannot be repeated in the manifest.
  - There cannot be an extra empty line before any header.
  - A line must not be longer than 72 bytes.
  - Use only a colon followed by a white space between the header and its value. Don't use TAB (\t).
  - Use only a white space (not TAB) at the beginning of a line to indicate continuation of the previous line.
  - There must be an extra new line at the end of the manifest.

4.10.3 Creating a JAR File

- Make sure you have included the manifest definition when you package the JAR file using the `jar` command. You always need to use the command in the form of `jar cmf Manifest bundle.jar contents`, otherwise important OSGi headers are left out of the resultant JAR file.
- Pack the JAR file so that the directory structure corresponds to the packages. For example, a bundle with the following layout won't work:

  ```
  META-INF/MANIFEST.MF
  /home/joe/project/com/acme/util/LinkedList.class
  /home/joe/project/com/acme/util/BTree.class
  ```

  because `/home/joe/project` is obviously not part of the package name.
- You can include anything in the bundle JAR file, such as the original source files (`.java` files) and the manifest stub. Although these entries are ignored by the framework when the bundle is installed and activated, they can be handy if sources are needed for rebuilding the bundle.
- When in doubt, you can unpack the bundle JAR file in a temporary directory, and examine whether `META-INF/MANIFEST.MF` indeed correctly contains the headers you intend to declare.

CHAPTER 5

Cooperation among Service Bundles

IN the traditional library-based software environment, we can always count on the class library to be there. Because library-based software is usually layered, it is impossible to build the next layer if the layer beneath it is not present.

This reassuring static configuration is no longer the norm with the component-based model used by the OSGi framework. We have learned that bundles can be started or stopped and services can be registered or unregistered, which makes for a rather dynamic run-time environment. This chapter provides general guidelines on how to cope with the challenge that during the active life span of your bundle, other bundles and services on which you rely may go away. We propose several solutions and comment on their strengths and weaknesses in various application scenarios. Because framework event dispatching and handling is the central mechanism that enables cooperation of bundles and services, we describe how they work in this chapter as well.

5.1 Event Handling

The OSGi event types and event listeners follow the event model introduced in JDK software version 1.x. There are three types of events, and their event classes are defined in the `org.osgi.framework` package:

1. **FrameworkEvent**. A framework event occurs when the framework is launched or an error has occurred asynchronously during execution of the framework.
2. **BundleEvent**. A bundle event occurs after a bundle life cycle action takes place.

3. **ServiceEvent**. A service event occurs in response to a service registration, unregistration, or property change.

A named constant is used to identify further a condition in one of the three event types. For example, `BundleEvent.STARTED` indicates the bundle event of a bundle that has been activated. Table 5.1 illustrates the types of events, when they are fired, and the methods of their corresponding event listeners that are invoked.

Table 5.1 OSGi Framework Events

Event Type		When the Event Is Fired	Listener Method Invoked
FrameworkEvent	STARTED	The framework starts up.	FrameworkListener.frameworkEvent
	ERROR	An error has been raised within the framework.	
BundleEvent	INSTALLED	A bundle has been installed in the framework.	BundleListener.bundleChanged
	STARTED	A bundle has been activated.	
	STOPPED	A bundle has been deactivated.	
	UPDATED	A bundle has been updated.	
	UNINSTALLED	A bundle has been uninstalled.	
ServiceEvent	REGISTERED	A service has been registered.	ServiceListener.serviceChanged
	UNREGISTERING	A service is being unregistered.	
	MODIFIED	The properties of a service have been modified.	

Because the framework must be launched before bundles can be hosted, how is it possible for a bundle's listener to receive the `FrameworkEvent.STARTED` event? The answer is during framework restart. The framework records which bundles were active before shutdown. When it is restarted, it first reactivates those bundles, which can be notified of the `FrameworkEvent.STARTED` event at the end of the framework restart process.

The following example bundle, when started, listens to any events generated within the framework. It demonstrates how to add and remove listeners, and how to implement listener methods. Code in bold type calls out relevant APIs.

Its manifest is straightforward:

```
BundleActivator: com.acme.event.Activator
```

The activator also serves as the listener for all three types of events:

```java
package com.acme.event;
import org.osgi.framework.*;

public class Activator implements BundleActivator,
   FrameworkListener, BundleListener, ServiceListener {

   public void start(BundleContext ctxt) {
      ctxt.addFrameworkListener(this);
      ctxt.addBundleListener(this);
      ctxt.addServiceListener(this);
   }

   public void stop(BundleContext ctxt) {
      ctxt.removeFrameworkListener(this);
      ctxt.removeBundleListener(this);
      ctxt.removeServiceListener(this);
   }

   /**
    * Implementation of FrameworkListener
    */
   public void frameworkEvent(FrameworkEvent e) {
      switch (e.getType()) {
      case FrameworkEvent.STARTED:
         System.out.println("The framework has been started.");
         break;
      case FrameworkEvent.ERROR:
         Bundle b = e.getBundle();
         Throwable t = e.getThrowable();
         System.err.println("Error occurred in bundle " +
            b.getLocation() + ", stack trace follows: ");
         t.printStackTrace();
```

```
        break;
    }
}

/**
 * Implementation of BundleListener
 */
public void bundleChanged(BundleEvent e) {
  Bundle bundle = e.getBundle();
  String location = bundle.getLocation();
  switch (e.getType()) {
  case BundleEvent.INSTALLED:
     System.out.println(location + " has been installed");
     break;
  case BundleEvent.UNINSTALLED:
     System.out.println(location + " has been uninstalled");
     break;
  case BundleEvent.STARTED:
     System.out.println(location + " has been activated");
     break;
  case BundleEvent.STOPPED:
     System.out.println(location + " has been deactivated");
     break;
  case BundleEvent.UPDATED:
     System.out.println(location + " has been updated");
     break;
  }
}

/**
 * Implementation of ServiceListener
 */
public void serviceChanged(ServiceEvent e) {
  ServiceReference ref = e.getServiceReference();
  switch (e.getType()) {
  case ServiceEvent.REGISTERED:
     System.out.println(ref + " has been registered");
     break;
```

```
            case ServiceEvent.UNREGISTERING:
               System.out.println(ref + " is being unregistered");
               break;
            case ServiceEvent.MODIFIED:
               System.out.println("the properties of "+ref+
               " have been modified");
               break;
         }
      }
   }
```

The framework automatically removes any event listeners added by a bundle when the bundle is stopped, in the same way it unregisters any services on the bundle's behalf. Therefore, the activator stop method may very well be empty:

```
   public void stop(BundleContext ctxt) {
      // We do not need to remove the listeners added by this
      // bundle because the framework will automatically remove
      // them for us.
   }
```

5.2 Bundle State and Service Registration

In the last chapter, we explained that a bundle usually registers a service when it is started, and it unregisters the service when it is stopped. It is important to realize whether the service registered *coincides* with the bundle being activated, but this coincidence is not required.

On the one hand, it is perfectly legal for a bundle to be active without having registered its services, or to register them some time after it is first started. It is also permissible that an active bundle unregisters services at any time, even if it is not going to be stopped in the foreseeable future.

On the other hand, when a client bundle has been successfully resolved (that is, its Import-Package declaration has been satisfied by some exporter in the framework), it may not necessarily be able to obtain the services it needs. This is because although the service-providing bundle has exported the package, it may not have registered the service yet.

For the client bundle, to monitor and handle the service events is the only means that can be used to deal with this uncertainty.

5.3 Synchronous and Asynchronous Events

The service events are guaranteed to be delivered synchronously, whereas the framework and bundle events do not have such a guarantee. Figure 5.1 illustrates synchronous service event dispatching when a service is unregistered.

Evidently, the framework waits for all listeners to complete their work before it proceeds with the service unregistration process. This is designed to give client bundles an opportunity to prepare for the consequences of registration, unregistration, or the property change of another service in their service listeners.

Delivery of other types of events (namely bundle events and framework events) does not have such characteristics. They are asynchronous, because the framework places a pending event in an event queue and returns immediately. It does not wait for an invocation of every listener to be completed. A separate and

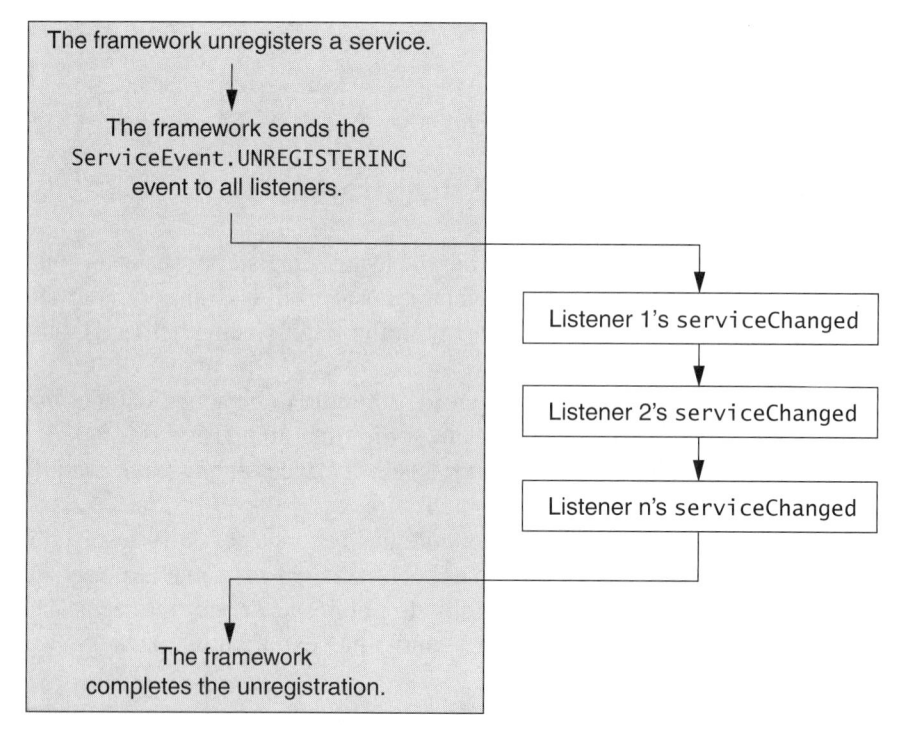

Figure 5.1 Synchronous service event dispatching. The shaded area is code belonging to the framework implementation.

dedicated event dispatcher thread picks up the next event from the queue and notifies all interested listeners. This scenario is depicted in Figure 5.2, where a bundle is uninstalled.

Although the bundle events and framework events are delivered asynchronously, they are not delivered out of order by the Java Embedded Server framework. For example, if bundle A is installed, then an active bundle B is updated, and finally A is uninstalled. Bundle event listeners are guaranteed to get this sequence of events in order: BundleEvent.INSTALLED event caused by A's installation, BundleEvent.STOPPED, BundleEvent.UPDATED, BundleEvent.STARTED events caused by B's update, and BundleEvent.UNINSTALLED event caused by A's removal.

If a bundle registers and unregisters a service in its activator, it poses an interesting situation in which a mix of asynchronous and synchronous events are involved. With respect to any one bundle, a listener is always notified in the following sequence: ServiceEvent.REGISTERED before BundleEvent.STARTED, ServiceEvent.UNREGISTERING before BundleEvent.STOPPED events. In both cases, the framework won't queue the bundle events before all service listeners have been notified. Otherwise, the dispatch order should not be assumed among asynchronous and synchronous events.

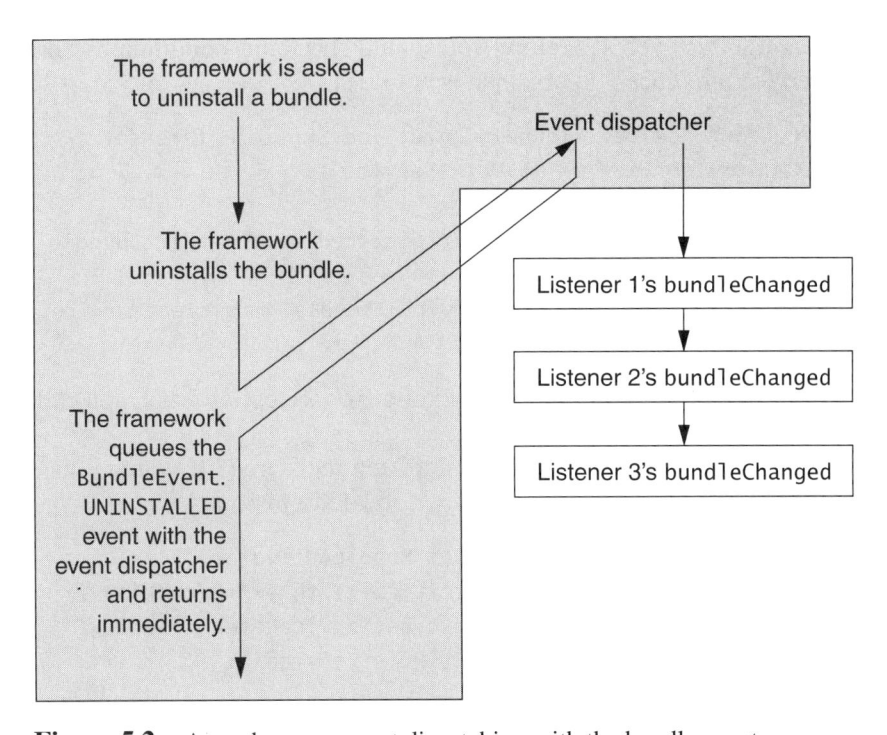

Figure 5.2 Asynchronous event dispatching with the bundle event

5.4 Dealing with Service Unregistration

If your service depends on the presence of another service, and there is a realistic chance that the other service may be unregistered at some point in time—perhaps because the service-providing bundle undergoes an update—you should program your service to protect yourself[1] from that event.

Such safeguard measures add quite a bit of complexity to your service, but the complexity is inherent in the component-based model. In the world of the OSGi framework, the earth does stand on top of giant tortoises, and you do not want to be thrown flat on your face when the ground moves away from under your feet!

The following sections list several solutions. Evaluate their advantages and disadvantages before deciding which one is the best for your application. We do not encourage you to use a single one for all your bundles.

5.4.1 Don't Start without the Service

When you have package dependency on another bundle, and the other bundle has exported the packages you declare to import, your bundle is resolved. However, it is possible, as we have explained in earlier sections, that the other bundle has not registered the service yet. Therefore, you should check this condition by verifying that the service reference you obtained is not `null`:

```
ServiceReference ref = bundleContext.getServiceReference(
    "com.acme.service.print.PrintService");
if (ref == null) {
    // the service has not been registered by the print bundle yet.
} else {
    PrintService svc = (PrintService) bundleContext.getService(ref);
}
```

Otherwise, you will get a `NullPointerException` exception when you call `getService` with a `null` service reference.

What can you do if the service has not been registered? If you are inside the activator's `start` method, you can simply throw `Exception`:

```
public class Activator implements BundleActivator {
    public void start(BundleContext ctxt) throws Exception {
        ServiceReference ref = ctxt.getServiceReference(
            "com.acme.service.print.PrintService");
        if (ref == null)
```

---

[1] That is, put yourself in the shoes of the client bundle in this chapter.

```
            throw new Exception("Required service " + ref +
                " has not been registered.");
        }
        ...
    }
    ...
}
```

As a result, your bundle won't start if the service you need is not registered. Taking this approach leaves the coordination responsibility to administrative software, which should then attempt to reactivate your bundle when it knows that the service is likely to have been registered.

This "solution" does not address the general problem of a service getting unregistered some time *after* you have obtained it, however. The situation is not unlike you telling your boss that you cannot start working unless a computer is provided; yet once you get started, it is still possible that your computer breaks down or is taken away.

5.4.2 Discovering Stale Service

After you succeed in obtaining the service by calling getService, you get a reference[2] to the service object itself. Some time elapses, and the registering bundle chooses to unregister the service. At this time, the service object in your possession is still a valid object in the Java virtual machine, and in all likelihood will continue to work. Figure 5.3 illustrates this situation.

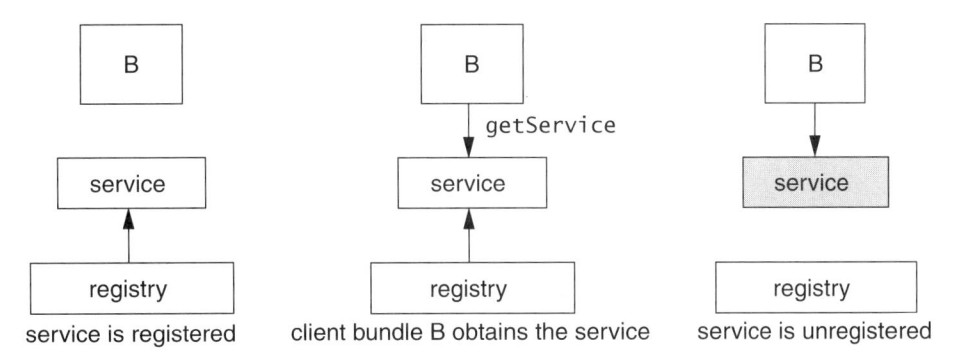

Figure 5.3 Bundle B gets a reference to a service from the registry. Some time later, the service is unregistered, leaving B with a stale reference.

---

[2] Don't confuse this with the service reference, which is an instance of ServiceReference.

However, when the service-providing bundle unregisters its services, it may signify the client bundles, based on certain application logic, that they should no longer use the service. For example, when a printer runs out of paper, the print service may get unregistered; or a preference service may be unregistered when its back-end directory server needs an upgrade. Undesirable consequences may ensue if client bundles disregard this fact and continue to hold on to the service object they have acquired.

We say that the service object is stale if the service is unregistered some time after a client bundle has obtained it. Figure 5.4 illustrates the time line.

To find out whether a service has become stale, you can call the `getBundle` method on the service reference to the service:

```
if (serviceReference.getBundle() == null) {
    // the service referenced by serviceReference
    // has been unregistered
}
```

The `getBundle` method returns the bundle that has registered the service. If the service is unregistered at a later time, this method returns `null`.

5.4.3 Carrying On without the Service

In many applications, your bundle or service is tolerant enough to be able to continue functioning, even though the service on which you depend has been unregistered. It is a lot like even though we occasionally experience power outages, we can usually keep up with our daily routine, although less effectively.

In such situations, you need to program your bundle or service as a state machine with two states: how it should work when the needed service is available and what it should do when the service is not. Furthermore, you must listen to `ServiceEvent` to figure out whether the service in which you are interested is going away or has come back.

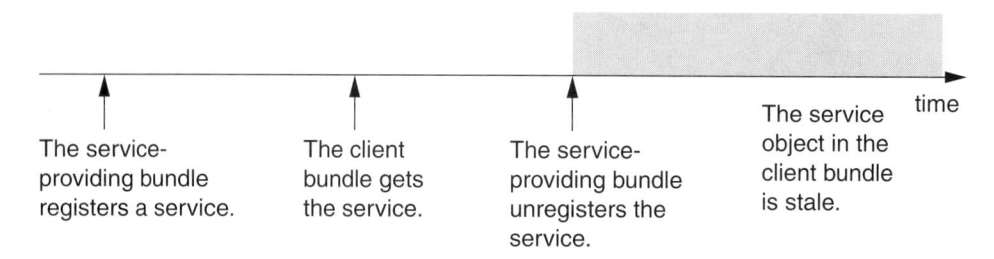

Figure 5.4 The time line of how a service obtained by the client bundle becomes stale

As an example, consider a memo service that uses the print service. The memo service enlists the help of a service event listener, `ServiceMonitor`, to monitor the status of the print service:

```
package com.acme.service.memo;
import org.osgi.framework.*;
import com.acme.service.print.PrintService;

class ServiceMonitor implements ServiceListener {
   static final String PRINT_SERVICE_NAME =
      "com.acme.service.print.PrintService";
   private BundleContext context;
   private ServiceReference currentRef = null;
   PrintService printService = null;

   ServiceMonitor(BundleContext ctxt) {
      this.context = ctxt;
   }

   /**
    * Monitor service events for the print service,
    * and flag its availability accordingly.
    */
   public synchronized void serviceChanged(ServiceEvent e) {
      if (e.getType() == ServiceEvent.UNREGISTERING) {
         if (e.getServiceReference().equals(currentRef)) {
            // the print service we are using is going away
            context.ungetService(currentRef);
            this.currentRef = null;
            this.printService = null;
         }
      } else if (e.getType() == ServiceEvent.REGISTERED) {
         // print service is registered
         if (this.printService == null) {
            this.currentRef = e.getServiceReference();
            this.printService = (PrintService)
               context.getService(currentRef);
         }
      }
   }
}
```

```
      synchronized void init() {
        try {
          context.addServiceListener(this,
             "(objectClass=" + PRINT_SERVICE_NAME +")");
        } catch (InvalidSyntaxException e) {
          // won't happen
        }
        ServiceReference ref =
          context.getServiceReference(PRINT_SERVICE_NAME);
        if (ref != null) {
          this.currentRef = ref;
          this.printService =
              (PrintService)context.getService(ref);
        }
      }
    }
```

The monitor's job is quite obvious: It maintains a reference to the print service, nullifies it when the print service is being unregistered, and reestablishes it when the print service has been registered. Its `init` method sets the initial state of the print service.

Here is the activator for the memo service bundle:

```
package com.acme.service.memo;
import org.osgi.framework.*;

public class Activator implements BundleActivator {

    public void start(BundleContext ctxt) {
       ServiceMonitor monitor = new ServiceMonitor(ctxt);
       monitor.init();
       MemoService memo = new MemoServiceImpl(monitor);
       ctxt.registerService(
          "com.acme.service.memo.MemoService", memo, null);
    }

    public void stop(BundleContext ctxt) {
       // The listener will be removed automatically
    }
}
```

This bundle is always started regardless of whether the print service is registered. In the activator, we add the service listener that listens for service registration or unregistration events of `com.acme.service.print.PrintService`. As shown earlier, this is achieved by calling `addServiceListener` and by supplying an LDAP filter parameter to narrow the number of service events delivered to the listener.

The print service may have already been registered before our listener is added. We find this out by attempting to obtain the service and, if successful, initializing the internal state of the listener. Notice that this is done in a synchronized method to avoid a nasty race condition under which another thread may unregister the service right after we have checked the condition

```
if (ref != null)
```

but before we add the listener. Here is why: While we are inside the `init` method and the lock is being held on the service listener (`monitor`), the framework's attempt to call back to the listener's synchronized `serviceChanged` method from another thread is blocked. It is not able to deliver the `ServiceEvent.UNREGISTERING` event. This prevents the framework from finishing its unregistration routine, because it must wait for the synchronous delivery of `ServiceEvent` to return. As soon as we are done with the initialization and release the lock, the service listener is in place and is notified of the unregistration. If the `init` method is not synchronized, our listener may miss this unregistration notification, leaving the listener with an incorrect initial state.

We use `currentRef` to identify the service reference to the service currently in use. Beware if more than one service instance has registered with the specified service interface. In that case, `ServiceMonitor` is notified when a service under the same interface, but not used by your bundle, is unregistered. Generally, you can take two measures to rule out irrelevant service events:

1. Use additional service properties in the filter. For example, suppose there are two print services, one for the local printer and the other for the network printer. If the network printer is the one you are using, you can add a differentiating condition, `implType`, to the filter:

   ```
   ctxt.addServiceListener(listener, "(&(objectClass=" +
       serviceName + ")(implType=network printer))");
   ```

2. Make additional checks within the service listener's `serviceChanged` method, which is as follows:

```
public void serviceChanged(ServiceEvent e) {
   ServiceReference ref = e.getServiceReference();
   if (!"network printer".equals(ref.getProperty("implType"))) {
      // not the instance of print service we are
      // interested in; ignore.
      return;
   }
   ...
}
```

How would the memo service use the print service under the new circumstances? We have seen that the service monitor is passed into `MemoServiceImpl` when it is constructed in the activator. Thus it may call the print service with the following sequence:

```
synchronized (monitor) {
   if (monitor.printService != null) {
      monitor.printService.print(...);
   } else {
      display("The print service is temporarily unavailable." +
         " Try later!");
   }
}
```

Note that accessing and modifying the reference to the print service should be synchronized on the service listener, because while the memo service is checking the availability of the print service, another thread may be in the process of unregistering it.

In summary, to keep your bundle active while some service on which you depend comes and goes, you need to program your bundle with the following five guidelines in mind:

1. Think through the application logic in two cases: what your bundle does when the needed service is registered and what is does when the needed service is unregistered.

2. Set up `ServiceEventListener` to monitor the needed service. Maintain an availability condition in the listener. When the `ServiceEvent.REGISTERED`

event happens, get the service; when the `ServiceEvent.UNREGISTERING` event happens, unget the service. Change the availability condition accordingly.

3. On bundle activation, call `getService` to see whether the service has already been registered and initialize the availability condition.

4. Synchronize on the event listener object whenever you need to check or modify the availability condition.

5. In your code where you invoke methods on the service, check the availability condition first. Branch into two execution paths accordingly.

5.4.4 Picking an Alternative

Within the framework, multiple services with the same service interface may be present. They differ only in implementation. In this situation you may want to obtain another service instance when the one you have been using is getting unregistered. An analogy from daily life is to take the train when the plane is grounded.

Most of the code in the previous section is still applicable, because you still need to prepare yourself for the situation when all the needed services are unregistered. The following is the revised `ServiceListener` implementation. The code in bold type reflects the new behaviors:

```
package com.acme.service.memo;
import org.osgi.framework.*;
import com.acme.service.print.PrintService;

class ServiceMonitor implements ServiceListener {
   static final String PRINT_SERVICE_NAME =
      "com.acme.service.print.PrintService";
   private BundleContext context;
   private ServiceReference currentRef = null;
   PrintService printService = null;

   ServiceMonitor(BundleContext ctxt) {
      this.context = ctxt;
   }

   /**
    * Monitor service events for the print service,
    * and flag its availability accordingly.
    */
```

```
    public synchronized void serviceChanged(ServiceEvent e) {
        if (e.getType() == ServiceEvent.UNREGISTERING) {
            // print service is about to go away
            if (!e.getServiceReference().equals(currentRef)) {
                // it is not the print service we're using; ignore.
                return;
            }
            context.ungetService(currentRef);
            // pick an alternative
            this.currentRef =
                context.getServiceReference(PRINT_SERVICE_NAME);
            if (currentRef != null) {
                this.printService = (PrintService)
                    context.getService(currentRef);
            } else {
                this.printService = null;
                this.currentRef = null;
            }
        } else if (e.getType() == ServiceEvent.REGISTERED) {
            // print service is registered
            if (this.printService != null) {
                // one more service instance is registered, but we
                // are happy with the one we have been using.
                return;
            }
            ServiceReference ref = e.getServiceReference();
            this.printService =
                (PrintService) context.getService(ref);
            this.currentRef = ref;
        }
    }

    synchronized void init() { ... }
}
```

The listener must remember the service reference representing the service instance currently being used. As in the previous example, this is maintained in currentRef. When we are notified that an instance of the print service is being unregistered, we first determine whether it is the instance we have been using. If it isn't, then the unregistration does not affect us. If it is, we must select an alternative. At this time, the outgoing service has already been unregistered. Therefore, we can simply get a service reference to another currently registered print service. A `null` return value means that none is available; otherwise, we switch to the new print service.

When we are notified that a print service is registered, we don't need to do anything if we are currently holding a valid service instance.

Taking this approach usually implies that the alternative service instances perform similar operations and have been designed to be used interchangeably. Their internal integrity must be preserved when any one of them takes over the task at some point in time. For example, suppose you have two log services that store records in a remote database for auditing purposes. One serves as the backup of the other. In this situation, time stamping each record allows you to get a complete trace after merging the entries separately recorded by the two service instances.

5.4.5 Cascading Service Registration

There are situations when the service on which you depend is unregistered, it is impossible for your bundle to continue. This is similar to the situation when your suppliers quit, you cannot open for business. If this is so, you may unregister the services provided by your bundle when the needed service is unregistered.

Suppose `PrintService` cannot print without `FontService`, which provides basic fonts and can install fancier ones. If the font service is unavailable, the presence of the print service may be misleading to its clients, which may choose to keep trying—in vain. If the print service is also unregistered, its clients may understand that the problem is not transient. `PrintService` monitors service events pertinent to `FontService` by adding an event listener as before.

The following is the revised service listener that monitors the font service to handle this scenario:

```
package com.acme.service.print;
import org.osgi.framework.*;
import com.acme.service.font.FontService;

class ServiceMonitor implements ServiceListener {
    static final String PRINT_SERVICE_NAME =
        "com.acme.service.print.PrintService";
    private ServiceRegistration printReg;
    private BundleContext context;
    private ServiceReference currentRef = null;
    FontService fontService = null;

    ServiceMonitor(BundleContext ctxt) {
        this.context = ctxt;
    }
```

```java
/**
 * Monitor service events for the font service,
 * and flag its availability accordingly.
 */
public synchronized void serviceChanged(ServiceEvent e) {
   if (e.getType() == ServiceEvent.UNREGISTERING) {
      if (e.getServiceReference().equals(currentRef)) {
         // we withdraw PrintService because
         // needed FontService is going away
         if (printReg != null) {
            printReg.unregister();
            printReg = null;
         }
         context.ungetService(e.getServiceReference());
         this.currentRef = null;
         this.fontService = null;
      }
   } else if (e.getType() == ServiceEvent.REGISTERED) {
      // font service is registered
      if (this.fontService == null) {
         this.currentRef = e.getServiceReference();
         this.fontService = (FontService)
            context.getService(currentRef);
         printReg =
            context.registerService(PRINT_SERVICE_NAME,
            new PrintServiceImpl(), null);
      }
   }
}

synchronized void init() {
   String fontServiceName = FontService.class.getName();
   try {
      context.addServiceListener(this,
         "(objectClass=" + fontServiceName +")");
   } catch (InvalidSyntaxException e) {
      // won't happen
   }
   ServiceReference ref =
      context.getServiceReference(fontServiceName);
```

```
        if (ref != null) {
            currentRef = ref;
            printReg = context.registerService(PRINT_SERVICE_NAME,
                new PrintServiceImpl(), null);
        }
    }
}
```

If you take this approach, you should know its domino effect. Assume we have bundles A, B, C, and D, intending to register services `AService`, `BService`, `CService`, and `DService`, respectively. `AService` needs `BService`, which needs `CService`, which in turn needs `DService`. And further assume that A, B, and C all adopt the cascading registration approach.

Now if D is not started, bundles A, B, and C can still be activated, but none of them will register any services. As soon as D is started and registers `DService`, a mini whirlwind of service registrations takes place as it triggers `CService`, `BService`, and `AService` to be automatically registered by their respective bundles.

Similarly, the deactivation of bundle D also causes the services from the other three bundles to be unregistered. This could be very disruptive to the overall operations of the gateway, and should be considered carefully.

This approach may also result in a deadlock if circular service dependency exists among bundles. For example, assume bundle A registers `AService` but needs `BService` in bundle B, which in turn registers `BService` but needs `AService`. No matter how you activate bundles A or B, their services will never get registered: Bundle A is waiting for the service registration event of `BService`, which never comes, because bundle B is waiting for the service registration event of `AService`. Notice this is a "benign" deadlock, because no thread is being held up, and the framework and unrelated bundles still function normally.

5.4.6 Refusing Service

In the previous examples we have shown that the calling bundle is responsible for preparing for the possibility that the service it needs may go away. In this section we demonstrate that service-providing bundles also have options of warning the callers when their services (the callees) are unregistered. If so, they can refuse to honor any call to their methods:

```
package com.acme.impl.print;
import org.osgi.framework.*;
import com.acme.service.print.PrintService;
```

```java
public class Activator implements BundleActivator {
    static final String PRINT_SERVICE_NAME =
        "com.acme.service.print.PrintService";
    private ServiceRegistration printReg;
    private PrintService printService;

    public void start(BundleContext ctxt) {
        printService = new PrintServiceImpl(ctxt);
        printReg = ctxt.registerService(PRINT_SERVICE_NAME,
            printService, null);
    }

    public void stop(BundleContext ctxt) {
        // give client bundles a chance to release their
        // use of the print service
        printReg.unregister();
        // invalidate this instance of the print service
        ((PrintServiceImpl) printService).invalidate();
    }
}
```

The following is the new implementation of `PrintService`:

```java
// imports
class PrintServiceImpl implements PrintService {
    private boolean amIRegistered;
    private BundleContext context;

    PrintServiceImpl(BundleContext ctxt) {
        this.context = ctxt;
        amIRegistered = true;
    }

    public void print(String printer, InputStream src)
        throws IOException
    {
        if (! amIRegistered)
            throw new IllegalStateException("Cannot print because " +
                "the service has been unregistered");
        ...
    }
```

```java
    public String getStatus(String printer)
       throws IOException
{
    if (! amIRegistered)
       throw new IllegalStateException("Cannot get status " +
          "because this service has been unregistered");
    ...
}

void invalidate() {
    amIRegistered = false;
}
}
```

In this example, the service object has an internal flag indicating whether it *itself* is registered. When its bundle unregisters the service, it invalidates itself by setting the flag accordingly. Notice that we explicitly unregister the print service to give client bundles an opportunity to stop using it. If this step is omitted, the framework belatedly broadcasts the `ServiceEvent.UNREGISTERING` event after we have invalidated the print service, which could cause the calling bundles to fail unexpectedly.

This is a defensive mechanism for the callee, and may very well produce a harmful effect on the callers, because usually callers are not prepared to catch an instance of `RuntimeException` when they invoke a method on a service. There are three workarounds:

1. Declare a checked exception to indicate that the service object is stale, so that callers have to handle it.

2. Throw one of the existing checked exceptions if appropriate. In the previous example, the print service may just throw `IOException` in both methods when `amIRegistered` is found to be `false`, because from the client bundle's point of view, it appears as if the printer has been disconnected. The client bundle can then adopt the strategy of releasing the print service after a certain number of unsuccessful tries, and can get another from the service registry.

3. Make the calling bundles implement one of the mechanisms suggested prior to this section for dealing with service unregistration.

Despite this disadvantage, the refusal of service approach predictably denies execution of methods on a unregistered service object, and may be valuable in preventing random outcome and protecting the correctness of certain application logic for some services.

5.5 Cooperation with Asynchronous Events

`BundleEvents` and `FrameworkEvents` are useful for administrative bundles. For example, a management bundle may present a user interface that enumerates all bundles currently installed in the framework. By listening to `BundleEvents`, it can dynamically update the list—remove an entry when the bundle is uninstalled, add an entry when a new bundle is installed, or change the status when a bundle is activated.

As another example, some diagnostic bundle may listen to `FrameworkEvent.ERROR` events and may report error conditions raised that way.

Let us demonstrate, in the following example, how bundles can cooperate using `BundleEvent`, and what to look for when dealing with asynchronously delivered events. Recall the bundle that registers a parameter service factory from "Service Factory" on page 66 in the previous chapter. We explained that the parameter bundle maintains a property file as the persistent storage for each client bundle in its own data area. We also showed that when a client bundle is stopped, its parameters are saved, and when it is restarted its parameters are restored. However, we left one problem unsolved: When a client bundle is uninstalled, the parameter bundle still keeps its property file, which is never used again.

The parameter bundle can use `BundleListener` to find out that a client bundle is gone, and can then call `ParameterStore`'s `clear` method to clean up accordingly:

```
...
public class Activator implements BundleActivator {

   public void start(final BundleContext ctxt) {
      final ParameterStore store = new ParameterStore(ctxt);
      // add a bundle listener listening to
      // uninstallation of client bundles
      ctxt.addBundleListener(new BundleListener() {
         public void bundleChanged(BundleEvent e) {
            // we are only interested in bundle uninstalled event
            if (e.getType() != BundleEvent.UNINSTALLED)
               return;
            store.clear(e.getBundle());
         }
      });
      ParameterServiceFactory factory =
         new ParameterServiceFactory(store);
```

```
    ctxt.registerService(
       "com.acme.service.param.ParameterService",
       factory, null);
  }

  public void stop(BundleContext ctxt) {
    // nothing needs to be done
  }
}
```

We add the bundle listener, which is defined as an anonymous inner class. `ParameterStore`'s `clear` method does the following: It first obtains the ID of the given bundle. Because we use the bundle ID as the directory name for each client bundle in the parameter bundle's data area, we check whether the bundle ID of the uninstalled bundle appears as the name of one of the directories. If so, one of the client bundles has been uninstalled, and we proceed to remove its parameter files. Otherwise, the uninstalled bundle has never requested `ParameterService` and thus is of no interest to the cleanup task at hand.

Recall that events other than `ServiceEvent` are delivered asynchronously, meaning that the framework, which fires the events, does not wait for the event listener methods to finish. Imagine in the previous example that while `BundleListener` is handling the `BundleEvent.UNINSTALLED` event by removing the parameter files for the uninstalled bundle, the same bundle is getting installed and activated by the framework again, and in the process is asking `ParameterService` to recreate those parameter files. Our implementation works fine in this circumstance because the framework generates a unique ID for the reinstalled bundle. However, if instead of using the bundle ID we had used some other naming convention that has no uniqueness guarantee, our bundle event handler would potentially have clashed with the framework operations in this particular scenario.

CHAPTER 6

Design Patterns and Pitfalls

WORKING with the component-based model of the OSGi framework introduces some unique design issues as well as a host of pitfalls and traps that may frustrate the unwary. This chapter provides recommendations and guidelines on these subjects.

6.1 Designing the Service

6.1.1 Separating Service Interface and Implementation

The service should be designed with the interface and implementation separated. The characteristics and benefits of this practice are

- The interface between the caller and the callee is well defined

- The interface is the only coupling point between the caller and the callee

- Any change made to the implementation portion of the callee does not impact the caller. We know that software always evolves. This minimizes the impact by bug fixes or feature enhancements, and significantly contributes to the stability of the entire software system.

- We can apply useful abstractions. For example, a file system service can offer its callers simple abstractions of reading, writing, and listing files, but one can be implemented on top of local hard disks while another is implemented over networked file systems such as Network File System.

- One implementation can be devoted to a very specific approach to maximize efficiency and performance without worrying about sacrificing generalization, which has already been captured in the interface. We are not excluding any alternatives because we can always supply another implementation. For example, a video service can provide a `getFeed` API. One implementation can concentrate on error correction and compensation with sophisticated image-processing techniques if the feed comes from a slow parallel port; another implementation can be spared this complexity altogether with a high bandwidth FireWire connection.

As a result, separation of interface and implementation encourages software reuse, improves flexibility, and reduces maintenance costs.

The OSGi framework provides further incentives for separating interface and implementation, because bundles are developed by different service providers (thus their implementation should be isolated), and they are expected to cooperate in a dynamic environment in which each may undergo life cycle transitions (hence their interfaces should be well defined and stable).

With standard interfaces defined, many bundles can be *developed*, but they needn't all be *deployed*. Some may serve as "spare parts" and may be taken off the shelf when their specific applications are called for. Having a software component market is not a new idea, but its practice is far from being widespread. That is perhaps one of the reasons why we begin by writing software but end up *rewriting* it, and software development remains to be a labor-intensive effort. But we digress.

It may be worth reviewing that the interface and implementation classes are separated in different packages, and only the packages containing service interface classes are exported. The implementation classes are kept private to the service-providing bundle. In the Java Embedded Server product, such behavior is realized through class loaders. Each installed bundle has its own class loader. By default, it can only load classes from within the same bundle. However, with the `Export-Package` manifest header, a bundle can instruct its class loader to export the specified classes to the framework. When another bundle declares `Import-Package` in its manifest, its class loader is "linked" with that of the exporter. That is, the importer delegates the loading and resolution of any class in the imported packages to the class loader of the exporting bundle. For example, assume bundle A exports the package `foo`, which bundle B imports. After the two bundles are started, when bundle B attempts to load class `foo.ServiceA`, system classes and CLASSPATH are searched. Failing that, B tries the exported packages, and succeeds in loading the class from A.

6.1.2 Challenges in Designing a Service Interface

Although the separation of interface from implementation offers many benefits, it also poses a challenge to the developer: The interface must be useful and stable. If the interface is changed often, the callers as well as the implementations are affected, and the benefits we have outlined are defeated.

Designing a good interface is hard. One must grasp the *intrinsic* functionality offered by the service, and *foresee* how it can be used. If the interface is too narrowly defined, many applications that could have used it can find it lacking. They are left with two awkward options: creating a new service interface that duplicates what most of the existing interface does, with the needed, additional API; or pushing for revision of the existing interface. The former may lead to a proliferation of similar interfaces; the latter results in interface changes that may break backward compatibility. Both cause a lost chance for algorithmic integration: Had all use scenarios of the interface been taken into consideration, similar behaviors or data structures could have been integrated, resulting in a more succinct and functional interface. When common factors reveal themselves after the interface has been set loose, you can only add new and possibly redundant APIs and constructs to your interface.

These challenges are not readily obvious to developers new to the component-based model. We are used to designing as we code on the fly, and few habits are more detrimental when it comes to interface design. Aiming to define interfaces that last and having disciplines in practice is the first step to designing services properly.

6.1.3 Approaching an Interface Design

What would be a good approach to designing interfaces? We have explained that it can be disastrous to design interfaces haphazardly or carelessly. However, it is also obvious that it takes an eternity to design *the* perfect interface. Things always evolve, and humans are not all knowing. The dilemma is not unlike the one faced by the trio in the following story:

Once three men were asked to walk through a field and pick the fullest wheat by the time they reach the far end. They could only make one choice and were not allowed to retrace their steps. The first man took the first large wheat he laid his eyes on, and regretted his pick for the rest of his trip because he saw many fuller ones. The second man resisted temptation and put off a decision, expecting a better catch down the road, only to settle for a small one near the end of the field. The third man made mental notes as he walked the field, and at about the middle, he selected the fullest one up to that point. He ended up with the fullest wheat among all three men, although his probably wasn't the biggest in the entire field.

The last approach appears to be a good rule of thumb for interface design as well. Although it is impossible to produce the perfect interface, it is possible to produce a good interface and to evolve the interface in large stages. This is preferred over designing the interface piecemeal and releasing it incrementally. Here are a few guidelines on designing service interfaces:

First, address the fundamental question, *What* exactly does the service do? It must be considered independently of *how* it is done.

For instance, determining the height of a building is what needs to be achieved. Measuring the atmospheric pressure with a barometer, timing its free fall from the top of the building, and trading it for the data from the building administrator are three ways of how to do it.

Let's look at a more tangible example. Suppose we want to create a file system service and the following interface is one cut of the design:

```
public interface FilesystemService {

    /** Gets the disk offset of the file. */
    public long getDiskOffset(String fileName);

    /**
     * Creates a file in the file system;
     * returns the disk offset for the new file.
     */
    public long createFile(String fileName);

    /**
     * Writes data read from the input stream to a file
     * at the specified disk offset.
     */
    public void writeFile(long offset, InputStream in);

    /** Reads a file at the specified disk offset. */
    public InputStream readFile(long offset);

    /**
     * Inspects the physical media at the specified offset range.
     * Fix problems automatically.
     */
    void verifyMedia(long startOffset, long endOffset);
}
```

The problem with this design is that it exposes the implementation aspect of the service through the service interface. The disk offset should not be a concern to the clients of this service. Having it as a parameter in the API and a conceptual entity makes the job of this service's caller more difficult. Removing the getDiskOffset and createFile methods and referring to files with their names in the writeFile and readFile methods would be a better solution. Exactly how the filename as a string is mapped to the physical address on the disk is up to the implementation of this service.

The inclusion of the `verifyMedia` API in this design is another problem. The applications that call this service to read or write files as part of their normal operation are quite different from utilities that perform maintenance duties. The former may be a tax calculator; the latter may be a disk "doctor." Therefore, it is worth separating the `verifyMedia` API into a dedicated `FilesystemDiagnostic` service, where more focused and powerful features such as defragmentation and compression APIs can be added.

The service interface API should cover a category of use and should be made "as simple as possible, but not simpler," as Albert Einstein put it.

Second, balance the generality of the service by considering the scope of use by potential clients.

Recall the print service example. It has the following service interface:

```
public interface PrintService {
   /** Gets status of the print queue. */
   public String getStatus(String queue) throws IOException;

   /** Prints the contents from the source to the print queue. */
   public void print(String queue, URL source) throws IOException;
}
```

The `print` API reads the source contents from a URL. This is an example of incorporating generality in consideration of potential uses of the client. A first attempt was to use `java.io.File` as the parameter. However, this design restricts the print service to print local files. What if the gateway does not have a local file system? What if the application would like to print directly from a link on the Web? Clearly the URL argument can cover more ground and is more flexible.

Third, consider all known forms of incarnations of a service and generalize the interface to make it possible to implement them.

Imagine a synchronization service that is responsible for communicating with a back-end server. The following is a flawed interface:

```
public interface SyncService {
   /** Communicates with the back-end server. */
   public void download(Socket s);
}
```

By mandating that a socket be used as an end point of a communication channel, we are excluding other potential implementations such as datagrams via UDP in cases that require efficiency and tolerate data loss (for example, streaming media), or transactions using HTTP in situations in which the data must tunnel through firewalls. Using the socket also reveals the intended implementation of the service. One possible solution is to use URL to identify the remote server.

Fourth, factor out common functionality into an independent service. The necessity of this usually reveals itself when you set out to implement a service. If a functional module turns out to be needed by multiple services, it is probably logical to create a separate service. For example, if we were to write a suite of network server services such as FTP, IMAP, and HTTP, it may be valuable to create auxiliary services such as a connection manager service that manges a pool of threads for handling each incoming TCP/IP connection, instead of duplicating the same logic in each service.

Fifth, exclude the configuration aspect of a service. Generally, configuration is more closely tied to the implementation of a service. Consider the following proposed `LogService` interface:

```
public interface LogService {
   /** Logs the message. */
   public void log(String msg);
   /** Sets the remote URL where log entries are sent and stored. */
   public void setRemoteURL(URL u);
   /** Gets the remote URL where the log entries are stored. */
   public URL getRemoteURL();
   /** Sets the name for the local log file. */
   public void setLogFilename(String name);
   /** Sets the maximum size in bytes of the local log file. */
   public void setMaxLogSize(long size);
   ...
}
```

`LogService` intends to allow for two different implementations: One is to save the log entries locally to a file; another is to deliver the log entries remotely to a URL. Depending on which implementation is used, different configuration parameters are called for. In a local log file implementation, it makes sense to configure filename and size, which does not make sense in the remote log implementation. This is why the configuration aspects of a service generally should not appear in the service interface.

Sometimes it is okay to put configuration methods into the interface because they do not vary based on implementations. However, including a large number of `get/set` methods in the service interface obscures the essential functionality of the service and clutters the interface. For example, consider the following version of `HttpService`:

```
public interface HttpService {
   void registerServlet(String alias, Servlet servlet, ...);
   void setPort(int port);
```

```
    int getPort();
    void setMimeTypes(String[] mimeTypes);
    ...
}
```

In any event, you may very well have a dedicated configuration service responsible for configuring parameters of various services.

Sixth, do not reinvent APIs. In Chapter 4 we discussed a mailer example that does not register any service of its own and sends e-mail messages directly using the JavaMail API. However, it is always tempting to create your own service interface. For example,

```
public interface MailService {

    /** Sends e-mail. */
    public void sendMail(String recipient, String sender,
        String subject, String messageBody);

    /** Opens a folder on a mail host to retrieve messages. */
    public Folder open(String mailHost, int port);
    // ...
}
```

Before you proceed, it is important to assess what value is added by this service interface over the published JavaMail API. Most such undertakings go forward under the pretext of simplifying the API on which they are built, but we must consider that yet another API usually increases the amount of learning a developer needs to do, duplicates the design effort that has already been made, and may very well miss important requirements or features. For example, the proposed interface would not be able to handle multipart multipurpose Internet mail extension (MIME) messages.

Programmers have a tendency to distrust code from their peers and wouldn't hesitate to put in their own creations. This may raise a hurdle to effective development work within our programming framework.

Seventh, document the interface thoroughly. An interface is often called a "contract," because it stipulates the semantics of the functionality it provides, and usually it is the only thing exposed to clients. For this reason it is important to accompany the interface definition with ample comments. The following parts of the interface should always be documented using the documentation comments recognizable by the `javadoc` tool:

- The interface itself. The functionality of the service should be stated as well as its limitations, assumptions, and other general information the client may need to know.

- Each method. Essential aspects that need documentation are what the method does, what parameters it takes, what return value it produces, any exceptions it throws under what kind of situations, and so forth. It may also be important to document whether the method is thread safe.

Eighth, and last, apply binary compatible changes to interfaces to minimize impact. The Java programming language allows certain changes to be made to an interface while preserving binary compatibility. For example, consider again our `PrintService` interface. After compilation, we end up with the `PrintService.class` file, which is loaded by a client bundle that needs to use it. Now suppose an enhancement is needed, and a new API

```
/** Cancels the specified print job. */
public void cancel(int jobNumber) throws IOException;
```

is added to the interface. We can recompile the print service (including the implementation classes), and obtain a new version of the binary class file `PrintService.class`. If we replace the previous version with this class, the client bundle does not have trouble accessing it.

Now, as an afterthought, we decide that it would be convenient to have the original `print` method return the print job number as follows:

```
/**
 * Prints the contents from the source to the print queue.
 * Return the print job number.
 */
public int print(String queue, URL source) throws IOException;
```

Thus we can easily cancel an ongoing job with our new API. Unfortunately, a client bundle unaware of this change breaks and raises `java.lang.NoSuchMethodError`.

We have seen that adding a new method to an existing interface does not break binary compatibility, but changing the return type of an existing method does. The complete specification of binary compatibility can be found in Chapter 13 of *The Java Language Specification* [17].

Version specifications in the `Export-Package` and `Import-Package` manifest headers do not help us with incompatible interface evolution. A higher version is expected to be backward compatible with a lower one for the same package. This is because the version number specified in the Import-Package header is the minimum, not the exact one required of the package.

Although certain changes to the interface will not break existing clients, these clients will not be able to take advantage of the new features. Therefore, service interface designers should not lessen their rigor by using these as a rectification mechanism if they want their design to be enduring and effective.

In summary, a good service interface should capture the essential functionality of what it ought to do. It should be general enough to allow room for multiple implementations and various demands from its clients, it should be minimal, and its function should be unambiguously documented. If changes to an interface are unavoidable, they should be applied in a binary-compatible fashion.

6.1.4 The Social Aspect

The process of producing a good interface is usually filled with debate, what-if brainstorming, and trade-offs among conflicting feature demands. Many of us find this distasteful because we are accustomed to making coding decisions on our own and seeing things happen right away. The planning is frustrating because we don't consider any progress has been made until the coding phase has begun.

But agreeing on an interface is most likely a collective effort, because Alice and Bob cannot proceed with their service implementations unless Charlie's service interface, on which both Alice and Bob rely, has become stable. The component-based model dictates that the team members must cooperate more explicitly on the interface design. In fact, this process is a mini standardization effort, not at the level of companies, industries, or international bodies, but within the scope of your project team, and possibly your customers. It is not surprising that designing interfaces has the similar pain and benefits associated with standardization.

Therefore, it is only normal that considerable time may be spent on arguing the merits of an interface. The initial deliberation is well worth the effort if the interface turns out to be well conceived and can stand the test of changes and diverse use cases. It saves time in the long run. As a matter of fact, we think that an interface without much scrutiny is highly suspicious of defects and needs to be revisited.

6.2 Designing Library Bundles

Recall that library bundles export utility classes but do not register services of their own. Selectively exporting some of the packages inside a library bundle makes it possible for callers to benefit from the changes immediately after an update. To accomplish this, you can design the library in an interface-provider fashion. For example, consider the following bundle:

```
META-INF/MANIFEST.MF
com/acme/util/Sort.class
com/acme/util/impl/QuickSort.class
com/acme/util/impl/BubbleSort.class
com/acme/util/impl/MergeSort.class
```

You may then declare

```
Export-Package: com.acme.util
```

in the manifest to export only the `com.acme.util` package containing the class `Sort`. A caller can pick an algorithm for sorting by writing code such as

```
Sort s = Sort.getInstance("QuickSort");
s.sort(anArray);
```

The specific sorting algorithm implementations are hidden in the `com.acme.util.impl` package, which cannot be accessed by callers from other bundles. When the implementations of the library bundle are updated, the changes can take effect immediately without requiring framework restart.

6.3 Delegation and Callback

Component-based design is "divide and conquer" with clear-cut compartmentalization: Sharing among bundles and services is strictly controlled. This poses a challenge to designing services that work together. For multiple callers to use a service, they must go through the *same* interface provided by the callee; at the same time, they may all want the callee in slightly *different* ways.

Suppose we are to design a news service, `NewsService`, whose HTML contents are needed by services for a pager, a touch panel, and a PC. The data are from the same source, but how they are displayed varies: text only on the pager, no dynamic contents on the touch panel, and full media on the PC.

The news service has a few options to deal with the variation of demands from its clients. First, it can expose a carefully designed service interface to accommodate the use scenarios of the callers. For example, the news service may be defined as

```
public interface NewsService {
    static final int TEXT_ONLY = 0;
    static final int STATIC_CONTENT = 1;
```

```
    static final int UNABRIDGED = 3;
    /**
     * Gets news from the source, requesting appropriate
     * content transformation.
     */
    public InputStream getNews(int contentTransformType);
}
```

Then the service for the pager would call

```
InputStream src = newsService.getNews(NewsService.TEXT_ONLY);
```

to obtain the plain text contents from the news service.

Second, register multiple instances of the service, each providing a different implementation, to satisfy callers with different needs. For example, we could define the NewsService interface simply as

```
public interface NewsService {
    public InputStream getNews();
}
```

and supply a number of implementations based on target devices:

```
/** The first news service impl: text only */
class TextOnlyNewsImpl implements NewsService {
    public InputStream getNews() {
        // strip anything but text from the source and
        // return the stream.
    }
}
/** The second news service impl: no dynamic content */
class StaticContentNewsImpl implements NewsService { ... }

/** The third news service impl: unabridged content */
class UnabridgedNewsImpl implements NewsService { ... }
```

If all three forms of the news services are registered along with the property contentTransformType, used to distinguish the three, the service for the pager would perform the following sequence of calls to get news:

```
ServiceReference[] ref = bundleContext.getServiceReferences(
   "NewsService", "(contentTransformType=text-only)");
NewsService newsService =
```

```
(NewsService) bundleContext.getService(ref);
InputStream src = newsService.getNews();
```

But no matter how hard the callee tries, we can always sense some degree of tension between the callers, who clamor for customization, and the callee that offers a unified interface. For instance, the first alternative requires the definition of a predetermined set of content-transforming type constants; the second alternative requires the implementation of multiple news services.

Rather than put the burden entirely on the callee, we can delegate whatever customization is needed to its callers. In other words, services on the pager, the touch panel, and the desktop now have to assume the responsibility of implementing their own particular application logic, and register with the news service. At the time the news service gets news on behalf of its callers, it calls back to them to have specialized decisions made. Here is one possible design:

```
public interface NewsService {
    InputStream getNews(ContentTransformer ct);
}
```

The `ContentTransformer` parameter may be defined as

```
public interface ContentTransformer {
   /** Returns a set of HTML tags to be stripped from
    * the source content.
    */
   public String[] getTagsForRemoval();
}
```

Now the service for the pager would use the news service like this:

```
ContentTransformer ct = new ContentTransformer() {
   public String[] getTagsForRemoval() {
      // remove image, applet, and script tags
      String[] tags = new String[] {
         "img", "applet", "script" };
      return tags;
   }
};
InputStream src = newsService.getNews(ct);
```

Similarly, the service for the touch panel would do

```
ContentTransformer ct = new ContentTransformer() {
   public String[] getTagsForRemoval() {
```

```
      // remove applet and script tags; image tags okay
      String[] tags = new String[] { "applet", "script" };
      return tags;
   }
};
InputStream src = newsService.getNews(ct);
```

And, finally, the service for the PC would do

```
ContentTransformer ct = new ContentTransformer() {
   public String[] getTagsForRemoval() {
      // nothing to remove
      return null;
   }
};
InputStream src = newsService.getNews(ct);
```

The news service, before returning any content to the caller, determines the unwanted tags from the `ContentTransformer` object supplied by the caller and removes them as specified.

This design strategy puts customization close to where it is needed: in the calling services. The callers pass an implementation of a well-known interface to the callee, informing the latter how they want a particular behavior carried out. The callee duly calls back to the callers to learn their wishes before completing the requests.

In the next chapter, we see that the standard OSGi HTTP service interface is a design typical of this kind.

6.4 Leveraging the Service Registry

We have seen that the framework maintains a service registry to which a bundle can publish its service by calling the `registerService` method and from which another can get the service by calling the `getServiceReference(s)` then `getService` methods on the `BundleContext` interface. However, it may not be apparent that you can in fact register *any* type of object with the registry.

For example, the following snippet is entirely valid, although probably not useful:

```
for (int i = 0; i < 100; i++)
   bundleContext.registerService(
         "java.lang.Integer", new Integer(i));
```

And the following call would then return 100 service references to `Integer` objects in the array

```
ServiceReference[] ref = bundleContext.getServiceReferences(
    null, "(objectClass=java.lang.Integer)");
```

This post-and-pick-up feature (also known as the **white board approach**) opens up a design possibility. To illustrate, we present an example of leveraging the frameworkwide service registry to implement an event dispatching and handling mechanism among bundles.

As we have learned, the framework fires three types of events: service events, bundle events, and framework events. However, how a bundle notifies another of certain application-specific events is not specified. One possible design is as follows:

Suppose the print service wants to send out a notification when the printer malfunctions, and the report service wants to know. The `EventListener` interface and the `Event` class are defined respectively as follows:

```
package com.acme.event.print;
public interface MalfunctionEventListener {
    public void printFailed(MalfunctionEvent e);
}

public class MalfunctionEvent extends java.util.EventObject {
    /** The reasons for malfunction. */
    public static final int OUT_OF_PAPER = 0;
    public static final int PAPER_JAM = 1;
    public static final int TONER_LOW = 2;
    private int reason;

    public MalfunctionEvent(String q, int r) {
        super(q);  // set event source to the print queue name
        this.reason = r;
    }
    /** Gets the name of the troubled print queue. */
    public String getQueue() {
        return (String) getSource();
    }

    /** Gets the reason for the malfunction. */
    public int getReason() { return reason; }
}
```

The report service may register a listener with the registry like this:

```
Properties props = new Properties();
props.put("event source", "com.acme.service.print.PrintService");
props.put("event type", "com.acme.event.print.MalfunctionEvent");
bundleContext.registerService(
   "com.acme.event.print.MalfunctionEventListener",
      new MalfunctionEventListener() { ... }, props);
```

This registration indicates that it is interested in learning that `com.acme.event.print.MalfunctionEvent` originated in the print service.

Now when the print service detects an out-of-paper problem, it can warn all the listeners like this:

```
ServiceReference[] ref =
   bundleContext.getServiceReferences(
      "com.acme.event.print.MalfunctionEventListener",
      "(&(event source=com.acme.service.print.PrintService)" +
      "(event type=com.acme.event.print.MalfunctionEvent))");
for (int i=0; i<ref.length; i++) {
   MalfunctionEventListener listener =
      (MalfunctionEventListener) bundleContext.getService(ref[i]);
   listener.printFailed(new MalfunctionEvent("tree-killer",
      MalfunctionEvent.OUT_OF_PAPER));
}
```

By sufficiently restricting the results with the LDAP filter, we make sure that we get the exact set of listeners for our purpose from the registry.

The print service bundle needs to export the `com.acme.event.print` package, which is to be imported by any bundle interested in the events.

Leveraging the registry this way can be a double-edged sword. Imagine that a mischievous bundle gleans all the malfunction event listeners and invokes them just for the heck of it. The effect is more harmful than randomly calling a "normal" service, such as the print service, because the listener is designed to be called only from a specific application context (that is, the printer malfunctions), whereas a service, by design, can usually be called under any circumstances without violating its intended application logic.

You should also be very cautious in registering instances of `ServiceRegistration` or `BundleContext` that are private to your bundle. Publishing them to the service registry allows others to unregister your service or charge service use to your bundle.

Of course, from a general security perspective, no object in the service registry, be it a service or not, should be used improperly. We can ensure this by subjecting callers to permission checks. For example, we can assign a special permission to the print service bundle so that it is the only one allowed to retrieve the listeners of the specific type from the registry. More details are presented in Chapter 9 when we discuss permissions.

6.5 Threading

A bundle or service can create and start any number of threads, and the duration of their execution depends on the operations defined in each thread's run method. Threads are especially useful because many callbacks from the framework are required to return promptly. For example, if you are to perform some long-running operation in the bundle activator's start method, you should spawn a thread to carry it out.

However, we also know that both the bundle and the service have life spans: For a bundle it is from when it is started to the time it is stopped; for a service it lasts from when the service is registered until it is unregistered. Consequently, it is important to program threads to cooperate with the life cycle of the bundle and service to prevent resource waste caused by runaway threads and to ensure the correctness of application logic.

6.5.1 Preventing Runaway Threads

Threads should be programmed so that they terminate naturally when the bundle or service that has created them is stopped or unregistered respectively. Let's see how this is done through an example.

Here is a bundle that finds all prime numbers in a specified integral range when it is started. First, here is the thread that does the computation:

```
package com.acme.apps.prime;

class PrimeFinder extends Thread {
   private volatile boolean running = true;

   public void run() {
      try {
         String maxprop =
            System.getProperty("com.acme.apps.prime.max");
         int max = Integer.parseInt(maxprop);
```

```
        for (int n = 2; n <= max && running; n++) {
            if (isPrime(n))
                System.out.println(n);
        }
    } catch (NumberFormatException e) {
    }
}

void terminate() {
    running = false;
}

private boolean isPrime(int n) {
    // implementation of algorithm to determine
    // if a number is prime
}
}
```

The maximum range of numbers from which to find primes is read from the system property com.acme.apps.prime.max. The following is the bundle activator:

```
package com.acme.apps.math;
import org.osgi.framework.BundleActivator;
import org.osgi.framework.BundleContext;

public class NumberCrunchingActivator implements BundleActivator {
    PrimeFinder t;
    public void start(BundleContext ctxt) {
        t = new PrimeFinder();
        t.start();
    }

    public void stop(BundleContext ctxt) {
        t.terminate();
    }
}
```

To ensure that the start method returns expediently, the lengthy computation is performed in a dedicated thread, which is set off to run in the start method. When the bundle is stopped, the stop method cleans up by terminating the computation thread naturally if it has not terminated already.

We only need to define the `Bundle-Activator` manifest header to complete this bundle:

```
Bundle-Activator: com.acme.apps.math.NumberCrunchingActivator
```

Install this bundle. Before you start it, set the range using the `set` command from the command console like this:

```
> set com.acme.apps.prime.max=1000
```

If as part of your service implementation you need to create separate threads, you should monitor the unregistering event of the service so that you can terminate the running thread in a similar fashion when the service is about to be unregistered.

6.5.2 Writing a Multithread Server Bundle

Writing a TCP/IP server is a common task in today's networked applications. A server is usually launched to wait on a well-known port. When a client connects to the server, the server spawns a dedicated thread to handle that particular request, and returns to wait for the next incoming request. In this way the server can handle multiple clients concurrently and thus achieve high performance and scalability.

If a bundle launches such a server, it should ensure that the server is shut down properly when it is deactivated. The following three aspects must be considered:

1. Create a separate thread to launch the server from the activator's `start` method. As we have explained previously, the `start` method must return promptly, and it must not be tied up by the server thread that waits for incoming requests.

2. When the activator's `stop` method is called, terminate the server's waiting thread, and force the `ServerSocket`'s `accept` method to return.

3. Keep track of all threads that are handling client requests, and terminate them naturally as well.

The following example code skeleton illustrates what we've just discussed. We are going to use such a server in Chapter 9 to accept administrative commands from a remote host.

First, here is the bundle's activator:

```
public class Activator implements BundleActivator {
    private ServerThread server = null;
```

```java
    public void start(BundleContext ctxt) throws IOException {
        ServerThread server = new ServerThread();
        server.start();
    }

    public void stop(BundleContext ctxt) throws IOException {
        if (server != null) {
            server.terminate();
        }
    }
}
```

ServerThread creates ServerSocket and waits for incoming connections. It returns from accept when a connection is established, and ConnectionThread is constructed and started to handle the connection.

The following is a typical setup for a multithread server:

```java
class ServerThread extends Thread {
    private boolean running = true;
    private ServerSocket serverSocket = null;

    ServerThread() throws IOException {
        serverSocket = new ServerSocket(8082, 16);
    }

    public void run() {
        while (this.running) {
            try {
                Socket socket = this.serverSocket.accept();
                if (!this.running)
                    break;
                ConnectionThread conn = new ConnectionThread(socket);
                conn.start();
            } catch (IOException e) {
            }
        }
    }

    void terminate() {
        this.running = false;
    }
}
```

The `terminate` method intends to make the server quit its waiting loop, but chances are the server is blocking at the `accept` call. This implementation does not terminate the server thread until a client makes one more connection. To force the server to return from the `accept` call, you may close the server socket outright:

```
void terminate() throws IOException {
   this.running = false;
   if (this.serverSocket != null) {
      this.serverSocket.close();
   }
}
```

Closing the server socket causes `SocketException` to be thrown by the `accept` method, which can be ignored.

An alternative scheme is to connect to the server socket from within the `terminate` method to mimic a client request:

```
void terminate() throws IOException {
   this.running = false;
   if (this.serverSocket != null) {
      InetAddress addr = InetAddress.getLocalHost();
      int port = this.serverSocket.getLocalPort();
      Socket s = new Socket(addr, port);
      s.close();
   }
}
```

With the second scheme, we must check the `running` flag after `accept` returns in the `run` method in `ServerThread` to distinguish whether the connection was made by a legitimate client or a "wake-up call" from `terminate`. That's what the following lines of code are for:

```
...
Socket socket = this.serverSocket.accept();
if (!this.running)
   break;
...
```

Finally, all `ConnectionThread` instances should be terminated as well during shutdown. A similar `terminate` method can be defined in `ConnectionThread`. As each `ConnectionThread` is created, it is added to a collection. Once it has run its course, it is removed from the collection. `ServerThread` is modified to make this happen:

```
class ServerThread extends Thread {
private boolean running = true;
private ServerSocket serverSocket;
private Vector clientConnections = new Vector(16);

class ConnectionThread extends Thread {
   private Socket socket;

   ConnectionThread(Socket s) {
      this.socket = s;
   }

   public void run() {
      ...
      // this should be the last statement in this
      // method body; the thread has completed its run
      clientConnections.removeElement(this);
   }

   void terminate() throws IOException {
      ... // other application-specific cleanup
      socket.close();  // close connection to this client
   }
} // end of ConnectionThread class definition

public void run() {
   while (this.running) {
      try {
         Socket socket = this.serverSocket.accept();
         ConnectionThread conn =
            this.new ConnectionThread(socket);
         clientConnections.addElement(conn);
         conn.start();
      } catch (IOException e) {
      }
   }
}
```

```
        void terminate() throws IOException {
          // terminate every outstanding client thread
          for (int i=0; i<clientConnections.size(); i++) {
            ConnectionThread conn = (ConnectionThread)
              clientConnections.elementAt(i);
            conn.terminate();
          }
          clientConnections.removeAllElements();
          this.running = false;
          // force the server thread to return from the accept call
          if (this.serverSocket != null)
            this.serverSocket.close();
        }
      }
```

The thread for handling a client request (`ConnectionThread`) is defined as a member inner class nested in the `ServerThread` class, which makes it convenient for the client thread to access the collection `clientConnections` directly.

6.5.3 Using a Thread Pool

You cannot kill a thread externally. The `stop` method on the `Thread` class can be dangerous to the integrity of the execution and has been deprecated. The `interrupt` method on the `Thread` class can only interrupt a thread that is sleeping, waiting to be notified, or doing input/output. Even then, if the thread chooses to catch `InterruptedException` and resumes execution of the thread, there's nothing that the "terminator" can do.

Why would you ever want to kill a running thread? Maybe it has been discovered to be trapped in an infinite loop, or maybe it has exceeded allowed execution time. If an ill-behaved bundle activator `start` method does not return, its invocation will hang the entire Java Embedded Server framework, and no other bundle can be managed.

As we have seen, because a runaway thread cannot be effectively killed externally, it becomes a lost cause and the system resource it consumes cannot be recovered. On the other hand, it is clearly unacceptable that the miscarriage of one thread should bring down the entire framework software. One way to increase the robustness and efficiency in this event is to use a thread pool.

Within a bundle we can create a few threads ahead of time. When a time-consuming and unsafe task needs to be run, we assign a thread to perform the operation. If that thread fails to return after some reasonable time, we give up the lost thread and continue to operate on the remaining threads. In the meantime, we may warn the administrator that something has gone wrong, so that measures can be taken to correct the situation. Of course, if all threads are lost, we're in trouble. But the thread pool gives us room to recover from problematic conditions and increases our chances of surviving misbehaving threads. It is not unlike the case where a ship that can withstand five torpedoes is much preferred over one that sinks after being hit by just one.

A variation of the same scheme is to allocate one thread each time after the previous one has timed out. This way we do not waste resources maintaining multiple idle threads (misbehaving threads are expected to be rare).

The following shows an implementation of the thread pool as a utility class. It is also possible to make it an independent service:

```
public class ThreadPool {
   private PoolThread[] threads;

   /**
    * Create a thread pool with the specified initial number of
    * active threads.
    */
   public ThreadPool(int initCapacity) {
      threads = new PoolThread[initCapacity];
      for (int i=0; i<threads.length; i++) {
         threads[i] = new PoolThread();   // allocate the threads
         threads[i].start();              // start them
      }
   }

   /**
    * Return a thread from the pool to execute the run method of
    * the specified Runnable object. Return null if no thread is
    * available in the pool.
    */
   public synchronized Thread getThread(Runnable task) {
      PoolThread t = null;
      for (int i=0; i<threads.length; i++)
         if (threads[i].isReady()) {
            t = threads[i];
            break;
         }
      if (t != null)
         t.setRunnable(task);   // assign the task to the thread
```

```java
            return t;
        }
    }

    /**
     * A thread in the thread pool.
     */
    class PoolThread extends Thread {
        // the task to be performed by the thread
        private Runnable task = null;

        /**
         * Associate the task with this thread.
         */
        synchronized void setRunnable(Runnable t) {
            this.task = t;   // assign the new task
            notifyAll();     // wake up this thread to perform the task
        }

        /**
         * Return whether the thread is available for a task.
         */
        synchronized boolean isReady() {
            return task == null;
        }

        public void run() {
            while (true) {
                synchronized (this) {
                    while (task == null) {
                        // wait while no task is assigned
                        try {
                            wait();
                        } catch (InterruptedException e) {
                        }
                    }
                    task.run();   // executing the task
                    task = null;
                }
            }
        }
    }
}
```

The thread pool creates and starts a set of threads. Each thread contains a task as a `Runnable` object. Initially, all threads' tasks are `null`, which puts them to sleep, waiting for tasks to be assigned.

A caller requesting a thread to run its number-crunching operation would write code like

```
Runnable numberCrunchingTask = new Runnable() {
    public void run() {
        // number crunching
    }
};
ThreadPool pool = new ThreadPool(10);
pool.getThread(numberCrunchingTask);
```

The first waiting thread in the pool is assigned the task and is woken to execute its run method. If all threads in the pool are busy, `getThread` returns `null`, and the specified task is not executed.

Because the threads in the pool have all been created and activated, the lead time spent on such a setup is no longer a liability for any caller that asks for a thread to get some task done. If callers follow the rule of always requesting a thread from the pool rather than instantiating a `java.lang.Thread` object themselves, we can achieve manageability to a significant extent.

Many enhancements can be made to this implementation, including wait with the option of time-out when no thread is available and error handling. We challenge you with these exercises.

6.6 Managing Object Allocation

The Java virtual machine reclaims unused objects with garbage collection, which is not deterministic and cannot be forced to happen in the Java virtual machine.[1] An object is unused if it is not referenced by anyone. Thus, care must be taken to ensure that references to unused objects are removed so that the garbage collector can recover the memory occupied by these objects.

Because a bundle can be stopped and uninstalled, it is especially important not to leave behind any objects that have been allocated by the stopped bundle. In many situations, a bundle may need to be restarted multiple times, or it may be

---

[1] The gc method on the `java.lang.System` class can be invoked to run the garbage collector, which makes a best effort to reclaim the memory occupied by unused objects. Its effect is specific to the Java virtual machine implementation.

updated. If each time it is stopped, some of its objects continue to take up memory, the gateway will run out of memory very quickly. This is clearly unacceptable for the intended application of a gateway, which is expected to be up and running for months, even years, to come.

This section provides some suggestions on how to keep object allocation under control.

6.6.1 Nullify References After Use

Because the existence of a reference to it prevents an object from being "garbage collected," you should keep track of the object use and nullify the references to an object when it is no longer of use.

Explicitly assigning `null` to a reference often is not necessary. However, doing so helps you maintain the discipline of managing object allocations and writing nonmemory-leaking code. It may also make it easier for certain garbage collectors to spot "garbage."

We know that the bundle activator is the first object to be instantiated when the bundle is started. You are responsible for whatever objects are created in the activator and subsequently within the services (because the earliest time a service can be registered is in the activator), and you should make sure that they are no longer referenced when the bundle is stopped. For example,

```
import java.util.*;
import org.osgi.framework.*;

public class Activator implements BundleActivator {
    private ServiceRegistration reg;
    private Object service;
    private Properties props;

    public void start(BundleContext ctxt) {
        service = new MyService();
        props = new Properties();
        props.put("description","The greatest service of all times");
        reg = ctxt.registerService("MyService", service, props);
    }

    public void stop(BundleContext ctxt) {
        if (reg != null)
            reg.unregister();
```

```
            reg = null;
            props = null;
            service = null;
    }
}
```

Although not strictly necessary, this practice makes it obvious that all three objects we have created in the `start` method—`service`, `props`, and `reg`—are all nullified in the `stop` method. As long as the service implementation itself cleans up properly (which we address in the next section), we can rest assured that our bundle won't leak memory.

The scope and access control enforced by the Java programming language is a great help in managing object references. Data members with `private` modifiers are only accessible within the same class. Data members with package-level access control won't be accessed outside their package. These all narrow the scope in which we need to keep track of object allocation.

6.6.2 Managing References among Bundles

Although cleaning up references within a bundle is relatively straightforward, managing them across bundles can be complicated. The primary mechanism by which a bundle gets a reference to a service object in another bundle is the `getService` call. Figure 6.1 shows the process.

Assume the type of the service under discussion is `FooService`. Reference s1 is created when bundle b1 instantiated an instance of `FooService` like

```
FooService s1 = new FooServiceImpl();
```

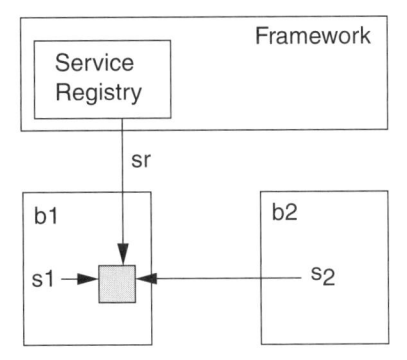

Figure 6.1   References to a service

Reference sr is established when b1 registers s1 with the registry:

```
bundleContext.registerService("FooService", s, null);
```

Reference s2 is established when bundle b2 calls `getService` and obtains the service from the registry:

```
ServiceReference ref =
   bundleContext.getServiceReference("FooService");
FooService s2 = (FooService) bundleContext.getService(ref);
```

The service object occupies memory as long as the three references remain pointing to it. To allow the garbage collector to reclaim the memory used by the service when bundle b1 is uninstalled, you must make sure that

1. b1 unregisters the service in the `stop` method of its activator. This removes reference sr, which is done automatically.

2. b1 removes the reference s1 by assigning `null` to it

3. b2 calls `ungetService` and also removes the reference s2 by assigning `null` to it. For this to work, b2 must listen to service unregistration events so that it can be notified when b1 unregisters its service.

If b2 is the bundle to be stopped, it should simply call `ungetService` and nullify its reference to the service object. This removes reference s2.

If bundle b1 registers a service factory rather than a service with the registry, you still need to follow the previously mentioned steps to ensure proper cleanup of the references. Figure 6.2 illustrates this new situation.

The reference sf is established by b1 instantiating a service factory:

```
ServiceFactory sf = new MyServiceFactory();
```

The reference sr is established by b1 registering the service factory:

```
bundleContext.registerService("FooService", sf, null);
```

The reference s is established in b2 by

```
ServiceReference ref =
   bundleContext.getServiceReference("FooService");
FooService s = (FooService) bundleContext.getService(ref);
```

For the last step, the framework calls the service factory to create a service, and caches it internally. The reference sc points to this cached service instance.

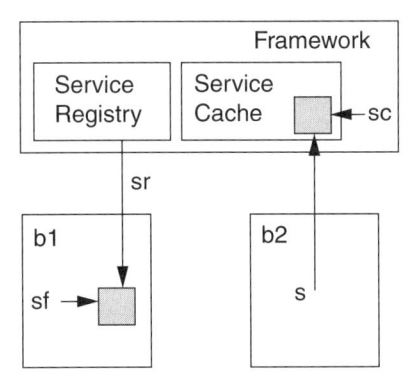

Figure 6.2 The references when b1 registers a service factory

Suppose b1 is going away. In this case, when b1 unregisters its service factory sf, it removes reference sr; it removes reference sf by assigning `null` to it. When bundle b2 calls `ungetService`, the framework removes the reference to the cached service sc, and b2 removes reference s by assigning `null` to it.

If b2 is going away, it then calls `ungetService` and nullifies its reference to the service, which removes references sc and s.

This discussion makes it clear that we should use service as the only coupling mechanism among bundles, because clean decoupling strategies are in place so that unused object references always get a chance to be removed.

We have just discussed a technique of using delegation and callback, which demands extra care with respect to cleaning up cross-bundle object references. In these circumstances, the caller usually passes an object to the callee as one of the parameters, or the callee returns an object to the caller as the return value. Let's take another look at our news service example. The following could be an implementation of the `getNews` method of `NewsService`:

```
class NewsServiceImpl implements NewsService {
   public InputStream getNews(ContentTransformer ct) {
      String[] tags = ct.getTagsForRemoval();
      ...
      stream = new TagFilteredInputStream(...);
      return stream;
   }
}
```

The reference `ct` points to an object created in the calling bundle. If `NewsService` does not further reference it within itself (as is the case earlier, because ct is a reference local to the scope of the method and is popped off the stack as the method returns), the calling bundle has full control of its disuse. However, if for some reason, NewsService assigns ct to some data member, then the calling bundle can no longer reclaim the object all by itself. Therefore, don't reference an object passed in from another bundle without good reason.

Conversely, after the calling bundle obtained the returned InputStream object, it should read from the stream, then close the stream, and nullify the reference:

```
InputStream in = null;
try {
   in = newsService.getNews(ct);
   // read from the input stream
} catch (Exception e) {
   // handle exception
} finally {
   if (in != null) {
      try {
         in.close();
      } catch (IOException e) { }
      in = null;
   }
}
```

By consciously cleaning up cross-bundle object references, we can develop well-behaved bundles that do not hamper the work of the garbage collector and that do not accumulate useless objects in the Java virtual machine over time.

CHAPTER 7

Standard Services

OSGI Service Gateway Specification 1.0 has defined APIs for two standard services: the Log service and the HTTP service. The Log service is a mandatory service that you can expect to be present on any vendor's implementation. The HTTP service, on the other hand, is optional. We next look at how a bundle can use these two services.

7.1 The Log Service

The main purpose of the Log service is to record events and errors, and to retrieve them afterward. Unlike desktop systems, residential gateways usually do not have conventional input/output devices such as keyboard and display. As a result, when an error occurs in the framework, we often cannot hope to display an error message to the user and get his intervention to correct the erroneous condition.

The Log service is a good place to save error and other messages so that remote administrators can analyze them either manually or through the use of a tool. The Log bundle registers two services: `LogService` for writing logs and `LogReaderService` for retrieving them.

7.1.1 Using `LogService` to Write Logs

To use `LogService`, your bundle must do the following:

1. In your manifest, declare the `LogService` package in the `Import-Package` header:

    ```
    Import-Package: org.osgi.service.log
    ```

2. In your bundle or service (usually in the activator), get an instance of `LogService`:

   ```
   import org.osgi.service.log.LogService;
   ...
   ServiceReference ref = bundleContext.getServiceReference(
       "org.osgi.service.log.LogService");
   LogService logService = (LogService) bundleContext.getService(ref);
   ```

The `LogService` interface provides APIs with which you can write log entries. How the log entries are processed and saved is up to the implementation of `LogService`. They may be saved on the disk locally if the gateway is so equipped, or they may be sent to a remote server over the network.

`LogService` also defines severity levels. When you call one of the `log` methods to write an entry to the log, you need to specify a level that indicates how important the entry is in your call. The predefined levels are

- `LogService.LOG_DEBUG`: a debugging message
- `LogService.LOG_INFO`: an informational message
- `LogService.LOG_WARNING`: a warning message
- `LogService.LOG_ERROR`: an error message

The level can be used by the `LogService` implementation to filter out log requests below a certain cutoff. For example, the Log service may want only to accept any log requests more severe than `LOG_DEBUG` during real deployment, but may lower the threshold to include `LOG_DEBUG` requests during development and maintenance.

We present some examples of how to perform logging by calling the Log service API. The following code logs a debugging message that reports the user's login/account name.

```
logService.log(LogService.LOG_DEBUG,
   "The value of user.name system property is " +
     System.getProperty("user.name"));
```

The following code logs an error message when an attempt to download data from a URL fails:

```
try {
  URL url = new URL(destination);
  URLConnection conn = url.openURLConnection();
```

```
    ...
} catch (Exception e) {
   logService.log(LogService.LOG_ERROR,
      "Cannot download from URL " + destination, e);
}
```

The following code logs a warning message if the print queue is crowded, and logs an error when we fail to print through the print service. In this example, we include the service reference to `PrintService` in `printRef` as part of the `log` method call, indicating the service associated with the log entry being produced:

```
ServiceReference printRef = bundleContext.getServiceReference(
      "com.acme.service.print.PrintService");
PrintService svc = (PrintService)
   bundleContext.getService(printRef);
String printer = "tree-killer";
String source = "file:/home/joe/memo";
try {
   // get status from the printer "tree-killer"
   String status = svc.getStatus(printer);
   if (status != null)
      logService.log(LogService.WARNING,
         "print queue " + printer + " is not empty.");
   svc.print(printer, new URL(source));
} catch (IOException e) {
   logService.log(printRef, LogService.LOG_ERROR,
      "failed to print file " + source, e);
}
```

7.1.2 Using `LogReaderService` to Get Logs

You can use `LogReaderService` to read entries that have been logged or to monitor logs as soon as they are written. Because the service is defined in the same package as `LogService`, you don't need to add anything to the `Import-Package` manifest header in your bundle. The following code gets `LogReaderService`:

```
ServiceReference logReaderRef = bundleContext.getServiceReference(
      "org.osgi.service.log.LogReaderService");
LogReaderService logReader = (LogReaderService)
      bundleContext.getService(logReaderRef);
```

With `LogReaderService`, you can achieve the following two tasks:

1. Get all the log entries that have been created so far. The Log service in the Java Embedded Server product has a size limit on the number of entries being kept; older entries are discarded.

2. Add a listener so that you can be notified whenever a log entry is written.

7.1.2.1 Getting a Snapshot of the Logs

By calling the `getLog` method on `LogReaderService`, you get an enumeration of log entries. A log entry, as defined by the `LogEntry` interface, contains the information provided to `LogService`'s `log` call when the entry was created. For example,

```
Enumeration enum = logReader.getLog();
while (enum.hasMoreElements()) {
   LogEntry entry = (LogEntry) enum.nextElement();
   displayLogEntry(entry);
}
```

where the method `displayLogEntry` may be defined as

```
void displayLogEntry(LogEntry entry) {
   Date timeStamp = new Date(entry.getTime());
   System.out.print(timeStamp + " ");
   switch (entry.getLevel()) {
      case LogService.LOG_DEBUG:
         System.out.print("debug ");
         break;
      case LogService.LOG_INFO:
         System.out.print("info ");
         break;
      case LogService.LOG_WARNING:
         System.out.print("warning ");
         break;
      case LogService.LOG_ERROR:
         System.out.println("error ");
         break;
   }
   Bundle b = entry.getBundle();
   System.out.print(b == null ? "" : b.getLocation());
   ServiceReference ref = entry.getServiceReference();
```

```
        if (ref != null)
           System.out.print(" "+ref);
        System.out.println(": " + entry.getMessage());
        Throwable t = entry.getException();
        if (t != null)
           t.printStackTrace();
    }
```

7.1.2.2 Monitoring Logs

You can add an implementation of `LogListener` so that it will be notified whenever a log entry is created. For example,

```
LogListener myLogListener = new LogListener() {
    public void logged(LogEntry entry) {
        displayLogEntry(entry);
    }
};
logReader.addLogListener(myLogListener);
```

You can remove `LogListener` when you no longer need to monitor logs:

```
logReader.removeLogListener(myLogListener);
```

The Log bundle automatically removes the listeners added by a bundle when that bundle goes away (gets stopped or uninstalled). It also removes all instances of `LogListener` when it itself goes away.

7.1.3 Performing Persistent Logging

The `LogService` implementation in the Java Embedded Server product keeps the log entries in memory. Oldest entries are overwritten and lost as new entries are added. It is often desirable to commit log records to persistent storage locally to disk or at a remote host, so that administrators can trace the history for purposes of auditing or performance analysis.

In this section we look at an implementation of `LogListener` that transfers log entries to an HTTP servlet on a remote Web server for safekeeping:

```
import java.io.*;
import java.net.*;
import java.util.Date;
import org.osgi.framework.*;
import org.osgi.service.log.*;
```

```java
class HttpLogListener implements LogListener {
    private URL serverURL;      // URL to remote HTTP servlet
    private LogEntry[] entries; // buffer of log entries
    private int index = 0;   // current index in log entry buffer

    public void logged(LogEntry entry) {
        if (index < entries.length) {
            // cache the log entry in the buffer
            entries[index++] = entry;
            return;
        }
        // the log entry buffer is full;
        // post to the remote HTTP servlet
        if (serverURL != null) {
            try {
                HttpURLConnection conn = (HttpURLConnection)
                    serverURL.openConnection();
                conn.setRequestMethod("POST");
                conn.setDoOutput(true);
                OutputStream os = conn.getOutputStream();
                DataOutputStream out = new DataOutputStream(os);
                sendLogs(out);
                // discard whatever the Web server returns
                conn.getInputStream().close();
                out.close();
            } catch (IOException e) {
                // log entries will be lost
            }
        }
        // store the new log entry
        index = 0;
        entries[index++] = entry;
    }

    HttpLogListener(URL u, int bufferSize) {
        this.serverURL = u;
        this.entries = new LogEntry[bufferSize];
    }
```

```java
    private void sendLogs(DataOutputStream out) throws IOException {
        for (int i=0; i<entries.length; i++) {
            String date = new Date(entries[i].getTime()).toString();
            String bundlestr = "";
            Bundle bundle = entries[i].getBundle();
            if (bundle != null)
                bundlestr = bundle.toString();
            String refstr = "";
            ServiceReference ref = entries[i].getServiceReference();
            if (ref != null) refstr = ref.toString();
            out.writeUTF(date);
            out.writeUTF(bundlestr);
            out.writeUTF(refstr);
            out.writeLong(entries[i].getLevel());
            out.writeUTF(entries[i].getMessage());
            Throwable t = entries[i].getException();
            String exception = "";
            if (t != null) {
                StringWriter sw = new StringWriter();
                t.printStackTrace(new PrintWriter(sw));
                exception = sw.toString();
            }
            out.writeUTF(exception);
            out.writeUTF("\n");
        }
        out.flush();
    }
}
```

The listener maintains a simple buffer so that a number of log entries can be posted to the remote server all at once to improve efficiency and to reduce network traffic. The URL to the receiving remote servlet and the maximum buffer size are initialized when the listener is instantiated.

We also define a marshalling protocol so that the various ingredients in a log entry—date, bundle, service reference, level, and exception—are converted into strings before being delivered over the wire. An empty line ('\n') is used as the separator between log entries.

Many enhancements can be made to the listener. For instance, we may use the persistent connection offered by the HTTP 1.1 protocol to improve network efficiency. We should check the status of the HTTP response to ensure our posting has indeed succeeded. We may also use a few backup URLs to which to send log entries in case the primary one fails. The servlet code that accepts the log entries is not shown. We leave that as an exercise for you.

It is not difficult to imagine alternative strategies by which the log entries may be saved to a local disk or sent to a remote plain socket end point.

Lastly, the standard services are not untouchables. You are free to reimplement any service interface to suit your own needs. For instance, you could rewrite implementations for `LogService` and `LogReaderService` entirely to do persistent logging directly. Instead of using the Log bundle provided by the Java Embedded Server product, you would install and activate your own Log bundle.

7.2 The HTTP Service

The HTTP service in the Java Embedded Server product is a lightweight HTTP server. By having it on the gateway, information can be retrieved from and controls can be directed to the gateway through standardized technology such as the Java™ Servlet API and HTML. We also benefit from one of the most universal front-end user interfaces: the Web browser. This saves us from a tremendous amount of effort in creating proprietary solutions that are slow to develop and unfamiliar to end users.

We first look at how to use the OSGi standard `HttpService` API, and then we look at the extended features provided by the Java Embedded Server implementation.

7.2.1 The Standard `HttpService` API

The `HttpService` API allows you to register servlets or resources from your bundle to be made accessible to remote clients through HTTP.

Servlets[1] run on the HTTP server side. They can be programmed to perform operations on the server and to generate dynamic content. The servlet provides the same functionality as the Common Gateway Interface (CGI) programs, only in a more robust and efficient way. Traditionally, it has become one of the most popular choices to construct middleware between a Web-based front end like a browser and some type of enterprise back end such as an application server. In our domain, the back end usually involves certain operations of the gateway instead. We assume you are familiar with how servlets work for the following discussion.

Resources are usually static data such as HTML pages, images, and so on. You generally package servlets and resources within a bundle and then register with `HttpService` to export them through HTTP. In the case of the resource, you may also make a portion of your local file system accessible through `HttpService`.

---

[1] Tutorials of Java Servlet can be found at `http://java.sun.com/docs/books/tutorial/servlets/`.

7.2.1.1 The Alias Namespace

The servlet or resource is registered with HttpService under an alias. HttpService maps the alias to its corresponding registered servlet or resource. The alias is used by HTTP clients to form URLs to invoke the servlet or to access the resource. For example, if a servlet is registered under the alias /foo and an HTML document is registered under the alias /bar, an HTTP client would use URLs such as http://mybox:8080/foo and http://mybox:8080/bar to access the servlet and the HTML page, respectively. In this example, mybox would be the host name and 8080 would be the port number where HttpService accepts requests. Generally, HttpService takes the URL from every incoming request, maps the alias portion of the URL to the corresponding servlet or resource, carries out operations defined by the servlet if one is called for, and returns static or generated contents. Figure 7.1 illustrates such a setup.

The allocation of the alias namespace is on a first-come-first-serve basis. If a servlet or a piece of resource has registered under an alias, subsequent requests to register anything under the same alias will fail and result in NamespaceException.

Valid aliases are slash-separated names. Suppose servlet A is registered under the /utilities alias, then any request to aliases beneath the /utilities tree

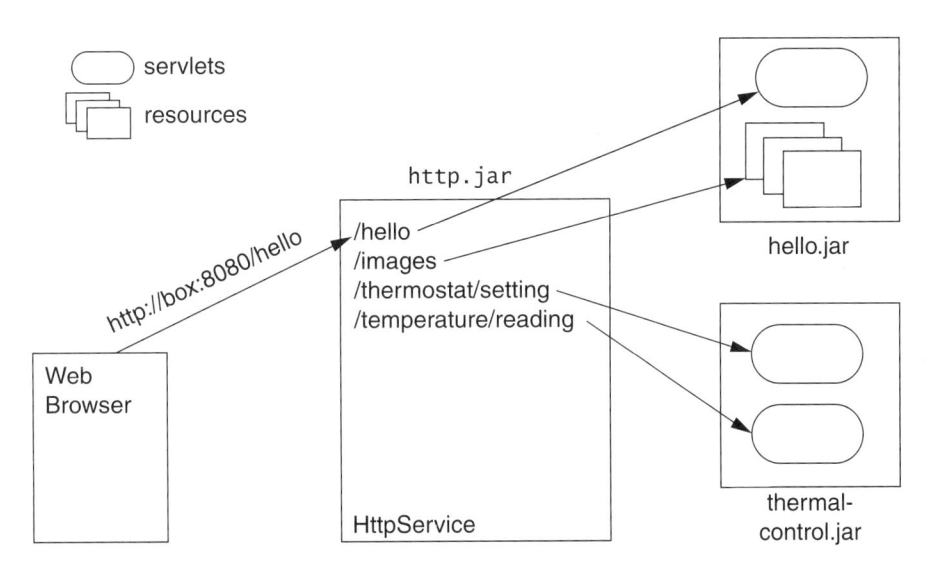

Figure 7.1 Servlet/resource registration and alias mapping by HttpService

would be directed to servlet A. In other words, the following requests all invoke servlet A:

```
http://mybox:8080/utilities/gas/readings
http://mybox:8080/utilities/water/
http://mybox:8080/utilities
```

However, if servlet B is subsequently registered at a more "specific" alias under the /utilities tree, say, /utilities/gas, then the more specific alias prevails. In other words, the following requests invoke servlet B but not servlet A:

```
http://mybox:8080/utilities/gas
http://mybox:8080/utilities/gas/readings
```

whereas the following requests are still sent to servlet A:

```
http://mybox:8080/utilities/water
http://mybox:8080/utilities
```

Notice that servlet registration and resource registration share the same alias namespace. Thus, if a servlet has occupied the alias /welcome.html, a resource registration is not able to claim it anymore.

A common misconception is that these aliases refer to some directory paths in the file system. People sometimes are frustrated by not finding the welcome.html file, not realizing that it is simply a name mapped to some dynamic content to be generated programmatically.

7.2.1.2 Getting and Using `HttpService`

To use the standard `HttpService`, follow these steps in your bundle:

1. Declare to import the Java Servlet and `org.osgi.service.http` packages in your manifest:

    ```
    Import-Package: javax.servlet; specification-version=2.1,
        javax.servlet.http; specification-version=2.1,
        org.osgi.service.http
    ```

   Import the Java Servlet packages because most likely you will be developing servlets in your bundle. The Java Servlet API is provided in a library bundle called `servlet.jar` in the Java Embedded Server distribution (you need to install and activate the servlet bundle first).

2. Obtain `HttpService` in your bundle:

   ```
   import org.osgi.service.http.HttpService;
   ...
   ServiceReference httpRef = bundleContext.getServiceReference(
       "org.osgi.service.http.HttpService");
   HttpService httpService = (HttpService)
           bundleContext.getService(httpRef);
   ```

3. Register the servlet or resource using the `registerServlet` or `register-Resources` methods of the `HttpService` interface respectively.

4. Unregister your servlet or resource when your bundle is to be stopped.

7.2.1.3 Registering a Servlet

`HttpService` provides the following API for registering servlets:

```
public void registerServlet(
    String alias,
    javax.servlet.Servlet servlet,
    java.util.Dictionary initParams,
    HttpContext httpCtxt) throws NamespaceException
```

For example,

```
httpService.registerServlet("/hello", new HelloServlet(),
    null, servletContext);
```

registers `HelloServlet` under the alias /hello, without any initial servlet parameters (hence the third parameter is `null`), and `HttpContext` (explained later). The servlet's `init` method is called to carry out any necessary initialization.

An HTTP client can later invoke this servlet by connecting to it at the URL http://*host*:*port*/**hello**. The bold type shows the correspondence between the registration alias and the URL that accesses the servlet.

7.2.1.4 Registering a Resource

`HttpService` defines the following API for registering resources:

```
public void registerResources(
    String alias
    String name,
    HttpContext httpCtxt) throws NamespaceException
```

For example,

```
HttpContext imgContext = new MyResourceContext();
httpService.registerResources("/hello/image",
    "/com/acme/servlet/image", imgContext);
```

This call registers images located by the name /com/acme/servlet/image under the alias /hello/image. What is /com/acme/servlet/image? It is a resource name whose interpretation is further determined by the HttpContext object, imgContext, which we investigate shortly.

An HTTP client can then fetch the images through the URL http://*host*:*port*/**hello/image**/pict.jpg. The bold type shows the correspondence between the registration alias and the URL that accesses the resource.

7.2.1.5 Unregistering Servlets or Resources

You can unregister any of the registered servlets or resources by calling the unregister method of the HttpService interface, and passing in the same alias used at the time of registration. For example,

```
httpService.unregister("/hello/image"); // unregister the resource
httpService.unregister("/hello");       // unregister the servlet
```

For a servlet, unregister invokes the servlet's destroy method to perform any required cleanup. If you do not unregister your servlet or resource, the HTTP service does so automatically. However, your servlet's destroy method is *not* called.

7.2.1.6 Example: Servlet and Resource Registration

Let's look at a complete example by creating a bundle that registers a servlet and an image included as a resource in the bundle. When accessed from a browser, the servlet generates an HTML page with an in-line picture (Figure 7.2).

The majority of the work is done in our bundle's activator. When the bundle is started, it obtains the HTTP service and registers a servlet. It also defines HttpContext, which is used in the servlet and image registration. The introduction of the HttpContext object adds a twist to how the HTTP service fetches the image as a resource. That is why we indicate in bold type the portion of the code that sets up the image resource for retrieval to be analyzed afterward:

```
package com.acme.servlet;
import org.osgi.framework.*;
import org.osgi.service.http.*;
import java.net.*;
```

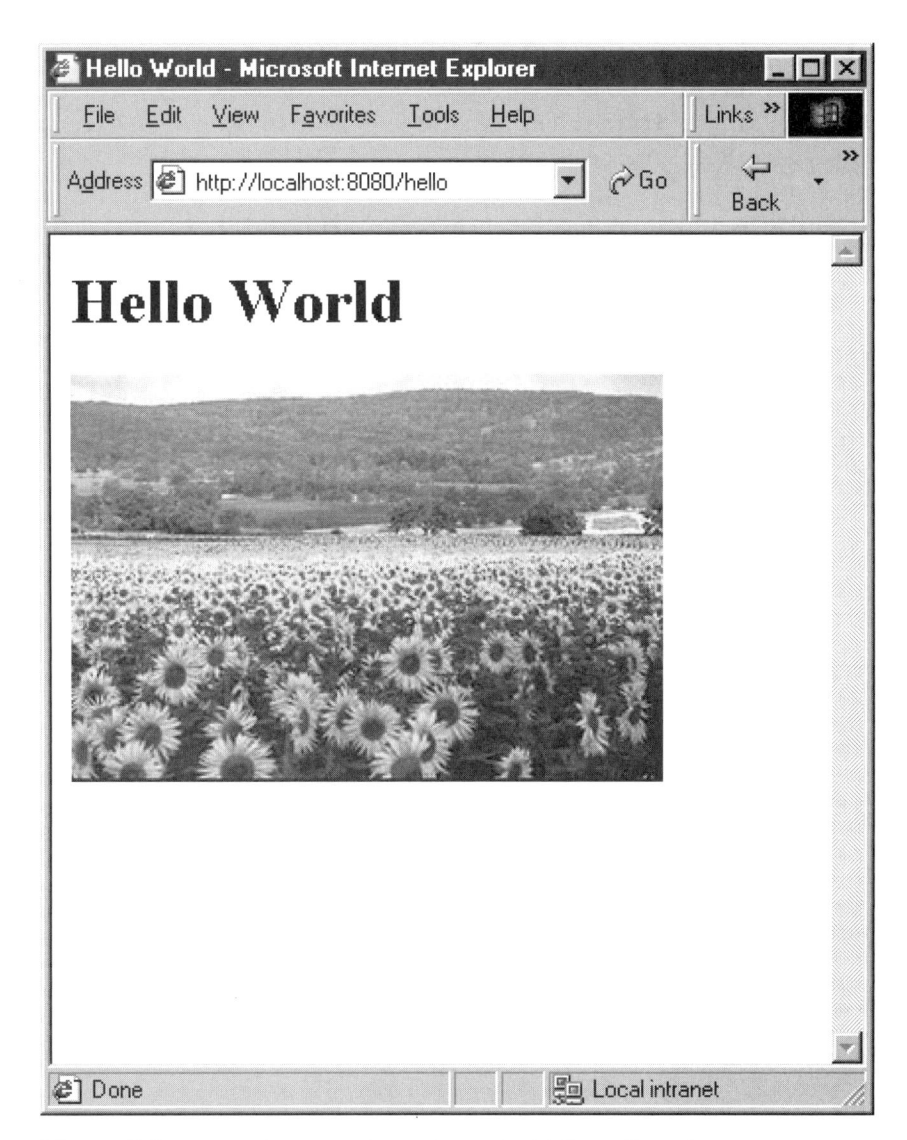

Figure 7.2 Accessing a servlet registered with `HttpService`

```
import java.io.IOException;
import javax.servlet.*;
import javax.servlet.http.*;
```

```java
public class Activator implements BundleActivator {
    final static String IMAGE_ALIAS = "/hello/image";
    final static String SERVLET_ALIAS = "/hello";
    private HttpService http;

    public void start(BundleContext context) throws Exception {
        ServiceReference ref = context.getServiceReference(
            "org.osgi.service.http.HttpService");
        http = (HttpService) context.getService(ref);
        HttpContext hc = new HttpContext() {
            public String getMimeType(String name) {
                return null;   // let HttpService decide
            }

            public boolean handleSecurity(HttpServletRequest req,
                HttpServletResponse resp) throws IOException
            {
                return true;   // no authentication needed
            }

            public URL getResource(String name) {
                // get the named resource from the bundle JAR
                URL u = this.getClass().getResource(name);
                return u;
            }
        };
        http.registerResources(IMAGE_ALIAS,
            "/com/acme/servlet/image", hc);
        http.registerServlet(SERVLET_ALIAS,
            new HelloServlet(), null, hc);
    }

    public void stop(BundleContext context) throws Exception {
        if (http != null) {
            http.unregister(IMAGE_ALIAS);
            http.unregister(SERVLET_ALIAS);
        }
    }
}
```

The following code shows the `HelloServlet` implementation:

```
package com.acme.servlet;
import javax.servlet.*;
import javax.servlet.http.*;
import java.io.*;
import java.util.Date;

/**
 * This servlet responds to HTTP GET requests for the URL under which
 * this servlet is registered with HttpService. It generates a
 * message in HTML and returns it to the client.
 */
class HelloServlet extends HttpServlet {

    public void doGet(HttpServletRequest req,
        HttpServletResponse resp)
        throws ServletException, IOException
    {
        String html =
            "<HTML>\n" +
            "<title>Hello World</title>\n" +
            "<body bgcolor=\"#ffffff\">\n" +
            "<h1>Hello World</h1>\n\n" +
            "<img src=\"" + Activator.IMAGE_ALIAS +
            "/sunflower.jpg\"><br>\n" +
            "</body></HTML>\n";
        ServletOutputStream out = resp.getOutputStream();
        resp.setContentType("text/html");
        out.println(html);
        out.close();
    }
}
```

The `doGet` and `doPost` methods are probably the most important ones to override in the `HttpServlet` class. They process two common types of requests defined in the HTTP protocol, GET and POST respectively. Normally when you enter a URL directly into a browser's Location field to access the servlet, you send a GET request; if you submit a form, however, you supply the data with a POST request. We have a chance to see an example of handling the POST request in a servlet in Chapter 9.

To continue with our example, the following are the manifest definitions:

```
Bundle-Activator: com.acme.servlet.Activator
Import-Package: javax.servlet; specification-version=2.1,
 javax.servlet.http; specification-version=2.1,
 org.osgi.service.http
```

Finally, here are the contents of the bundle JAR file:

```
META-INF/MANIFEST.MF
com/acme/servlet/Activator.class
com/acme/servlet/Activator$1.class
com/acme/servlet/HelloServlet.class
com/acme/servlet/image/sunflower.jpg
```
[2]

Let's walk through the request/response cycles. Suppose the HTTP service is listening at mybox port 8080, and this bundle is activated. When a browser sends the request http://mybox:8080/hello, the HTTP service accepts the incoming request, extracts /hello, and looks it up in its registrants. No doubt HelloServlet is matched, and its doGet method is invoked. The HTML page is generated and returned to the browser.

The browser then encounters the following line while parsing and rendering the HTML page:

```
<img src="/hello/image/sunflower.jpg">
```

As a result, the browser comes back to the HTTP service with a second request: http://mybox:8080/hello/image/sunflower.jpg. Now, to make things easier, let's trace the rest of the process in a flow chart (Figure 7.3).

The HTTP service calls not only the getResource method, but also the getMimeType and handleSecurity methods of the HttpContext interface. In this example, we chose to do minimal customization for these methods, as described by the comments in the source code.

7.2.1.7 The HttpContext Interface

Both the servlet and the resource registration take an HttpContext argument. This interface is designed to give a registering bundle flexibility to customize how a request is handled in three aspects: deciding the returned MIME type, checking authentication, and finding a resource. At the time when the servlet or resource is accessed, the methods in this interface get a callback from the HTTP service to

---

[2] You can substitute any JPEG image here and modify the code to use its filename.

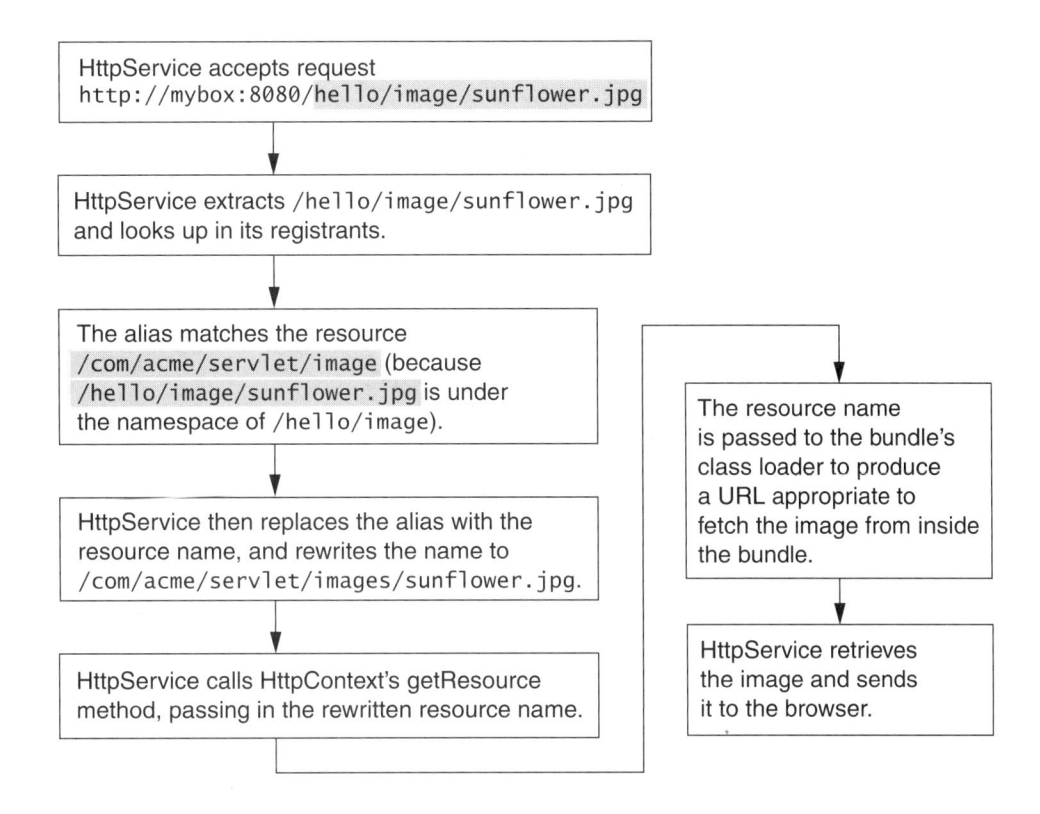

```
┌─────────────────────────────────────┐
│ HttpService accepts request         │
│ http://mybox:8080/hello/image/sunflower.jpg │
└─────────────────────────────────────┘
                 │
                 ▼
┌─────────────────────────────────────┐
│ HttpService extracts /hello/image/sunflower.jpg │
│ and looks up in its registrants.    │
└─────────────────────────────────────┘
                 │
                 ▼
┌─────────────────────────────────────┐
│ The alias matches the resource      │
│ /com/acme/servlet/image (because    │
│ /hello/image/sunflower.jpg is under │
│ the namespace of /hello/image).     │
└─────────────────────────────────────┘
                 │
                 ▼
┌─────────────────────────────────────┐
│ HttpService then replaces the alias with the │
│ resource name, and rewrites the name to      │
│ /com/acme/servlet/images/sunflower.jpg.      │
└─────────────────────────────────────┘
                 │
                 ▼
┌─────────────────────────────────────┐        ┌─────────────────────────────┐
│ HttpService calls HttpContext's getResource │──▶│ The resource name           │
│ method, passing in the rewritten resource name. │ │ is passed to the bundle's  │
└─────────────────────────────────────┘        │ class loader to produce     │
                                                │ a URL appropriate to        │
                                                │ fetch the image from inside │
                                                │ the bundle.                 │
                                                └─────────────────────────────┘
                                                              │
                                                              ▼
                                                ┌─────────────────────────────┐
                                                │ HttpService retrieves       │
                                                │ the image and sends         │
                                                │ it to the browser.          │
                                                └─────────────────────────────┘
```

Figure 7.3 How a resource is retrieved

assist in making decisions in these areas. This is an example of the design pattern "Delegation and Callback," described in Chapter 6.

The `HttpContext` API provides functionality similar in general but different in details for servlet and resource registrations. In the servlet registration, `Http-Context` is an interface meant to represent `javax.servlet.ServletContext` for the servlet. In fact, `HttpContext` has a one-to-one mapping to `javax.servlet.ServletContext`. Any servlets sharing the same instance of `HttpContext` belong to the same `ServletContext`. Obviously, such semantics do not apply to resource registration.

public String getMimeType(String name)

For Servlet Registration

This method allows you to define MIME[3] types based on the name obtained from the request. For example, a name ending with .html usually maps to a MIME type of text/html, .jpg to image/jpeg, and so on. You should implement this method if the contents produced by your servlet are of some special content type. In this case, the call to the getMimeType method of javax.servlet.Servlet-Context is delegated to your implementation of the getMimeType method in the HttpContext interface. Otherwise, simply have this method return null and ask the HTTP service to select an appropriate MIME type.

For Resource Registration

This method serves the same purpose as in the servlet registration. The MIME type is set in the Content-Type header of the response by the HTTP service. Return null if you'd like the HTTP service to select the best MIME type.

public boolean handleSecurity(HttpServletRequest req, HttpServletResponse resp)

Usually sensitive operations or data are protected and can only be accessed by authorized users. To determine the user, you can use some authentication techniques. One of those most frequently used is HTTP basic authentication [23], whereby a simple username/password pair is expected from the client.

This method allows authentication for each request, and works the same for both types of registrations. It returns true if a request has been authenticated, and returns false otherwise.

If you do not need such protection, always return true from this method. Otherwise, the steps to implement this method are as follows:

1. Get and parse the username and password carried in the request. If none is present, send the client a challenge and ask for credentials.

2. Compare the username and password in the request against a database of legitimate users. The user database may be maintained by the bundle that has registered the servlet or by a centralized service in the framework.

3. Return true if the credential checks out, and HttpService will proceed to invoke the servlet's service method. Otherwise, return false, and send the appropriate error code to the client.

---

[3] MIME defines formats for multipart, textual, and nontextual messages. See RFCs 2045 [18], 2046 [19], 2047 [20], 2048 [21], and 2049 [22] for more details.

With the Java Embedded Server product, you can perform the authentication using the `BasicSchemeHandler` service provided in the `httpauth.jar` bundle, and can maintain your own user database using the `httpusers.jar` bundle. A detailed example is presented in the next section.

Another much stronger security mechanism is the secure socket layer (SSL). SSL uses public key cryptography to authenticate the client and the server engaged in a communication session. It also encrypts the messages as they are exchanged over the network to protect data privacy. SSL is on top of the TCP/IP layer but beneath application protocols. HTTPS refers to HTTP over an SSL channel. If HTTPS is enabled for both client and server, you may not need to worry about implementing the `handleSecurity` method. However, if you do not have client authentication, you may use a combination of HTTP basic authentication with HTTPS.

The Java Embedded Server product provides an SSL bundle to enable secure HTTP communication. For more information, consult the product documentation.

public String getResource(String name)

For Servlet Registration
The call to `ServletContext.getResource` is forwarded to your implementation of the `getResource` method in the `HttpContext` interface.

For Resource Registration
This method has quite different semantics from those for servlets. In resource registration, this method is expected to do additional name translation, depending on from where the resource comes. When you register a resource, you map the resource name to an alias. In our previous example:

```
http.registerResources(IMAGE_ALIAS,
     "/com/acme/servlet/image", hc);
```

where the resource name is the string /com/acme/servlet/image. When the resource is accessed, how and where this name is mapped is further determined by the `getResource` implementation of `hc`.

If the intention is to retrieve a resource included inside the bundle JAR file, you should ask the bundle's class loader to return a URL that identifies the resource. For example,

```
HttpContext hc = new HttpContext() {
    ...
    public URL getResource(String name) {
```

```
            return this.getClass().getResource(name);
      }
};
```

The URL is used internally to retrieve resources from bundle JAR files, and is understood only by the framework, which has implemented and installed a URL stream handler for it. If you were to expose its external form to a remote browser, you would have confused the browser utterly. Therefore, do not embed the URL in the HTML generated by your servlet, because it is sent to the remote client and won't be recognized.

The resource name can also refer to other types of resources. If our intention is to use `HttpService` as a conventional Web server and to export a portion of our file system as the document root, we would implement the `getResource` method quite differently:

```
class FileContext implements HttpContext {
   public String getMimeType(String name) { return null; }

   public boolean handleSecurity(
      HttpServletRequest req,
      HttpServletResponse resp) throws IOException
   {
      return true;
   }
   public URL getResource(String name) {
      return new URL("file", name);
   }
}
```

We would then register this resource in the following way:

```
httpService.registerResource("/web", "/wwwroot",
      new FileContext());
```

At run-time, the client request URL `http://mybox:8080/web/index.html` causes `index.html` to be passed to the `getResource` method via the `name` parameter and is eventually translated into `file:/wwwroot/index.html`, causing the file /wwwroot/index.html in the local file system to be returned.

To summarize, we compare the usage of `HttpContext` in both servlet and resource registration in Table 7.1.

Table 7.1 Comparison of `HttpContext` Usage in Servlet and Resource Registration

Method	HttpContext in Servlet Registration	HttpContext in Resource Registration
getMimeType	Return the appropriate MIME type based on the request. Within the servlet, calls to `javax.servlet.ServletContext.getMimeType` is delegated to this method.	Return the appropriate MIME type based on the request. The MIME type is set in the Content-Type HTTP header.
handleSecurity	The same	
getResource	Within the servlet, calls to `javax.servlet.ServletContext.getResource` is delegated to this method.	Used to translate further the requested resource name to a resource that is retrievable with a URL.

7.2.2 Performing Basic Authentication

Web sites frequently use a username/password pair to authenticate users. We have explained that a servlet or resource can achieve this by implementing the `handleSecurity` method on `HttpContext`. The Java Embedded Server product provides a `BasicSchemeHandler` service that makes your job much easier.

In the following example, suppose accessing our servlet requires a username of "admin" and a password of "secret." Furthermore, the "admin" user belongs to the "acme" realm. You only need to follow these steps to enable basic authentication:

1. Declare to import the basic scheme handler's service interface package in the manifest:

    ```
    Bundle-Activator: com.acme.servlet.Activator
    Import-Package: javax.servlet; specification-version=2.1,
     javax.servlet.http; specification-version=2.1,
     org.osgi.service.http, com.sun.jes.service.http.auth.basic
    ```

182 CHAPTER 7 STANDARD SERVICES

2. Get an instance of `BasicSchemeHandler` to parse the username and password from the HTTP client and to send challenges back when needed:

```
package com.acme.servlet;
... // Other imports
import com.sun.jes.service.http.auth.basic.*;

public class Activator implements BundleActivator {
   private HttpService http;
   private final String SERVLET_ALIAS = "/hello";
   ...

   public void start(BundleContext context) throws Exception {
      ...
      // Obtain BasicSchemeHandler
      ServiceReference basicRef = context.getServiceReference(
         BasicSchemeHandler.class.getName())
      final BasicSchemeHandler basicAuth = basicRef != null ?
         (BasicSchemeHandler)context.getService(basicRef) :
         null;
      ...
      HttpContext hc = new HttpContext() {
         String realm = "acme";

         public String getMimeType(String name) { ... }

         public URL getResource(String name) { ... }

         public boolean handleSecurity(HttpServletRequest req,
               HttpServletResponse resp)
            throws IOException
         {
            if (basicAuth == null) {
               // always deny access if
               // we can't perform authentication
               resp.sendError(resp.SC_UNAUTHORIZED);
               return false;
            }
            BasicSchemeHandler.Response response =
```

```
                    basicAuth.getResponse(req);
                if ( response == null ) {
                    // no credential is present;
                    // send a challenge back to the client
                    basicAuth.sendChallenge(resp, realm);
                    // deny access to the client:
                    return false;
                }
                // Check username and password,
                // challenge the client if the check fails
                String user = response.getName();
                String password = response.getPassword();
                if (!"admin".equals(user) ||
                    !"secret".equals(password) )
                {
                    basicAuth.sendChallenge(resp, realm);
                    return false;
                }
                // Set the request attributes for the servlet
                req.setAttribute(
                    "org.osgi.service.http.remote.user", user);
                req.setAttribute("org.osgi.service.http.auth.type",
                    "basic");
                // Grant access
                return true;
            }
        };
        http.registerServlet(SERVLET_ALIAS,
            new HelloServlet(), null, hc);
        ...
    }

    public void stop(BundleContext context) {
        ...
    }
}
```

This version of handleSecurity only allows one user from a single realm to access the servlet, because the valid username and realm are hard coded in the HttpContext implementation. If you have a large number of users from several realms, you may want to resort to a dedicated service for user management.

handleSecurity is invoked for every request and response. BasicScheme-Handler's sendChallenge method sends the realm to the HTTP client when expected credentials are not present. In the case of a browser, this generally causes a dialog to pop up, prompting for username and password. Its getResponse method then extracts the returned credentials for verification.

The setAttribute calls are workarounds. They communicate the information of the authenticated user and authentication method used back to the servlet. Imagine that you want to display, in the Web page generated in the servlet's doGet method, the user who is currently logged in. You can do so with the following code:

```
String user = (String) req.getAttribute(
   "org.osgi.service.http.remote.user");
out.println("<P>The current user is <b>" + user + "</b>");
```

In the next release of the Java Embedded Server product, you can simply call HttpServletRequest's getRemoteUser and getAuthType methods to retrieve the values set for the org.osgi.service.http.remote.user and org.osgi.service.http.auth.type attributes, respectively. These two attribute names are expected to be standardized in the future.

7.2.3 The Extended HTTP Service

The Java Embedded Server product's implementation of the HTTP service extends the functionality of the HttpService defined by the OSGi in two ways:

1. The extended alias syntax that allows a servlet or resource to be registered on any host (if multihome) or port of the gateway. A multihome machine has more than one network interface card (NIC) installed, each with its own IP address and host name. A service gateway can naturally double as a network gateway by using one NIC for the subnet inside the house while using another for connecting to the Internet at large.

2. An additional service interface, com.sun.jes.service.http.HttpAdmin, which reports servlet and resource registration status of HttpService.

The semantics of the alias parameter have been enriched to allow for registration on different hosts and ports as well as using HTTPS. The extended syntax is a superset of that specified in the OSGi HttpService API. The full syntax is

```
http[s]://host:port/alias
```

The various scenarios made possible by this syntax are summarized in Table 7.2. In the example, we assume that a host has two host names: `myhost` and `myhost1`. The default host name is `myhost` and the default port number is 8080. We are to register a home portal servlet with the HTTP service running on the host.

Table 7.2 Extended Alias Syntax

Alias Used at Registration	URL for Accessing the Servlet or Resource	Notes
`/HomePortal`	`http://myhost:8080/HomePortal`	Use default host and port number.
`http://*:7070/HomePortal`	`http://myhost:7070/HomePortal` `http://myhost1:7070/HomePortal`	On a multihome host, the same servlet can be accessed through any of the hosts on port 7070. In the example, one host has two host names: myhost and myhost1.
`http://myhost1:6060/HomePortal`	`http://myhost1:6060/HomePortal`	Specify a specific host only on the multihome host.
`https://myhost:443/HomePortal`	`https://myhost:443/HomePortal`	`HttpService` is communicating with clients over HTTPS connections on port 443.

The same alias registered on one host/port does not conflict with that on another.

Another augmented functionality is that the HTTP bundle registers a second service, `com.sun.jes.service.http.HttpAdmin`, in addition to the standard `HttpService`. The new API allows you to find out how many servlets or resources have been registered so far, what aliases have been used, and so on. Management applications may need to access such information.

To take advantage of this service, add the following to a client bundle:

1. Declare to import the `com.sun.jes.service.http` package:

    ```
    Import-Package: javax.servlet; specification-version=2.1,
        javax.servlet.http; specification-version=2.1,
        org.osgi.service.http, com.sun.jes.service.http
    ```

2. Obtain a reference to the `HttpAdmin` service:

    ```
    import com.sun.jes.service.http.HttpAdmin;
    import com.sun.jes.service.http.HttpRegistration;
    ...
    ```

```
ServiceReference adminRef = bundleContext.getServiceReference(
    "com.sun.jes.service.http.HttpAdmin");
HttpAdmin httpAdmin = (HttpAdmin)
    bundleContext.getService(adminRef);
```

This service allows you to get an array of either servlet registrations or resource registrations. From each of the returned registration objects you can find out more details. The following code demonstrates this:

```
HttpRegistration[] regs = httpAdmin.getServletRegistrations();
for (int i=0; i<regs.length; i++) {
    System.out.println("Registered servlet #" + i + ":");
    System.out.println("Alias: " + regs[i].getAlias());
    System.out.println("URL: " + regs[i].getURL("*"));
    System.out.println("Initial servlet parameters:");
    Servlet servlet = regs[i].getServlet();
    ...
    System.out.println();
}
```

Because these APIs reveal a great deal of sensitive information, the caller must have administrative permission to use them. We cover security in Chapter 9.

CHAPTER 8

Device Access

COMMUNICATING with and controlling devices are the primary applications of a service gateway. The device access (DA) allows bundles to interact with devices as objects in the Java virtual machine. It is an optional OSGi component and defines a framework in its own right. It is not used as a service like the Log service or the HTTP service. We first discuss what it intends to achieve (and what it is *not* designed to do), then explain how it works not only conceptually but also with a hands-on exercise, and lastly provide a comprehensive example in which we configure the serial port through a Web interface using the HTTP service.

8.1 Introduction

Before we introduce DA, let's revisit our overall architectural makeup and zoom in on the details made important by accessing devices on the native platform.

8.1.1 The Software Stack in Device Access

To access physical devices, applications written in the Java programming language need to go through several layers of indirection. Through the JNI, they can talk to the underlying operating system, which can communicate with the hardware through device drivers. Figure 8.1 shows a few possibilities for bundles to access the devices in an OSGi framework.

A client bundle such as C1 can either interact with a device service provided by bundle D1, which turns around and talks to a library L as part of the Java platform, or it may talk to the API exposed by L directly. A typical example of such a library is the standard Java™ Communications API defined in the `javax.comm` package that allows programs to access the serial and parallel ports. The library has a wrapper interfacing callers from the Java platform on one side and uses the JNI to engage the native driver on the other side.

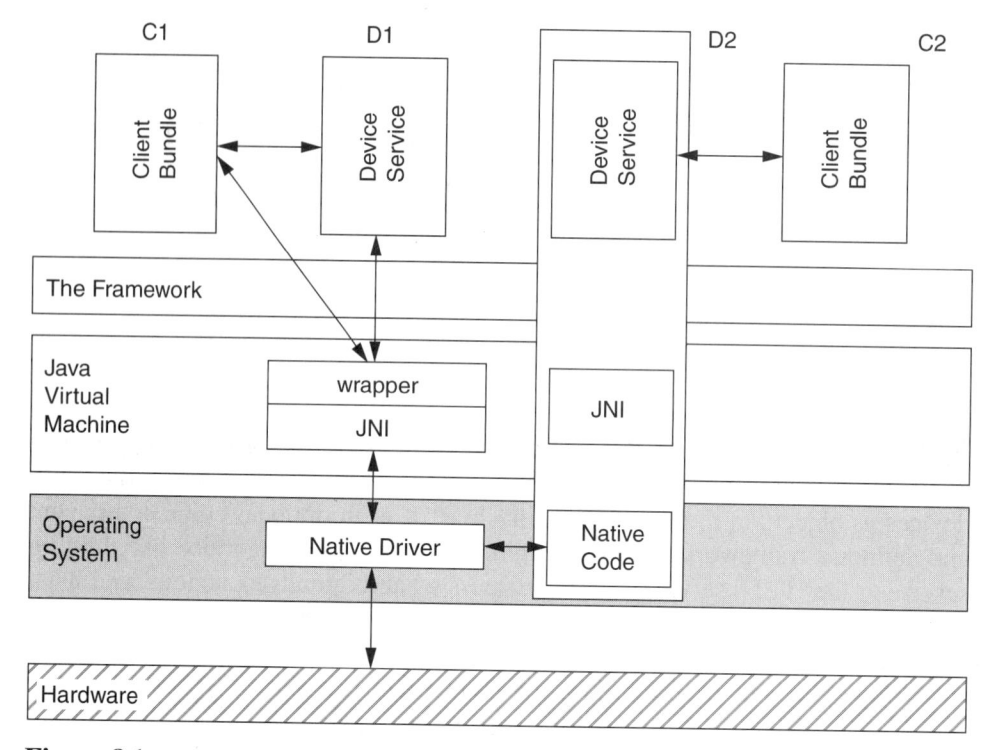

Figure 8.1 Accessing hardware devices from bundles C1 and C2 before DA enters the picture

Another client bundle such as C2 can interact with a device service provided by bundle D2, which includes both the device service written in the Java programming language and the native code to access the driver. This is exactly what we showed in the native code example in Chapter 4.

From the client bundle's perspective, it generally accesses the device through a service provided by another bundle (we show the service as "Device Service" in Figure 8.1; the precise definition is forthcoming). This is highly desirable because it makes accessing a device no more different from getting and calling any service in the OSGi framework.

8.1.2 What Device Access Is *Not*

To understand what DA is, it may be illuminating first to understand what it is not. The mere name may conjure up misconceptions, which warrant clarification up front.

DA is not about writing low-level device drivers. Device drivers, the software that enables applications to access physical devices, are usually part of the operating system. Because they serve as the bridges between software and hardware, they are highly specific to the native platforms and are mostly written in programming languages such as C or assembly. Additionally, configuration at the operating system level is almost always required to have the newly installed driver take effect. For example, to install an Ethernet card driver on your PC, you usually need to run a setup utility provided by the vendor. The utility probably updates Windows registry entries, installs software files onto system directories, and requires you to reboot the computer.

DA is part of the OSGi solution using the Java platform, and the Java programming language, designed specifically to be platform neutral, is not well suited to deal with the functional and operational aspects just described. Therefore, DA is not designed to facilitate writing or deploying low-level device drivers. Mostly, DA expects the native drivers to have been installed and configured beforehand.

DA is not about programming any particular device interfaces or protocols. Based on your application requirements and hardware capabilities, you may want to write software that communicates with devices through a USB interface, or exchanges data using FireWire, or talks to mobile phones with BlueTooth. DA is agnostic to the particulars of these protocols, and is designed to accommodate them all.

DA is not another Jini technology or UPnP. Jini technology and UPnP are designed to enable interconnectivity and interoperability of any device. They offer mechanisms for a device to discover another's presence and capabilities dynamically, so that they can utilize each other's functionality. DA does not favor one or the other and does not aim to solve as broad a class of problems. Potentially it may take advantage of both or either within its architecture.

The device access emphasizes "access," and not so much "device." We already have numerous types of devices as well as interfacing and connecting technologies. DA attempts to integrate them in one coherent framework as specified by the OSGi consortium.

8.2 Motivation

If you have ever installed a printer or a modem, you know that simply connecting them to a computer probably won't work. On many occasions you have to download and set up drivers, configure operating systems, and reboot the machine. Along the way you gain a lot of unwanted knowledge of buses, ports, speeds, connector genders, and interrupt request numbers when you really want to print documents or surf the Web. That's why plug-and-play is a great feature to have.

The following is probably a more pleasant experience. Suppose you want to get the pictures that you've taken out of a digital camera. You extract the flash RAM card, fit it into an adapter, and insert it into a laptop's PC Card slot. The computer beeps and a dialog pops up to say a new device has been detected. You find that the memory card appears as another icon of a hard drive, with which you can copy the images, just like you would with any regular disk drive. Once you are done, you eject the card, and the laptop acknowledges its removal. How painless!

What are some features that bring about such seamless operation? First, automatic detection of devices without interrupting operation. There is no need to reboot the system. Second, consistent representation of the device. The card appears as an icon, just like any other operable object in the desktop environment. Thus, a user will have no trouble figuring out how to interact with it. Third, abstraction. The memory card is certainly not a disk drive, but making it look and operate like one relieves a user from learning the details of a new type of device.

DA has been designed to achieve similar characteristics. When a device comes online, it is represented as a **device service** within the framework, just like the memory card was an icon on the desktop. For example, a ZIP drive connected to a parallel port can cause `ParallelService` to be registered.

As soon as a device service is found to have been registered, a **device refinement process** is attempted to provide a better abstraction (or refinement) for the new device service, just like the memory card is abstracted to a disk drive. The central character in device refinement is the **device manager,** which keeps a lookout for device service registrations. It involves **driver services,** which understand the particulars of certain types of devices and if better abstractions are available. To continue with our example, the device manager asks existing driver services to refine the newly registered `ParallelService`. One driver may know about the parallel port ZIP drive, so it responds positively and eventually is selected by the device manager to register another device service, `ZipDiskService`. Other drivers do not have the knowledge of this device setup. They may be able to handle a mouse attached to a USB port, a printer to a parallel port, or a ZIP drive to a SCSI interface, but not a ZIP drive to a parallel port. That is why they are queried, but are not chosen.

To reiterate, the device refinement process starts with the registration of a device service. It ends with the registration of another device service, which is considered a better abstraction of the previous one. The device manager moves the entire process along. It consults many driver services and selects the best driver. The selected driver then registers the refined device service.

There are, of course, more details to this, but as you read along, don't lose sight of the big picture.

8.3 Cast of Characters

DA consists of a single device manager, a number of device services, driver locator services, and driver services. Briefly, DA performs the following duties:

- **Device detection**. With the aid of native drivers, DA can detect whether a device is connected and can register a device service to represent its functionality.
- **Device refinement**. The device manager automatically refines a device service by consulting drivers and registering new device services. In the meantime, the device manager also asks **driver locators** to find and download new drivers on the fly to participate in this process.
- **Reconfiguration**. When no driver can be found in the device refinement process to represent a device in one way, the device manager may try alternative device services to represent the device in a different way.

Let's first look at each of the main entities in DA and what role they play at a high level, then we'll get our hands dirty examining them in action.

8.3.1 Device Service

A device service exposes the functionality provided by a physical device through its service interface. It must extend the `org.osgi.service.device.Device` interface. For example, `ParallelService`, whose service interface represents operations on a parallel port, may look like this:

```
/**
 * ParallelService accesses data using the parallel port.
 */
public interface ParallelService
   extends org.osgi.service.device.Device
{
   /**
    * Gets the output stream to write to the specified parallel port.
    * Closing the stream closes the port.
    * @param port the specification for the parallel port.
    */
   public OutputStream getOutputStream(String port);
```

```
    /** Gets the input stream to read from the parallel port. */
    public InputStream getInputStream(String port);
}
```

The `org.osgi.service.device.Device` interface defines only one method:

```
public void noDriverFound();
```

This method is used in the reconfiguration process for a device, which is described later in this chapter. It does not represent device operations, and implementations not concerned with the reconfiguration scenario should provide an empty method body.

In DA, registration and unregistration of the device service corresponds to the attachment and detachment of the physical device. For example, when you plug an external ZIP disk drive into the parallel port, `ParallelService` is registered with the framework and can be obtained and invoked by any client bundle that wishes to access the port. Later, when you unplug the ZIP drive, `ParallelService` is then unregistered in accordance with the changed reality in the physical world.[1]

By monitoring `ParallelService` unregistration events, the client bundles can find out that the parallel port is vacated and can take suitable action using techniques described in Chapter 5.

From the client bundle's perspective, it is often desirable to access the device at different levels. For example, most applications care about retrieving and storing files when they use a ZIP drive, rather than transferring bits directly through the parallel port using `ParallelService`. They probably would prefer `ZipDiskService` at a higher level of abstraction, like this:

```
public interface ZipDiskService extends
    org.osgi.service.device.Device {

    /** Gets input stream to read from a file. */
    public InputStream readFile(String fileName);

    /**
     * Gets input stream to read from the file locked with a password.
     */
    public InputStream readFile(String fileName, String password);

    /** Locks the file with a password. */
    public void LockFile(String fileName, String password);
```

---

[1] `ParallelService`'s unregistration does not mean the parallel port is gone. It means that no device is connected to the port, so there's no need to provide a service designed to communicate through the parallel interface.

```
    ...
}
```

In this sense, we say `ParallelService` is refined by `ZipDiskService`. If both are registered, client bundles now can access the same device at different levels of abstraction as needed. A ZIP diagnostic utility may call `ParallelService` to send or get raw bits from the parallel port; an image downloading service, on the other hand, would call `ZipDiskService` to save files to the ZIP drive without knowing the parallel channel at the lower layer.

When a device service is registered, it must be registered with at least one service property under the name `DEVICE_CATEGORY`. For instance, the parallel service could be registered with the property `DEVICE_CATEGORY=parallel`, whereas `ZipDiskService` could be registered with `DEVICE_CATEGORY=removable_disk`. In addition, the following properties may also be included:

- `DEVICE_CLASS`
- `DEVICE_MODEL`
- `DEVICE_MAKE`
- `DEVICE_SERIAL`
- `DEVICE_REVISION`

These service properties help define the nature of the device, and serve as the basis for the device refinement process.

The OSGi consortium intends to work with appropriate organizations to standardize many device service interface APIs. For example, there may be a USB device service interface, a modem device service interface, a switch device service interface, and so on, in the future. At the time of this writing, neither a standard device service API nor a standard device category exists. We look at a few device service interface in later sections, but they are by no means standard.

Driver services are responsible for evaluating an existing device service and registering other device services to refine it.

8.3.2 Driver Services

In DA parlance, the term **driver** means not just the low-level device drivers in the operating system. The low-level drivers, such as the one that you would download from Iomega's Web site and enables access to your parallel ZIP drive, are entities outside the OSGi framework and are referred to as the **base drivers** in the specification. Base drivers are responsible for detecting devices. For example, a base driver can poll a parallel port periodically to see whether a device is connected, and if so, register `ParallelService`.

Within DA, there are other entities also referred to as drivers. The job of these drivers is to register the appropriate device services in an attempt to refine the existing device service with new ones that offer richer semantics or different levels of abstraction. For example, semantically, `ZipDiskService` is at a higher level than `ParallelService`. Because drivers within DA make refinement of device services happen, they are called the **refinement drivers** in the specification.

A refinement driver usually comes with its own bundle.[2] The driver bundle registers an `org.osgi.service.device.Driver` service when it is started and usually carries a number of device services in the bundle as candidates for refining certain kinds of device services registered in the framework. Figure 8.2 shows the structure of a driver bundle used to refine `ParallelService` to `ZipDiskService`. Let's call it the parallel-zip driver.

Driver bundles can be installed and activated beforehand, or they may be downloaded, installed, and activated on the fly by driver locators (which are explained in the next section).

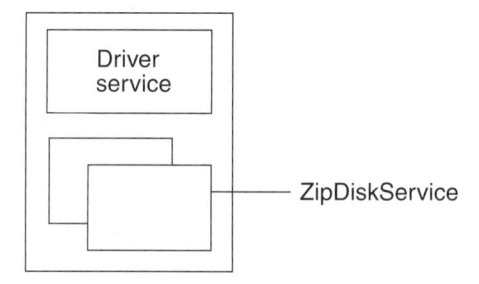

Figure 8.2 A driver bundle. It registers the `Driver` service when it is first started and carries `ZipDiskService` as a candidate for refining `ParallelService` when asked.

---

[2] We use **driver** and **driver service** without defining their difference. The former is equated to a driver bundle, which registers the latter. If the driver is selected by the device manager, it is also responsible for registering the refined device service.

Each refining driver is uniquely identified by its driver ID. If two drivers differ in any one of the following aspects, their driver IDs must be different as well:

- **Vendor.** Driver IDs of IEEE 1394 drivers from Apple and Sony must differ.
- **Type.** IDs of modem drivers must be different from those of serial drivers.
- **Revisions.** Drivers from the same vendor for the same type of device must have different driver IDs if they have different revision numbers.

The driver ID is required to be one of the service properties when a `Driver` service is registered with the framework.

The `Driver` service is an "expert" on the capabilities of the device services contained in the driver bundle and what kind of device services registered in the framework can be refined by them. It stands ready to advise the device manager in the device refinement process. The device manager asks: Given the device service just registered, how well can the device services you know of further refine it? All existing `Driver` services are queried with the following method defined in the `Driver` interface:

```
public int match(ServiceReference sr) throws Exception;
```

The service reference `sr` belongs to the device service to be refined, and a return value from this call indicates the confidence level of the driver to refine it. For example, when asked to match `ParallelService`, the parallel-zip driver yields a big integer value (Use me!), because it knows that `ZipDiskService` refines `ParallelService` perfectly. However, it returns zero if `EthernetService` is refined, because it knows that `ZipDiskService` cannot be accessed through Ethernet at all.

Based on the `Driver` services' replies, the device manager selects the highest bidder and instructs it to register the new device services. This is achieved by the other method defined in the `Driver` service interface:

```
public String attach(ServiceReference sr) throws Exception;
```

This method should register the new device services and return `null`. In so doing, it attaches the driver to the existing device service. In our example, the parallel-zip driver is chosen to register `ZipDiskService` and is attached to `ParallelService`.

This API also serves a secondary function: referring other drivers. If the current driver chosen by the device manager knows of another driver that can better attach to the device service, it returns a non-`null` referral driver ID, informing the device manager to use the other driver rather than register any device services itself.

8.3.3 Driver Locator

Refinement drivers may be present already when the device manager makes its round to query each. However, if a driver locator service is registered, the device manager asks the driver locator service to find and download driver bundles on the fly, and the new drivers still get a chance to participate in the device refinement process.

The driver locator service encapsulates the knowledge of the whereabouts of refinement drivers for a particular device service. Multiple driver locators can be present in the framework, and each may implement a different search strategy or target repository.

The `org.osgi.service.device.DriverLocator` interface defines the following method for finding drivers:

```
public String[] findDrivers(Dictionary prop);
```

The dictionary `prop` contains the service properties for the device service whose refining drivers are sought. The method returns a set of driver IDs to the device manager.

The other method defined in the `DriverLocator` interface is

```
public InputStream loadDriver(String driverID) throws IOException;
```

With the driver ID obtained from the `findDrivers` call, the device manager downloads the driver bundle from the input stream returned by this method and installs and starts it in the framework.

8.3.4 Device Manager

The device manager is the conductor orchestrating the actions of device services, drivers, and driver locators. It is an invisible player because it does not register any service of its own. It drives the refinement process in the following sequence:

1. The device manager monitors device service registrations.

2. When it is notified that a device service has been registered, it asks all available driver locators to download appropriate drivers that can refine the device service.

3. The device manager then queries all existing drivers regarding how well they can refine the device.

4. Of the replies the device manager selects the best driver and instructs that driver to register its device services as a refinement.

You may have noticed that in step 4, registration of refined device services causes step 2 to be repeated. The process continues until step 3, when none of the refinement drivers returns a positive bid. Figure 8.3 shows one iteration in the refinement process.

The design of the DA attempts to reuse as many mechanisms from the OSGi framework as possible. Essentially, it is about mapping the physical devices, which are dynamic and versatile, to services in the OSGi framework, which are equally dynamic and flexible.

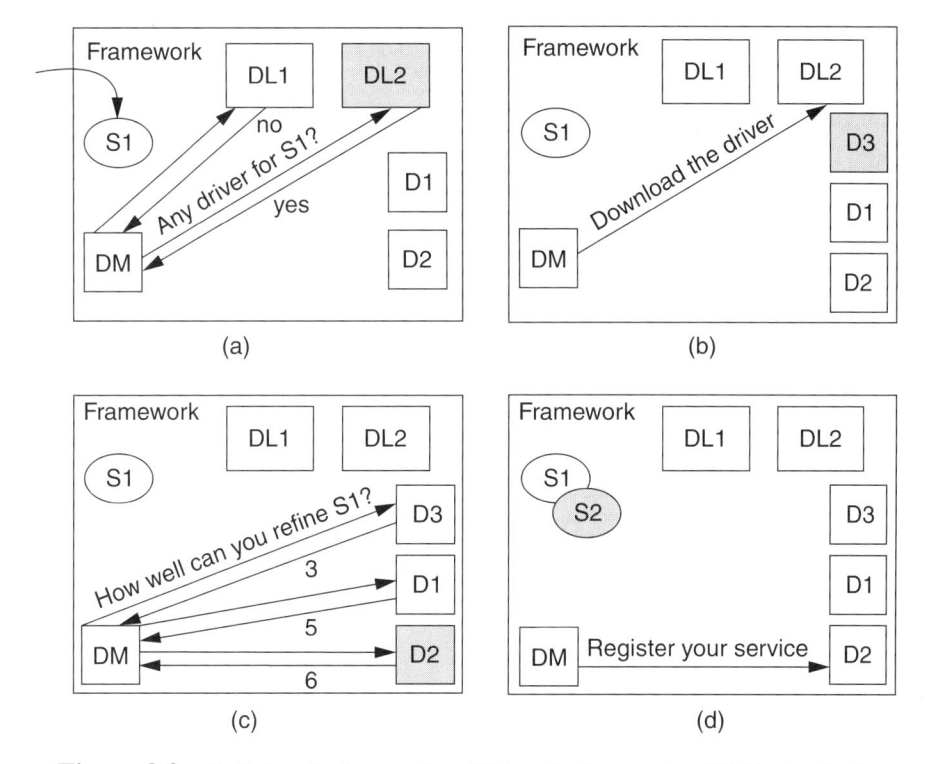

Figure 8.3 Refining device service. S1 is a device service, DM is the device manager, DL1 and DL2 are driver locator services, and D1 and D2 are driver services. (a) A device service S1 is registered in the framework, triggering DM to ask the two existing driver locators whether they know any driver that can refine S1. DL2 replies positively. (b) DM asks DL2 to download the driver, which DM installs and activates in the framework, resulting in the registration of a new driver service, D3. (c) DM queries each of the drivers regarding how well it can refine S1. Driver D2 yields the highest bid. (d) DM selects D2, which registers a refined service S2 for S1. This sequence repeats itself for S2.

8.4 Writing DA Services

In this section we learn how to develop device services, driver services, and driver locator services for the serial port. These services are fully operational, which will help you understand DA in concrete terms.

The example we are about to develop consists of a serial service bundle and a driver bundle. Figure 8.4 shows how they are packaged.

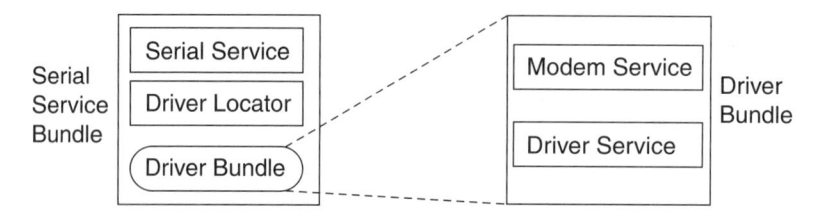

Figure 8.4 The serial service bundle contains a serial device service, a driver locator that knows where to find the driver bundle—inside its own bundle. The blowup on the right shows that the driver bundle contains a modem device service and driver service.

The serial port is a 25-pin or 9-pin D-shaped socket usually found at the back of the gateway. It transmits data one bit at a time asynchronously. The serial port is often used to connect to peripherals like mice, modems, and digital cameras.

The hardware requirement for our experiment is simple: You need a computer equipped with serial ports and a NULL modem. A NULL modem is a converter or a cable that allows two serial ports to talk to each other directly by mapping the transmitting pins on one end to the receiving pins on the other. It is readily available from most computer hardware stores. Figure 8.5 shows the hardware setup.

In the Solaris system, use the `tip(1)` command to verify that they are connected properly. Use the HyperTerminal program in Windows to do the same thing.

8.4.1 The Base Driver

The device driver from the operating system and Java Communications API[3] together make up the base driver for the serial port. It is obviously outside the

---

[3] You can download an implementation of the API from http://java.sun.com/products/javacomm/index.html.

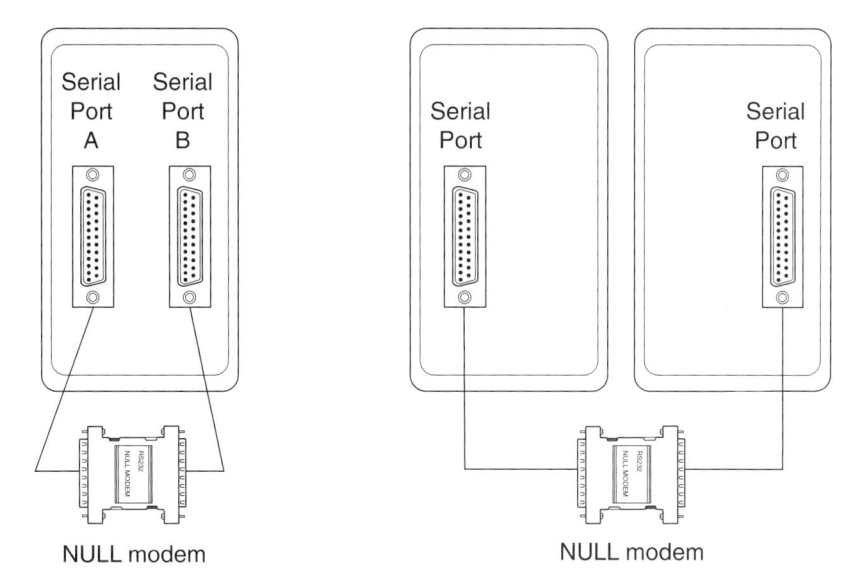

Figure 8.5 You can connect one serial port to another on the same machine through the NULL modem, or you can connect two serial ports on two different machines through the NULL modem. Make sure you get the proper cables with matching genders.

environment of the OSGi framework. To start the framework using the serial base driver on Windows, do the following:

```
set CLASSPATH=comm_dir\comm.jar;jes_path\lib\framework.jar
java[4] -Djava.library.path=comm_dir com.sun.jes.impl.framework.Main
```

where *comm_dir* is where you installed the Java Communications API files, and *jes_path* is where you installed the Java Embedded Server software. You also need to tell the Java runtime environment where to load the native shared library win32com.dll (libSolarisSerialPallel.so on the Solaris system) with either the java.library .path system property or the appropriate environment variable in the operating system (LD_LIBRARY_PATH for UNIX, PATH for Windows).

Once the framework is up and running, you can install and start the log and DA bundles from the console:

```
> start jes_path/bundles/log.jar, jes_path/bundles/device.jar
```

---

[4] On the Solaris system, you need to launch the Java virtual machine using native threads by specifying the -native switch after java (not necessary in Windows because native threads are used by default).

The bundle `device.jar` contains the implementation of DA, which depends on the Log service.

8.4.2 Device Detection

We first develop a bundle that contains a device service representing the serial port. The service is registered when the NULL modem is plugged into the serial port, and it is unregistered when the NULL modem is unplugged, automatically.

Like any service in the framework, we begin with the service interface definition:

```
package com.acme.service.device.serial;
import org.osgi.service.device.Device;

public interface SerialService extends Device {
   /**
    * Gets the SerialPort object for the port.
    */
   public javax.comm.SerialPort getPort();

   /**
    * Adds an event listener for SerialPortEvents.
    */
   public void addEventListener(
      javax.comm.SerialPortEventListener l);

   /**
    * Removes the event listener for SerialPortEvents.
    */
   public void removeEventListener(
      javax.comm.SerialPortEventListener l);
}
```

As specified by DA, `SerialService` extends the `org.osgi.service.device.Device` interface. An instance of this service represents a serial port available to bundles in the framework. If multiple serial ports are available, each corresponds to an instance of the service. The `getPort` method gives you access to the serial port itself, whereas the other two methods allow you to add and remove listeners for serial port events. The `javax.comm.SerialPort` API allows you to add only one serial event listener, and internally we have used it for detecting devices. To work around this restriction, we make it possible to add/remove listeners through the `SerialService` interface. No other operations need to be defined because the Java Communications API has already served that purpose. It does not make sense to reinvent APIs (see the discussion in Chapter 6).

The activator enumerates all known serial ports on the host and finds the ones that are not owned by other applications. For each available port, we add a serial event listener:

```
package com.acme.impl.device.serial;
import javax.comm.CommPortIdentifier;
import javax.comm.SerialPort;
...  // other imports

public class Activator implements BundleActivator {
   private Vector ports = new Vector(4);

   public void start(BundleContext ctxt)
      throws Exception
   {
      for (Enumeration enum =
         CommPortIdentifier.getPortIdentifiers();
         enum.hasMoreElements(); )
      {
         CommPortIdentifier portId =
            (CommPortIdentifier) enum.nextElement();
         if (portId.getPortType() ==
            CommPortIdentifier.PORT_SERIAL) {
            try {
               SerialPort port = (SerialPort)
                  portId.open("SerialService", 2000);
               port.notifyOnCTS(true);
               SerialListener serialListener =
                  new SerialListener(ctxt);
               port.addEventListener(serialListener);
               ports.addElement(port);
            } catch (PortInUseException e) {
                // the serial port has been occupied; skip it
            } catch (TooManyListenersException e) {
                // can't happen
            }
         }
      }
   }
}
```

CHAPTER 8 DEVICE ACCESS

```
      public void stop(BundleContext ctxt)
        throws Exception
   {
      for (int i=0; i<ports.size(); i++) {
           SerialPort port = (SerialPort) ports.elementAt(i);
           port.removeEventListener();
           port.close();
      }
   }
}
```

Because we are interested in the signal on the Clear To Send (CTS) pin of the serial interface, we tell the serial port not to mask any event on that pin but to send it to our listener:

```
port.notifyOnCTS(true);
port.addEventListener(serialListener);
```

The activator's `stop` method is self-explanatory: When the bundle is deactivated, we clean up by removing the serial event listener and close the serial ports. The complete source of the activator can be found in Appendix A, section A.2.1.5.

The serial event listener is at the heart of device detection, and its implementation is as follows:

```
class SerialListener implements SerialPortEventListener {
   private BundleContext context;
   private ServiceRegistration serialReg = null;
   private SerialServiceImpl serialService = null;
   private String[] deviceClazzes = {
      "com.acme.service.device.serial.SerialService",
      "org.osgi.service.device.Device" };

   SerialListener(BundleContext ctxt) {
      this.context = ctxt;
   }

   public synchronized void serialEvent(SerialPortEvent e) {
      SerialPort port = (SerialPort) e.getSource();
      int t = e.getEventType();
```

```
        if (t == SerialPortEvent.CTS) {
            // listen to CTS pin of the serial interface
            boolean plugged = e.getNewValue();
            if (plugged) {
                // register a serial device service when a
                // device is connected to the serial port
                Properties props = new Properties();
                props.put("DEVICE_CATEGORY", "serial");
                props.put("DEVICE_MAKE", "Acme");
                props.put("Port", port.getName());
                serialService = new SerialServiceImpl(port);
                serialReg = context.registerService(deviceClazzes,
                    serialService, props);
            } else {
                // unregister the serial device service when
                // the device is disconnected from the serial
                // port
                if (serialReg != null) {
                    serialReg.unregister();
                    serialReg = null;
                    serialService = null;
                }
            }
        }
    }
}
```

SerialListener's serialEvent method is called if an event occurs on the serial port. If the CTS pin is turned on (getNewValue returns true), a device is connected to the port; if it goes off (SerialEvent's getNewValue method returns false), the device is disconnected from the port.

Once we discover that a device is connected to the serial port, we register an instance of SerialService to represent the port, along with the service properties DEVICE_CATEGORY, DEVICE_MAKE, and Port. Conversely, if the device is found to be disconnected, we unregister the service accordingly.

The SerialServiceImpl class is a straightforward implementation of the SerialService interface. Its source is listed in Appendix A, section A.2.1.2, and is not shown here.

204 CHAPTER 8 DEVICE ACCESS

The manifest is defined as follows. Because we reference DA interfaces, we need to import the DA package:

```
Bundle-Activator: com.acme.impl.device.serial.Activator
Import-Package: org.osgi.service.device
```

Compile the source and pack the classes into a bundle named `serial.jar`. Its contents should look like

```
META-INF/MANIFEST.MF
com/acme/service/device/serial/SerialService.class
com/acme/impl/device/serial/Activator.class
com/acme/impl/device/serial/SerialListener.class
com/acme/impl/device/serial/SerialServiceImpl.class
```

It's time to see things in action. From the console, install and start the `serial.jar` bundle, then examine the list of registered services:

```
> start serial.jar
> services
[org.osgi.service.log.LogService]
    description=The standard OSGi Log service
[org.osgi.service.log.LogReaderService]
    description=The standard OSGi LogReader service
```

This output shows that only the services from the log bundle are registered within the framework.

Plug the NULL modem into one of the serial ports at the back of the machine, and reissue the `services` command in the console:

```
> services
[org.osgi.service.log.LogService]
    description=The standard OSGi Log service
[org.osgi.service.log.LogReaderService]
    description=The standard OSGi LogReader service
[org.osgi.service.device.Device,com.acme.service.device.serial↵
.SerialService]
    Port=COM2
    DEVICE_CATEGORY=serial
    DEVICE_MAKE=Acme
```

A new `SerialService` has been automatically registered! Unplug the serial cable and verify that the service is unregistered.

Obviously, every type of device has its own way of detecting whether a device is connected. This example presents the mechanism tailored for the serial interface made available to us from the Java Communications API. This is why, in many situations, device detection hinges on the capability from the native drivers.

8.4.3 Device Refinement

Registering a device service kicks off a device refinement process controlled by the device manager. To many applications, bare-bone `SerialService` provides functionality that is at an inappropriately low level. For example, a service of a bulletin board system would be much more comfortable with `ModemService`, which communicates through the serial port, than dealing with `SerialService` directly.

8.4.3.1 The Confidence Level for Matching a Device

First, we need to add a few constants to the `SerialService` interface to indicate how well the device can be matched by a driver:

```
public interface SerialService extends Device {
   public static final int MATCH_OK = 1;
   // the rest of the interface remains the same
}
```

You may specify multiple levels of matching values from a minimum to a maximum integer. In our example, the scale is binary: Either match or not. Thus, we only define one constant here. These constants are used by the `Driver` service, which is explained in Section 8.4.3.3.

8.4.3.2 The Driver Locator Service

We next add a `DriverLocator` implementation to our serial bundle. The `DriverLocator` service knows where to find and download drivers capable of refining `SerialService`:

```
package com.acme.impl.locator;
// imports
public class DriverLocatorImpl implements DriverLocator {

   // map a device category to IDs of refining drivers
   private Hashtable categoryMap;
   // map driver IDs to their URLs
   private Hashtable driverMap;
```

```
      static final String DRIVER_ID_PREFIX =
         "com.acme.device.drivers";

   public String[] findDrivers(Dictionary props) {
      String make = (String) props.get("DEVICE_MAKE");
      String category = (String) props.get("DEVICE_CATEGORY");
      if (!"Acme".equalsIgnoreCase(make))
      return null;
      String[] ids = (String[]) categoryMap.get(category);
      return ids;
   }

   public InputStream loadDriver(String id) throws IOException {
      URL u = (URL) driverMap.get(id);
      if (u != null) {
            return u.openStream();
      }
      return null;
   }

   public DriverLocatorImpl() {
      categoryMap = new Hashtable(3);
      categoryMap.put("serial", new String[] {
         DRIVER_ID_PREFIX + ".serial.modem.0" });
      driverMap = new Hashtable(3);
      driverMap.put(DRIVER_ID_PREFIX + ".serial.modem.0",
         this.getClass().getResource("/drivers/driver.jar"));
   }
}
```

First, the driver locator knows where to find any refining drivers for a given set of device service properties. The drivers are identified by their driver IDs. In the previous example, we use a very specific naming convention for driver IDs:

com.acme.device.drivers.<origin device category>.<refined device category>.<version number>

where com.acme.device.drivers is the prefix for all drivers written by Acme, <origin device category> refers to the device category as the basis for refinement, <refined device category> indicates the target of refinement, and <version number> distinguishes various incarnations of the same driver. For example, the driver with an ID of com.acme.device.drivers.serial.modem.0 indicates that the driver written by Acme can refine the serial device category to the modem category. To find refining drivers for a device service, the findDrivers method first obtains the device category from the service properties, and checks whether it can be used as the basis for any refinement based on the naming convention of the driver IDs.

Second, the driver locator service knows where to download the driver if any is found. In our example, the driver bundle is stored as a resource in the serial bundle. The internal data structure driverMap maps the driver ID to the URL of the bundle.

The policy of how and where to locate drivers in this example is admittedly simplistic, yet it represents only one of numerous strategies. You are free to implement as many driver locator services as you need. Your drivers may be stored at a centralized server accessible through URLs, or you may have elaborate matching criteria to determine to which device categories a given category can be refined. These aspects are intentionally left undefined in the standard to allow you the maximum flexibility.

The serial bundle's activator needs to register the newly added driver locator service when it is started. The code in bold type shows the new additions; other code remains the same:

```
package com.acme.impl.device.serial;
// imports
public class Activator implements BundleActivator {
    ...
    public void start(BundleContext ctxt) {
        Properties locatorProps = new Properties();
        locatorProps.put("description",
            "Locate refining drivers for the serial device category.");
        ctxt.registerService(
            "org.osgi.service.device.DriverLocator",
            new DriverLocatorImpl(), locatorProps);
        ...
    }

    public void stop(BundleContext ctxt) {
        ...
    }
}
```

The contents of the new serial bundle then show the following layout:

```
META-INF/MANIFEST.MF
com/acme/service/device/serial/SerialService.class
com/acme/impl/device/serial/Activator.class
com/acme/impl/device/serial/SerialServiceImpl.class
com/acme/impl/locator/DriverLocatorImpl.class
drivers/driver.jar
```

The entry drivers/driver.jar is a mystery to us at this point. This is the driver that is used to refine serial device category services and is retrieved by the driver locator during refinement. But what exactly is involved? Let's leave the serial bundle aside for a moment and delve into the world of refining drivers.

8.4.3.3 The Driver Service

Many drivers may be available to provide refinement for a device category. The most appropriate driver is selected by the device manager by calling its match method. Once a winner is selected, its attach method is called to register the new device service.

Here is the implementation of the driver service in our example:

```
package com.acme.impl.driver;
// imports
class DriverImpl implements Driver {
   private BundleContext context;
   private ServiceRegistration reg = null;

   public int match(ServiceReference sr) throws Exception {
      String category =
         (String) sr.getProperty("DEVICE_CATEGORY");
      if ("serial".equals(category))
           return SerialService.MATCH_OK;
      return Device.MATCH_NONE;
   }

   public String attach(ServiceReference sr) throws Exception {
      String[] deviceClazzes = new String[] {
           "org.osgi.service.device.Device",
           "com.acme.service.device.modem.ModemService" };
      Properties props = new Properties();
      props.put("DEVICE_CATEGORY", "modem");
      props.put("DEVICE_MAKE", "Acme");
```

```
      reg = context.registerService(deviceClazzes,
         new ModemServiceImpl(), props);
      return null;
   }

   DriverImpl(BundleContext ctxt) {
      this.context = ctxt;
   }
}
```

When this driver is asked how well it can match the device service (represented by the `ServiceReference` instance `sr` on entering the `match` method), it first checks to which device category the device belongs. The driver knows that it can refine the serial category well, therefore it returns the `match_OK` value if the service reference represents a serial device. Otherwise, it reports that it can match none, with `Device.MATCH_NONE` as the return value.

After gleaning match values from all drivers (in our case, the driver service is the only one), the device manager selects the highest bidder and calls its `attach` method. In our example, we register the refined `ModemService` under the "modem" device category, and therefore complete our mission of refining `SerialService` to the next level.

The driver bundle's activator performs the task of registering the driver service when the bundle is started, and unregistering it when it is stopped:

```
package com.acme.impl.driver;
// imports
public class Activator implements BundleActivator {
   private ServiceRegistration reg;

   public void start(BundleContext ctxt) {
      Properties props = new Properties();
      props.put("DRIVER_ID",
         "com.acme.device.drivers.serial.modem.0");
      props.put("description", "The driver that refines " +
         "a serial device to a modem device.");
      reg = ctxt.registerService("org.osgi.service.device.Driver",
            new DriverImpl(ctxt), props);
   }
```

```
        public void stop(BundleContext ctxt) {
            if (reg != null)
                reg.unregister();
        }
    }
```

`ModemService` exposes operations expected of a modem. The main part of its interface is as follows:

```
package com.acme.service.device.modem;
import org.osgi.service.device.Device;

public interface ModemService extends Device {
    /**
     * The data connection to a connected modem.
     */
    interface DataConnection { ... }

    /**
     * Dials up a modem with the given phone number.
     */
    public DataConnection dialup(String phoneNumber) throws
        IOException;

    /**
     * Gets information about the modem.
     */
    public String getInfo() throws IOException;

    /**
     * Hangs up the modem.
     */
    public void hangup() throws IOException;
    /**
     * Configures the volume of the modem's speaker.
     */
    public void configureSpeaker(int mode) throws IOException;

    /**
     * Gets the value of the given S register.
     */
    public byte getSRegister(int r) throws IOException;
```

```
    /**
     * Sets the value for the given S register.
     */
    public void setSRegister(int r, byte value) throws IOException;
}
```

The implementation class `ModemServiceImpl` is shown in Appendix A, section A.2.2.4.

Now we are ready to show the complete layout of the driver bundle:

```
META-INF/MANIFEST.MF
com/acme/service/device/modem/ModemService.class
com/acme/impl/device/modem/ModemServiceImpl.class
com/acme/impl/driver/
com/acme/impl/driver/DriverImpl.class
com/acme/impl/driver/Activator.class
```

With the changes in place, we can now witness the refinement process in action. Unplug the NULL modem from the serial port and restart the framework. From the framework console, update the serial bundle to incorporate the new contents:

```
> update serial.jar
```

Plug the NULL modem back into the serial port. This act causes the following chain of events to take place:

1. The base driver notices that a device is plugged into the serial port via `SerialPortEventListener`.

2. The listener registers `SerialService` with the framework.

3. Because `SerialService` is also registered under the `org.osgi.service.device.Device` type, the device manager provided by the DA bundle is notified.

4. The device manager looks into the framework's service registry for driver locator services. It finds the one registered by the serial bundle.

5. The device manager invokes the driver locator's `findDrivers` method, passing in the `SerialService`'s service reference. The service property `DEVICE_CATEGORY` shows that its device category is "serial," so the method returns the driver ID `com.acme.device.drivers.serial.modem.0`.

6. The device manager then asks the driver locator for the location of the driver bundle corresponding to the ID. Because the driver is included within the serial bundle, a bundle resource URL is returned to obtain the input stream to the driver.

7. The device manager downloads the driver from the input stream and installs and starts the driver bundle, at which time a Driver service is registered with the framework.

8. The device manager calls the Driver service's match method, passing in the SerialService's service reference. Based on the serial device service's category, a SerialService.MATCH_OK value is returned, indicating that the driver is capable of refining the serial service.

9. The device manager then calls the Driver service's attach method, which registers the ModemService included in the driver bundle with the framework.

10. As in step 3, the device manager is notified of the ModemService registration, because it is also registered under the org.osgi.service.device.Device type. As a result, the preceding process is repeated.

11. The device manager again checks the driver locator, which has no driver to install for the modem service.

12. The device manager then consults the only driver service by calling its match method. Having discovered that the device category is "modem," the method reports Device.MATCH_NONE to indicate that it is clueless as how to refine ModemService further. This ends the refinement process.

At the console, issue the following command:

```
> bundles
ID  STATE   LOCATION
--  ------  ----------------------------
1   ACTIVE  file:jes_path/bundles/log.jar
2   ACTIVE  file:jes_path/bundles/device.jar
6   ACTIVE  file:/home/joe/bundles/serial/serial.jar
7   ACTIVE  com.acme.device.drivers.serial.modem.0
```

Bundle 7 is the driver bundle that is found by the driver locator service and is installed by the device manager automatically in step 7.

Now check the service registration:

```
> services
[org.osgi.service.device.Driver]
        DRIVER_ID=com.acme.device.drivers.serial.modem.0
        description=The driver that refines a serial device to a ↵
modem device.
[org.osgi.service.device.Device,
    com.acme.service.device.modem.ModemService]
        DEVICE_CATEGORY=modem
        DEVICE_MAKE=Acme
        Port=COM2
[org.osgi.service.device.DriverLocator]
        description=Locate refining drivers↵
for the serial device category.
[org.osgi.service.device.Device,com.acme.service.device.serial.↵
SerialService]
        DEVICE_CATEGORY=serial
        DEVICE_MAKE=Acme
        Port=COM2
[org.osgi.service.log.LogService]
        description=The standard OSGi Log service
[org.osgi.service.log.LogReaderService]
        description=The standard OSGi LogReader service
```

The output makes it clear that in response to the attachment of the serial cable, a driver service is registered in step 7, and a refined device service, ModemService, is also registered with the framework in step 9.

8.4.3.4 A Smarter Refining Driver

Our example so far assumes that whenever a device is attached, it must be a modem. What if it is not a modem but a serial connection used simply to transfer data? In this section, we make our refining driver smarter not only by trusting the device category from the device service properties, but also by talking to the underlying device briefly to make sure. If the driver satisfies itself that the device is indeed a modem, ModemService is registered.

To be certain that the device attached is indeed a modem, we modify the driver's match method to send an AT command through the serial port. If we get OK back as the response, we know it is a modem:

```
package com.acme.impl.driver;
// imports
```

```java
class DriverImpl implements Driver {
  private BundleContext context;
  ...
  public int match(ServiceReference sr) throws Exception {
    String category =
      (String) sr.getProperty("DEVICE_CATEGORY");
    if ("serial".equals(category)) {
      if (modemAccessed(sr)) {
        return SerialService.MATCH_OK;
      }
    }
    return Device.MATCH_NONE;
  }

  // The rest of the code remains the same

  private boolean modemAccessed(ServiceReference sr) {
    boolean isModem = false;
    SerialService ss = (SerialService) context.getService(sr);
    SerialPort port = ss.getPort();
    try {
      // send AT command to the serial port
      // if we get OK as reply, set isModem to true
    } finally {
      context.ungetService(sr);
    }
    return isModem;
  }
}
```

With this enhancement, if you simply attach a NULL modem, `SerialService` is registered, but the device refinement process does not go any further. Only when a full-featured modem is connected to the serial port is `ModemService` registered.

Note that calling `SerialService` is a temporary act. Therefore, we must be sure to "unget" the service after we are done in the `modemAccessed` method.

8.4.3.5 Disconnecting the Device

In our discussion so far, we know that when the serial cable is disconnected from the port, `SerialListener` is notified and unregisters `SerialService`. However, the driver has registered `ModemService` as the refinement for `SerialService`. It is logical to withdraw `ModemService` too when `SerialService` is gone.

The responsibility lies with the refining driver, which monitors service events to find out whether `SerialService` is about to be unregistered. The following code in bold type shows the new additions; the remaining code is the same:

```java
package com.acme.impl.driver;
// imports
class DriverImpl implements Driver {
    private BundleContext context;
    private ServiceRegistration modemReg = null;
    private ServiceReference serialRef;

    public int match(ServiceReference sr) throws Exception {
        ...
    }

    public String attach(ServiceReference sr) throws Exception {
        serialRef=sr;
    }

    DriverImpl(BundleContext ctxt) {
        this.context = ctxt;
        try {
            String filter = "(objectClass=" +
                "com.acme.service.device.serial.SerialService)";
            this.context.addServiceListener(new ServiceListener() {
                public void serviceChanged(ServiceEvent e) {
                    if (e.getType() == ServiceEvent.UNREGISTERING) {
                        if (e.getServiceReference().equals(serialRef)
                            &&modemReg != null) {
                            modemReg.unregister();
                            modemReg = null; }
                    }
                }
            }, filter);
        } catch (InvalidSyntaxException e) {
            // can't happen
        }
    }
}
```

With the revised driver, when you unplug the serial cable and examine the registered services, you will find that both `SerialService` and `ModemService` are unregistered.

8.4.4 The Reconfiguration Process

Many devices have composite configurations. For instance, a home theater system consists of video and audio components. It can function as one entity when you play a movie on DVD with surround sound. Its components, however, may also function independently: Only the stereo system is used when you listen to a music CD.

DA is designed with such scenarios in mind. It allows a comprehensive device representation (home theater) to be registered first. If no other driver is found to refine the device, the driver that has registered the comprehensive device service may withdraw the service and attempt to register devices representing its subcomponents (a video service and a stereo service).

Let's look at the driver designed to handle reconfigurations:

```
import org.osgi.service.device.*;
class ReconfigDriver implements Driver {
   private ServiceRegistration reg = null;
   private BundleContext context;

   ReconfigDriver(BundleContext ctxt) {
      context = ctxt;
   }

   public int match(ServiceReference sr) throws Exception {
      String category =
         (String) sr.getProperty("DEVICE_CATEGORY");
      if ("havi".equals(category))   // can refine a HAVi service
         return HaviService.MATCH_OK;
      return Device.MATCH_NONE;
   }

   public String attach(ServiceReference sr) throws Exception {
      String[] deviceClazzes = new String[] {
         "org.osgi.service.device.Device",
         "com.acme.service.device.av.HomeTheatre" };
      // the HAVi service is refined to a HomeTheatre service
```

```
            reg = context.registerService(deviceClazzes,
               new HomeThreatreImpl(this), props);
            return null;
      }

      void changeConfiguration() {
         if (reg != null) {
            reg.unregister();   // unregister HomeTheatre
            reg=null; }
            ...
            // register a video and an audio service instead
            context.registerService(videoClazzes,
               new VideoServiceImpl(), videoProps);
            context.registerService(audioClazzes,
               new AudioServiceImpl(), audioProps);
      }
   }
```

Here are the partial definitions of the home theater service, service interface first:

```
   public interface HomeTheatre
      extends org.osgi.service.device.Device
   {
      // methods pertaining to functions of a home theatre
      ...
   }
```

And here is the implementation class:

```
   class HomeTheatreImpl implements HomeTheatre {
      private ReconfigDriver driver;

      public void noDriverFound() {
         // No driver can further refine HomeTheatre;
         // change device configurations
         this.driver.changeConfiguration();
      }

      // implementation of the methods pertaining to a home theatre
      ...
```

```
    HomeTheatreImpl(ReconfigDriver d) {
        this.driver = d;
    }
}
```

The reconfiguration driver can refine the HAVi service to a refined home theater service. However, further refinement is not available. At this point the driver has two options: (1) be satisfied with the latest refinement and do nothing or (2) realize that the latest refinement is a dead end and try different configurations. Let's see how the latter is done using the previous example.

When no refining driver can be found for `HomeTheatre` service, the `noDriverFound` method on the `HomeTheatre` service is invoked. The method turns around and calls back to the `changeConfiguration` method on the reconfiguration driver. The driver unregisters the `HomeTheatre` service and registers two of its components: a video service and an audio service.

The device can call back to its registering driver, because a reference to the driver is passed into `HomeTheatre` through its constructor.

8.5 Putting It Together

In this section we give a comprehensive example showing how the standard services we have covered so far can be used together. We develop a bundle that registers a servlet with the HTTP service and allows you to configure the serial ports through a Web interface as shown in Figure 8.6.

The servlet looks up the framework service registry for instances of `SerialServices`. It then presents the parameters—baud rate, data bits, stop bits, and parity—for each `SerialService`'s serial port in an HTML form. A user can select different settings using the pull-down menu and can effect the change by pressing the Set button.

This servlet is only responsible for serial ports that have some device attached to them, because it searches for `SerialService` instances. This exemplifies how a client bundle can work with DA.

In the bundle's activator, the servlet is registered with the HTTP service. The `BundleContext` object is passed to the servlet's constructor, because the servlet needs to access the service registry and to get/unget the serial services. (The full listing is located in Appendix A, section A.2.3.1.)

PUTTING IT TOGETHER **219**

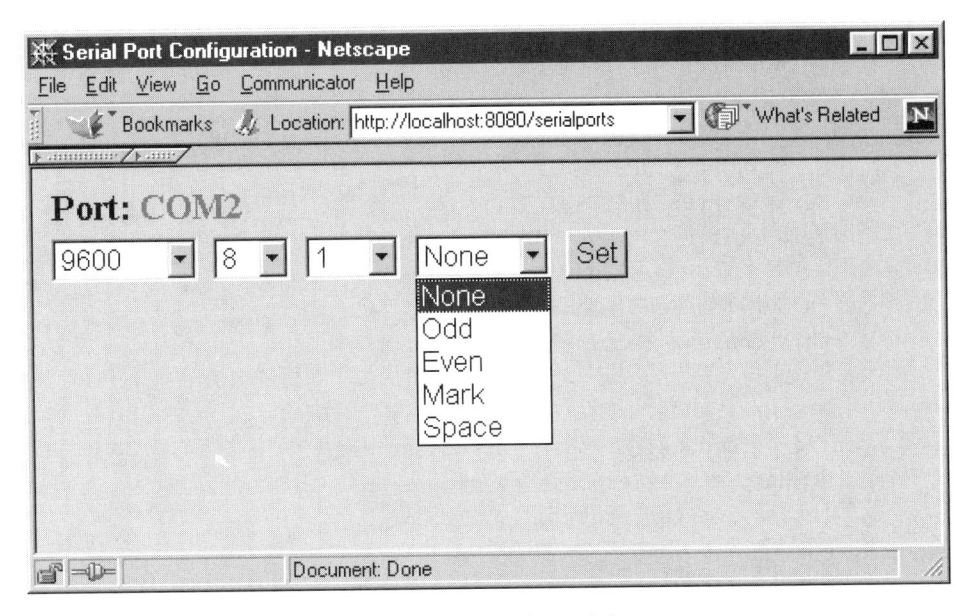

Figure 8.6 A Web interface for configuring the serial port

Here is the source code for the servlet. As part of response to a GET request, it displays a user interface in HTML. It changes the settings on the serial port when a POST is received:

```
package com.acme.gui.serial;
// imports

class SerialServlet extends HttpServlet {

   private BundleContext context;
   private static int[] bauds = { 2400, 4800, 9600, 19200,
      28800, 38400, 57600, 115200 };
   private static int[] dataBits = { SerialPort.DATABITS_5,
      SerialPort.DATABITS_6,
      SerialPort.DATABITS_7,
      SerialPort.DATABITS_8 };
   private static String[] dataBitsLabel = { "5", "6", "7", "8" };
   private static int[] parity = { SerialPort.PARITY_NONE,
      SerialPort.PARITY_ODD,
      SerialPort.PARITY_EVEN,
      SerialPort.PARITY_MARK,
```

```java
      SerialPort.PARITY_SPACE };
   private static String[] parityLabel = { "None", "Odd", "Even",
      "Mark","Space" };
   private static int[] stopBits = { SerialPort.STOPBITS_1,
      SerialPort.STOPBITS_2,
      SerialPort.STOPBITS_1_5 };
   private static String[] stopBitsLabel = { "1", "2", "1.5" };

   SerialServlet(BundleContext ctxt) {
      this.context = ctxt;
   }

   public void doGet(HttpServletRequest req,
         HttpServletResponse resp)
      throws ServletException, IOException
   {
      ServletOutputStream out = resp.getOutputStream();
      resp.setContentType("text/html");
      displayHeader(out);
      try {
         ServiceReference[] refs = context.getServiceReferences(
            "com.acme.service.device.serial.SerialService",
             null);
         if (refs == null) {
            out.println("<i>No device is found to be attached "+
                  "to any of the serial ports.</i>");
         } else {
            for (int i=0; i<refs.length; i++)
               displayControl(out, refs[i]);
         }
      } catch (InvalidSyntaxException e) {
      }
      displayFooter(out);
      out.close();
   }

   public void doPost(HttpServletRequest req,
           HttpServletResponse resp)
      throws ServletException, IOException
   {
      String message = null;
```

```java
        String portName = req.getParameter("port");
        try {
            ServiceReference[] refs = context.getServiceReferences(
                "com.acme.service.device.serial.SerialService",
                "(Port=" + portName + ")");
            if (refs != null) {
                SerialService ss = (SerialService)
                    context.getService(refs[0]);
                SerialPort port = ss.getPort();
                int baud = Integer.parseInt(
                    req.getParameter("baud_select"));
                int databits = Integer.parseInt(
                    req.getParameter("databits_select"));
                int stopbits = Integer.parseInt(
                    req.getParameter("stopbits_select"));
                int parity = Integer.parseInt(
                    req.getParameter("parity_select"));
                 port.setSerialPortParams(baud, databits,
                    stopbits, parity);
            } else {
                message = "<i>Could not set serial port parameters: "+
                    "no device is attached to " + portName +
                    " any longer.</i>";
            }
        } catch (InvalidSyntaxException e) {
        } catch (UnsupportedCommOperationException e) {
            message = "<i>Failed to set serial port parameters: "+
            e.toString() + "</i>";
         }
        if (message != null) {
            ServletOutputStream out = resp.getOutputStream();
            resp.setContentType("text/html");
            displayHeader(out);
            out.println(message);
            displayFooter(out);
            out.close();
        } else {
            resp.sendRedirect("/serialports");
        }
    }
```

```
        private void displayControl(ServletOutputStream out,
            ServiceReference ref)
          throws ServletException, IOException
        {
          SerialService ss = (SerialService) context.getService(ref);
          SerialPort port = ss.getPort();
          String name = port.getName();
          // display an HTML form
          // present four <select> pull-down menus with valid options
          // for baud rate, data bits, stop bits, and parity
          // call port.getBaudRate(), port.getDataBits(),
          // port.getStopBits(), and port.getParity() to
          // obtain the current settings
          // select the current settings in the four pull-down menus
          context.ungetService(ref);
        }

        private void displayHeader(ServletOutputStream out)
          throws ServletException, IOException
        {
          // display HTML headers
        }

        private void displayFooter(ServletOutputStream out)
          throws ServletException, IOException
        {
          // display HTML footers
         }
    }
```

This example depends on DA-related bundles: log.jar, device.jar, and serial.jar, as well as HTTP-related bundles: servlet.jar and http.jar. Their packages needs to be imported to this bundle, whose manifest is defined as follows:

```
Bundle-Activator: com.acme.gui.serial.Activator
Import-Package: org.osgi.service.http,
 com.acme.service.device.serial,
 javax.servlet, javax.servlet.http
```

The serial service may come and go. As a result, the servlet is designed to be stateless. Each time it needs to query or modify the parameters for a serial service instance, it retrieves it anew from the framework service registry. If the intended service has disappeared, an error message is displayed in the browser.

A more sophisticated scheme is to maintain up-to-date state of the serial services in the servlet, which can be achieved by listening to the registration/unregistration events of the service. If we program an applet to receive the events, we can provide the user with real-time usage of the serial port. With an HTML-based front end, however, it does not buy us much, because the user has to hit the Reload button on the browser anyway.

Perhaps the most important lesson we can learn from this example is how to expose the control interface through the browser using servlets. On the back end, it may be a thermostat, a gas meter, or a lamp module. Regardless, a flexible and familiar Web user interface can be put together just as easily.

CHAPTER 9

Permission-based Security and Administration

SECURITY is an essential requirement for residential gateway applications. Security also involves many different aspects. In this chapter we focus on granting and enforcing permissions to bundles using the policy-based fine-grained access control mechanisms of the Java 2 platform.

We begin by refreshing our memory on how permission-based security works in the Java 2 Runtime Environment. We then examine the new permissions defined by the OSGi Service Gateway Specification 1.0. Lastly we outline the steps to run the Java Embedded Server software with security enabled, and discuss how to use permissions in your own services with examples.

Because administration is considered a privileged operation and therefore requires an administrative permission to be carried out, we discuss how to perform common administrative tasks in this chapter as well.

9.1 Permission-based Security inside the Java 2 Platform

Permission-based security is used to make access control decisions. Given a piece of code, the security mechanism ensures that it is authorized to do what it wants to do. Let's review the entities and process involved in reaching such a decision. For a complete treatment of the subject, consult *Inside Java™ 2 Platform Security* [24].

9.1.1 Code Source

In the Java runtime environment, the object that is under security scrutiny is an instance of a class, with security-related characteristics that are encapsulated by its **code source.** The code source identifies the following two aspects of a class:

1. **The origin of the class.** This is represented by a URL that points to where the class was loaded. This piece of information carries weight in measuring the trustworthiness of the class: If it is loaded from a local hard disk inaccessible from the network, it is probably more secure than if it is loaded from the open Internet.

2. **The signers of the class.** This information is indirectly conveyed in a set of certificates in the code source. The certificates contain the public keys of the signers, whose corresponding private keys were used to sign the class. If the certificates have been issued by a trusted certificate authority, they vouch for the fact that the public keys do belong to the signers.

The code source is represented by the `java.security.CodeSource` class.

9.1.2 Permission

Permission is the authority to access some resource (for example, reading or modifying certain properties) or to perform some operation (for example, shutting down the Java virtual machine and therefore terminating the application in execution). The `java.security.Permission` class and its subclasses are used to represent permissions. In the following example,

```
PropertyPermission propPerm =
    new PropertyPermission("java.vendor", "read");
```

`propPerm` represents the permission to read the `java.vendor` system property. Both the target resource (`java.vendor` system property) and how it is to be accessed (`read`) must be specified for this permission.

Here is another example:

```
RuntimePermission exitPerm = new RuntimePermission("exitVM");
```

`exitPerm` represents the permission to shut down the Java virtual machine. It only requires an operation (`exitVM`) to be specified; no additional parameters are needed.

The bearer of a permission is allowed to access a resource or to perform an operation specified in the permission, and the lack of it denies the caller an access or operation.

A set of permission classes have been predefined. You can create new permissions particular to your application context by extending the `Permission` class. The OSGi framework did exactly that by defining three new permission classes: `AdminPermission`, `ServicePermission`, and `PackagePermission` in the `org.osgi.framework` package.

A collection of permissions with the *same type* can be grouped into a `PermissionCollection`; multiple instances of `PermissionCollection` can be grouped into a `Permissions` object. As a result, a `Permissions` collection may hold heterogeneous permissions. These collection classes are convenient because an application class usually has many permissions, which need to be dealt with as a group.

9.1.3 Policy

There is no such thing as absolute and universal security. What is secure is determined by assumptions of trust, weighed against tolerance for risks, and balanced with cost and convenience of use. For example, possession of a bank card and its personal identification number (PIN) gives one access to cash at an automatic teller machine (ATM). It is probably more secure to require that one show a photo ID and the account information to a human to get the money, but that would increase the cost to the bank and reduce the convenience for the customer. Further restrictions on limiting the maximum amount of cash that can be withdrawn per day lowers the risk factor if one loses the card and divulges the PIN. These considerations make the ATM a secure alternative to banking in most circumstances.

Specifying who can do what is captured by a **policy.** The `java.security.Policy` class defines a configurable access control matrix. There is exactly one `Policy` object per Java virtual machine, and it maps the class's code source (which establishes trust) to a set of permissions that the instances of the class can have. Essentially, a policy specifies rules of the following form:

> *If a class is from Charles Schwab and is signed by the brokerage, allow it to access my account.*

> *If a class is from RealNetworks, allow it to play a piece of streaming media.*

> *If an applet class is from TurboTax, allow it to print to the printer.*

The `java.security.Policy` class is an abstract class. Its default implementation in the Java 2 SDK is a plain text file. We look at policy file syntax shortly.

9.1.4 Granting Permissions to Classes

Permissions are not assigned directly to classes; rather, they are granted to **protection domains** represented by java.security.ProtectionDomain. Classes "inherit" their granted permissions by belonging to protection domains.

When a class, say Foo, is being loaded and defined by the secure class loader (a subclass of java.security.SecureClassLoader), the following will take place:

1. The secure class loader consults the Policy object, providing it with Foo's CodeSource.

2. Policy looks up its access control matrix according to Foo's CodeSource and returns the permissions granted to Foo.

3. Based on Foo's CodeSource and granted permissions, the secure class loader assigns the class to the appropriate ProtectionDomain.

ProtectionDomain encapsulates a class's CodeSource and its granted permissions. Each class can only belong to one ProtectionDomain. All classes in the same ProtectionDomain are from the same CodeSource and are granted the same permissions. Figure 9.1 shows the process of granting permissions to a class.

It is important to understand that a class's permissions have already been assigned prior to its being referenced as a type inside the Java virtual machine.

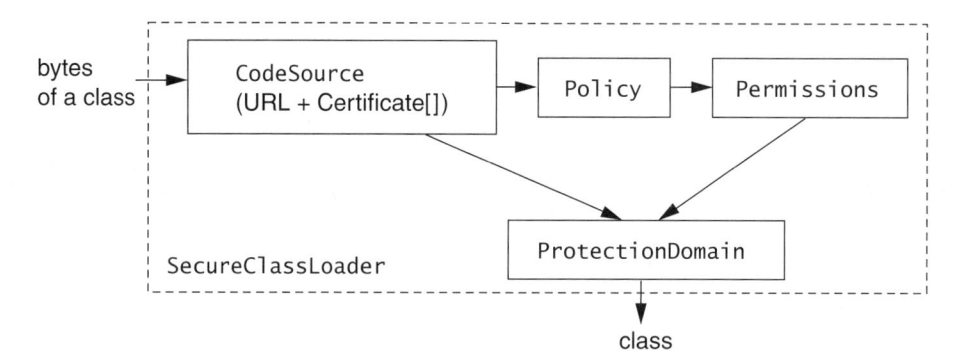

Figure 9.1 ProtectionDomain is identified by CodeSource and granted permissions (after consulting the Policy object). The class is assigned to ProtectionDomain when it is loaded and defined by SecureClassLoader.

9.1.5 Security Manager

So far we have looked at one side of the coin: granting permissions. The flip side is to enforce them. A **security manager** performs the actual checking when a specific operation is to be carried out at run-time. It does so by examining the set of permissions owned by a calling class against the required permission. As an analogy, if the permission is a visa, then the secure class loader acts like the consulate that issues the visa, and the security manager is the customs official who verifies the visa on entry to the destination country.

If a class has the needed permission, the execution proceeds silently; otherwise, `java.security.SecurityException` is raised at the checkpoint.

In the Java 2 Runtime Environment, the security manager delegates permission checking to `java.security.AccessController`, which carries out a predefined access control algorithm. We discuss this algorithm later in "Performing Privileged Actions."

When you develop services, you probably will not need to use classes such as `CodeSource`, `ProtectionDomain`, or `SecureClassLoader`, but you may need to understand how to check the caller for required permissions (Section 9.4.1) and how to perform privileged operations by asserting the permissions of your own code (Section 9.4.2).

9.2 OSGi Permissions

The OSGi framework defines the following new permissions, all of which are subclasses of `java.security.BasicPermission`.

9.2.1 `AdminPermission`

This class represents the permission to perform administrative operations in the framework. You can instantiate `AdminPermission` as follows:

```
AdminPermission adminPerm = new AdminPermission();
```

For example, if a class has the permission `adminPerm`, it is permitted to perform bundle life cycle operations.

9.2.2 `ServicePermission`

This class represents a permission to register a service to or to get a service from the service registry. The service's fully qualified class name (optionally with wildcard), and an action must be specified. The action is either "get" or "register." For example,

```
ServicePermission sp1 =
    new ServicePermission("com.acme.service.*", "get");
```

If a class has the permission `sp1`, it is allowed to get any service whose class name begins with `com.acme.service`. Such a permission may be granted exclusively to bundles of Acme's paying customers in a real deployment scenario.

```
ServicePermission sp2 =
    new ServicePermission("com.acme.TaxService", "register");
```

Only the class with permission `sp2` can register `TaxService`. Suppose `TaxService` calculates taxes. Without enforcing this permission, a malicious bundle could register an alleged `TaxService`, but in fact quietly steal your financial information as part of its implementation. By granting the permission judiciously, you can prevent distrusted bundles from publishing a Trojan horse service.

9.2.3 PackagePermission

This class represents a permission to import or to export a package. A package name (optionally with wildcard), and an action must be specified. The action is either "import" or "export."

```
PackagePermission pp1 =
    new PackagePermission("com.acme.service.print", "export");
```

Permission `pp1` allows one to export the `com.acme.service.print` package. If one has `PackagePermission` to export a package, one also has `PackagePermission` to import the same package. In other words, for the same set of packages, the "export" `PackagePermission` implies the "import" `PackagePermission`.

```
PackagePermission pp2 =
    new PackagePermission("*", "import");
```

Permission `pp2` allows one to import any package.

9.2.4 Permission Required by the Framework APIs

Calling many framework APIs requires that the calling class have one of the previous permissions. Which permission is needed by which API is summarized in Table 9.1.

Table 9.1 The Framework APIs and the Permissions They Require

Permissions	Interface	API
AdminPermission	BundleContext	installBundle
	Bundle	start
		update
		stop
		uninstall
		getHeaders
		getLocation
ServicePermission	BundleContext	registerService
		getServiceReference(s)
		getService
PackagePermission	Not applicable	Not applicable

Obviously, for methods on the BundleContext interface, registerService requires that the caller have the "register" ServicePermission, whereas getServiceReference(s) and getService requires the "get" ServicePermission.

Although not shown in Table 9.1, the behavior of ServiceListener is also affected by ServicePermission. Recall that when a service is registered, unregistered, or its service properties are modified, ServiceEvent is broadcast to the listeners. However, the broadcast is discriminatory: Only those bundles that have ServicePermission to "get" the service are notified through their service listeners. A bundle not permitted to get the service in the first place should not be allowed to learn any occurrence to the service either.

PackagePermission is checked when a bundle's package dependencies are resolved by the framework. There is no corresponding API.

9.3 Enabling Security

In this section, in addition to your role as a developer, you assume the responsibility of an administrator for learning and practicing purposes. However, in real-life deployment situations, the two duties usually are not shared by a single person, because

- The service providers are independent of the gateway operators from an operational perspective.

- Merging the two roles would constitute conflicts of interest, because each service would like to have as little security restrictions as possible, which is usually not acceptable for overall security. Bear in mind that services from competitors are likely to coexist in the framework, and it won't be fair to allow one to regulate security, possibly at the sacrifice of another.

Undoubtedly developers and the administrator must cooperate with one another. A developer's concerns with security are mostly local to one's particular service, whereas an administrator must plan for the security of the overall system consisting of many services. Each developer usually communicates to the administrator the permissions that are required by one's service, but the administrator is the policy maker.

To enable security for the Java Embedded Server software, the administrator must do the following:

1. Set up policy to grant necessary permissions.
2. Launch the framework with the default security manager installed.

9.3.1 Setting Up a Policy

In JDK, policies are defined using a flat text file, and can be retrieved through a URL. Multiple policy files can be used to specify a composite policy. The policies to be applied are specified by the security configuration file *java_home*/lib/security/java.security, where *java_home* points to the Java runtime environment on the system.

By default, JDK uses *java_home*/lib/security/java.policy, which defines the systemwide policy, and *user_home*/.java.policy, which defines the per-user policy, where *user_home* points to a user's home directory.

In this discussion, we use an additional application-specific policy, with a location that is specified with the system property java.security.policy. Let's refer to our policy file as *jes_policy*.

9.3.2 Running with Security Enabled

To enable security, we must install the default security manager when we launch the framework. Otherwise, the Java runtime environment reverts to the "sandbox" model, in which all local classes are fully trusted. Furthermore, we want to grant the framework implementation code all permissions; therefore, we define the following policy file as a starting point:

```
grant codeBase "file:jes_path/lib/*" {
    permission java.security.AllPermission;
};
```

Make sure you include the semicolon at the end after the closing brace, and save this file as *jes_policy*. The following command line is used to start the Java Embedded Server software:

```
java -Djava.security.manager -Djava.security.policy=jes_policy
    com.sun.jes.impl.framework.Main
```

You see the same screen that you did in Chapter 2. Issue the `help` command to confirm that security is indeed enabled:

```
Java Embedded Server 2.0

Copyright 1998, 1999 and 2000 Sun Microsystems, Inc.
All rights reserved.
Use is subject to license terms.

Type h[elp] for a list of commands.
> help
...

JES cache directory:    /home/joe/jescache
Bundle base URL:        file:/home/joe/jes2.0/bundles
Java 2 security support: Yes
```

How will things work differently now that security has been enabled? Let's attempt to install and activate the Log bundle to find out:

```
> start jes_path/bundles/log.jar
Error: Could not start bundle jes_path/bundles/log.jar:
org.osgi.framework.BundleException: BundleActivator (start)↵
failed for bundle ...
Nested exception: java.security.AccessControlException: access↵
denied (java.util.PropertyPermission com.sun.jes.service.log.size↵
read)
```

Alas! We are no longer able to perform an innocuous function of activating a standard bundle. The culprit is the Log bundle's lack of a few permissions. From the previous message it needs `PropertyPermission` to read property `com.sun.jes.service.log.size` as part of its activation routine.

To fix this problem, we need to append the following entries to *jes_policy*:

```
...
grant codeBase "jes_path/bundles/log.jar" {
   permission java.util.PropertyPermission
      "com.sun.jes.service.log.*", "read,write";
   permission org.osgi.framework.ServicePermission
      "org.osgi.service.log.*", "register";
   permission org.osgi.framework.PackagePermission
      "org.osgi.service.log", "export";
};
```

This definition grants the Log bundle `PropertyPermission` to read and to write any properties prefixed with `com.sun.jes.service.log`. It also permits the Log bundle to register its own services; namely, `org.osgi.service.log.LogService` and `org.osgi.service.log.LogReaderService`. Lastly, we permit the Log bundle to export the `org.osgi.service.log` package, which automatically allows it to import that same package.

How can we be certain that these permissions are granted to the Log bundle and not something else? We put the location string as the code base in the `grant` clause in the policy file, and use it to identify the code source of the classes from the Log bundle only. This location string is the same as the one we used to install the Log bundle in the console previously.

Similarly, we have to inspect other bundles and grant appropriate permissions individually. It is tempting to avoid the hassle and grant broad permissions at a coarse granularity. For example, grant `java.security.AllPermission` to all code. In doing so we effectively cancel out the protection afforded by Java 2 Platform security. Convenience and security usually demand competing priorities, and you have to make a trade-off.

9.4 Using Permissions in Your Service

In this section, we return to the unfinished design of the parameter service (`ParameterService`) from Chapter 4 and see how permissions can be used in this service.

9.4.1 Checking Permissions

Recall that the parameter service allows other bundles to access their parameter settings and handles the task of persistently saving them to and restoring them from a file. Because we used the service factory technique, each bundle can read, create, or modify its own parameters. However, oftentimes an administrative bundle may want to configure the parameters *on behalf of* another bundle. For instance, the administrative bundle can set the sender, recipient, and mail host parameters for the mailer example, or the printer parameter for the print service, avoiding the expediency of using system properties, as we did earlier.

Based on this requirement, we need to define another service for the parameter bundle, the `ParameterAdmin` service:

```
package com.acme.service.param;
import java.util.Properties;
import java.io.IOException;
/**
 * This service allows an administrative caller to get or set
 * parameters on behalf of another bundle.
 */
public interface ParameterAdmin {
   /**
    * Stores a parameter set for a bundle.
    * @param bundleLocation the location of the bundle.
    * @param props the parameter set.
    * @exception java.io.IOException if saving to the property file
    *       fails.
    * @exception java.security.SecurityException if the caller does
    *       not have AdminPermission and the Java runtime supports
    *       permissions.
    */
   public void set(String bundleLocation, Properties props)
      throws IOException;

   /**
    * Retrieves the parameter set for a bundle.
    *
    * @exception java.security.SecurityException if the caller does
    *       not have AdminPermission and the Java runtime supports
    *       permissions.
    */
```

```
        public Properties get(String bundleLocation)
            throws IOException;
}
```

With this service added, the parameter bundle has two types of client bundles:

1. The "ordinary" bundles, which access their own parameters
2. The administrative bundles, which can access anyone's parameters

To distinguish the latter from the former, the parameter bundle must check their permissions; otherwise, chaos ensues if just about anyone can change anyone else's parameters. Figure 9.2 shows the new use scenario for the parameter bundle.

The following is the `ParameterAdmin` service implementation:

```
package com.acme.impl.param;
import org.osgi.framework.AdminPermission;
// other imports
```

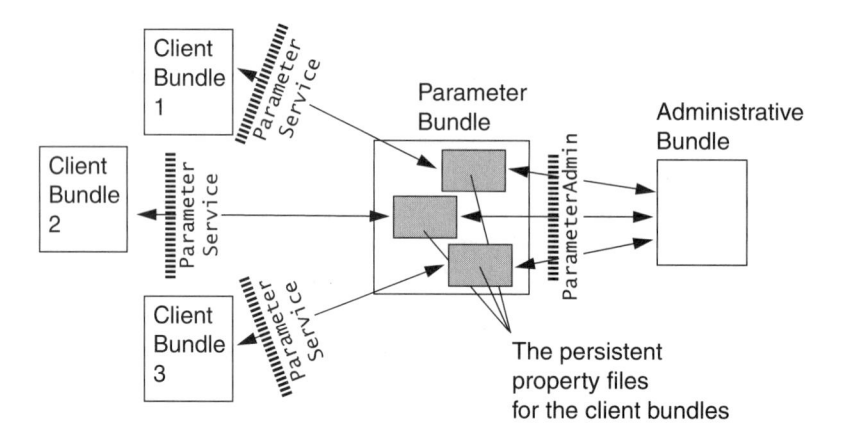

Figure 9.2 The two types of client bundles for the parameter bundle. The "ordinary" client bundles are on the left. They each have their own copy of `ParameterService` produced by the service factory. The administrative bundle is on the right. It can access any bundle's persistent property file directly through the `ParameterAdmin` service.

```
class ParameterAdminImpl implements ParameterAdmin {
   private static AdminPermission adminPermission =
      new AdminPermission();
   ...
   private ParameterStore store;

   ParameterAdminImpl(BundleContext ctxt, ParameterStore store) {
      ...
      this.store = store;
   }

   public void set(String loc, Properties props)
      throws IOException
   {
      SecurityManager sm = System.getSecurityManager();
      if (sm != null) {
         sm.checkPermission(adminPermission);
      }
      Bundle b = getBundle(loc); // given its loc, find the bundle
      ...
      store.save(b, props);
   }

   public synchronized Properties get(String loc)
      throws IOException
   {
      SecurityManager sm = System.getSecurityManager();
      if (sm != null) {
         sm.checkPermission(adminPermission);
      }
      Bundle b = getBundle(loc); // given its loc, find the bundle
      ...
      return store.load(b);
   }
   ...
}
```

As shown by the implementation code, we check the caller for `AdminPermission` before we proceed to retrieve or store the properties for a given bundle. An "ordinary" bundle would fail this check, causing `SecurityException` to be thrown, because it does not have `AdminPermission`.

238 CHAPTER 9 PERMISSION-BASED SECURITY AND ADMINISTRATION

As a rule, we perform the permission checking only when a security manager has been installed. This makes it possible for the bundle to run successfully if we do not specify -Djava.security.manager on the command line when launching the framework and therefore choose not to enforce security at all.

What remains to be done is to instantiate a `ParameterAdmin` service in the activator and register it:

```
...
public void start(BundleContext ctxt) {
    ParameterStore store = new ParameterStore(ctxt);
    ...
    ParameterAdmin paramAdmin = new ParameterAdminImpl(ctxt, store);
    ctxt.registerService("com.acme.service.param.ParameterAdmin",
        paramAdmin, null);
}
...
```

Unlike `ParameterService`, the `ParameterAdmin` service is registered as an ordinary service, not a service factory.

The parameter bundle needs to be granted the following permissions:

```
...
grant codeBase "file:/home/joe/bundles/param.jar" {
    permission org.osgi.framework.ServicePermission
        "com.acme.service.param.*", "register";
    permission org.osgi.framework.PackagePermission
        "com.acme.service.param", "import,export";
    // we need to call Bundle's getLocation method, which
    // requires AdminPermission
    permission org.osgi.framework.AdminPermission;
}
```

The framework automatically grants the parameter bundle access permission to its own data directory, which is used to maintain property files for all client bundles.

9.4.2 Performing Privileged Actions

With the `ParameterAdmin` service in place, we turn to developing its client, the administrative bundle. A variety of designs are possible. Let's provide a Web interface using a servlet, which interacts with the `ParameterAdmin` service to set or retrieve parameters for any bundle in the framework. In this section, we look at only the code pertaining to permissions; the complete code listing can be found in Appendix A, section A.3.2.

The administrative bundle does the following to set properties for a bundle with a location found in bundleLoc:

```
ServiceReference ref = bundleContext.getServiceReference(
    "com.acme.service.param.ParameterAdmin");
if (ref != null) {
   ParameterAdmin admin =
      (ParameterAdmin) bundleContext.getService(ref);
   Properties props = new Properties();
   props.put("printer","kontakt");
   admin.set(bundleLoc, props);
}
```

To be able to perform these operations, the administrative bundle must be granted the following permissions:

```
grant "file:/home/joe/bundles/admin.jar" {
   permission org.osgi.framework.ServicePermission
      "com.acme.service.param.ParameterAdmin", "get";
   permission org.osgi.framework.PackagePermission
      "com.acme.service.param", "import";
   permission org.osgi.framework.AdminPermission;
}
```

Not surprisingly, AdminPermission must be granted to the administrative bundle.

Install and activate the admin.jar bundle, and point your browser to its URL:

```
http://localhost:8080/admin/parameters
```

You will see a list of currently installed bundles, each identified by its location, as shown in Figure 9.3.

Click on the link to the Log bundle to configure its parameters. You can modify an existing property in place, or create a new property by filling in the empty input fields (Figure 9.4).

So far so good. Unfortunately, when you initiate the parameter-setting operation, you are confronted with the following messages:

```
java.security.AccessControlException: access denied
   (java.io.FilePermission /home/joe/jescache/bundle1/data/2 read)
  at java.security.AccessControlContext.checkPermission
    (AccessControlContext.java, Compiled Code)
```

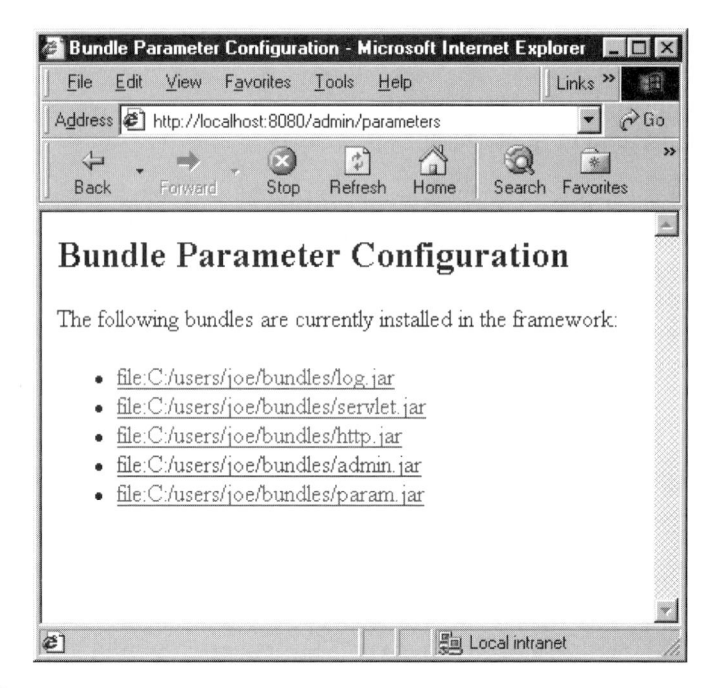

Figure 9.3 A list of installed bundles by the administrative bundle whose parameters can be configured

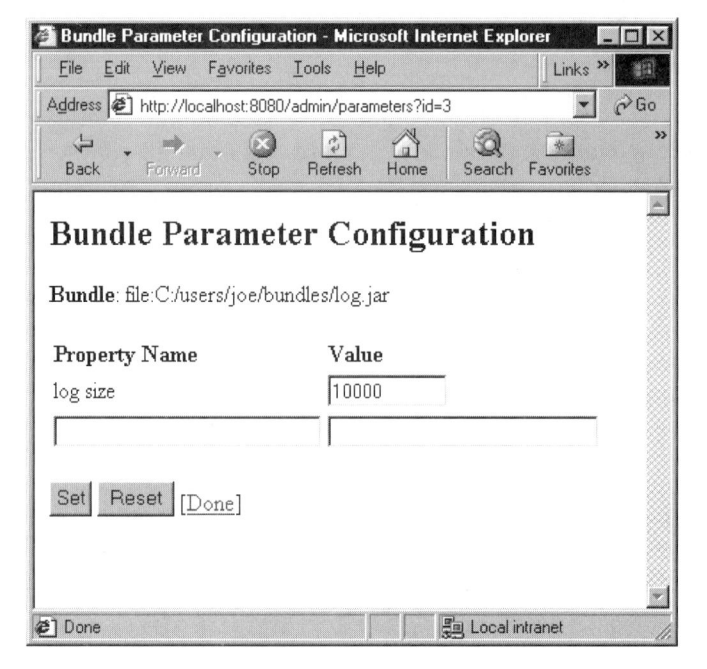

Figure 9.4 Setting parameters for the Log bundle using the administrative bundle

```
    at java.security.AccessController.checkPermission
       (AccessController.java, Compiled Code)
    at java.lang.SecurityManager.checkPermission
       (SecurityManager.java, Compiled Code)
    at java.lang.SecurityManager.checkRead
       (SecurityManager.java, Compiled Code)
    at java.io.File.exists(File.java, Compiled Code)
    at com.acme.impl.param.ParameterStore.save
       (ParameterStore.java, Compiled Code)
    at com.acme.impl.param.ParameterAdminImpl.set
       (ParameterAdminImpl.java, Compiled Code)
    at com.acme.admin.param.AdminServlet.doPost
       (AdminServlet.java, Compiled Code)
    ...
```

At a glance, the exception messages appear to complain that the `ParameterAdmin` code does not have `FilePermission` to read the data area belonging to its own bundle! However, we specifically mentioned that the framework will grant this permission. What has gone wrong? It has to do with the algorithm used by the Java 2 Runtime Environment to enforce access control for a thread that crosses multiple protection domains.

In the framework, all classes of a bundle belong to the same protection domain because they share the same origin and are granted the same set of permissions. If class `Foo` belongs to bundle A, and class `Bar` belongs to bundle B, then `Foo` and `Bar` belong to different protection domains. When a method of `Bar` calls a method of `Foo`, this execution thread traverses two domains. To determine whether the execution is authorized to perform an action, Java runtime environment not only checks whether the class of the current domain has the permission, but also traces the calling stack to ensure *all* the preceding callers have the permission as well. This is to prevent a less privileged class from acquiring the permissions of a more privileged class by calling into that class, which would cause a security breach.

Stack trace in Figure 9.5 illustrates exactly such a situation: The execution goes from the class in the administrative bundle (`com.acme.admin.param.AdminServlet.doPost`) into the parameter bundle (`com.acme.impl.param.ParameterAdminImpl.set`). Although the parameter bundle has the needed `FilePermission` to read its own data area, its caller—the administrative bundle—does not. As a result, we failed the file permission check when we attempted to verify whether the property file already existed.

Analogously, a bank teller has permission to access any customer's account. If he obeys whoever walks up to the counter and executes transactions as he's told,

```
at java.security.AccessControlContext.checkPermission
at java.security.AccessController.checkPermission
at java.lang.SecurityManager.checkPermission
at java.lang.SecurityManager.checkRead
at java.io.File.exists

at com.acme.impl.param.ParameterStore.save
at com.acme.impl.param.ParameterAdminImpl.set

at com.acme.admin.param.AdminServlet.doPost
```

System Domain

Domain boundaries

Protection domain of the administrative bundle. It does not have `FilePermission` to access the parameter bundle's data area.

Protection domain of the parameter bundle. It has `FilePermission` to access the parameter bundle's data area.

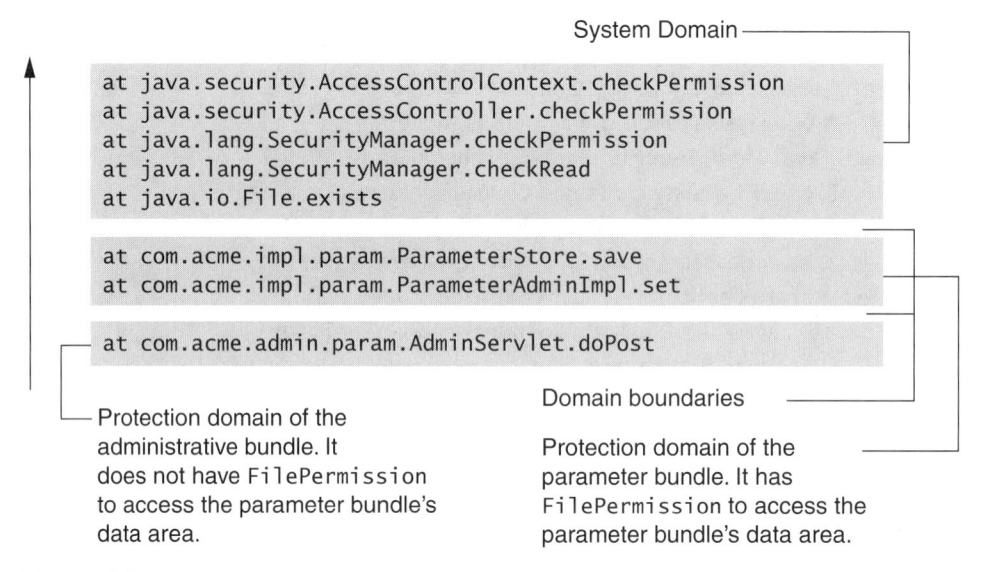

Figure 9.5 The stack status when the administrative bundle called the parameter bundle, and the read access to the latter's data area was denied.

then anybody, authorized or not, can initiate random actions through him, which is clearly unacceptable.

However, although this strategy is secure, it is overly conservative. A bank teller can render privileged services that a customer is never permitted to do herself. For example, only a cashier can issue a money order. In other words, under some circumstances, it is okay for the cashier to execute a transaction under his own permission even though the customer does not have that permission. What are these circumstances? The cashier must first verify the customer's bank card or credentials to ensure that she is not an imposter and is thus entitled to the service.

Now the relationship between the administrative and the parameter bundles is quite similar: The latter has the permission to access its own data area, but the former does not. However, the parameter bundle has already checked the caller for `AdminPermission`, so it knows that the caller is authorized and it is safe to carry out the file operation on the caller's behalf. Therefore, the `ParameterAdmin` service needs to assert its own permissions when it calls `ParameterStore`'s `save` method with the `doPrivileged` construct introduced in the Java 2 Platform:

```
...
try {
    AccessController.doPrivileged(new PrivilegedExceptionAction() {
```

```
        public Object run() throws IOException {
            ...
            FileOutputStream fos = new FileOutputStream(paramFile);
            props.save(fos, "...");
            fos.close();
            return null;
        }
    });
} catch (PrivilegedActionException e) {
    throw (IOException) e.getException();
}
```

The same construct should be wrapped around the file operations in `ParameterStore` as well. Because the file operations may potentially raise `IOException`, we need to implement the `PrivilegedExceptionAction` interface with an anonymous inner class. We can implement `PrivilegedAction` if the privileged code block does not throw checked exceptions. Other variations of using the `doPrivileged` construct are not discussed further.

A final note on the administrative bundle is that its servlet should perform authentication by implementing `HttpContext`'s `handleSecurity` method. See "Performing Basic Authentication" on page 181 for one way of doing this. In a real deployment situation, without authenticating a request from a browser, all our efforts in permission enforcement would be in vain, because anyone could perform configurations by accessing the administrative servlet's URL. As the saying goes, "the security of the entire system is as strong as its weakest link."

In our examples so far we have determined whether a class is secure based exclusively on its origin. Classes can also be digitally signed by a principal (a person or a corporation) to establish their trustworthiness. JDK provides security tools to assist in key management, and JAR file signing and verification. `keytool` is used to generate public/private key pairs and self-signed certificates. It also maintains a key store file as the key database. `jarsigner` is used to sign a JAR file using the private key from the key store and can verify that a signed JAR file has not subsequently been tampered with in any way.

When classes are digitally signed, we can grant permissions based on who are the signers. For example, our policy file may have the following entry:

```
grant codeBase "file:jes_path/bundles/log.jar", signedBy "Sun" {
    permission java.util.PropertyPermission "*", "read,write";
};
```

Good tutorials are available on how this is done at http://java.sun.com/docs/books/tutorial/security1.2/index.html.

Earlier we examined a design pattern of using delegation and callbacks. Specifically, we gave the example of a caller that passes a ContentTransformer object to NewsService's getNews method to have its result customized. Let's explore this scenario a bit further to reveal a security issue concerning privileged actions.

Suppose the service for the pager named Fetcher needs to read a system property to determine which tags should be removed and is granted the permission to access the system property. It would implement its ContentTransformer as follows:

```
ContentTransformer ct = new ContentTransformer() {
    public String[] getTagsForRemoval() {
        String tagstr = System.getProperty("pager.tags.removal");
        String[] tags = null;
        // 'tagstr' contains comma separated tags;
        // extract each and add them to the array 'tags'.
        return tags;
    }
};
InputStream src = newsService.getNews(ct);
```

As it calls the getNews method, SecurityException is thrown, complaining that the access to the system property is denied. The calling stack is shown in Figure 9.6.

As is evident from Figure 9.6, the callback takes a "round-trip" from the fetcher's domain to the news service's domain and back. Because the news ser-

```
Exception in thread "main"
java.security.AccessControlException: access denied
(java.util.PropertyPermission pager.tags.removal read)
java.security.AccessController.checkPermission
java.lang.SecurityManager.checkPermission
java.lang.SecurityManager.checkPropertyAccess
java.lang.System.getProperty
pager.Fetcher$1.getTagsForRemoval
com.acme.service.news.NewsService.getNews
pager.Fetcher.run
```

NewsService's domain does not have PropertyPermission

Figure 9.6 The stack status of the callback

vice's domain is inserted into the call stack, its lack of necessary permissions leads to denied access.

The solution is that the callback implementation should assert its own permissions. Thus, `ContentTransformer`'s implementation should wrap the system property access code in a `doPrivileged` block.

Does applying `doPrivileged` in callbacks constitute any security risk? Generally, no, because when the fetcher passes the `ContentTransformer` object to `NewsService`, its very intention is to invite the latter to call it back. Therefore, the callback implementation knows clearly who the caller is going to be and trusts it fully.

This situation applies not only to interservices calls, but also to any context involving callbacks, particularly when you program an OSGi event listener or a service factory in your bundle. In these cases, consider using `doPrivileged`, because the framework will call your listener or service factory, but it may not have the required permissions.

9.4.3 Creating Your Own Permission Types

When it comes to customizing security policy, you have the following choices:

1. "Subclassing" the default `SecurityManager` and overriding the `checkPermission` method
2. Providing your own implementation of the `Policy` class
3. Creating your own permission types

The first two options are only available to administrators, not to you as a bundle programmer, because there is only one security manager installed and one policy object instantiated in the entire Java virtual machine, and changes to them affect all bundles in the framework. Therefore, let's see how you can define your own permission type correctly through an example.

Suppose your service insists on not being called during certain operational hours in a day. Let's define `WorkHourPermission` that takes a time span. For example,

```
WorkHourPermission w = new WorkHourPermission("9-17");
```

means holder of the permission is allowed access from 9 AM to 5 PM. The semantics of the permission are implemented by its `PermissionCollection`'s `implies` method. To understand this, you must understand how `checkPermission` works.

We learned that when a class is loaded, it is put into a protection domain, which has a set of permissions. Suppose the class is granted `FilePermission("/tmp/-", "read,write")` for the first time. `FilePermission`'s `newPermissionCollection` method is called to create `FilePermissionCollection` for holding permissions of the same type, and the first granted permission is added to the collection. Subsequently, if another `FilePermission("/etc/-", "read")` is granted to the same class, it is again added to the existing `FilePermissionCollection`.

Assume that the class above is permission checked as follows:

```
if (sm != null) {
   Permission requestedPermission =
      new FilePermission("/tmp/junk.txt", "write");
   sm.checkPermission(requestedPermission);
}
```

`checkPermission` calls `FilePermissionCollection`'s `implies` method. What's being determined is whether the set of file permissions granted to the class implies the `requestedPermission`. The implication is true if any one permission in the permission collection implies the requested permission. In other words, the following evaluations take place:

```
FilePermission("/tmp/-", "read,write") →
   FilePermission("/tmp/junk.txt", "write") = true
FilePermission("/etc/-", "read") →
   FilePermission("/tmp/junk.txt", "write") = false
```

Because the class is permitted to read or write any files below /tmp and only to read files under /etc, it is certainly allowed to write a particular file junk.txt under /tmp. Therefore, the permission check succeeds, and the class is given the green light to perform the file operation.

With an understanding of the principle behind permission checking, let's proceed with our `WorkHourPermission` definition:

```
import java.security.*;
import java.util.*;

public final class WorkHourPermission extends BasicPermission {
   private int startHour;
   private int endHour;

   public WorkHourPermission(String name) {
      super(name);
```

```
   String h = name.trim();
   if (h.equals(""))
        throw new IllegalArgumentException("Work hour cannot be
empty");
   String startHourStr = h;
   String endHourStr   = h;
   int dashPos = h.indexOf('-');
   if (dashPos == 0) {
        startHourStr = "0";
        endHourStr   = h.substring(dashPos+1);
   } else if (dashPos == h.length()-1) {
        startHourStr = h.substring(0, dashPos);
        endHourStr   = "23";
   } else if (dashPos > 0) {
        startHourStr = h.substring(0, dashPos);
        endHourStr   = h.substring(dashPos+1);
   }
   // the following will throw NumberFormatException
   // if the work hour is not a legal integer string and
   // cannot be parsed
   this.startHour = Integer.parseInt(startHourStr);
   this.endHour   = Integer.parseInt(endHourStr);
   if (this.startHour > this.endHour)
      throw new IllegalArgumentException(
         "start hour cannot be after end hour");
   if (this.startHour >23 || this.startHour <0 ||
      this.endHour >23 || this.endHOur<0)
      throw new IllegalArgumentException(
         "start or end hour not 0-23 inclusive");
}

public WorkHourPermission(String name, String action) {
   this(name);
}

public boolean implies(Permission p) {
   if (!(p instanceof WorkHourPermission))
        return false;
   WorkHourPermission that = (WorkHourPermission) p;
   return (this.startHour <= that.startHour &&
      this.endHour >= that.endHour);
```

```
      }

      public String getActions() {
         // no action associated with this permission
           return "";
      }

      public boolean equals(Object obj) {
         if (obj == this)
             return true;
         if (! (obj instanceof WorkHourPermission))
             return false;
         WorkHourPermission that = (WorkHourPermission) obj;
         return (this.startHour == that.startHour &&
            this.endHour == that.endHour);
      }

      public int hashCode() {
         return this.startHour << 5 | this.endHour;
      }

      public PermissionCollection newPermissionCollection() {
         return new WorkHourPermissionCollection();
      }
   }
```

We extend `java.security.BasicPermission` because it takes a name and an action, which maps to the policy file syntax in a straightforward way. This allows us to grant easily WorkHourPermission in the policy file.

We use the name parameter to specify the time span. Therefore, "8-18" means 8 AM to 6 PM inclusive, "-12" means at or before 12 PM, and "9-" means at or after 9 AM. The string parsing is done in the constructor. Because permission class implementation has serious security consequences, we must take extra care to ensure it is watertight: We must prevent an invalid time parameter from being entered, and we must always ensure that the two permission instances are of the same WorkHourPermission type in the equals and implies methods. We have no use for the action parameter, thus its canonical name is an empty string as returned by the getActions method.

For one WorkHourPermission to imply another, the former's time span must be wider than the latter. For example, a 9-17 WorkHourPermission implies those with the following time spans: 9, 17, 12, 12-14, 9-10, and 11-17, to name a few.

We know that granted permissions are put into a collection for WorkHourPermissions and the collection's `implies` method is the one used in actual permission checking. Thus we construct the collection in WorkHourPermission's newPermissionCollection method, and define the WorkHourPermissionCollection class as follows:

```
final class WorkHourPermissionCollection
    extends PermissionCollection
{
    private Vector perms;

    public WorkHourPermissionCollection() {
        perms = new Vector(11);
    }

    public void add(Permission permission) {
        if (! (permission instanceof WorkHourPermission))
            throw new IllegalArgumentException(
                "invalid permission: " + permission);
        if (isReadOnly())
            throw new SecurityException("attempt to add a " +
                "Permission to a readonly PermissionCollection");
        perms.addElement((WorkHourPermission) permission);
    }

    public Enumeration elements()
    {
        return perms.elements();
    }

    public boolean implies(Permission permission) {
        if (! (permission instanceof WorkHourPermission))
            return false;
        WorkHourPermission whp = (WorkHourPermission) permission;
        for (int i=0; i<perms.size(); i++) {
            WorkHourPermission p =
                (WorkHourPermission) perms.elementAt(i);
            if (p.implies(whp))
                return true;
        }
        return false;
```

        }
    }

The all-important `implies` method enumerates all `WorkHourPermissions` granted to the class and checks to see whether the requested `WorkHourPermission` is implied by at least one of them. If so, the permission check succeeds; otherwise, it fails.

Equipped with the new permission class, we can grant `WorkHourPermission` to classes with the following entry in the policy file:

```
grant ... {
   // The class has permission to use a service 9 AM-5 PM only
   permission WorkHourPermission "9-17";
};
```

And during any hour of the day, the caller can be checked with the following segment of code:

```
SecurityManager sm = System.getSecurityManager();
if (sm != null) {
   Calendar cal = Calendar.newInstance();
   int currentHour = cal.get(Calendar.HOUR_OF_DAY);
   String hourStr = Integer.toString(currentHour);
   sm.checkPermission(new WorkHourPermission(hourStr));
}
```

9.5 Administration

The OSGi specification provides APIs for getting various status information and initiating administrative actions. For example, you can find out about all the currently installed bundles, their IDs, states, and locations; you can get a rundown of a bundle's manifest headers; and you can install and start other bundles. The command console is built on these very same APIs, and it allows you to perform administrative tasks interactively. A bundle with sufficient permissions can also assume the same administrative role programmatically.

We do not attempt to address the general issue of management. That job deals with provisioning for and managing numerous gateways running the Java Embedded Server software over the Internet in a distributed fashion and must consider scalability and reliability requirements seriously. This is referred to as **macro management**. As a contrast, we discuss **micro management**—local administration of one gateway, and in particular, how to resolve a group of bundles automatically.

9.5.1 Resolving Bundles Dynamically

We have learned that for a bundle to be resolved, the packages it imports must be exported in the framework by some other bundles, and the exported packages must have compatible versions, meaning an exported package's version must be equal to or greater than the version required for importing that package. So far we have been keeping track of the package dependency manually: Before we start admin.jar, for example, we first install and start servlet.jar, http.jar, and param.jar in the console, knowing that the administrative bundle depends on the parameter bundle for accessing the parameter storage area and the HTTP bundle for registering the servlet that presents the Web user interface. The HTTP bundle in turn relies on the servlet bundle for the Java Servlet library classes. These relationships form a treelike graph, as shown in Figure 9.7. Won't it be convenient to automate this process? That is, when a bundle is installed, other bundles that it needs are automatically found, installed, and activated, so that the bundle in question can be resolved successfully.

To begin, installing and activating the needed bundles cannot be done by the bundle itself, because it cannot be started, let alone get anything done, without them in the first place. A separate facilitator must act as the go-between, which provides the following functionalities:

- Encapsulating the knowledge of interbundle package dependency relationships.
- Resolving bundles recursively. If bundle A depends on bundle B, we must examine whether B further needs bundle C, C needs D, and so on. In computer science jargon, we need to resolve the **transitive closure** of bundles starting from A.

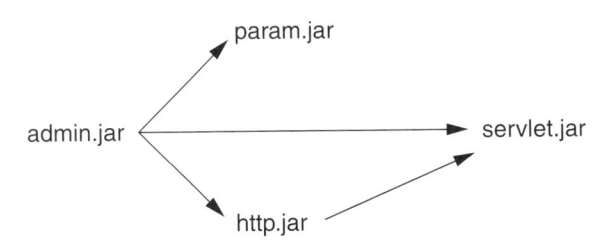

Figure 9.7 The package dependency tree for the administrative bundle

- If the resolution process fails at some point, reporting the package whose exporter either is not found or exports it at an incompatible version, as well as the unsatisfied bundle that is in need of the package.

Package dependency can be expressed as a map, as shown in Table 9.2. It basically answers the following question: Given a package, what is the location of the bundle that exports the package and at what version? We call this relation the **package exporter map.**

Table 9.2 Package Exporter Map

Package	Version	Location of the Exporting Bundle
org.osgi.service.http	1.0	file:*jes_path*/bundles/http.jar
javax.servlet	2.1.1	file:*jes_path*/bundles/servlet.jar
javax.servlet.http	2.1.1	file:*jes_path*/bundles/servlet.jar
org.osgi.service.log	1.0	file:*jes_path*/bundles/log.jar
com.acme.service.param	0.0	file:/home/joe/bundles/param.jar

The map is implemented as a property file. The property name is the package name, the property value contains the location, a comma, and the version. The version can be omitted, in which case, it is assumed to be zero. For example, the first row in Table 9.2 corresponds to this entry in the property file:

```
org.osgi.service.http=file:jes_path/bundles/http.jar, 1.0
```

Next, the facilitator is designed to carry out the following resolution algorithm:

1. Install the bundle whose location is given. Examine its Import-Package header by calling the getHeaders method of the Bundle interface. Parse the header and obtain a set of package names.

2. Consult the package exporter map and find the locations of the bundles that export the packages. If the map yields nothing, or if the package version for export is incompatible with the one needed for import, the resolution fails.

3. Install the newly found bundles.

4. Repeat this process recursively for the bundles installed in step 3.

The termination condition for the recursion is as follows: At step 1, if a bundle's Import-Package header is empty, or the needed packages are available from CLASSPATH, then the bundle does not depend on another and is said to be a **leaf** in the **dependency tree.**

Before we look at the facilitator implementation, let's get a sense of how it is typically used. Let's assume we want to resolve admin.jar, whose location is given in url:

```
Facilitator f = new Facilitator(bundleContext);
if ( ! f.resolve(url)) {
   System.out.println("Failed to resolve bundle from " + url);
   Enumeration unsatisfiedBundles = f.getUnsatisfiedBundles();
   while (unsatisfiedBundles.hasMoreElements()) {
      Bundle b = (Bundle) unsatisfiedBundles.nextElement();
      String[] pkgs = f.getMissingPackages(b);
      System.out.println("Bundle (" + b.getLocation() + ")" +
         " needs the following missing packages:");
      for (int i=0; i<pkgs.length; i++)
         System.out.println("   " + pkgs[i]);
   }
}
f.reset(); // now f is ready to resolve another bundle
```

The getMissingPackages and getUnsatisfiedBundles methods return why and where the resolution fails. The following is the main part of the implementation. To highlight the resolution portion of the code, we omit the error-reporting methods. The complete listing is in Appendix A (section A.3.3.1):

```
class Facilitator {
   private BundleContext context;
   private Properties packageExporterMap;
   // Flag a visited bundle to prevent following circular dependency
   // during recursion.
   private Hashtable visited;

   Facilitator(BundleContext ctxt) throws IOException {
      this.context = ctxt;
      this.packageExporterMap = new Properties();
      String resourceName =
         "/com/acme/admin/resolv/package-exporters.map";
      InputStream in =
         this.getClass().getResourceAsStream(resourceName);
      packageExporterMap.load(in);
      this.visited = new Hashtable();
```

```java
        }

        boolean resolve(String urlstr) throws BundleException {
            if (urlstr == null)
                return false;
            if (visited.get(urlstr) != null) {
                // if a bundle is processed, don't run in circles
                return true;
            }
            Bundle b = context.installBundle(urlstr);
            // flag that the bundle has been processed
            visited.put(urlstr, Boolean.TRUE);
            Dictionary headers = b.getHeaders();
            String imports = (String) headers.get("Import-Package");
            boolean r = true;
            if (imports != null) {
                String[] loc = findExporters(imports, b);
                for (int i=0; i<loc.length; i++) {
                    // use bitwise & to prevent short-circuit
                    // behavior associated with logical &&
                    r = r & resolve(loc[i]);
                }
            }
            if (r) {
                b.start();
            }
            return r;
        }

        private String[] findExporters(String imports, Bundle b) {
            StringTokenizer st = new StringTokenizer(imports, ",");
            Vector v = new Vector(st.countTokens());
            while (st.hasMoreTokens()) {  // enumerate each package
                String token = st.nextToken().trim();
                // separate package name and import version
                int semicolonPos = token.indexOf(';');
                    String pkgname = token;
                    String importVersion = "";
                    if (semicolonPos != -1) {
                        pkgname = token.substring(0, semicolonPos).trim();
                        int eqPos = token.indexOf('=', semicolonPos);
```

```java
                importVersion = token.substring(eqPos + 1);
            }
        if (isFromClasspath(pkgname))
            continue;
        String loc = (String) packageExporterMap.get(pkgname);
        if (loc != null) {
            // separate bundle location and export version
            String exportVersion = "";
            int commaPos = loc.indexOf(',');
            if (commaPos != -1) {
                exportVersion = loc.substring(commaPos + 1);
                loc = loc.substring(0, commaPos);
            }
            if (! areVersionsCompatible(importVersion,
                exportVersion))
            {
                loc = null;
            }
        }
        if (loc == null) {
            // save current package 'pkgname'
            // to be returned by getMissingPackages method.
            ...
        }
        v.addElement(loc);
    } // while
    String[] locations = new String[v.size()];
    v.copyInto(locations);
    // save all missing packages for the bundle 'b'
    ...
    return locations;
}

private boolean isFromClasspath(String pkg) {
    URL u = ClassLoader.getSystemResource(
        pkg.replace('.','/') + "/");
    return u != null;
}

private boolean areVersionsCompatible(String impVerStr,
    String expVerStr)
{
```

```
                // The package version for export must be equal to or
                // greater than the package version needed for import
                ...
        }
}
```

In the constructor, the package exporter map is read from a static property file included in the facilitator bundle. The `resolve` method implements the resolution algorithm just presented. If the current bundle and all the bundles on which it depends have been resolved, then the bundle is started. Notice that resolved bundles are activated on return from recursion to ensure that child bundles in the dependency tree are activated before their parents and ancestors.

If bundle A needs to import packages from bundle B, which directly or indirectly also needs to import packages from bundle A, a circular dependency is formed. The resolution routine runs infinitely if this situation arises and is unchecked. The `visited` hash table is used to break the cycle by not repeating resolution of a bundle if it has been marked as having been processed.

Much of the `findExporters` method is responsible for parsing the `Import-Package` header for a set of package names, looking up the locations of exporting bundles from the package exporter map and ensuring that the package's export version is compatible with its import version.

The `isFromClasspath` method reports whether a package is available from CLASSPATH. If so, there is no need to locate an exporter for that package. `ClassLoader.getSystemResource` returns non-null URL for system classes on the CLASSPATH, but `null` for classes loaded from another bundle. This check is necessary because according to the OSGi specification, packages with names that do not begin with `java.` must be declared in the `Import-Package` header, even though they are available from CLASSPATH.

What is not shown is how to interact with the facilitator. In our example, we implement a multithread server so that we can connect to the Java Embedded Server software from another host over a TCP/IP channel, install a bundle, and resolve it remotely. We depart from using our favorite servlet solution, because the facilitator, which is charged with the job of resolving other bundles, should be self-sufficient to be effective. The complete source code is shown in Appendix A, section A.3.3.2.

First, let's install and activate the facilitator bundle, which starts a server listening on port 8082:

```
> start file:/home/joe/bundles/facilitator.jar
> bundles
ID   STATE    LOCATION
--   ------   ---------------------------
```

```
1   ACTIVE  file:/home/joe/bundles/facilitator.jar
>
```

Then start a session using the standard `telnet` command[1] as the client. Enter a location string for the bundle you'd like to resolve after the prompt. Note that the location string is referring to a location on the host where the Java Embedded Server software is running:

```
% telnet mybox 8082
Trying 129.144.175.65...
Connected to mybox.
Escape character is '^]'.

Bundle Resolution

Enter the bundle's URL: file:/home/joe/bundles/admin.jar

OK

Connection closed by foreign host.
```

From the console we can verify the result by issuing the `bundles` command:

```
> bundles
ID   STATE   LOCATION
--   ------  ----------------------------
1    ACTIVE  file:/home/joe/bundles/facilitator.jar
2    ACTIVE  file:/home/joe/bundles/admin.jar
3    ACTIVE  file:jes_path/bundles/http.jar
4    ACTIVE  file:jes_path/bundles/servlet.jar
5    ACTIVE  file:/home/joe/bundles/param.jar
```

Just as we expected, the facilitator automatically installed and activated the `servlet.jar`, `param.jar`, `http.jar`, and `admin.jar` in the right order so that every bundle is resolved and started successfully all at once.

The previous implementation attempts to resolve as many bundles as possible. For instance, suppose the dependency map has the following entry missing, meaning it does not know which bundle exports the `com.acme.service.param` package:

```
com.acme.service.param=file:jes_path/bundles/param.jar
```

---

[1] To see your typing in Windows systems, turn on "Local Echo" of the telnet program from Menu Terminal → Preferences → Local Echo.

The algorithm will install and activate `servlet.jar` and `http.jar` in addition to `admin.jar` before reporting the resolution failure. It allows us to activate all the bundles in a subtree, even though bundles below another branch have resolution problems.

When the resolution fails, a partial set of bundles is left installed or activated in the framework. This is fine because the installation and activation operations are both idempotent: If an installed bundle is to be installed, or an active bundle is to be activated a second time, the framework detects this situation and does nothing. However, if transactional behavior is desired, we can remember the set of installed and activated bundles and undo them by deactivating and uninstalling them if the resolution fails eventually. Another way is to examine the manifest headers directly from the source without installing the bundles at all until the complete set of bundles is resolved.

The package exporter map is at the heart of the resolution algorithm. However, its static nature is limiting for the usefulness of the solution. A tool can be developed to construct the map automatically for a given set of bundles. Assuming the locations of the bundles under inspection are saved in an array `locations`, the following code fragment shows how to do this:

```
import java.util.jar.*;
...

Properties packageExporterMap = new Properties();
for (int i=0; i<locations.length(); i++) {
   Attributes headers = null;
   try {
      URL bundleURL = new URL(locations[i]);
      InputStream in =
         bundleURL.openConnection().getInputStream();
      JarInputStream jis = new JarInputStream(in);
      // get the bundle's manifest
      Manifest manifest = jis.getManifest();
      // get the manifest headers
      Attributes headers = manifest.getMainAttributes();
   } catch (IOException e) {
   } finally {
      try { jis.close(); } catch (IOException e) {}
   }
   if (headers == null)
      continue;
   // get the value for the Export-Package header
```

```
        String exports = headers.getValue("Export-Package");
        // parse the header for package names and version spec
        StringTokenizer st = new StringTokenizer(exports, ",");
        while (st.hasMoreTokens()) {
            // enumerate each package for export
            String token = st.nextToken().trim();
            int semicolonPos = token.indexOf(';');
            String pkgname = token;
            String exportVersion = null;
            if (semicolonPos != -1) {
                // parse the version spec
                pkgname = token.substring(0, semicolonPos).trim();
                int eqPos = token.indexOf('=', semiconlonPos);
                if (eqPos != -1) {
                    exportVersion = token.substring(eqPos+1).trim();
                }
            }
            String val = locations[i];
            if (exportVersion != null)
                val += ", " + exportVersion;
            packageExporterMap.put(pkgname, val);
        }
    }
}
```

We directly read and interpret the manifest of a bundle JAR file from its source URL using the classes in the `java.util.jar` package available since JDK 1.2.

An optimization can be done by partially applying the resolution logic to the previous process, so that we can determine whether any dependency cannot be satisfied early on. For example, we can additionally read and parse the Import-Package header of a bundle. If it imports certain packages not exported by any other bundles in the set, we already know this group of bundles will not resolve when they are deployed to a framework all by themselves.

Additional complications may occur because many bundles can declare to export the same package with the same version. Until the bundles are actually installed and resolved in the framework at run-time, there is no way of determining which bundle will be picked as the exporter. Moreover, because bundles can be started and stopped in various orders, a selected exporter may not be the winner the next time the framework is restarted and the same package is to be exported. The good news is that as long as at least one bundle exists and offers the needed package at the compatible version, the importers will be able to get resolved.

Let's look at this situation with a concrete example. The DA bundle `device.jar` imports the `org.osgi.service.log` package, which is offered by two bundles: the Log bundle and the HTTP bundle. The HTTP bundle does this to ensure it can always be resolved even when the Log bundle is absent. If we attempt to set up the dependency among these three bundles, two equally legal outcomes may emerge. The first version of the package exporter map is presented in Table 9.3.

Table 9.3 First Version of the Exporter Map among the Log, HTTP, and Device Bundles

Package	Location of the Exporting Bundle
`org.osgi.service.log`	`file:jes_path/bundles/log.jar`
`org.osgi.service.http`	`file:jes_path/bundles/http.jar`
`org.osgi.service.device`	`file:jes_path/bundles/device.jar`

If you start the Device bundle, the Log bundle is automatically started. This is usually what is expected. However, a second result is also possible (Table 9.4).

Table 9.4 Second Version of the Exporter Map among the Log, HTTP, and Device Bundles

Package	Location of the Exporting Bundle
`org.osgi.service.log`	`file:jes_path/bundles/http.jar`
`org.osgi.service.http`	`file:jes_path/bundles/http.jar`
`org.osgi.service.device`	`file:jes_path/bundles/device.jar`

The only difference from the first outcome is that the `org.osgi.service.log` package is shown to be exported by the HTTP bundle. As a result, if you start the device bundle, the HTTP bundle is automatically started. This is usually not what is intended, because the HTTP bundle does not provide the Log services. Yet as far as bundle resolution is concerned, the Device is resolved and can be started. It is then up to the Device bundle to handle the missing service situation using techniques from Chapter 5. In this case, it may choose simply to display log messages to the display until the Log bundle comes along some time later and registers its services.

9.5.2 Relevant APIs

Now let's summarize the manifest headers and APIs that allow you to provide and retrieve information about the bundles and services, which is essential to administrative applications.

9.5.2.1 Bundle Interface

The `Bundle` interface represents an installed bundle in the framework. The following APIs return various information about the bundle.

public Dictionary getHeaders()

We have grown familiar with the important manifest headers such as `Bundle-Activator`, `Import-Package`, `Export-Package`, `Bundle-ClassPath`, and `Bundle-NativeCode`. Here we look at a group of additional headers that serve informational and advisory purposes (Table 9.5).

Table 9.5 Informational Manifest Headers

Manifest Headers	Meaning
Bundle-Name	The name of a bundle
Bundle-Vendor	The name of the bundle vendor
Bundle-Version	The version of a bundle
Bundle-Description	The description of a bundle
Bundle-DocURL	The URL to a bundle's documentation
Bundle-ContactAddress	The e-mail address to contact about a bundle
Export-Service	The services that are to be registered by a bundle
Import-Service	The services a bundle is to get

For example, we can add the following to the administrative bundle's manifest definition:

```
Bundle-Name: The Administrative Bundle
Bundle-Description: This bundle can access and modify parameters for
  other bundles. It requires org.osgi.framework.AdminPermission, and
  provides a web user interface at http://<host>:8080/admin.
Bundle-Vendor: Acme Systems, Inc.
Bundle-Version: 1.0
Bundle-DocURL: http://www.acme.com/bundles/admin/index.html
```

```
Bundle-ContactAddress: support@acme.com
Import-Service: com.acme.service.param.ParameterAdmin
```

A management application can retrieve the information as follows, assuming bundle refers to the administrative bundle:

```
Dictionary headers = bundle.getHeaders();
System.out.println("Bundle: " + headers.get("Bundle-Name") +
    " " + headers.get("Bundle-Version"));
System.out.println("description: " +
    headers.get("Bundle-Description"));
```

Unlike Import-Package and Export-Package, the Import-Service and Export-Service manifest headers are advisory. Their presence simply indicates that *at some point in time*, the bundle needs to get or is going to register the specified service. Conceivably, a "resolution" process (similar to what we have just attempted with package dependency) can be implemented based on the Import-Service and Export-Service headers. However, even activating bundles following the order thus generated still has no guarantee that each bundle will register the service before another tries to get it. Therefore, the usefulness of these headers is quite limited, and they are no substitute for the techniques described in Chapter 5.

public long getBundleId()

This method returns the unique ID of the bundle installed in the framework.

public String getLocation()

This method returns the location string from which the bundle is installed. If the bundle has been installed directly from InputStream, the location identifier string passed into BundleContext's installBundle method is returned.

public int getState()

This method returns the current state of the bundle. It will be one of Bundle.INSTALLED, Bundle.UNINSTALLED, Bundle.RESOLVED, Bundle.STARTING, Bundle.STOPPING, and Bundle.ACTIVE. To check whether a bundle is in one of multiple states, use the following statement:

```
if (bundle.getState() &
    (Bundle.STARTING | Bundle.STOPPING | Bundle.ACTIVE) != 0)
```

public ServiceReference[] getRegisteredServices()

This method returns an array of service references of services registered by this bundle.

public ServiceReference[] getServicesInUse()

This method returns an array of service references of services that are being used by this bundle.

public boolean hasPermission(Object permission)

This method checks whether this bundle has the given permission. If the given permission is implied by the collection of permissions granted to the bundle, the method returns `true`.

9.5.2.2 BundleContext Interface

public Bundle getBundle()

If `BundleContext` is passed to a bundle's activator, calling `getBundle` returns the `Bundle` object representing the receiving bundle. Quite a mouthful for a simple operation. It is mostly used by a bundle to find out information about itself. For example,

```
public class Activator implements BundleActivator {
   public void start(BundleContext ctxt) {
      Bundle self = ctxt.getBundle();
      System.out.println("I was from " + self.getLocation() +
         " and assigned an ID of " + self.getBundleId());
      System.out.println("Am I being started? " +
         (self.getState() == Bundle.STARTING));
}
   ...
```

reports the following messages on bundle activation:

```
I was from file:/somewhere/foo.jar and assigned an ID of 5
Am I being started? true
```

public Bundle getBundle(long bundleID)

Get the installed bundle with the given `bundleID`. This is mostly used by an administrative bundle to perform a life cycle operation on another bundle or to obtain its location or state.

public Bundle[] getBundles()

This method gets all currently installed bundles in the framework.

public String getProperty(String name)

This method gets the value of an OSGi framework environment property. We covered the following standard properties in Chapter 4. They reflect various attributes of the underlying native platform:

- `org.osgi.framework.processor`
- `org.osgi.framework.os.name`
- `org.osgi.framework.os.version`
- `org.osgi.framework.language`

CHAPTER 10

Future Directions

TECHNOLOGY moves at an amazing speed, especially for the burgeoning service gateway market. Since the release of the 1.0 specification, the OSGi Core Platform Expert Group (formerly the Java Expert Group) has been actively working on existing issues and new features. In this chapter, we briefly look at the nature of some of the issues and examine other major technical areas into which OSGi is branching.

10.1 Removing Phantom Bundles

Earlier we learned that the exported packages remain in effect even when the exporting bundle has been updated, stopped, or uninstalled. Although this behavior is deterministic, it does leave behind "zombies"—inaccessible bundles that consume valuable resources. The following user session reveals this situation:

```
> start jes_path/bundles/log.jar, jes_path/bundles/device.jar
> bundles
ID   STATE   LOCATION
--   ------  ----------------------------
0    ACTIVE  System Bundle
1    ACTIVE  file:jes_path/bundles/log.jar
2    ACTIVE  file:jes_path/bundles/device.jar
> exportedpackages
Package: org.osgi.service.device (0.0.0)
  Exported by: 2 (file:jes_path/bundles/device.jar)
  Imported by: 2 (file:jes_path/bundles/device.jar)
Package: org.osgi.service.log (1.0.0)
  Exported by: 1 (file:jes_path/bundles/log.jar)
  Imported by: 1 (file:jes_path/bundles/log.jar)
               2 (file:jes_path/bundles/device.jar)
```

The device bundle imports the `org.osgi.service.log` package from the Log bundle. After both bundles were resolved and started, we witnessed that this is indeed so from the `exportedpackages` command output.

We next uninstall the Log bundle and reexamine the exported packages:

```
> uninstall 1
> exportedpackages
Package: org.osgi.service.device (0.0.0)
   Exported by: 2 (file:jes_path/bundles/device.jar)
   Imported by: 2 (file:jes_path/bundles/device.jar)
Package: org.osgi.service.log (1.0.0)
   Exported by: 1 (file:jes_path/bundles/log.jar)
   Imported by: 2 (file:jes_path/bundles/device.jar)
```

Although the Log bundle has been uninstalled, the line of `exportedpackages` output in bold type shows that its packages remain exported as before.

Finally, we reinstall and restart the Log bundle.

In Figure 10.1, a new bundle ID (3) was assigned to the installed and restarted Log bundle. The highlighted part of the `exportedpackages` output shows that the uninstalled Log bundle, whose ID is 1, still hangs around: The Device bundle imports the `org.osgi.service.log` package from bundle 1, and so does the

```
> start jes_path/bundles/log.jar
> bundles
ID   STATE     LOCATION
--   ------    -----------------------------
0    ACTIVE    System Bundle
2    ACTIVE    file:jes_path/bundles/device.jar
3    ACTIVE    file:jes_path/bundles/log.jar
> exportedpackages
Package: org.osgi.service.device (0.0.0)
   Exported by: 2 (file:jes_path/bundles/device.jar)
   Imported by: 2 (file:jes_path/bundles/device.jar)
Package: org.osgi.service.log (1.0.0)
   Exported by: 1 (file:jes_path/bundles/log.jar)
   Imported by: 2 (file:jes_path/bundles/device.jar)
                 3 (file:jes_path/bundles/log.jar)
```

Figure 10.1 The phantom Log bundle with ID 1 is still exporting the `org.osgi.service.log` package.

newly activated Log bundle 3 because its package export attempt was blocked because of bundle 1.

This situation is not optimal. Bundle 1 is a phantom because it does not appear in the bundles output and is not usable anymore. Bundle 3 is fully capable of taking over and exporting the needed packages. Even worse, it may be offering a newer version of the log package after bug fixes for export, but is not given a chance to do so. With the OSGi 1.0 framework, one has to relaunch the framework to clean up the likes of bundle 1. Work is under way to provide a mechanism that allows an administrator to perform the cleanup without necessarily shutting down the framework.

10.2 Dynamic Permissions

In the default implementation of JDK, the policy definition and granted permissions are mostly static. We explained in Chapter 9 that the Policy object in the Java virtual machine is initialized from a predefined policy file, which requires administrators to foresee *all* the permissions that a bundle may ever need before it is installed and resolved. Although the active Policy can be explicitly refreshed as follows:

```
Policy policy = Policy.getPolicy();   // get the only Policy in JVM
policy.refresh();                     // reread the policy file
```

the new rules in the policy file only apply to classes loaded after the refresh. Existing protection domains are not affected by any changes to the Policy, because they take a snapshot of the permissions granted to them by the Policy at the time they are created and remain oblivious to updates to the Policy thereafter.

When bundles are deployed to a large number of residential gateways in the field, managing bundle permissions is a complex undertaking. Obviously, not allowing dynamic permission update is unreasonable, because in real life, circumstances change, and so should security policies. A solution to enable dynamic permission administration is being worked.

10.3 Preferences

To be able to store and retrieve preferences persistently is a common requirement for many applications. It is also highly desirable to use a more expressive hierarchical structure than a flat property file. A treelike hierarchy can organize categories of attributes naturally. For instance, if we were to manage a user's Netscape preferences, we would have a tree with the layout presented in Figure 10.2.

Each node in the tree is named with a *path* similar to that of a file system. For example, /Mail/Identity refers the node that contains Joe's name and e-mail address. Different users usually have different sets of preferences. Therefore, each user can have her own preference tree, not unlike the multiple user profile feature

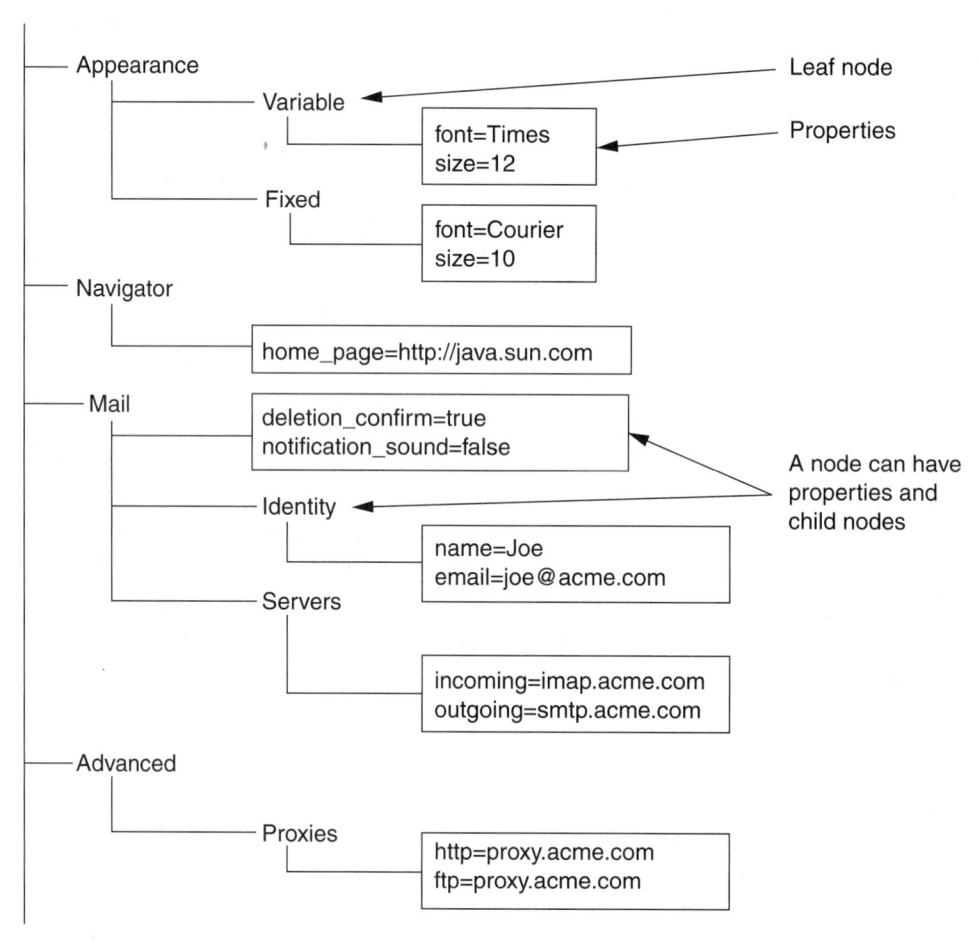

Figure 10.2 A preference tree

of the Netscape browser. In addition, a system preference tree is available for system attributes. Modeled after the Preferences API (`http://java.sun.com/aboutJava/communityprocess/review/jsr010`) being standardized in the Java community process, such a service is in the works.

10.4 User Administration

In Chapter 9 we discussed how to grant permissions to bundles based on *where* they come from, but not on *whose* behalf they run. For example, before giving out an employee's payroll information, you must ensure the user is indeed the employee herself. Knowing where the request is originated—even from a trusted location—is insufficient.

To establish the identify of a user, or to **authenticate** a user, is the prerequisite for making **authorization** decisions, for only after you have ascertained the identity of the user can you determine to what he is entitled. Authentication is achieved by verifying something a user has (fingerprint) or knows (password).

The Java 2 runtime environment has been supporting authorization based on the source of the code and who has signed it since the Java 2 SDK 1.2. In subsequent releases of the Java SDK, user-based authentication and authorization, known as the Java™ Authentication and Authorization Service (JAAS), was introduced (`http://java.sun.com/products/jaas`). Although the code source-based access control mechanism in the Java 2 Platform has been adopted by the OSGi specification 1.0, JAAS is considered too "heavy" for service gateway applications. As a result, a user administration service is being worked out. It will rely on existing mechanisms (such as `HttpService`'s `handleSecurity` implementation) to authenticate users, maintain a database of users, and assist in making authorization decisions.

10.5 Configuration Management

In earlier chapters we discussed the parameter bundle, which is used to access simple parameters for bundles. Two types of bundles can be its clients: ordinary bundles that need to be configured and administrative bundles that configure properties on behalf of other bundles. However, it is more a coding example on various framework features than a general and sophisticated solution for configuration management. Such a standard service can be expected in the future.

10.6 What's Next

If you have gotten this far, you're probably thinking, *This hardly feels like the conclusion!* and we would agree. The foundation is still being laid, and the work continues.

The OSGi enjoys continued growth. Currently it has expert groups working in the areas of core platform, remote management, security architecture, and vehicle-specific requirements. The deployment of service gateway technology to the automotive world is an interesting and exciting direction.

Although industry heavyweights are pushing forward standards and products, the success of the residential gateway market and the OSGi depends very much on the inventive and exciting services that current and future developers like yourself create. We hope we have provided you with sufficient building blocks to embark on this venture.

APPENDIX A

Code Examples

This appendix lists the complete source listings for examples used in the book. The examples have been tested on both the Solaris version 2.x system and Windows NT 4.0 operating systems with Sun Microsystems' Java 2 SDK.

A.1 Chapter 4—Developing Bundles

A.1.1 The LPD Print Service

A.1.1.1 com/acme/service/print/PrintService.java

```java
package com.acme.service.print;
import java.io.IOException;
import java.net.URL;
/**
 * The PrintService prints contents from a URL or
 * gets status of a print queue.
 */
public interface PrintService {
  /**
   * Prints the contents from the source to the specified printer.
   * @param printer the name of the destination printer
   * @param source the source of the contents to be printed
   * @exception IOException if printing fails
   */
  public void print(String printer, URL source) throws IOException;
  /**
   * Gets the status of the specified printer.
   * @param printer the name of the printer
```

```
     * @return the status of the print queue as an array,
     * one element per print job;
     * null if no entries are present in the queue
     */
    public String[] getStatus(String printer) throws IOException;
}
```

A.1.1.2 com/acme/impl/print/Printer.java

```java
package com.acme.impl.print;
import java.io.*;
import java.net.*;

class Printer {
   private String printServer;

   Printer(String ps) {
      this.printServer = ps;
   }

   /**
    * Sends a request to the printer daemon.
    * @param command a number representing a command
    * @param queue the name of the print queue
    * @param operand the operand needed by the command
    * @return a connection to the printer daemon.
    * @exception java.io.IOException if communication to the daemon
    * fails.
    */
   PrintConnection request(int command, String queue,
      String operand) throws IOException
   {
      Socket s = new Socket(printServer, 515);
      OutputStream out = s.getOutputStream();
      out.write(command);
      out.write(queue.getBytes());
      out.write(32); // write a white space SP
      if (operand != null) {
            out.write(operand.getBytes());
      }
```

```
            out.write(10); // write a line feed char LF
            out.flush();
            return new PrintConnection(queue, s);
      }
   }
```

A.1.1.3 com/acme/impl/print/PrintServiceImpl.java

```
   package com.acme.impl.print;
   import java.net.*;
   import java.io.*;
   import java.util.*;
   import com.acme.service.print.PrintService;

   class PrintServiceImpl implements PrintService {
      private final static int SEND_QUEUE_STATE = 4;
      private final static int RECEIVE_PRINT_JOB = 2;
      private Printer printer;
      private static int jobNumber = 100;

      PrintServiceImpl() {
         printer = new Printer("kontakt");
      }

      public String[] status(String printQueue) throws IOException {
         Vector v = new Vector();
         PrintConnection conn =
            printer.request(SEND_QUEUE_STATE, printQueue, null);
         BufferedReader r = new BufferedReader(conn.getReader());
         String line;
         while ( (line = r.readLine()) != null) {
            v.addElement(line);
         }
         r.close();
         String[] s = null;
         if (v.size() > 0) {
            String entry0 = (String) v.elementAt(0);
            if (! "no entries".equals(entry0)) {
               s = new String[v.size()];
               v.copyInto(s);
            }
```

```java
      }
      return s;
   }

   public void print(String printQueue, URL src)
      throws IOException
   {
      PrintConnection conn = printer.request(RECEIVE_PRINT_JOB,
            printQueue, null);
      int ack = conn.getAck();
      if (ack != 0)
         throw new IOException("Sending print job to " +
            printQueue + " failed.");
      conn.sendControl(jobNumber, src);
      conn.sendData(jobNumber, src);
      conn.close();
      // generate the next 3-digit job number
      jobNumber = (jobNumber + 1) % 1000;
   }
}
```

A.1.1.4 com/acme/impl/print/PrintConnection.java

```java
package com.acme.impl.print;
import java.net.*;
import java.io.*;

class PrintConnection {
   private static int RECEIVE_CONTROL = 2;
   private static int RECEIVE_DATA = 3;
   private Socket sock;
   private String host;
   private String printQueue;

   PrintConnection(String q, Socket s) throws IOException {
      this.sock = s;
      this.host = InetAddress.getLocalHost().getHostName();
      this.printQueue = q;
   }
```

```java
// Gets messages from the daemon.
Reader getReader() throws IOException {
    InputStream in = sock.getInputStream();
    return new BufferedReader(new InputStreamReader(in));
}

// Gets byte streams from the daemon.
InputStream getInputStream() throws IOException {
    return sock.getInputStream();
}

// Gets an acknowledge byte from the daemon. 0 means success.
int getAck() throws IOException {
    return sock.getInputStream().read();
}

// Sends control sequences to the daemon.
// This identifies the data that follow and their size.
void sendControl(int jobNumber, URL src)
    throws IOException
{
    String ctrlName = "cfA" + jobNumber + host;
    String df_file = "dfA" + jobNumber + host;
    String[] ctrlSeq = new String[] {
            "H" + host,
            "P" + System.getProperty("user.name"),
            "f" + df_file,
            "N" + src.toExternalForm()
    };
    int count = 0;
    for (int i=0; i<ctrlSeq.length; i++) {
        count += ctrlSeq[i].getBytes().length;
    }
    count += ctrlSeq.length;
    OutputStream out = sock.getOutputStream();
    out.write(RECEIVE_CONTROL);
    out.write(Integer.toString(count).getBytes());
    out.write(32);
    out.write(ctrlName.getBytes());
    out.write(10);
    out.flush();
```

```java
      if (getAck() != 0)
         throw new IOException("Couldn't start sending control "+
             " file to " + printQueue);
      for (int i=0; i<ctrlSeq.length; i++) {
        out.write(ctrlSeq[i].getBytes());
        out.write(10);
      }
      out.write(0);
      out.flush();
      if (getAck() != 0)
         throw new IOException("Failed sending control " +
             "sequence to " + printQueue);
   }

   // Sends data to the daemon. The data source can be a local file
   // or from a URL pointing to a remote location.
   void sendData(int jobNumber,URL src) throws IOException {
      String dataName = "dfA" + jobNumber + host;
      RandomAccessFile raf = null;
      URLConnection uconn = null;
      int count = -1;
      if ("file".equals(src.getProtocol())) {
            raf = new RandomAccessFile(src.getFile(), "r");
            count = (int) raf.length();
      } else {
            uconn = src.openConnection();
            count = uconn.getContentLength();
      }
      if (count == -1)
         throw new IOException("Couldn't determine the length " +
               "of source contents.");
      OutputStream out = sock.getOutputStream();
      out.write(RECEIVE_DATA);
      out.write(Integer.toString(count).getBytes());
      out.write(32);
      out.write(dataName.getBytes());
      out.write(10);
      out.flush();
      if (getAck() != 0)
         throw new IOException("Couldn't start sending " +
             "data file to " + printQueue);
```

```
      byte[] buf = new byte[10240];
      int byteRead;
      if ("file".equals(src.getProtocol())) {
         while ( (byteRead = raf.read(buf)) > 0)
            out.write(buf, 0, byteRead);
         raf.close();
      } else {
         BufferedInputStream in =
            new BufferedInputStream(uconn.getInputStream());
         while ( (byteRead = in.read(buf)) > 0)
         out.write(buf, 0, byteRead);
         in.close();
      }
      out.write(0);
      out.flush();
      int ack = getAck();
      if (ack != 0)
         throw new IOException("Failed to send data file to "+
            printQueue);

   }

   // Closes connection to the daemon.
   void close() throws IOException {
      sock.close();
   }
}
```

A.1.1.5 com/acme/impl/print/Activator.java

```
package com.acme.impl.print;
import java.util.Properties;
import org.osgi.framework.*;
import com.acme.service.print.PrintService;

public class Activator implements BundleActivator {
   private ServiceRegistration reg;

   public void start(BundleContext ctxt) {
      PrintService svc = new PrintServiceImpl();
      Properties props = new Properties();
```

```
      props.put("description", "A sample print service");
      reg = ctxt.registerService(
         "com.acme.service.print.PrintService", svc, props);
   }

   public void stop(BundleContext ctxt) {
      if (reg != null)
         reg.unregister();
   }
}
```

A.1.1.6 com/acme/impl/print/Manifest

```
Bundle-Activator: com/acme/impl/print/Activator
Export-Package: com.acme.service.print
```

A.2   Chapter 8—Device Access

A.2.1   Serial Service and Driver Locator

A.2.1.1 com/acme/service/device/serial/SerialService.java

```
package com.acme.service.device.serial;
import javax.comm.SerialPortEventListener;
import org.osgi.service.device.Device;

/**
 * The serial device service represents an available serial port
 * on the host. If multiple ports are available, we claim
 * ownership for them and register an instance of this service
 * for each of the ports.
 *
 * It also allows multiple event listeners to be added for
 * SerialPortEvents, which are delivered to the listeners
 * synchronously.
 *
 * Do not disable the CTS event notification, because DA relies on
 * that to detect if a device is connected to or disconnected from the
 * serial port.
 */
```

```java
public interface SerialService extends Device {

   /**
    * The confidence values used by the driver to match this service.
    */
   public static final int MATCH_OK = 1;

   /**
    * Gets the SerialPort object for the port.
    */
   public javax.comm.SerialPort getPort();

   /**
    * Adds an event listener for SerialPortEvents.
    */
   public void addEventListener(SerialPortEventListener l);

   /**
    * Removes the event listener for SerialPortEvents.
    */
   public void removeEventListener(SerialPortEventListener l);
}
```

A.2.1.2 com/acme/impl/device/serial/SerialServiceImpl.java

```java
package com.acme.impl.device.serial;
import java.util.*;
import javax.comm.SerialPort;
import javax.comm.SerialPortEvent;
import javax.comm.SerialPortEventListener;
import com.acme.service.device.serial.SerialService;

class SerialServiceImpl implements SerialService {
   private SerialPort port;
   private Vector listeners;

   public SerialPort getPort() {
      return this.port;
   }
```

```java
    public void addEventListener(SerialPortEventListener l) {
        listeners.addElement(l);
    }

    public void removeEventListener(SerialPortEventListener l) {
        listeners.removeElement(l);
    }

    public void noDriverFound() {
    }

    void fireEvent(SerialPortEvent e) {
        synchronized (listeners) {
            for (int i=0; i<listeners.size(); i++) {
                SerialPortEventListener l = (SerialPortEventListener)
                    listeners.elementAt(i);
                l.serialEvent(e);
            }
        }
    }

    SerialServiceImpl(SerialPort port) {
        this.port = port;
        this.listeners = new Vector(4);
    }
}
```

A.2.1.3 com/acme/impl/device/serial/SerialListener.java

```java
package com.acme.impl.device.serial;
import java.util.Properties;
import javax.comm.*;
import org.osgi.framework.*;

class SerialListener implements SerialPortEventListener {
    private BundleContext context;
    private ServiceRegistration serialReg = null;
    private SerialServiceImpl serialService = null;
    private String[] deviceClazzes = {
        "com.acme.service.device.serial.SerialService",
        "org.osgi.service.device.Device" };
```

```java
      SerialListener(BundleContext ctxt) {
         this.context = ctxt;
      }

      public void serialEvent(SerialPortEvent e) {
         SerialPort port = (SerialPort) e.getSource();
         int t = e.getEventType();
         if (t == SerialPortEvent.CTS) {
            // listen to CTS pin of the serial interface
            boolean plugged = e.getNewValue();
            if (plugged) {
               // register a serial device service when a
               // device is connected to the serial port
               Properties props = new Properties();
               props.put("DEVICE_CATEGORY", "serial");
               props.put("DEVICE_MAKE", "Acme");
               props.put("Port", port.getName());
               serialService = new SerialServiceImpl(port);
               serialReg = context.registerService(deviceClazzes,
                   serialService, props);
            } else {
               // unregister the serial device service when
               // the device is disconnected from the serial
               // port
               if (serialReg != null) {
                  serialReg.unregister();
                  serialReg = null;
                  serialService = null;
               }
            }
         } else {
            if (serialService != null)
               serialService.fireEvent(e);
         }
      }
   }
}
```

A.2.1.4 com/acme/impl/locator/DriverLocatorImpl.java

```java
package com.acme.impl.locator;
import java.util.*;
```

```java
import java.net.URL;
import java.io.InputStream;
import java.io.IOException;
import org.osgi.service.device.*;

/**
 * This driver locator tries to find a refining driver for the
 * serial device category in its own bundle as a resource.
 */
public class DriverLocatorImpl implements DriverLocator {
   // Map a device category to IDs of refining drivers
   private Hashtable categoryMap;
   // Map a driver ID to a URL to the driver bundle
   private Hashtable driverMap;
   static final String DRIVER_ID_PREFIX = "com.acme.device.drivers";

   public String[] findDrivers(Dictionary props) {
      String category = (String) props.get("DEVICE_CATEGORY");
      String make = (String) props.get("DEVICE_MAKE");
      if (!"Acme".equalsIgnoreCase(make))
         return null;
      String[] ids = (String []) categoryMap.get(category);
      return ids;
   }

   public InputStream loadDriver(String id) throws IOException {
      URL u = (URL) driverMap.get(id);
      if (u != null) {
         return u.openStream();
      }
      return null;
   }

   public DriverLocatorImpl() {
      categoryMap = new Hashtable(3);
      categoryMap.put("serial",
         new String[] { DRIVER_ID_PREFIX + ".serial.modem.0"});
      driverMap = new Hashtable(3);
      driverMap.put(DRIVER_ID_PREFIX + ".serial.modem.0",
            this.getClass().getResource("/drivers/driver.jar"));
```

        }
    }

A.2.1.5 com/acme/impl/device/serial/Activator.java

```
package com.acme.impl.device.serial;
import java.util.*;
import javax.comm.*;
import org.osgi.framework.*;
import com.acme.impl.locator.DriverLocatorImpl;

/**
 * The bundle activator registers a driver locator service,
 * finds all available serial ports, and defines a listener
 * for each port, detecting if a device is connected to
 * the serial port.
 */
public class Activator implements BundleActivator {
    private Vector ports = new Vector(4);

    public void start(BundleContext ctxt) throws Exception {
        // register a driver locator
        Properties props = new Properties();
        props.put("description",
            "Locating refining drivers for " +
            "the serial device category.");
        ctxt.registerService(
            "org.osgi.service.device.DriverLocator",
            new DriverLocatorImpl(), props);
        for (Enumeration enum =
            CommPortIdentifier.getPortIdentifiers();
            enum.hasMoreElements(); )
        {
            CommPortIdentifier portId =
                (CommPortIdentifier) enum.nextElement();
            if (portId.getPortType() ==
                CommPortIdentifier.PORT_SERIAL) {
                try {
                    SerialPort port = (SerialPort)
                        portId.open("SerialService", 2000);
                    port.notifyOnCTS(true);
```

```
                    SerialListener serialListener =
                        new SerialListener(ctxt);
                    port.addEventListener(serialListener);
                    ports.addElement(port);
                    if (port.isCTS()) {
                        SerialPortEvent event = new SerialPortEvent(
                            port, SerialPortEvent.CTS, false, true);
                        serialListener.serialEvent(event);
                    }
                } catch (PortInUseException e) {
                    // the serial port has been occupied; skip it
                } catch (TooManyListenersException e) {
                    // can't happen
                }
            }
        }
    }

    public void stop(BundleContext ctxt) throws Exception {
        for (int i=0; i<ports.size(); i++) {
            SerialPort port = (SerialPort) ports.elementAt(i);
            port.removeEventListener();
            port.close();
        }
    }
}
```

A.2.1.6 Manifest

```
Bundle-Activator: com.acme.impl.device.serial.Activator
Export-Package: com.acme.service.device.serial
Import-Package: org.osgi.service.device
```

A.2.2 Driver Service and Modem Service

A.2.2.1 com/acme/impl/driver/DriverImpl.java

```
package com.acme.impl.driver;
import java.util.Properties;
import java.io.*;
import javax.comm.*;
```

CODE EXAMPLES

```
import org.osgi.framework.*;
import org.osgi.service.device.*;
import com.acme.service.device.serial.SerialService;
import com.acme.impl.device.modem.ModemServiceImpl;

class DriverImpl implements Driver {
   private BundleContext context;
   private ServiceRegistration reg;
   private ServiceReference serialRef;

   public int match(ServiceReference sr) throws Exception {
      String category =
         (String) sr.getProperty("DEVICE_CATEGORY");
      if ("serial".equals(category)) {
         if (modemAccessed(sr))
            return SerialService.MATCH_OK;
      }
      return Device.MATCH_NONE;
   }

   public String attach(ServiceReference sr) throws Exception {
      String[] deviceClazzes = new String[] {
         "org.osgi.service.device.Device",
         "com.acme.service.device.modem.ModemService" };
      Properties props = new Properties();
      props.put("DEVICE_CATEGORY", "modem");
      props.put("DEVICE_MAKE", "Acme");
      props.put("Port", sr.getProperty("Port"));
      serialRef=sr;
      SerialService serialService = (SerialService)
            context.getService(sr);
      reg = context.registerService(deviceClazzes,
               new ModemServiceImpl(serialService),
               props);
      return null;
   }

   DriverImpl(BundleContext ctxt) {
      this.context = ctxt;
      try {
         String filter = "(objectClass=" +
```

```
            "com.acme.service.device.serial.SerialService)";
          context.addServiceListener(new ServiceListener() {
            public void serviceChanged(ServiceEvent e) {
              if (e.getType() == ServiceEvent.UNREGISTERING) {
                if (e.getServiceReference().equals(serialRef)&&
                    reg != null {
                    reg.unregister();
                    reg = null;
                    serialRef = null;
                }
              }
            }
          }, filter);
      } catch (InvalidSyntaxException e) {
        // can't happen
      }
    }

    private boolean modemAccessed(ServiceReference sr) {
      boolean isModem = false;
      SerialService ss = (SerialService) context.getService(sr);
      SerialPort port = ss.getPort();
      try {
        OutputStream out = port.getOutputStream();
        InputStream in = port.getInputStream();
        out.write("ATE0\r\n".getBytes());
        out.flush();
        // ReceiveTimeout is set so that we won't block forever
        // in case it's not a modem
        port.enableReceiveTimeout(3000);
        byte[] buf = new byte[20];
        int byteRead;
        while (true) {
          byteRead = in.read(buf);
          if (byteRead == 0)
            break;
          String s = new String(buf, 0, byteRead);
          if (s.indexOf("\r\nOK\r\n") >= 0) {
            isModem = true;
            break;
          } else if (s.indexOf("\r\nERROR\r\n") >=0)
            break;
        }
```

```java
      } catch (Exception e) {
      } finally {
         context.ungetService(sr);
      }
      return isModem;
   }
}
```

A.2.2.2 com/acme/impl/driver/Activator.java

```java
package com.acme.impl.driver;
import java.util.Properties;
import org.osgi.framework.*;

public class Activator implements BundleActivator {
   private ServiceRegistration reg;

   public void start(BundleContext ctxt) {
      Properties props = new Properties();
      props.put("DRIVER_ID",
         "com.acme.device.drivers.serial.modem.0");
      props.put("description",
         "The driver that refines a serial device to a modem device.");
      reg = ctxt.registerService("org.osgi.service.device.Driver",
         new DriverImpl(ctxt), props);
   }

   public void stop(BundleContext ctxt) {
      if (reg != null)
         reg.unregister();
   }
}
```

A.2.2.3 com/acme/service/device/modem/ModemService.java

```java
package com.acme.service.device.modem;
import java.io.*;
import org.osgi.service.device.Device;

/**
 * ModemService allows access to a modem.
 */
public interface ModemService extends Device {
```

APPENDIX A CODE EXAMPLES

```
/**
 * The data connection to a connected modem.
 */
interface DataConnection {
   public OutputStream getOutputStream() throws IOException;
   public InputStream getInputStream() throws IOException;
   public void returnToCommandMode();
}

/** Disables the modem's speaker */
public static final int SPEAKER_DISABLED = 0;
/** Sets the volume of the modem's speaker to the default level */
public static final int SPEAKER_DEFAULT = 1;

/**
 * Dials up a modem with the given phone number.
 */
public DataConnection dialup(String phoneNumber)
   throws IOException;

/**
 * Hangs up the modem.
 */
public void hangup() throws IOException;

/**
 * Gets information about the modem.
 */
public String getInfo() throws IOException;

/**
 * Configures the volume of the modem's speaker.
 * @param mode the volume level of the speaker. Must be either
 * SPEAKER_DISABLED or SPEAKER_DEFAULT.
 */
public void configureSpeaker(int mode) throws IOException;

/**
 * Gets the value of the given S register.
 */
public byte getSRegister(int r) throws IOException;
```

```
    /**
     * Sets the value for the given S register.
     */
    public void setSRegister(int r, byte value) throws IOException;
}
```

A.2.2.4 com/acme/impl/device/modem/ModemServiceImpl.java

```
package com.acme.impl.device.modem;
import java.io.*;
import javax.comm.*;
import com.acme.service.device.modem.ModemService;
import com.acme.service.device.serial.SerialService;

public class ModemServiceImpl implements ModemService {
    private SerialPort port;

    public void noDriverFound() {
    }

    public ModemService.DataConnection dialup(String phoneNumber)
        throws IOException
    {
        String rc = sendCommand("ATDT"+phoneNumber+"\r\n");
        if (rc.indexOf("CONNECT") != -1) {
            return this.new DataConnectionImpl();
        }
        return null;
    }

    public void hangup() throws IOException {
        sendCommand("ATH\r\n");
    }

    public String getInfo() throws IOException {
        String rc = sendCommand("ATI4\r\n");
        int pos = rc.indexOf("\r\n", 2);
        if (pos != -1)
            rc = rc.substring(2, pos);
        return rc;
    }
```

APPENDIX A   CODE EXAMPLES

```java
public void configureSpeaker(int mode) throws IOException {
   sendCommand("ATM" + mode + "\r\n");
}

public byte getSRegister(int n) throws IOException {
   String rc = sendCommand("ATS" + n + "?\r\n");
   int pos = rc.indexOf("\r\n", 2);
   if (pos != -1)
      rc = rc.substring(2, pos);
   return Byte.parseByte(rc);
}

public void setSRegister(int n, byte value) throws IOException {
   String r = sendCommand("ATS" + n + "=" + value);
}

public ModemServiceImpl(SerialService ss)
   throws UnsupportedCommOperationException
{
   this.port = ss.getPort();
   port.enableReceiveTimeout(5000);
}

private String sendCommand(String cmd) throws IOException {
   InputStream in = port.getInputStream();
   int byteRead;
   int off = 0;
   byte[] buf = new byte[1024];
   StringBuffer sb = new StringBuffer();
   while (true) {
      byteRead = in.read(buf);
      if (byteRead == 0)
         break;
      String s = new String(buf, 0, byteRead);
      sb.append(s);
      if (s.indexOf("\r\nOK\r\n") >= 0)
         break;
      else if (s.indexOf("\r\nERROR\r\n") >=0)
         throw new IOException(sb.toString());
   }
```

```
            return sb.toString();
    }

    class DataConnectionImpl
        implements ModemService.DataConnection
    {
        public OutputStream getOutputStream() throws IOException {
            return port.getOutputStream();
        }

        public InputStream getInputStream() throws IOException {
            return port.getInputStream();
        }

        public void returnToCommandMode() {
            try {
                getOutputStream().write("+++".getBytes());
            } catch (IOException e) {
            }
        }
    }
}
```

A.2.2.5 Manifest

```
Bundle-Activator: com.acme.impl.driver.Activator
Export-Package: com.acme.service.device.modem
Import-Package: org.osgi.service.device,
 com.acme.service.device.serial
```

A.2.3 Web Interface to the Serial Ports

A.2.3.1 com/acme/gui/serial/SerialServlet.java

```
package com.acme.gui.serial;
import java.io.*;
import javax.servlet.*;
import javax.servlet.http.*;
import javax.comm.*;
import org.osgi.framework.*;
import com.acme.service.device.serial.*;
```

```java
class SerialServlet extends HttpServlet {
   private BundleContext context;
   private static int[] bauds = { 2400, 4800, 9600, 19200,
      28800, 38400, 57600, 115200 };
   private static int[] dataBits = {
      SerialPort.DATABITS_5, SerialPort.DATABITS_6,
      SerialPort.DATABITS_7, SerialPort.DATABITS_8 };
   private static String[] dataBitsLabel = { "5", "6", "7", "8" };
   private static int[] parity = { SerialPort.PARITY_NONE,
      SerialPort.PARITY_ODD, SerialPort.PARITY_EVEN,
      SerialPort.PARITY_MARK, SerialPort.PARITY_SPACE };
   private static String[] parityLabel = {
      "None", "Odd", "Even", "Mark", "Space" };
   private static int[] stopBits = { SerialPort.STOPBITS_1,
      SerialPort.STOPBITS_2, SerialPort.STOPBITS_1_5 };
   private static String[] stopBitsLabel = { "1", "2", "1.5" };

   SerialServlet(BundleContext ctxt) {
      this.context = ctxt;
   }

   public void doGet(HttpServletRequest req,
      HttpServletResponse resp)
      throws ServletException, IOException
   {
      ServletOutputStream out = resp.getOutputStream();
      resp.setContentType("text/html");
      displayHeader(out);
      try {
         ServiceReference[] refs = context.getServiceReferences(
            "com.acme.service.device.serial.SerialService",
            null);
         if (refs == null) {
            out.println("<i>No device is found to be attached "+
               "to any of the serial ports.</i>");
         } else {
            // display serial port settings for each port found
            for (int i=0; i<refs.length; i++)
               displayControl(out, refs[i]);
         }
```

```java
      } catch (InvalidSyntaxException e) {
      }
      displayFooter(out);
      out.close();
   }

   public void doPost(HttpServletRequest req,
      HttpServletResponse resp)
      throws ServletException, IOException
   {
      String message = null;
      String portName = req.getParameter("port");
      try {
         ServiceReference[] refs = context.getServiceReferences(
            "com.acme.service.device.serial.SerialService",
            "(Port=" + portName + ")");
         if (refs != null) {
            SerialService ss =
               (SerialService) context.getService(refs[0]);
            SerialPort port = ss.getPort();
            // receive new settings posted from the browser
            int baud = Integer.parseInt(
               req.getParameter("baud_select"));
            int databits = Integer.parseInt(
               req.getParameter("databits_select"));
            int stopbits = Integer.parseInt(
               req.getParameter("stopbits_select"));
            int parity = Integer.parseInt(
               req.getParameter("parity_select"));
            // set new parameters to the given serial port
             port.setSerialPortParams(baud, databits,
               stopbits, parity);
         } else {
            message = "<i>Could not set serial port parameters: "+
               "no device is attached to " + portName +
               " any longer.</i>";
         }
      } catch (InvalidSyntaxException e) {
      } catch (UnsupportedCommOperationException e) {
          message = "<i>Failed to set serial port parameters: "+
          e.toString() + "</i>";
```

294 APPENDIX A CODE EXAMPLES

```java
      }
      if (message != null) {
        ServletOutputStream out = resp.getOutputStream();
        resp.setContentType("text/html");
        displayHeader(out);
        out.println(message);
        displayFooter(out);
        out.close();
      } else {
        resp.sendRedirect("/serialports");
      }
    }

    // display parameters for a given serial port
    private void displayControl(ServletOutputStream out,
      ServiceReference ref)
      throws ServletException, IOException
    {
      SerialService ss = (SerialService) context.getService(ref);
      SerialPort port = ss.getPort();
      String name = port.getName();
      out.println("<form action=\"/serialports\" method=post>\n");
      out.println("<table border=0>\n" +
        "<tr><td colspan=5><b>Port: " +
        "<font color=green>" + name + "</font>" +
        "</b></td></tr>\n" +
        "<tr>\n" +
        "<td>" +
        displaySelect("baud_select",
            bauds, null, port.getBaudRate()) +
        "</td>\n" +
        "<td>" +
        displaySelect("databits_select",
            dataBits, dataBitsLabel,
            port.getDataBits()) +
        "</td>\n" +
        "<td>" +
        displaySelect("stopbits_select",
            stopBits, stopBitsLabel,
            port.getStopBits()) +
```

```java
                    "</td>\n" +
                    "<td>" +
                    displaySelect("parity_select",
                        parity, parityLabel, port.getParity()) +
                    "</td>\n" +
                    "<td>\n" +
                    "<input type=submit value=Set>\n" +
                    "</td>\n" +
                    "</tr>\n" +
                    "</table>\n" +
                    "<input type=hidden name=port value=\"" + name + "\">\n" +
                    "</form>");
        context.ungetService(ref);
    }

    private String displaySelect(String widgetId,
                int[] candidates,
                String[] labels,
                int value)
    {
        StringBuffer sb = new StringBuffer();
        sb.append("<select name=\"" + widgetId + "\">\n");
        for (int i=0; i<candidates.length; i++) {
            sb.append("<option value=\"" + candidates[i] + "\"" +
                (candidates[i] == value ? " selected" : "") + ">" +
                (labels != null ? labels[i] :
                  Integer.toString(candidates[i])) + "\n");
        }
        sb.append("</select>\n");
        return sb.toString();
    }

    private void displayHeader(ServletOutputStream out)
        throws ServletException, IOException
    {
        out.println("<HTML>\n" +
            "<HEAD>\n" +
            "<TITLE>Serial Port Configuration</TITLE>\n" +
            "</HEAD>\n" +
            "<BODY BGCOLOR=#cccccc>");
    }
```

```
        private void displayFooter(ServletOutputStream out)
           throws ServletException, IOException
     {
        out.println("</BODY>\n" +
           "</HTML>");
     }
  }
```

A.2.3.2 com/acme/gui/serial/Activator.java

```
package com.acme.gui.serial;
import java.net.*;
import java.io.IOException;
import javax.servlet.*;
import javax.servlet.http.*;
import org.osgi.framework.*;
import org.osgi.service.http.*;

public class Activator implements BundleActivator {
   private HttpService http;
   private final String SERVLET_ALIAS = "/serialports";

   public void start(BundleContext context)
      throws ServletException, NamespaceException
   {
      ServiceReference ref = context.getServiceReference(
            "org.osgi.service.http.HttpService");
      http = (HttpService) context.getService(ref);
      SerialServlet servlet = new SerialServlet(context);
      http.registerServlet(SERVLET_ALIAS, servlet, null, null);
   }

   public void stop(BundleContext context) {
      if (http != null) {
         http.unregister(SERVLET_ALIAS);
      }
   }
}
```

A.2.3.3 com/acme/gui/serial/Manifest

```
Bundle-Activator: com.acme.gui.serial.Activator
Import-Package: org.osgi.service.http,
 com.acme.service.device.serial,
 javax.servlet, javax.servlet.http
```

A.3 Chapter 9—Permission-based Security and Administration

A.3.1 Parameter Services

The parameter bundle provides a comprehensive example that illustrates the following features:

- Service factory
- Asynchronous event handling
- Permission checking
- Performing privileged actions

In a Java run-time environment that does not support permissions, comment out the security-related code.

A.3.1.1 com/acme/service/param/ParamService.java

```java
package com.acme.service.param;
/**
 * This service allows a caller to store and retrieve parameters
 * in the form of a key/value pair.
 */
public interface ParameterService {
   /**
    * Stores a parameter.
    * @param key the name of the parameter.
    * @param value the value of the parameter.
    */
   public void set(String key, String value);

   /**
    * Retrieves a parameter.
    */
```

```
        public String get(String key);
}
```

A.3.1.2 com/acme/service/param/ParameterAdmin.java

```
package com.acme.service.param;
import java.io.IOException;
import java.util.Properties;

public interface ParameterAdmin {
  /**
   * Stores a parameter set for a bundle.
   * @param bundleLocation the location of the bundle.
   * @param props the parameter set.
   * @exception java.io.IOException if saving to the property file
   *       fails.
   * @exception java.security.SecurityException if the caller does
   *       not have AdminPermission and the Java runtime supports
   *       permissions.
   */
  public void set(String bundleLocation, Properties props)
      throws IOException;

  /**
   * Retrieves the parameter set for a bundle.
   *
   * @exception java.security.SecurityException if the caller does
   *       not have AdminPermission and the Java runtime supports
   *       permissions.
   */
  public Properties get(String bundleLocation)
      throws IOException;
}
```

A.3.1.3 com/acme/impl/param/ParameterServiceImpl.java

```
package com.acme.impl.param;
import java.util.*;
import com.acme.service.param.ParameterService;

class ParameterServiceImpl implements ParameterService {
  Properties props;
```

```java
   public void set(String key, String value) {
      props.put(key, value);
   }

   public String get(String key) {
      return props.get(key);
   }

   ParameterServiceImpl(Properties initProps) {
      if (initProps != null) // copy initial parameters if any
         props = (Properties) initProps.clone();
      else
         props = new Properties();
   }
}
```

A.3.1.4 com/acme/impl/param/ParameterServiceFactory.java

```java
package com.acme.impl.param;
import java.io.IOException;
import java.util.Properties;
import org.osgi.framework.Bundle;
import org.osgi.framework.BundleContext;
import org.osgi.framework.ServiceFactory;
import org.osgi.framework.ServiceRegistration;

class ParameterServiceFactory implements ServiceFactory {
   private ParameterStore store;

   ParameterServiceFactory(ParameterStore store) {
      this.store = store;
   }

   // A client bundle starts using ParameterService.
   public Object getService(Bundle bundle, ServiceRegistration reg)
   {
      try {
         return new ParameterServiceImpl(store.load(bundle));
      } catch (IOException e) {
         // should log the exception
      }
```

```
            return new ParameterServiceImpl(null);
        }

        // The client bundle finishes using ParameterService.
        public void ungetService(Bundle bundle, ServiceRegistration reg,
                                 Object service)
        {
            ParameterServiceImpl ps = (ParameterServiceImpl) service;
            try {
                store.save(bundle, ps.props);
            } catch (IOException e) {
                // should log the exception
            }
        }
    }
```

A.3.1.5 com/acme/impl/param/ParameterAdminImpl.java

```
    package com.acme.impl.param;
    import java.util.Properties;
    import java.io.IOException;
    import org.osgi.framework.*;
    import com.acme.service.param.ParameterAdmin;

    class ParameterAdminImpl implements ParameterAdmin {
        private static AdminPermission adminPermission =
            new AdminPermission();
        private BundleContext context;
        private ParameterStore store;

        ParameterAdminImpl(BundleContext ctxt, ParameterStore store) {
            this.context = ctxt;
            this.store = store;
        }

        public void set(String loc, Properties props)
            throws IOException
        {
            sm = System.getSecurityManager();
            if (sm != null) {
                sm.checkPermission(adminPermission);
            }
```

```java
         Bundle b = getBundle(loc);
         if (b == null)
            throw new IOException("Bundle (" + loc +
               ") not installed");
         store.save(b, props);
      }

      public Properties get(String loc) throws IOException {
         SecurityManager sm = System.getSecurityManager();
         if (sm != null) {
            sm.checkPermission(adminPermission);
         }
         Bundle b = getBundle(loc);
         if (b == null)
            throw new IOException("Bundle (" + loc +
               ") not installed");
         return store.load(b);
      }

      private Bundle getBundle(String loc) {
         Bundle[] bundles = context.getBundles();
         for (int i=0; i<bundles.length; i++) {
            if (bundles[i].getLocation().equals(loc)) {
               return bundles[i];
            }
         }
         return null;
      }
   }
```

A.3.1.6 com/acme/impl/param/ParameterStore.java

```java
   package com.acme.impl.param;
   import java.io.*;
   import java.util.Properties;
   import java.security.*;
   import org.osgi.framework.*;

   class ParameterStore {
      static final String FILENAME = "parameters.properties";
      private File dataRoot;
```

```java
      ParameterStore(BundleContext ctxt) {
         this.dataRoot = ctxt.getDataFile("");
      }

      synchronized void save(final Bundle b, final Properties props)
         throws IOException
      {
         try {
            AccessController.doPrivileged(
               new PrivilegedExceptionAction() {
                  public Object run() throws IOException {
                     String id = Long.toString(b.getBundleId());
                     File paramDir = new File(dataRoot, id);
                     if (! paramDir.exists()) {
                        if (! paramDir.mkdir())
                           throw new IOException(
                              "Couldn't create dir: "+ paramDir);
                     }
                     File paramFile = new File(paramDir, FILENAME);
                     FileOutputStream out =
                        new FileOutputStream(paramFile);
                     props.save(out, "Parameters for " +
                        b.getLocation());
                     out.close();
                     return null;
                  }
               });
         } catch (PrivilegedActionException e) {
            throw (IOException) e.getException();
         }
      }

      synchronized Properties load(final Bundle b) throws IOException {
         Properties props = null;
         try {
            props = (Properties)
               AccessController.doPrivileged(
                  new PrivilegedExceptionAction()
                  {
                     public Object run() throws IOException {
                        Properties p = new Properties();
```

```java
               String id = Long.toString(b.getBundleId());
               File paramFile = new File(dataRoot,
                   id + File.separator +
                   FILENAME);
               if (!paramFile.exists())
                  return null;
               FileInputStream in =
                   new FileInputStream(paramFile);
               p.load(in);
               in.close();
               return p;
            }
         });
      } catch (PrivilegedActionException e) {
         throw (IOException) e.getException();
      }
      return props;
}

synchronized void clear(Bundle b) {
   final long id = b.getBundleId();
   String[] ids = dataRoot.list();
   for (int i=0; i<ids.length; i++) {
      try {
         if (id != Long.parseLong(ids[i]))
            continue;
         AccessController.doPrivileged(
            new PrivilegedAction()
         {
            public Object run() {
               File paramFile = new File(dataRoot, id +
                   File.separator + FILENAME);
               paramFile.delete();
               File paramDir = new File(dataRoot,
                   Long.toString(id));
               paramDir.delete();
               return null;
               }
         });
         break;
```

```
            } catch (NumberFormatException e) {
            }
         }
      }
   }
```

A.3.1.7 com/acme/impl/param/Activator.java

```
package com.acme.impl.param;
import java.io.*;
import org.osgi.framework.*;

public class Activator implements BundleActivator {
   private ServiceRegistration reg;

   public void start(BundleContext ctxt) {
      final ParameterStore store = new ParameterStore(ctxt);
      // add a bundle listener listening to
      // uninstallation of client bundles
      ctxt.addBundleListener(new BundleListener() {
         public void bundleChanged(BundleEvent e) {
            // we are only interested in bundle uninstalled event
            if (e.getType() != BundleEvent.UNINSTALLED)
               return;
            store.clear(e.getBundle());
         }
      });
      reg = ctxt.registerService(
         "com.acme.service.param.ParameterService",
         new ParameterServiceFactory(store), null);
      ctxt.registerService(
         "com.acme.service.param.ParameterAdmin",
         new ParameterAdminImpl(ctxt, store), null);
   }

   public void stop(BundleContext ctxt) {
      if (reg != null)
         reg.unregister();
   }
}
```

A.3.1.8 com/acme/impl/param/Manifest

```
Bundle-Activator: com.acme.impl.param.Activator
Export-Package: com.acme.service.param
```

A.3.2 Parameter Configuration Servlet

A.3.2.1 com/acme/admin/param/AdminServlet.java

```java
package com.acme.admin.param;
import java.util.*;
import java.io.*;
import javax.servlet.*;
import javax.servlet.http.*;
import org.osgi.framework.*;
import com.acme.service.param.ParameterAdmin;

class AdminServlet extends HttpServlet {
   private BundleContext context;
   static final String TAG_NEW_PROP_NAME =
      "com.acme.admin.new.property.name";
   static final String TAG_NEW_PROP_VALUE =
      "com.acme.admin.new.property.value";
   static final String TAG_BUNDLE_ID =
      "com.acme.admin.bundle.id";

   AdminServlet(BundleContext ctxt) {
      this.context = ctxt;
   }

   public void doGet(HttpServletRequest req,
         HttpServletResponse resp)
      throws ServletException, IOException
   {
      ServletOutputStream out = resp.getOutputStream();
      resp.setContentType("text/html");
      displayHeader(out);
      String idstr = req.getParameter("id");
      if (idstr == null) {
         displayAllBundles(out);
      } else {
```

```java
         long bundleId = Long.parseLong(idstr);
         displayForm(out, bundleId);
      }
      displayFooter(out);
      out.close();
   }

   public void doPost(HttpServletRequest req,
             HttpServletResponse resp)
      throws ServletException, IOException
   {
      Properties props = new Properties();
      String newPropName = null;
      String newPropVal  = null;
      Enumeration propNames = req.getParameterNames();
      while (propNames.hasMoreElements()) {
         String k = (String) propNames.nextElement();
         String v = req.getParameter(k);
         if (TAG_NEW_PROP_NAME.equals(k))
            newPropName = v;
         else if (TAG_NEW_PROP_VALUE.equals(k))
            newPropVal  = v;
         else if (! (TAG_BUNDLE_ID.equals(k))) {
            if (v.length() > 0)
               props.put(k, v);
         }
      }
      if (newPropName.length() > 0 && newPropVal.length() > 0)
         props.put(newPropName, newPropVal);
      ServiceReference ref = context.getServiceReference(
         "com.acme.service.param.ParameterAdmin");
      ParameterAdmin admin =
         (ParameterAdmin) context.getService(ref);
      long id = Long.parseLong(req.getParameter(TAG_BUNDLE_ID));
      Bundle b = context.getBundle(id);
      admin.set(b.getLocation(), props);
      context.ungetService(ref);
      resp.sendRedirect(Activator.SERVLET_ALIAS + "?id=" + id);
   }
```

```java
private void displayAllBundles(ServletOutputStream out)
   throws ServletException, IOException
{
   Bundle[] bundles = context.getBundles();
   if (bundles == null) {
      out.println("<i>No bundle is installed " +
         "in the framework.</i>");
   } else {
      out.println("The following bundles are currently " +
         "installed in the framework:\n" +
         "<p>\n" +
         "<ul>\n");
      for (int i=0; i<bundles.length; i++)
         out.println("<li>" +
            "<a href=\"" + Activator.SERVLET_ALIAS +
            "?id=" + bundles[i].getBundleId() +
            "\">" + bundles[i].getLocation() +
            "</a>\n");
      out.println("</ul>\n");
   }
}

private void displayForm(ServletOutputStream out, long id)
   throws ServletException, IOException
{
   Bundle b = context.getBundle(id);
   ServiceReference ref = context.getServiceReference(
      "com.acme.service.param.ParameterAdmin");
   ParameterAdmin admin =
      (ParameterAdmin) context.getService(ref);
   Properties props = admin.get(b.getLocation());
   context.ungetService(ref);
   out.println("<b>Bundle</b>: " + b.getLocation() + "<p>\n");
   if (props == null) {
      out.println("<i>There is no property " +
         "for this bundle.</i>");
   }
   out.println("<form action=\"" +
      Activator.SERVLET_ALIAS + "\" method=post>\n");
   out.println("<table border=0>\n" +
      "<tr><th align=left>Property Name</th>" +
```

```java
            "<th align=left>Value</th></tr>\n");
      if (props != null)
         for (Enumeration propNames = props.propertyNames();
            propNames.hasMoreElements(); )
         {
            String propName = (String) propNames.nextElement();
            String propVal  = props.getProperty(propName);
            out.println("<tr>\n" +
               "<td>" + propName + "</td>" +
               "<td><input name=\"" + propName + "\" " +
               "value=\"" + propVal + "\" size=" +
               (propVal.length() + 5) + "></td>\n" +
               "</tr>\n");
         }
      out.println("<tr>\n" +
         "<td><input name=\"" + TAG_NEW_PROP_NAME + "\" "+
         "size=25></td>" +
         "<td><input name=\"" + TAG_NEW_PROP_VALUE + "\" "+
         "size=25></td>\n" +
         "</tr>\n");
      out.println("</table><p>\n" +
         "<input type=hidden name=\"" + TAG_BUNDLE_ID + "\" " +
         "value=\"" + id + "\">\n" +
         "<input type=submit value=\"Set\"> " +
         "<input type=reset> " +
         "[<a href=\"" + Activator.SERVLET_ALIAS +
         "\">Done</a>]\n" +
         "</form>\n");
   }

   private void displayHeader(ServletOutputStream out)
      throws ServletException, IOException
   {
      out.println("<HTML>\n" +
         "<HEAD>\n" +
         "<TITLE>Bundle Parameter Configuration</TITLE>\n" +
         "</HEAD>\n" +
         "<BODY BGCOLOR=white>\n" +
         "<h2>Bundle Parameter Configuration</h2>\n" +
         "<p>\n");
   }
```

```java
      private void displayFooter(ServletOutputStream out)
         throws ServletException, IOException
   {
      out.println("</BODY>\n" +
         "</HTML>");
   }
}
```

A.3.2.2 com/acme/admin/param/Activator.java

```java
package com.acme.admin.param;
import java.net.*;
import java.io.IOException;
import javax.servlet.*;
import javax.servlet.http.*;
import org.osgi.framework.*;
import org.osgi.service.http.*;
import com.acme.service.param.ParameterAdmin;

public class Activator implements BundleActivator {
   private HttpService http;
   final static String SERVLET_ALIAS = "/admin/parameters";

   public void start(BundleContext context) throws Exception   {
      ServiceReference ref = context.getServiceReference(
         "org.osgi.service.http.HttpService");
      http = (HttpService) context.getService(ref);
         AdminServlet servlet = new AdminServlet(context);
         http.registerServlet(SERVLET_ALIAS, servlet, null, null);
   }

   public void stop(BundleContext context) throws Exception {
      if (http != null) {
         http.unregister(SERVLET_ALIAS);
      }
   }
}
```

A.3.2.3 com/acme/admin/param/Manifest

```
Bundle-Activator: com.acme.admin.param.Activator
Import-Package: com.acme.service.param,
```

```
      org.osgi.service.http,
     javax.servlet, javax.servlet.http
Bundle-Name: The Administrative Bundle
Bundle-Description: This bundle can access and modify parameters for
    other bundles. It requires org.osgi.framework.AdminPermission, and
    provides a web user interface at http://<host>:8080/admin.
Bundle-Vendor: Acme Systems, Inc.
Bundle-Version: 1.0
Bundle-DocURL: http://www.acme.com/bundles/admin/index.html
Bundle-ContactAddress: support@acme.com
Import-Service: com.acme.service.param.ParameterAdmin
```

A.3.3 Facilitator

A.3.3.1 com/acme/admin/resolv/Facilitator.java

```java
package com.acme.admin.resolv;
import java.util.*;
import java.net.*;
import java.io.*;
import org.osgi.framework.*;

/**
 * This class performs recursive bundle resolution. It parses a
 * bundle's Import-Package manifest header and installs/activates
 * the bundles that export the needed packages.
 */
class Facilitator {
   private BundleContext context;
   /**
    * The map that encapsulates the knowledge of given a package,
    * which bundle exports that package, and at what version. It maps
    * a package name to the exporting bundle's location and the
    * package version.
    */
   private Properties packageExporterMap;
   // Flag a visited bundle to prevent following circular dependency
   // during recursion.
   private Hashtable visited = new Hashtable();
   // Identify the unsatisfied bundle when resolution fails.
   // maps an unresolved bundle to a vector of missing package names
```

```java
   private Hashtable unsatisfiedBundles = new Hashtable();

/**
 * The constructor. It reads the package exporter map from a
 * property file inside this bundle.
 */
Facilitator(BundleContext ctxt) throws IOException {
   this.context = ctxt;
   this.packageExporterMap = new Properties();
   String resourceName =
      "/com/acme/admin/resolv/package-exporters.map";
   InputStream in =
      this.getClass().getResourceAsStream(resourceName);
   packageExporterMap.load(in);
}

/**
 * Reset the internal state so that the resolution process can be
 * run anew.
 */
void reset() {
   visited.clear();
   unsatisfiedBundles.clear();
}

/**
 * Resolve a bundle. It follows this algorithm: (1) install the
 * bundle whose location is given, (2) parse the bundle's
 * Import-Package manifest header, (3) based on the packages it
 * needs to import, look up the package exporter map to find
 * out what additional bundles should be installed,
 * (4) recursively perform this sequence until all bundles are
 * resolved or a bundle cannot be resolved.
 *
 * @param urlstr the location string of the bundle to be resolved.
 * @return true if all bundles are resolved, false otherwise. If
 * not resolved, the unsatisfied bundle can be retrieved by
 * calling getUnsatisfiedBundle and the missing package name is
 * returned by getMissingPackage method.
 */
```

```java
boolean resolve(String urlstr) throws BundleException {
   if (urlstr == null)
      return false;
   if (visited.get(urlstr) != null) {
      // if a bundle is processed, don't run in circles
      return true;
   }
   Bundle b = context.installBundle(urlstr);
   // flag that the bundle is processed
   visited.put(urlstr, Boolean.TRUE);
   Dictionary headers = b.getHeaders();
   String imports = (String) headers.get("Import-Package");
   boolean r = true;
   if (imports != null) {
      String[] loc = findExporters(imports, b);
      for (int i=0; i<loc.length; i++) {
         r = r & resolve(loc[i]);
      }
   }
   if (r) {
      b.start();
   }
   return r;
}

/**
 * Return the names of the missing packages for the given bundle,
 * or null if all bundles are resolved.
 */
String[] getMissingPackages(Bundle b) {
   if (b == null)
      return null;
   Vector pkgsVec = (Vector) unsatisfiedBundles.get(b);
   String[] pkgs = null;
   if (pkgsVec != null && pkgsVec.size() > 0) {
      pkgs = new String[pkgsVec.size()];
      pkgsVec.copyInto(pkgs);
   }
   return pkgs;
}
```

```java
/**
 * Return the unsatisfied bundles, or an empty enumeration if
 * all bundles are resolved.
 */
Enumeration getUnsatisfiedBundles() {
   return unsatisfiedBundles.keys();
}

/**
 * Find the exporters for the packages needed by the given bundle.
 *
 * @param imports the value of the Import-Package header.
 * @param b the bundle that defines the Import-Package header.
 * @return the locations of the bundles that export the needed
 * package at the compatible versions.
 */
private String[] findExporters(String imports, Bundle b) {
   StringTokenizer st = new StringTokenizer(imports, ",");
   Vector missingPkgs = null;
   Vector v = new Vector(st.countTokens());
   while (st.hasMoreTokens()) {
      String token = st.nextToken().trim();
      int semicolonPos = token.indexOf(';');
      String pkgname = token;
      String importVersion = "";
      if (semicolonPos != -1) {
         pkgname = token.substring(0, semicolonPos).trim();
         int eqPos = token.indexOf('=', semicolonPos);
         importVersion = token.substring(eqPos + 1);
      }
      if (isFromClasspath(pkgname))
         continue;
      String loc = (String) packageExporterMap.get(pkgname);
      if (loc != null) {
         String exportVersion = "";
         int commaPos = loc.indexOf(',');
         if (commaPos != -1) {
            exportVersion = loc.substring(commaPos + 1);
            loc = loc.substring(0, commaPos);
         }
```

```
                    if (! areVersionsCompatible(importVersion,
                        exportVersion))
                    {
                        loc = null;
                    }
                }
                if (loc == null) {
                    if (missingPkgs == null)
                        missingPkgs = new Vector();
                    missingPkgs.addElement(pkgname);
                }
                v.addElement(loc);
            }
            String[] locations = new String[v.size()];
                v.copyInto(locations);
            if (missingPkgs != null)
                unsatisfiedBundles.put(b, missingPkgs);
            return locations;
        }

        /**
         * Check if a package is on the CLASSPATH.
         */
        private boolean isFromClasspath(String pkg) {
            URL u = ClassLoader.getSystemResource(pkg.replace('.','/')
                + "/");
            return u != null;
        }

        /**
         * Check if a package version for export is equal to or greater
         * than the version required for importing the same package.
         *
         * @param impVerStr the package version string required for
         * import.
         * @param expVerStr the package version string for export.
         * @return true if the check passes, false otherwise.
         */
        private boolean areVersionsCompatible(String impVerStr,
            String expVerStr)
        {
```

```
            StringTokenizer impst = new StringTokenizer(impVerStr, ".");
            StringTokenizer expst = new StringTokenizer(expVerStr, ".");
            try {
                while (impst.hasMoreTokens() && expst.hasMoreTokens()) {
                    int iv = Integer.parseInt(impst.nextToken().trim());
                    int ev = Integer.parseInt(expst.nextToken().trim());
                    if (ev < iv) {
                        // E.g., if import needs 1.4.5, export is 1.3.6,
                        // then import > export and no need to scan
                        // further because at the second component, 4 > 3
                        return false;
                    } else if (ev > iv) {
                        // E.g., if import needs 1.4.5, export is
                        // 1.5.1, then import < export and no need to scan
                        // further because at the second component, 4 < 5
                        return true;
                    }
                }
                if (impst.hasMoreTokens()) {
                    // E.g., if import needs 1.4.5, export is 1.4, then
                    // import > export
                    return false;
                }
            } catch (NumberFormatException e) {
                return false;
            }
            return true;
        }
    }
```

A.3.3.2 com/acme/admin/resolv/Activator.java

```
    package com.acme.admin.resolv;
    import java.net.*;
    import java.io.*;
    import java.util.*;
    import org.osgi.framework.*;

    public class Activator implements BundleActivator {
        private ServerThread server;

        public void start(BundleContext context) throws IOException {
```

```java
      server = new ServerThread(context);
      server.start();
   }

   public void stop(BundleContext context) throws IOException {
      server.terminate();
   }
}

class ServerThread extends Thread {
   private Facilitator facilitator;
   private ServerSocket ss;
   private boolean running = true;
   private Vector clientConnections = new Vector(16);

   ServerThread(BundleContext ctxt) throws IOException {
      this.ss = new ServerSocket(8082, 5);
      facilitator = new Facilitator(ctxt);
   }

   public void run() {
      try {
         while(running) {
            Socket s = ss.accept();
            if (!running) {
               // server is being shut down
               break;
            }
            // accept a client connection
            ConnectionThread conn = this.new ConnectionThread(s);
            clientConnections.addElement(conn);
            // start a thread to handle it
            conn.start();
         }
         ss.close();
         ss = null;
      } catch (IOException e) {
         System.out.println(e);
      }
   }
}
```

```
// terminate the server and clean up
void terminate() throws IOException {
   // terminate each client connection
   for (int i=0; i<clientConnections.size(); i++) {
      ConnectionThread conn = (ConnectionThread)
         clientConnections.elementAt(i);
      conn.terminate();
   }
   clientConnections.removeAllElements();
   running = false;
   // force the server socket to return from accept
    if (ss != null) {
       ss.close();
    }
}

class ConnectionThread extends Thread {
   private Socket socket;

   ConnectionThread(Socket s) {
      this.socket  = s;
   }

   public void run() {
      PrintWriter out = null;
      try {
         InputStream  is = socket.getInputStream();
         OutputStream os = socket.getOutputStream();
         BufferedReader in  =
            new BufferedReader(new InputStreamReader(is));
         out = new PrintWriter(os, true);
         out.print("\nBundle Resolution\n" +
            "\nEnter the bundle's URL: ");
         out.flush();
         // get command from remote host
         String url = in.readLine();
         facilitator.reset();
         if (facilitator.resolve(url)) {
            out.println("\nOK");
         } else {
```

APPENDIX A   CODE EXAMPLES

```
                Enumeration e =
                    facilitator.getUnsatisfiedBundles();
                while (e.hasMoreElements()) {
                    Bundle b = (Bundle) e.nextElement();
                    String[] pkgs =
                        facilitator.getMissingPackages(b);
                    out.println("Bundle " + b.getLocation() +
                        " needs the missing packages below:");
                    for (int i=0; i<pkgs.length; i++) {
                        out.println("   " + pkgs[i]);
                    }
                }
            }
            out.println();
        } catch (BundleException e) {
            out.println("\n" + e);
            Throwable t = e.getNestedException();
            if (t != null)
                out.println("Nested exception: " + t);
            out.println();
        } catch (IOException e) {
        } finally {
            try {
                if (socket != null)
                    socket.close();
            } catch(IOException e) {}
            clientConnections.removeElement(this);
        }
    }

    void terminate() throws IOException {
        // this will cause IOException to be raised from the
        // readLine call in the client thread
        socket.close();
        socket = null;
    }
} // ConnectionThread
}
```

A.3.3.3 com/acme/admin/resolv/package-exporters.map

```
org.osgi.service.http=file:jes_path/bundles/http.jar
javax.servlet=file:jes_path/bundles/servlet.jar, 2.1.1
javax.servlet.http=file:jes_path/bundles/servlet.jar, 2.1.1
org.osgi.service.log=file:jes_path/bundles/log.jar, 1.0
com.acme.service.param=file:/home/joe/bundles/param.jar
```

A.3.3.4 com/acme/admin/resolv/Manifest

```
Bundle-Activator: com.acme.admin.resolv.Activator
```

APPENDIX B

OSGi Service Gateway Specification

Release 1.0
May 2000

org.osgi.framework 323
    AdminPermission. 332
    Bundle 335
    BundleActivator. 350
    BundleContext 352
    BundleEvent. 369
    BundleException 373
    BundleListener. 375
    Configurable. 376
    FrameworkEvent 378
    FrameworkListener 381
    InvalidSyntaxException 382
    PackagePermission. 384
    ServiceEvent 388
    ServiceFactory 391
    ServiceListener. 393
    ServicePermission 395
    ServiceReference 399
    ServiceRegistration 401
org.osgi.service.device 404
    Device 406
    Driver. 408
    DriverLocator. 411

org.osgi.service.http 413
    HttpContext 417
    HttpService. 420
    NamespaceException 424

org.osgi.service.log 426
    LogEntry. 429
    LogListener 431
    LogReaderService 432
    LogService 434

Package
org.osgi.framework

Description

The OSGi Java Services Framework.

Welcome to the Open Service Gateway Initiative (OSGi) Framework API. This page gives an overview of what this framework is intended for and what the overall structure is.

The purpose of the framework is to provide a context for application developers to write code for small devices that are continuously running. In these environments applications are swapped in and out, they are updated on the fly and they must communicate in a structured and dependable way with other applications. Obviously this is quite different from normal applications that are started from a command line or mouse click.

The OSGi Framework takes advantage of the Java^{TM} programming language's ability to download code from the network. It provides a rich and structured development platform for component-based architectures.

Goals

The primary goal of the framework is to provide an environment that supports:

1. Dynamic load or update applications on the fly without stopping the environment.

2. Be able to use in limited memory devices

3. Offer a concise and consistent component programming model for application developers

4. Manage dependencies between applications

5. Scalable.

The OSGi framework provides a life-cycle management framework that permits application developers to partition applications into small self-installable applications. These applications are called bundles in this context. Devices running the framework can download bundles on demand and remove them when they are no longer required. A bundle, when installed can register any number of services to be shared with other bundles under control of the framework.

The OSGi Framework also supports application developers in coping with scalability issues. This support is critical, because the framework is designed to run in a variety of devices; the different hardware characteristics of the devices could affect the scale of the services that they are able to support. The framework supports the development and use of services of varying scale by decoupling a service's specification from its implementation. By splitting the implementation of a service from its specification (its Java interface):

- Developers of service implementations can implement the same interface
- Developers who use a service can code against that service's interface without regard to its implementation

For example, in a high-end device, a logging service might be able to store log messages on a hard drive, while on a disk-less device, the log entries may have to be saved remotely. The developers of the two logging service implementations implement the same interface; the developers of services that use a logging service write code against the logging service interface, without regard to which implementation their service might use. The framework can fully hide and manage the different implementations from the bundles that use the service.

Concepts

The OSGi Framework is a lightweight framework for creating extensible services using the Java programming language. To take best advantage of the framework, developers should design an application as a set of services, with each service implementing a segment of the overall functionality. These services and other extension services are then packaged in a "bundle" and downloaded on demand by the target device. For example, a text editing application designed this way could rely on a spell-checking service. The editor would instruct its framework to download a spell-checker for it to use. The framework provides mechanisms to support this paradigm that are simple to use and help with the practical aspects of writing extensible applications. The key entities of the framework are:

- Services—Objects that provide a collection of methods providing some service
- Bundles—The infrastructure for delivering code
- Bundle contexts—The execution environments of the bundles

Services

In the OSGi Framework model, an application is built around a set of cooperating services: it can extend itself at runtime by requesting the services it requires. The framework maintains a set of mappings from services to their implementations and has a powerful query mechanism that enables an installed bundle to request and use the available services. The framework manages dependencies between services and bundles. For example, when a bundle is stopped, all the services that it registered will be unregistered automatically.

A standard group like the OSGi or a private group of developers define a service as an interface and publish it. Any developer can now offer this service by implementing this standard interface. Other developers can now write code that uses this interface and obtain implementations via the framework.

The framework provides an API that the developer then uses to register the service. A service can be registered with an optional set of properties describing the service. This could for example be the name of manufacturer, version, interfaces, or author. Any bundle that now wants to use a service can specify a filter string that can be used to filter the service registry for available services. The framework can be asked to pick any service that fulfills the filter or it can return a list of services.

The framework hands out references to services. These references can be queried for properties and other meta information. A reference to a desired service can be used to obtain the service object which implements the service. The framework tracks the services that are being used by each bundle.

Bundles

To be available to the framework, a service implementation must be packaged. Service implementations are packaged into entities called bundles. A bundle is a JAR file that:

- Contains the resources implementing zero or more services. These resources may be class files for the Java programming language, as well as any other data (such as HTML help files, icons, and so on).

- States static dependencies on some other resources, such as Java packages. If any dependencies are stated, the framework takes the appropriate actions to make the required resource available.

- Manifest header describing which class should be used to start() or stop() a service.

By packing all these items together in a single JAR file, the framework can uniformly download and control a bundle.

To write a bundle, the developer must put a tag in the manifest that defines the name of a class that implements the `BundleActivator` interface. This interface has a start and stop method to start/stop the bundle. In the start method the bundle should wait until all its requirements are fulfilled and then start registering its services or fulfilling its task.

Bundle Manifest Headers

The framework recognizes special headers in the bundle's manifest. These headers and their values contain important information about how the bundle will operate in the framework. Additional headers can be defined by a bundle programmer as needed. Headers and their values of all manifest headers can be retrieved with `Bundle.getHeaders()` method.

The following headers in the bundle's manifest have special meaning to the framework.

`Bundle-Activator: class-name`

> If present, this header names the class in the bundle which implements the `BundleActivator` interface. This class will used when the bundle is started and stopped. `class-name` must be a fully qualified Java class name.

`Bundle-Name: string`

> If present, this header contains a human readable string which is the name of the bundle. This information is available at runtime using the bundle's `Bundle.getHeaders()` method. The name string is the value of the key "Bundle-Name."

`Bundle-Vendor: string`

> If present, this header contains a human readable string describing the vendor of the bundle. This information is available at runtime using the bundle's `Bundle.getHeaders()` method. The vendor string is the value of the key "Bundle-Vendor."

`Bundle-Version: string`

> If present, this header contains a human readable string which is the version of the bundle. This information is available at runtime using the bundle's `Bundle.getHeaders()` method. The version string is the value of the key "Bundle-Version."

`Bundle-Description: string`

If present, this header contains a human readable string describing the purpose or function of the bundle. This information is available at runtime using the bundle's `Bundle.getHeaders()` method. The description string is the value of the key "Bundle-Description."

`Bundle-DocURL: string`

If present, this header contains a human readable string which is a URL which contains further information about the bundle. This information is available at runtime using the bundle's `Bundle.getHeaders()` method. The doc URL string is the value of the key "Bundle-DocURL."

`Bundle-ContactAddress: string`

If present, this header contains a human readable string which is an e-mail address which can be contacted regarding the bundle. This information is available at runtime using the bundle's `Bundle.getHeaders()` method. The contact address string is the value of the key "Bundle-ContactAddress."

`Bundle-UpdateLocation: string`

If present, this header contains a location string that will be used to locate an updated version of the bundle when the bundle is updated using the `Bundle.update()` method. If this header is not present, the bundle will be updated from its original location. The location string will typically be a URL.

`Bundle-ClassPath: path (, path )*`

If present, this header describes the classpath within the bundle. A bundle's JAR file can contain other JAR files within it. So the Bundle-ClassPath is used to describe the search order for classes. `path` can be either *dot* ('.') which represents the bundle's JAR file or it can be the path of a JAR file contained in the bundle's JAR file. If Bundle-ClassPath is not specified, the default value is *dot*. If Bundle-ClassPath is specified, but *dot* is not an element of the path, then the bundle's main JAR file will not be searched. Only the contained JAR files referenced by the path elements will be searched.

`Export-Package: package-description (, package-description )*`

> If present, this header describes the packages which the bundle offers for share with other bundles. `package-description` has the following format
>
> `package-name (; specification-version=version-number )`
>
> `package-name` is the fully qualifed name of a Java package. `version-number` is the version number of the package as specified by Java™ Product Versioning Specification (`http://java.sun.com/products/jdk/1.2/docs/guide/versioning/spec/VersioningSpecification.html#PackageVersionSpecification`). Since multiple bundles may offer to share the same package, the framework will select the bundle offering to share the package at the highest version. The framework guarantees that only one bundle will be selected to share a given package name.
>
> A bundle which offers to export a package must also import that package. If the bundle's manifest does not have an Import-Package header for the same package name, the bundle will automatically import the package using the same `package-description` it has offered for export.

`Import-Package: package-description (, package-description )*`

> If present, this header describes the packages which the bundle requires. These packages must be exported by another bundle. See Export-Package for the definition of `package-description`. If no bundles export the required packages, then this bundle is not permitted to offer packages for export.
>
> Packages that are part of the Java platform, such as those package names starting with "java." should not be referenced in the Import-Package header. For all other packages required by the bundle, the package names of those packages should be specified in the Import-Package header.

`Export-Service: class-name (, class-name )*`

> If present, this header describes the services the bundle may register. This header provides advisory information that is not used by the framework. It is intended for use by server-side management tools.

`Import-Service: class-name (, class-name )*`

> If present, this header describes the services the bundle may use. This header provides advisory information that is not used by the framework. It is intended for use by server-side management tools.

Bundle-NativeCode: nativecode-clause (,nativecode-clause)*

If present, this header describes the files which contain the implementation of the native methods used by classes in the bundle. `nativecode-clause` has the following format

```
nativecode-clause: nativepaths ( ; env-parameter )*
nativepaths: nativepath ( ; nativepath )*
env-parameter: ( processordef | osnamedef | osversiondef | languagedef )
processordef: processor=token
osnamedef: osname=token
osversiondef: osversion=token
languagedef: language=token
```

`nativepath` is the path of a file in the bundle's JAR file containing native methods. The `env-parameters` are compared against property values provided by `BundleContext.getProperty()`.

- `processor` is compared against `org.osgi.framework.processor`.
- `osname` is compared against `org.osgi.framework.os.name`.
- `osversion` is compared against `org.osgi.framework.os.version`.
- `language` is compared against `org.osgi.framework.language`.

If a group of specified `env-parameters` match the property values, the framework will make the files specified by the `nativepaths` preceding the `env-parameters` available to be loaded by `System.loadLibrary`.

Care should be taken to select a unique name for the file containing the native methods. The framework will extract the selected files from the bundle into a location where `System.loadLibrary` can find them. This location will be shared by all bundles.

When the framework starts and stops

When the framework is started. The following actions occur:

1. Event handling is enabled. Events can now be delivered to listeners.
2. The Framework persistently records whether an installed bundle has been started or stopped. When the framework is restarted, all installed bundles previously recorded as being active will be automatically started as described in

the `Bundle.start` method. Reports any exceptions that occur during startup using `FrameworkEvents`.

3. A `FrameworkEvent` of type STARTED is broadcast.

When the framework is stopped. The following actions occur:

1. Suspend all active bundles as described in the `Bundle.stop` method except that their persistently recorded states remain to be ACTIVE. These bundles will be restarted when the framework is next started. Reports any exceptions that occur during stopping using `FrameworkEvents`.

2. Event handling is disabled.

Conformance Statement

Conforming implementations must not add any new methods or fields to any of the classes or interfaces defined in the OSGi specification (though, they may add them to subclasses, or classes that implement the interfaces), nor may they add any new classes or packages to the org.osgi package tree.

Class Summary

Interfaces

`Bundle`	A bundle installed in a framework.
`BundleActivator`	Customizes the starting and stopping of a bundle.
`BundleContext`	Bundle's execution context.
`BundleListener`	BundleEvent listener.
`Configurable`	Interface implemented by services which support a configuration object.
`FrameworkListener`	FrameworkEvent listener.
`ServiceFactory`	Service factories allow services to provide customized service objects.
`ServiceListener`	ServiceEvent listener.
`ServiceReference`	A reference to a service.
`ServiceRegistration`	A registered service.

Class Summary

Classes

AdminPermission	The AdminPermission indicates the caller's right to perform life-cycle operations on or to get sensitive information about a bundle.
BundleEvent	Bundle life cycle change event.
FrameworkEvent	General framework event.
PackagePermission	PackagePermission indicates a bundle's right to import or export a package.
ServiceEvent	Service life cycle change event.
ServicePermission	ServicePermission indicates a bundle's right to register or get a service.

Exceptions

BundleException	Exception from the framework to indicate a bundle life cycle problem occurred.
InvalidSyntaxException	Exception from the framework to indicate a filter string parameter has an invalid syntax and cannot be parsed.

org.osgi.framework
AdminPermission

Syntax

public final class AdminPermission extends java.security.BasicPermission

```
java.lang.Object
  |
  +--java.security.Permission
        |
        +--java.security.BasicPermission
              |
              +--org.osgi.framework.AdminPermission
```

All Implemented Interfaces: java.security.Guard, java.io.Serializable

Description

The AdminPermission indicates the caller's right to perform life-cycle operations on or to get sensitive information about a bundle.

AdminPermission has no actions or target.

The `hashCode()` method of AdminPermission is inherited from java.security.BasicPermission. The hash code it returns is the hash code of the name "AdminPermission," which is always the same for all instances of AdminPermission.

Member Summary

Constructors

public AdminPermission()
: Creates a new AdminPermission object.

public AdminPermission(String, String)
: Creates a new AdminPermission object.

Member Summary

Methods

public boolean	`equals(Object)`	Checks two AdminPermission objects for equality.
public boolean	`implies(Permission)`	Checks if the specified permission is "implied" by this object.
public PermissionCollection	`newPermissionCollection()`	Returns a new PermissionCollection object for storing AdminPermission objects.

Constructors

AdminPermission()

public **AdminPermission**()

Creates a new AdminPermission object. Its name is set to "AdminPermission."

AdminPermission(String, String)

public **AdminPermission**(java.lang.String name,
         java.lang.String actions)

Creates a new AdminPermission object. This constructor exists for use by the `Policy` object to instantiate new Permission objects.

Parameters:
 name—Ignored; always set to "AdminPermission."

 actions—Ignored.

Methods

equals(Object)

public boolean **equals**(java.lang.Object obj)

Checks two AdminPermission objects for equality. Two AdminPermission objects are always equal.

Overrides: java.security.BasicPermission.equals(java.lang.Object) in class java.security.BasicPermission

Parameters:
    obj—the object we are testing for equality with this object.

Returns: `true` if *obj* is an AdminPermission, `false` otherwise.

implies(Permission)

`public boolean implies(java.security.Permission p)`

Checks if the specified permission is "implied" by this object. This method returns `true` if the specified permission is an instance of `AdminPermission`, and `false` otherwise.

Overrides: java.security.BasicPermission.implies(java.security.Permission) in class java.security.BasicPermission

Parameters:
    p—the permission to check against.

Returns: `true` if the permission is an instance of this class, `false` otherwise.

newPermissionCollection()

`public java.security.PermissionCollection newPermissionCollection()`

Returns a new PermissionCollection object for storing AdminPermission objects.

Overrides: java.security.BasicPermission.newPermissionCollection() in class java.security.BasicPermission

Returns: a new PermissionCollection object suitable for storing AdminPermissions.

org.osgi.framework
Bundle

Syntax
```
public interface Bundle
```

Description
A bundle installed in a framework. The bundle is the access point to define the life cycle of the bundle. Each bundle installed in the framework will have an associated Bundle object.

A bundle will have a unique identity, a `long`, chosen by the framework. This identity will not change during the life cycle of a bundle, even when the bundle is updated. Uninstalling and then reinstalling will create a new identity.

The Bundle has six states: UNINSTALLED, INSTALLED, RESOLVED, STARTING, STOPPING, and ACTIVE. The values assigned to these states have no specified ordering. They represent bit values that may be ORed together for the purposes of determining if a bundle is in one of a set of states.

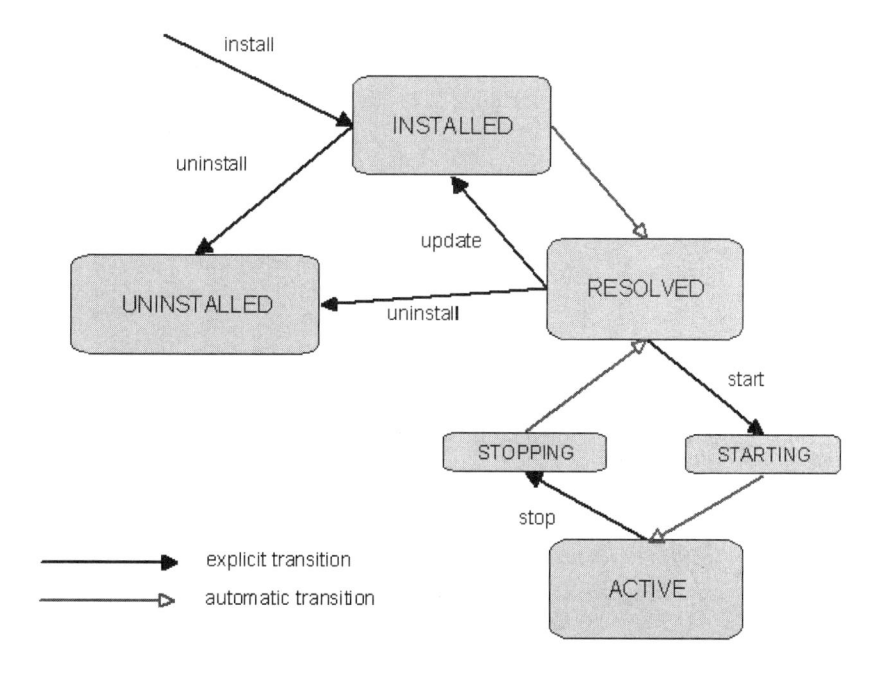

A bundle should only be executing code when its state is in { STARTING, ACTIVE, STOPPING }. An UNINSTALLED bundle can never go back to another state. It is a zombie and can only be reached because invalid references are kept somewhere. The framework is the only one that can create Bundle objects and these objects are only valid within the framework that created them.

Member Summary

Fields

    public static final ACTIVE
        Active state, the bundle is now running.

    public static final INSTALLED
        Installed state, the bundle is installed but not yet resolved.

    public static final RESOLVED
        Resolved state, the bundle is resolved and is able to be started.

    public static final STARTING
        Starting state, the bundle is in the process of starting.

    public static final STOPPING
        Stopping state, the bundle is in the process of stopping.

    public static final UNINSTALLED
        Uninstalled state, the bundle is uninstalled and may not be used.

Methods

    public long getBundleId()
        Retrieve the bundle's unique identifier, which the framework assigned to this bundle when it was installed.

    public Dictionary getHeaders()
        Return the bundle's manifest headers and values from the manifest's preliminary section.

    public String getLocation()
        Retrieve the location identifier of the bundle.

    public ServiceReference getRegisteredServices()
        Provides a list of ServiceReference s for the services registered by this bundle or null if the bundle has no registered services.

Member Summary

public ServiceReference	getServicesInUse() Provides a list of `ServiceReferences` for the services this bundle is using, or `null` if the bundle is not using any services.
public int	getState() Returns the current state of the bundle.
public boolean	hasPermission(Object) Determine whether the bundle has the requested permission.
public void	start() Start this bundle.
public void	stop() Stop this bundle.
public void	uninstall() Uninstall this bundle.
public void	update() Update this bundle.
public void	update(InputStream) Update this bundle from an InputStream.

Fields

ACTIVE

```
public static final int ACTIVE
```

Active state, the bundle is now running. The bundle is in the ACTIVE state when it has been successfully started.

The value of ACTIVE is 0x00000020.

INSTALLED

```
public static final int INSTALLED
```

Installed state, the bundle is installed but not yet resolved. The bundle is in the INSTALLED state when it has been installed in the framework but cannot run. This state is visible if the bundle's code dependencies are not resolved.

The framework may attempt to resolve an INSTALLED bundle's code dependencies and move the bundle to the RESOLVED state.

The value of INSTALLED is 0x00000002.

RESOLVED

`public static final int` **RESOLVED**

Resolved state, the bundle is resolved and is able to be started. The bundle is in the RESOLVED state when the framework has successfully resolved the bundle's code dependencies. These dependencies include:

- The bundle's class path from its `Bundle-ClassPath` manifest header.
- The bundle's native code from its `Bundle-NativeCode` manifest header.
- The bundle's package dependencies from its `Export-Package` and `Import-Package` manifest headers.

However, the bundle is not active yet. A bundle must be in the RESOLVED state before it can be started. The framework may attempt to resolve a bundle at any time.

The value of RESOLVED is 0x00000004.

STARTING

`public static final int` **STARTING**

Starting state, the bundle is in the process of starting. The bundle is in the STARTING state when the `start()` method is active. The bundle will be in this state when the bundle's `BundleActivator.start(BundleContext)` is called. If the `BundleActivator.start(BundleContext)` method completes without exception, the bundle has successfully started and will move to the ACTIVE state.

The value of STARTING is 0x00000008.

STOPPING

`public static final int` **STOPPING**

Stopping state, the bundle is in the process of stopping. The bundle is in the STOPPING state when the `stop()` method is active. The bundle will be in this state when the bundle's `BundleActivator.stop(BundleContext)` is called. When the `BundleActivator.stop(BundleContext)` method completes the bundle is stopped and will move to the RESOLVED state.

The value of STOPPING is 0x00000010.

UNINSTALLED

```
public static final int UNINSTALLED
```

Uninstalled state, the bundle is uninstalled and may not be used. The UNINSTALLED state is only be visible after a bundle is uninstalled. The bundle is in an unusable state and all references to the Bundle object should be released immediately.

The value of UNINSTALLED is 0x00000001.

Methods

getBundleId()

```
public long getBundleId()
```

Retrieve the bundle's unique identifier, which the framework assigned to this bundle when it was installed.

The unique identifier has the following attributes:

- It is unique and persistent.
- The identifier is a long.
- Once its value is assigned to a bundle, that value is not reused for another bundle, even after the bundle is uninstalled.
- Its value does not change as long as the bundle remains installed.
- Its value does not change when the bundle is updated

This method will continue to return the bundle's unique identifier when the bundle is in the UNINSTALLED state.

Returns: This bundle's unique identifier.

getHeaders()

```
public java.util.Dictionary getHeaders()
          throws java.lang.SecurityException
```

Return the bundle's manifest headers and values from the manifest's preliminary section. That is all the manifest's headers and values prior to the first blank line.

Manifest header names are case-insensitive. The methods of the returned `Dictionary` object will operate on header names in a case-insensitive manner.

For example, the following manifest headers and values are included if they are present in the manifest:

```
Bundle-Name
Bundle-Vendor
Bundle-Version
Bundle-Description
Bundle-DocURL
Bundle-ContactAddress
```

This method will continue to return this information when the bundle is in the UNINSTALLED state.

Returns: A `Dictionary` object containing the bundle's manifest headers and values.

Throws:
> `java.lang.SecurityException`—If the caller does not have the `AdminPermission` and the Java runtime environment supports permissions.

getLocation()

```
public java.lang.String getLocation()
        throws java.lang.SecurityException
```

Retrieve the location identifier of the bundle. This is typically the location passed to `BundleContext.installBundle(String)` when the bundle was installed. The location identifier of the bundle may change during bundle update. Calling this method while framework is updating the bundle results in undefined behavior.

This method will continue to return the bundle's location identifier when the bundle is in the UNINSTALLED state.

Returns: A string that is the location identifier of the bundle.

Throws:
> java.lang.SecurityException—If the caller does not have the AdminPermission and the Java runtime environment supports permissions.

getRegisteredServices()

> public ServiceReference[] **getRegisteredServices**()
>   throws java.lang.IllegalStateException

Provides a list of ServiceReference s for the services registered by this bundle or null if the bundle has no registered services.

If the Java runtime supports permissions, a ServiceReference to a service is included in the returned list if and only if the caller has the ServicePermission to "get" the service using at least one of the named classes the service was registered under.

The list is valid at the time of the call to this method, but the framework is a very dynamic environment and services can be modified or unregistered at anytime.

Returns: An array of ServiceReference or null.

Throws:
> java.lang.IllegalStateException—If the bundle has been uninstalled.

See Also: ServiceRegistration, ServiceReference

getServicesInUse()

> public ServiceReference[] **getServicesInUse**()
>   throws java.lang.IllegalStateException

Provides a list of ServiceReference s for the services this bundle is using, or null if the bundle is not using any services. A bundle is considered to be using a service if the bundle's use count for the service is greater than zero.

If the Java runtime supports permissions, a ServiceReference to a service is included in the returned list if and only if the caller has the ServicePermission to "get" the service using at least one of the named classes the service was registered under.

The list is valid at the time of the call to this method, but the framework is a very dynamic environment and services can be modified or unregistered at anytime.

Returns: An array of `ServiceReference` or `null`.

Throws:
   java.lang.IllegalStateException—If the bundle has been uninstalled.

See Also: `ServiceReference`

getState()

```
public int getState()
```

Returns the current state of the bundle. A bundle can only be in one state at any time.

Returns: element of {UNINSTALLED, INSTALLED, RESOLVED, STARTING, STOPPING, ACTIVE }

hasPermission(Object)

```
public boolean hasPermission(java.lang.Object permission)
        throws java.lang.IllegalStateException
```

Determine whether the bundle has the requested permission.

If the Java runtime environment does not support permissions this method always returns `true`. The permission parameter is of type `Object` to avoid referencing the `java.security.Permission` class directly. This is to allow the framework to be implemented in Java environments which do not support permissions.

Parameters:
   permission—The requested permission.

Returns: `true` if the bundle has the requested permission or the permissions possessed by the bundle imply the requested permission; `false` if the bundle does not have the permission or the permission parameter is not an `instanceof java.security.Permission`.

Throws:
   java.lang.IllegalStateException—If the bundle has been uninstalled.

start()

```
public void start()
          throws BundleException, java.lang.IllegalState-
          Exception, java.lang.SecurityException
```

Start this bundle.

The following steps are followed to start a bundle:

1. If the bundle is UNINSTALLED then an `IllegalStateException` is thrown.

2. If the bundle is STARTING or STOPPING then this method will wait for the bundle to change state before continuing. If this does not occur in a reasonable time, a `BundleException` is thrown to indicate the bundle was unable to be started.

3. If the bundle is ACTIVE then this method returns immediately.

4. If the bundle is not RESOLVED, an attempt is made to resolve the bundle. If the bundle cannot be resolved, a `BundleException` is thrown.

5. The state of the bundle is set to STARTING.

6. The `start(BundleContext)` method of the bundle's `BundleActivator`, if one is specified, is called. If the `BundleActivator` is invalid or throws an exception, the state of the bundle is set back to RESOLVED, the bundle's listeners, if any, are removed, service's registered by the bundle, if any, are unregistered, and service's used by the bundle, if any, are released. A `BundleException` is then thrown.

7. It is recorded that this bundle has been started, so that when the framework is restarted, this bundle will be automatically started.

8. The state of the bundle is set to ACTIVE.

9. A `BundleEvent` of type `BundleEvent.STARTED` is broadcast.

Preconditions
- getState() in { INSTALLED,RESOLVED }.

Postconditions, no exceptions thrown
- getState() in { ACTIVE }.

- `BundleActivator.start(BundleContext)` has been called and did not throw an exception.

Postconditions, when an exception is thrown
- getState() not in { STARTING, ACTIVE }.

Throws:
BundleException—If the bundle couldn't be started. This could be because a code dependency could not be resolved or the specified BundleActivator could not be loaded or threw an exception.

java.lang.IllegalStateException—If the bundle has been uninstalled or the bundle tries to change its own state.

java.lang.SecurityException—If the caller does not have the AdminPermission and the Java runtime environment supports permissions.

stop()

```
public void stop()
        throws BundleException, java.lang.IllegalState-
        Exception, java.lang.SecurityException
```

Stop this bundle. Any services registered by this bundle will be unregistered. Any services used by this bundle will be released. Any listeners registered by this bundle will be removed.

The following steps are followed to stop a bundle:

1. If the bundle is UNINSTALLED then an IllegalStateException is thrown.

2. If the bundle is STARTING or STOPPING then this method will wait for the bundle to change state before continuing. If this does not occur in a reasonable time, a BundleException is thrown to indicate the bundle was unable to be stopped.

3. If the bundle is not ACTIVE then this method returns immediately.

4. The state of the bundle is set to STOPPING.

5. It is recorded that this bundle has been stopped, so that when the framework is restarted, this bundle will not be automatically started.

6. The `stop(BundleContext)` method of the bundle's `BundleActivator`, if one is specified, is called. If the `BundleActivator` throws an exception, this method will continue to stop the bundle. A `BundleException` will be thrown after completion of the remaining steps.

7. The bundle's listeners, if any, are removed, service's registered by the bundle, if any, are unregistered, and service's used by the bundle, if any, are released.

8. The state of the bundle is set to RESOLVED.

9. A `BundleEvent` of type `BundleEvent.STOPPED` is broadcast.

Preconditions
- getState() in { ACTIVE }.

Postconditions, no exceptions thrown
- getState() not in { ACTIVE, STOPPING }.
- `BundleActivator.stop(BundleContext)` has been called and did not throw an exception.

Postconditions, when an exception is thrown
- None.

Throws:
BundleException—If the bundle's BundleActivator could not be loaded or threw an exception.

java.lang.IllegalStateException—If the bundle has been uninstalled or the bundle tries to change its own state.

java.lang.SecurityException—If the caller does not have the `AdminPermission` and the Java runtime environment supports permissions.

uninstall()

```
public void uninstall()
         throws BundleException, java.lang.IllegalState-
         Exception, java.lang.SecurityException
```

Uninstall this bundle.

This causes the framework to notify other bundles that this bundle is being uninstalled, and then to put this bundle into the UNINSTALLED state. The framework will remove any resources related to this bundle that it can.

If this bundle has been exporting any packages, the framework may either:

- continue to make all packages exported by this bundle available to the importing bundles until the framework is relaunched (at which time, the importing bundles will be bound to another bundle exporting a compatible package, or they will not be started); or

- remove all packages exported by this bundle, possibly stopping all importing bundles and putting them into the INSTALLED state until another bundle offering a compatible package for export has been selected by the framework.

The following steps are followed to uninstall a bundle:

1. If the bundle is UNINSTALLED then an IllegalStateException is thrown.

2. If the bundle is ACTIVE or STARTING, the bundle is stopped as described in the stop() method. If stop() throws an exception, a FrameworkEvent of type FrameworkEvent.ERROR is broadcast containing the exception.

3. A BundleEvent of type BundleEvent.UNINSTALLED is broadcast.

4. The state of the bundle is set to UNINSTALLED.

5. The bundle and the persistent storage area provided for the bundle by the framework, if any, is removed.

Preconditions
- getState() not in {UNINSTALLED }.

Postconditions, no exceptions thrown
- getState() in {UNINSTALLED }.
- The bundle has been uninstalled.

Postconditions, when an exception is thrown
- getState() not in {UNINSTALLED }.
- The bundle has not been uninstalled.

Throws:

BundleException—If the uninstall failed.

java.lang.IllegalStateException—If the bundle has been uninstalled or the bundle tries to change its own state.

java.lang.SecurityException—If the caller does not have the AdminPermission and the Java runtime environment supports permissions.

See Also: stop()

update()

```
public void update()
        throws BundleException, java.lang.IllegalState-
        Exception, java.lang.SecurityException
```

Update this bundle. If the bundle is ACTIVE, the bundle will be stopped before the update and started after the update successfully completes.

If the bundle that is being updated has exported any packages, it is the framework's responsibility to ensure that all bundles that are importing those packages (including the bundle that is exporting them) share the same version of the exported class files. In one implementation of the framework, updating a package may not have any effect on the importing bundles until the framework is restarted. Another framework implementation may choose to resolve all importing bundles against the updated class files, by possibly stopping and restarting them.

The following steps are followed to update a bundle:

1. If the bundle is UNINSTALLED then an IllegalStateException is thrown.

2. If the bundle is ACTIVE or STARTING, the bundle is stopped as described in the stop() method. If stop() throws an exception, the exception is rethrown terminating the update.

3. The location for the new version of the bundle is determined from either the manifest header Bundle-UpdateLocation if available or the original location.

4. The location is interpreted in an implementation dependent way (typically as a URL) and the new version of the bundle is obtained from the location.

5. The new version of the bundle is installed. If the framework is unable to install the new version of the bundle, the original version of the bundle will be restored and a BundleException will be thrown after completion of the remaining steps.

6. The state of the bundle is set to INSTALLED.

7. If the new version of the bundle was successfully installed, a BundleEvent of type BundleEvent.UPDATED is broadcast.

8. If the bundle was originally ACTIVE, the updated bundle is started as described in the start() method. If start() throws an exception, a FrameworkEvent of type FrameworkEvent.ERROR is broadcast containing the exception.

Preconditions
- getState() not in { UNINSTALLED }.

Postconditions, no exceptions thrown
- getState() in { INSTALLED,RESOLVED,ACTIVE }.
- The bundle has been updated.

Postconditions, when an exception is thrown
- getState() in { INSTALLED,RESOLVED,ACTIVE }.
- Original bundle is still used, no update took place.

Throws:
BundleException—If the update fails.

java.lang.IllegalStateException—If the bundle has been uninstalled or the bundle tries to change its own state.

java.lang.SecurityException—If the caller does not have the AdminPermission and the Java runtime environment supports permissions.

See Also: stop(), start()

update(InputStream)

```
public void update(java.io.InputStream in)
```

Update this bundle from an InputStream.

This method performs all the steps listed in update(), except the bundle will be read in through the supplied InputStream, rather than a URL.

This method will always close the InputStream when it is done, even if an exception is thrown.

Parameters:
    in—The InputStream from which to read the new bundle.

Throws:
    BundleException

See Also: update()

org.osgi.framework
BundleActivator

Syntax
`public interface BundleActivator`

Description
Customizes the starting and stopping of a bundle. BundleActivator is an interface that may be implemented by a bundle programmer that is called when the bundle is started or stopped. A bundle can only specify a single BundleActivator in the manifest.

When a bundle is started or stopped, the BundleActivator is called.

The framework can create instances of the bundle's BundleActivator as required. It is guaranteed, however, that if an instance's `start(BundleContext)` method executes successfully, that same instance's `stop(BundleContext)` method will be called when the bundle is to be stopped.

A bundle programmer specifies the BundleActivator through the `Bundle-Activator` Manifest header. The form of the header is:

`Bundle-Activator: class-name`

where `class-name` is a fully qualified Java classname. The specified BundleActivator class must have a public constructor that takes no parameters so that a BundleActivator object can be created by `Class.newInstance()`.

Member Summary

Methods

`public void start(BundleContext)`
Called when the bundle is started so that the bundle can perform any bundle specific activities to start the bundle.

`public void stop(BundleContext)`
Called when the bundle is stopped so that the bundle can perform any bundle specific activities necessary to stop the bundle.

Methods

start(BundleContext)

```
public void start(BundleContext context)
        throws java.lang.Exception
```

Called when the bundle is started so that the bundle can perform any bundle specific activities to start the bundle. Bundle programmers can use this method to register the bundle's services or to allocate any resources that the bundle needs.

This method must complete and return to its caller in a timely manner.

Parameters:
context—The execution context of the bundle being started.

Throws:
java.lang.Exception—If this method throws an exception, the bundle is marked as stopped and the framework will remove the bundle's listeners, unregister all service's registered by the bundle, release all service's used by the bundle.

See Also: Bundle.start()

stop(BundleContext)

```
public void stop(BundleContext context)
        throws java.lang.Exception
```

Called when the bundle is stopped so that the bundle can perform any bundle specific activities necessary to stop the bundle. In general, this method should undo the work that the start(BundleContext) method did. When this method returns the bundle should have no active threads. A stopped bundle should be stopped and should not be calling any framework objects.

This method must complete and return to its caller in a timely manner.

Parameters:
context—The execution context of the bundle being stopped.

Throws:
java.lang.Exception—If this method throws an exception, the bundle is still marked as stopped and the framework will remove the bundle's listeners, unregister all service's registered by the bundle, release all service's used by the bundle.

See Also: Bundle.stop()

org.osgi.framework
BundleContext

Syntax
public interface BundleContext

Description
Bundle's execution context. Represents the execution context of a bundle within the framework. The context provides methods which allow the bundle to interact with the framework.

The provided methods allow a bundle to:

- Subscribe to the events published by the framework.
- Register services in the framework's service registry.
- Retrieve references to service from the framework's service registry.
- Get and release the service objects for a referenced service.
- Install new bundles into the framework.
- Get the list of installed bundles.
- Get the Bundle object for a bundle.
- Create File objects for files in a persistent storage area provided for the bundle by the framework.

A BundleContext object will be created and provided to the bundle when the bundle is started (BundleActivator.start(BundleContext)). The same BundleContext object will be passed to the bundle when the bundle is stopped (BundleActivator.stop(BundleContext)). The context is for the private use of the bundle and, in general, is not meant to be shared with other bundles. The context is used when accounting for services and event listeners.

The BundleContext object is only valid during an execution instance of the bundle. That is during the period from when the bundle is called at BundleActivator.start(BundleContext) until after the bundle is called and returns from BundleActivator.stop(BundleContext) (or BundleActivator.start (BundleContext) terminates with an exception). If the context object is used after this, an `IllegalStateException` may be thrown. When the bundle is next restarted, a new BundleContext object will be created.

The framework is the only one that can create BundleContext objects and these objects are only valid within the framework that created them.

Note: A single virtual machine may host multiple framework instances at any given time, but objects created by one framework instance cannot be used by bundles running in the execution context of another framework instance.

Member Summary

Methods

public void	addBundleListener(BundleListener) Add a bundle listener.
public void	addFrameworkListener(FrameworkListener) Add a general framework listener.
public void	addServiceListener(ServiceListener) Add a service listener.
public void	addServiceListener(ServiceListener, String) Add a service listener with a filter.
public Bundle	getBundle() Retrieve the Bundle object for the context bundle.
public Bundle	getBundle(long) Retrieve the bundle that has the given unique identifier.
public Bundle	getBundles() Retrieve a list of all installed bundles.
public File	getDataFile(String) Creates a `File` object for a file in the persistent storage area provided for the bundle by the framework.
public String	getProperty(String) Retrieve the value of the named environment property.
public Object	getService(ServiceReference) Get a service's service object.
public ServiceReference	getServiceReference(String) Get a service reference.

Member Summary

public ServiceReference	getServiceReferences(String, String) Get a list of service references.
public Bundle	installBundle(String) Install a bundle from a location.
public Bundle	installBundle(String, InputStream) Install a bundle from an InputStream.
public ServiceRegistration	registerService(String[], Object, Dictionary) Register a service with multiple names.
public ServiceRegistration	registerService(String, Object, Dictionary) Register a service with a single name.
public void	removeBundleListener(BundleListener) Remove a bundle listener.
public void	removeFrameworkListener(FrameworkListener) Remove a framework listener.
public void	removeServiceListener(ServiceListener) Remove a service listener.
public boolean	ungetService(ServiceReference) Unget a service's service object.

Methods

addBundleListener(BundleListener)

```
public void addBundleListener(BundleListener listener)
         throws java.lang.IllegalStateException
```

Add a bundle listener. BundleListener s are notified when a bundle has a life cycle state change. The listener is added to the context bundle's list of listeners. See getBundle() for a definition of context bundle.

Parameters:
listener—The bundle listener to add.

Throws:
> java.lang.IllegalStateException—If the context bundle has stopped.

See Also: BundleEvent, BundleListener

addFrameworkListener(FrameworkListener)

```
public void addFrameworkListener(FrameworkListener listener)
        throws java.lang.IllegalStateException
```

Add a general framework listener. FrameworkListener s are notified of general framework events. The listener is added to the context bundle's list of listeners. See getBundle() for a definition of context bundle.

Parameters:
> listener—The framework listener to add.

Throws:
> java.lang.IllegalStateException—If the context bundle has stopped.

See Also: FrameworkEvent, FrameworkListener

addServiceListener(ServiceListener)

```
public void addServiceListener(ServiceListener listener)
```

Add a service listener.

This method is the same as calling addServiceListener(ServiceListener, String) with filter set to null.

See Also: addServiceListener(ServiceListener, String)

addServiceListener(ServiceListener, String)

```
public void addServiceListener(ServiceListener listener,
            java.lang.String filter)
      throws InvalidSyntaxException, java.lang.IllegalState-
      Exception
```

Add a service listener with a filter. `ServiceListener`s are notified when a service has a life cycle state change. See `getServiceReferences(String, String)` for a description of the filter syntax. The listener is added to the context bundle's list of listeners. See `getBundle()` for a definition of context bundle.

The listener is called if the filter criteria is met. To filter based upon the class of the service, the filter should reference the "objectClass" property. If the filter parameter is `null`, all services are considered to match the filter.

If the Java runtime environment supports permissions, the service listener will be notified of a service event only if the bundle that is registering it has the `ServicePermission` to `get` the service using at least one of the named classes the service was registered under.

Parameters:
　listener—The service listener to add.

　filter—The filter criteria.

Throws:
　InvalidSyntaxException—If the filter parameter contains an invalid filter string which cannot be parsed.

　java.lang.IllegalStateException—If the context bundle has stopped.

See Also: `ServiceEvent, ServiceListener`

getBundle()

```
public Bundle getBundle()
      throws java.lang.IllegalStateException
```

Retrieve the Bundle object for the context bundle.

The context bundle is defined as the bundle which is associated with this BundleContext. More specifically, the context bundle is defined to be the bundle which was given this BundleContext in its `BundleActivator`.

Returns: The context bundle's `Bundle` object.

OSGI SERVICE GATEWAY SPECIFICATION

Throws:
> java.lang.IllegalStateException—If the context bundle has stopped.

getBundle(long)

> public Bundle **getBundle**(long id)

Retrieve the bundle that has the given unique identifier.

Parameters:
> id—The identifier of the bundle to retrieve.

Returns: A Bundle object, or null if the identifier doesn't match any installed bundle.

getBundles()

> public Bundle[] **getBundles**()

Retrieve a list of all installed bundles. The list is valid at the time of the call to getBundles, but the framework is a very dynamic environment and bundles can be installed or uninstalled at anytime.

Returns: An array of Bundle objects, one object per installed bundle.

getDataFile(String)

> public java.io.File **getDataFile**(java.lang.String filename)
>   throws java.lang.IllegalStateException

Creates a File object for a file in the persistent storage area provided for the bundle by the framework. If the platform does not have file system support, this method will return null.

A File object for the base directory of the persistent storage area provided for the context bundle by the framework can be obtained by calling this method with the empty string ("") as the parameter. See getBundle() for a definition of context bundle.

If the Java runtime environment supports permissions, the framework will ensure that the bundle has the java.io.FilePermission with actions "read","write","execute","delete" for all files (recursively) in the persistent storage area provided for the context bundle by the framework.

Parameters:
> filename—A relative name to the file to be accessed.

Returns: A `File` object that represents the requested file or `null` if the platform does not have file system support.

Throws:

`java.lang.IllegalStateException`—If the context bundle has stopped.

getProperty(String)

```
public java.lang.String getProperty(java.lang.String key)
```

Retrieve the value of the named environment property. Values are provided for the following properties:

`org.osgi.framework.version`

The version of the framework.

`org.osgi.framework.vendor`

The vendor of this framework implementation.

`org.osgi.framework.language`

The language being used. See ISO 639 for possible values.

`org.osgi.framework.os.name`

The name of the operating system of the hosting computer.

`org.osgi.framework.os.version`

The version number of the operating system of the hosting computer.

`org.osgi.framework.processor`

The name of the processor of the hosting computer.

Note: These last four properties are used by the `Bundle-NativeCode` manifest header's matching algorithm for selecting native code.

Parameters:

key—The name of the requested property.

Returns: The value of the requested property, or `null` if the property is undefined.

getService(ServiceReference)

```
public java.lang.Object getService(ServiceReference reference)
         throws java.lang.SecurityException, java.lang.Illegal-
     StateException
```

Get a service's service object. Retrieves the service object for a service. A bundle's use of a service is tracked by a use count. Each time a service's service object is returned by `getService(ServiceReference)`, the context bundle's use count for the service is incremented by one. Each time the service is release by `ungetService(ServiceReference)`, the context bundle's use count for the service is decremented by one. When a bundle's use count for a service drops to zero, the bundle should no longer use the service. See `getBundle()` for a definition of context bundle.

This method will always return `null` when the service associated with this reference has been unregistered.

The following steps are followed to get the service object:

1. If the service has been unregistered, `null` is returned.

2. The context bundle's use count for this service is incremented by one.

3. If the context bundle's use count for the service is now one and the service was registered with a `ServiceFactory`, the `ServiceFactory.getService(Bundle, ServiceRegistration)` method is called to create a service object for the context bundle. This service object is cached by the framework. While the context bundle's use count for the service is greater than zero, subsequent calls to get the services's service object for the context bundle will return the cached service object.
   If the service object returned by the `ServiceFactory` is not an `instanceof` all the classes named when the service was registered or the `ServiceFactory` throws an exception, `null` is returned and a `FrameworkEvent` of type `FrameworkEvent.ERROR` is broadcast.

4. The service object for the service is returned.

Parameters:
reference—A reference to the service whose service object is desired.

Returns: A service object for the service associated with this reference, or `null` if the service is not registered.

Throws:
`java.lang.SecurityException`—If the caller does not have the `ServicePermission` to "get" the service using at least one of the named classes the service was registered under and the Java runtime environment supports permissions.

java.lang.IllegalStateException—If the context bundle has stopped.

See Also: ungetService(ServiceReference), ServiceFactory

getServiceReference(String)

```
public ServiceReference getServiceReference(java.lang.String
        clazz)
```

Get a service reference. Retrieves a ServiceReference for a service which implements the named class.

This reference is valid at the time of the call to this method, but since the framework is a very dynamic environment, services can be modified or unregistered at anytime.

This method is provided as a convenience for when the caller is interested in any service which implements a named class. This method is the same as calling getServiceReferences(String, String) with a null filter string but only a single ServiceReference is returned.

Parameters:
   clazz—The class name with which the service was registered.

Returns: A ServiceReference object, or null if no services are registered which implement the named class.

See Also: getServiceReferences(String, String)

getServiceReferences(String, String)

```
public ServiceReference[] getServiceReferences(java.lang.String
        clazz, java.lang.String filter)
    throws InvalidSyntaxException
```

Get a list of service references. Retrieves a list of ServiceReference s for services which implement and were registered under the named class and match the filter criteria.

The list is valid at the time of the call to this method, but the framework is a very dynamic environment and services can be modified or unregistered at anytime.

The filter parameter is used to select registered service whose properties objects contain keys and values which satisfy the filter. The syntax of the filter parameter is the string representation of LDAP search filters as defined in RFC 1960: A String Representation of LDAP Search Filters (http://www.ietf.org/

rfc/rfc1960.txt). It should be noted that RFC 2254: A String Representation of LDAP Search Filters (http://www.ietf.org/rfc/rfc2254.txt) supersedes RFC 1960 but only adds extensible matching and is not applicable for this API.

The string representation of an LDAP search filter is defined by the following grammar. It uses a prefix format.

```
<filter> ::= '(' <filtercomp> ')'
<filtercomp> ::= <and> | <or> | <not> | <item>
<and> ::= '&' <filterlist>
<or> ::= '|' <filterlist>
<not> ::= '!' <filter>
<filterlist> ::= <filter> | <filter> <filterlist>
<item> ::= <simple> | <present> | <substring>
<simple> ::= <attr> <filtertype> <value>
<filtertype> ::= <equal> | <approx> | <greater> | <less>
<equal> ::= '='
<approx> ::= '~='
<greater> ::= '>='
<less> ::= '<='
<present> ::= <attr> '=*'
<substring> ::= <attr> '=' <initial> <any> <final>
<initial> ::= NULL | <value>
<any> ::= '*' <starval>
<starval> ::= NULL | <value> '*' <starval>
<final> ::= NULL | <value>
```

<attr> is a string representing an attributte, or key, in the properties objects of the registered services. Attribute names are not case sensitive; that is cn and CN both refer to the same attribute. <value> is a string representing the value, or part of one, of a key in the properties objects of the registered services. If a <value> must contain one of the characters '*' or '(' or ')', these characters should be escaped by preceding them with the backslash '\' character. Note that although both the <substring> and <present> productions can produce the 'attr=*' construct, this construct is used only to denote a presence filter.

Examples of LDAP filters are:

```
(cn=Babs Jensen)
(!(cn=Tim Howes))
```

```
(&(objectClass=Person)(|(sn=Jensen)(cn=Babs J*)))
(o=univ*of*mich*)
```

If the filter parameter is `null`, all registered services are considered to match the filter.

If the filter cannot be parsed, an `InvalidSyntaxException` will be thrown with a human readable message where the filter became unparsable.

The approximate match (~=) is implementation specific but should at least ignore case and white space differences. Optional are codes like soundex or other smart "closeness" comparisons.

Comparison of values is not straightforward. Strings are compared differently than numbers and it is possible for a key to have multiple values. Note that that keys in the properties object must always be strings. The comparison is defined by the object type of the key's value. The following rules apply for comparison:

Property Value Type	Comparison Type
String	String comparison
Integer, Long, Float, Double, Byte, Short, BigInteger, BigDecimal	numerical comparison
Character	character comparison
Boolean	equality comparisons only
[] (array)	recursively applied to values
Vector	recursively applied to elements

Note: arrays of primitives are also supported.

A filter matches a property that has multiple values if it matches at least one of those values. For example,

```
Properties p = new Properties();
p.put( "cn", new String[] { "a", "b", "c" } );
```

p will match (cn=a) and also (cn=b)

A filter with unrecognizable data types will be evaluated to be `false`.

The following steps are followed to select a service:

1. If the Java runtime environment supports permissions, the caller is checked for the `ServicePermission` to "get" the service with the named class. If the caller does not have the permission, `null` is returned.

2. If the filter string is not `null`, the filter string is parsed and the set of registered services which satisfy the filter is produced. If the filter string is `null`, then all registered services are considered to satisfy the filter.

3. If the `clazz` parameter is not `null`, the set is further reduced to those services which are an `instanceof` and were registered under the named class.

4. An array of `ServiceReference` to the selected services is returned.

Parameters:
    `clazz`—The class name with which the service was registered, or `null` for all services.

    `filter`—The filter criteria.

Returns: An array of `ServiceReference` objects, or `null` if no services are registered which satisfy the search.

Throws:
    `InvalidSyntaxException`—If the filter parameter contains an invalid filter string which cannot be parsed.

installBundle(String)

```
public Bundle installBundle(java.lang.String location)
        throws BundleException, java.lang.SecurityException
```

Install a bundle from a location. The bundle is obtained from the location parameter as interpreted by the framework in an implementation dependent way. Typically, location will most likely be a URL.

The following steps are followed to install a bundle:

1. If a bundle having the same location is already installed, the `Bundle` object for that bundle is returned.

2. The bundle's content is read from the location. If this fails, a `BundleException` is thrown.

3. The bundle's associated resources are allocated. The associated resources consist of at least a unique identifier and a persistent storage area, if the platform has file system support. If this step fails, a `BundleException` is thrown.

4. The state of the bundle is set to `INSTALLED`.

5. A `BundleEvent` of type `BundleEvent.INSTALLED` is broadcast.

6. The `Bundle` object for the newly installed bundle is returned.

Postconditions, no exceptions thrown
- `getState()` in { `INSTALLED`, `RESOLVED` }.
- Bundle has a unique id.

Postconditions, when an exception is thrown
- Bundle is not installed and no trace of the bundle exists.

Parameters:
    `location`—The location identifier of the bundle to install.

Returns: The `Bundle` object of the installed bundle.

Throws:
    `BundleException`—If the install failed.

    `java.lang.SecurityException`—If the caller does not have the `AdminPermission` and the Java runtime environment supports permissions.

installBundle(String, InputStream)

```
public Bundle installBundle(java.lang.String location,
          java.io.InputStream in)
    throws BundleException
```

Install a bundle from an InputStream.

This method performs all the steps listed in `installBundle(String)`, except the bundle's content will be read from the InputStream. The location identifier specified will be used as the identity of the bundle.

This method will always close the InputStream, even if an exception is thrown.

Parameters:
    `location`—The location identifier of the bundle to install.

    `in`—The InputStream from which the bundle will be read.

Returns: The `Bundle` of the installed bundle.

Throws:
    `BundleException`—If the provided stream cannot be read.

See Also: installBundle(String)

registerService(String[], Object, Dictionary)

```
public ServiceRegistration registerService(java.lang.String[]
        clazzes, java.lang.Object service,
        java.util.Dictionary properties)
        throws java.lang.IllegalArgumentException, java.lang
        .SecurityException, java.lang.IllegalStateException
```

Register a service with multiple names. This method registers the given service object with the given properties under the given class names. A ServiceRegistration object is returned. The ServiceRegistration object is for the private use of the bundle registering the service and should not be shared with other bundles. The registering bundle is defined to be the context bundle. See getBundle() for a definition of context bundle. Other bundles can locate the service by using either the getServiceReferences(String, String) or getServiceReference(String) method.

A bundle can register a service object that implements the ServiceFactory interface to have more flexiblity in providing service objects to different bundles.

The following steps are followed to register a service:

1. If the service parameter is not a ServiceFactory, an IllegalArgumentException is thrown if the service parameter is not an instanceof all the classes named.

2. The service is added to the framework's service registry and may now be used by other bundles.

3. A ServiceEvent of type ServiceEvent.REGISTERED is synchronously sent.

4. A ServiceRegistration object for this registration is returned.

Parameters:
clazzes—The class names under which the service can be located. The class names in this array will be stored in the service's properties under the key "objectClass."

service—The service object or a ServiceFactory object.

properties—The properties for this service. The keys in the properties object must all be Strings. Changes should not be made to this object after calling this method. To update the service's properties call the `ServiceRegistration.setProperties(Dictionary)` method. This parameter may be `null` if the service has no properties.

Returns: A `ServiceRegistration` object for use by the bundle registering the service to update the service's properties or to unregister the service.

Throws:

`java.lang.IllegalArgumentException`—If one of the following is true:

- The service parameter is null.

- The service parameter is not a `ServiceFactory` and is not an `instanceof` all the named classes in the clazzes parameter.

  `java.lang.SecurityException`—If the caller does not have the `ServicePermission` to "register" the service for all the named classes and the Java runtime environment supports permissions.

  `java.lang.IllegalStateException`—If the context bundle has stopped.

See Also: `ServiceRegistration`, `ServiceFactory`

registerService(String, Object, Dictionary)

```
public ServiceRegistration registerService(java.lang.String clazz,
        java.lang.Object service,
        java.util.Dictionary properties)
```

Register a service with a single name. This method registers the given service object with the given properties under the given class name.

This method is otherwise identical to `registerService(String[], Object, Dictionary)` and is provided as a convenience when the service parameter will only be registered under a single class name.

See Also: `registerService(String[], Object, Dictionary)`

removeBundleListener(BundleListener)

```
public void removeBundleListener(BundleListener listener)
        throws java.lang.IllegalStateException
```

Remove a bundle listener. The listener is removed from the context bundle's list of listeners. See `getBundle()` for a definition of context bundle.

If this method is called with a listener which is not registered, then this method does nothing.

Parameters:
>listener—The bundle listener to remove.

Throws:
>java.lang.IllegalStateException—If the context bundle has stopped.

removeFrameworkListener(FrameworkListener)

>public void **removeFrameworkListener**(FrameworkListener listener)
>   throws java.lang.IllegalStateException

Remove a framework listener. The listener is removed from the context bundle's list of listeners. See getBundle() for a definition of context bundle.

If this method is called with a listener which is not registered, then this method does nothing.

Parameters:
>listener—The framework listener to remove.

Throws:
>java.lang.IllegalStateException—If the context bundle has stopped.

removeServiceListener(ServiceListener)

>public void **removeServiceListener**(ServiceListener listener)
>   throws java.lang.IllegalStateException

Remove a service listener. The listener is removed from the context bundle's list of listeners. See getBundle() for a definition of context bundle.

If this method is called with a listener which is not registered, then this method does nothing.

Parameters:
>listener—The service listener to remove.

Throws:
>java.lang.IllegalStateException—If the context bundle has stopped.

ungetService(ServiceReference)

```
public boolean ungetService(ServiceReference reference)
        throws java.lang.IllegalStateException
```

Unget a service's service object. Releases the service object for a service. If the context bundle's use count for the service is zero, this method returns `false`. Otherwise, the context bundle's use count for the service is decremented by one. See `getBundle()` for a definition of context bundle.

The service's service object should no longer be used and all references to it should be destroyed when a bundle's use count for the service drops to zero.

The following steps are followed to unget the service object:

1. If the context bundle's use count for the service is zero or the service has been unregistered, `false` is returned.

2. The context bundle's use count for this service is decremented by one.

3. If the context bundle's use count for the service is now zero and the service was registered with a `ServiceFactory`, the `ServiceFactory.ungetService (Bundle, ServiceRegistration, Object)` method is called to release the service object for the context bundle.

4. `true` is returned.

Parameters:
    `reference`—A reference to the service to be released.

Returns: `false` if the context bundle's use count for the service is zero or if the service has been unregistered, otherwise `true`.

Throws:
    `java.lang.IllegalStateException`—If the context bundle has stopped.

See Also: `getService(ServiceReference)`, `ServiceFactory`

org.osgi.framework
BundleEvent

Syntax
```
public class BundleEvent extends java.util.EventObject
```

```
java.lang.Object
  |
  +--java.util.EventObject
         |
         +--org.osgi.framework.BundleEvent
```

All Implemented Interfaces:
java.io.Serializable

Description
Bundle life cycle change event. BundleEvents are delivered to `BundleListener` s when a change occurs in the bundle's life cycle. A type code is used to identify the event for future extendability.

OSGi reserves the right to extend the set of types in the future.

Member Summary

Fields

```
public static final  INSTALLED
```
A bundle has been installed.

```
public static final  STARTED
```
A bundle has been started.

```
public static final  STOPPED
```
A bundle has been stopped.

```
public static final  UNINSTALLED
```
A bundle has been uninstalled.

```
public static final  UPDATED
```
A bundle has been updated.

Member Summary

Constructors

>   public BundleEvent(int, Bundle)
>   Construct a bundle event.

Methods

>   public Bundle getBundle()
>   Retrieve the bundle who had a change occur in its life cycle.

>   public int getType()
>   Retrieve the type of this event.

Fields

INSTALLED

public static final int **INSTALLED**

A bundle has been installed.

The value of INSTALLED is 0x00000001.

See Also: BundleContext.installBundle(String)

STARTED

public static final int **STARTED**

A bundle has been started.

The value of STARTED is 0x00000002.

See Also: Bundle.start()

STOPPED

public static final int **STOPPED**

A bundle has been stopped.

The value of STOPPED is 0x00000004.

See Also: Bundle.stop()

UNINSTALLED

   public static final int **UNINSTALLED**

   A bundle has been uninstalled.

   The value of UNINSTALLED is 0x00000010.

   See Also: Bundle.uninstall()

UPDATED

   public static final int **UPDATED**

   A bundle has been updated.

   The value of UPDATED is 0x00000008.

   See Also: Bundle.update()

Constructors

BundleEvent(int, Bundle)

   public **BundleEvent**(int type, Bundle bundle)

   Construct a bundle event.

   Parameters:
   type—The event type.

   bundle—The bundle who had a change occur in its life cycle.

Methods

getBundle()

   public Bundle **getBundle**()

   Retrieve the bundle who had a change occur in its life cycle. This bundle is the source of the event.

   Returns: The bundle who had a change occur in its life cycle.

getType()

   public int **getType**()

Retrieve the type of this event. The type values are INSTALLED, STARTED, STOPPED, UPDATED, UNINSTALLED.

Returns: The type of bundle life cycle change.

org.osgi.framework
BundleException

Syntax
```
public class BundleException extends java.lang.Exception

java.lang.Object
  |
  +--java.lang.Throwable
        |
        +--java.lang.Exception
              |
              +--org.osgi.framework.BundleException
```

All Implemented Interfaces:
java.io.Serializable

Description
Exception from the framework to indicate a bundle life cycle problem occurred. It is created by the framework to denote an exception condition in the life cycle of a bundle. BundleExceptions should not be created by bundle programmers.

Member Summary

Constructors

  public BundleException(String)
    Create a bundle exception with the given message.

  public BundleException(String, Throwable)
    Create a bundle exception that wraps another exception.

Methods

public Throwable getNestedException()
    Retrieve any nested exception included in this exception.

Constructors

BundleException(String)

```
public BundleException(java.lang.String msg)
```

Create a bundle exception with the given message.

Parameters:
msg—The message.

BundleException(String, Throwable)

```
public BundleException(java.lang.String msg,
           java.lang.Throwable throwable)
```

Create a bundle exception that wraps another exception.

Parameters:
msg—The associated message.

throwable—The nested exception.

Methods

getNestedException()

```
public java.lang.Throwable getNestedException()
```

Retrieve any nested exception included in this exception.

Returns: The nested exception, or **null** if there is no nested exception.

org.osgi.framework
BundleListener

Syntax
`public interface BundleListener extends java.util.EventListener`

All Superinterfaces:
java.util.EventListener

Description
BundleEvent listener. BundleListener is an interface that may be implemented by a bundle programmer. A BundleListener is registered with the framework using the `BundleContext.addBundleListener(BundleListener)` method. BundleListeners are called with a `BundleEvent` when a bundle has been installed, started, stopped, updated, or uninstalled.

See Also: `BundleEvent`

Member Summary
Methods
`public void bundleChanged(BundleEvent)`   Receive notification that a bundle has had a change occur in its life cycle.

Methods

bundleChanged(BundleEvent)

`public void bundleChanged(BundleEvent event)`

Receive notification that a bundle has had a change occur in its life cycle.

Parameters:
event—The BundleEvent.

org.osgi.framework
Configurable

Syntax
public interface Configurable

Description
Interface implemented by services which support a configuration object. Configurable is an interface that may be implemented by a bundle programmer. The implementation of a service that is configurable should implement this interface. Bundles that wish to configure a service may test to see if the service object is an instanceof Configurable.

Member Summary
Methods
public Object getConfigurationObject()   Retrieve the configuration object for a service.

Methods

getConfigurationObject()

```
public java.lang.Object getConfigurationObject()
            throws java.lang.SecurityException
```

Retrieve the configuration object for a service.

Services implementing this interface should be careful when returning their configuration object since this object is probably sensitive. If the Java runtime environment supports permissions, it is recommended that the caller is checked for an appropriate permission before returning the configuration object. It is recommended that callers possessing the AdminPermission always be allowed to retrieve the configuration object.

Returns: The configuration object for the service.

Throws:
> `java.lang.SecurityException`—If the caller does not have an appropriate permission and the Java runtime environment supports permissions.

org.osgi.framework
FrameworkEvent

Syntax
```
public class FrameworkEvent extends java.util.EventObject

java.lang.Object
   |
   +--java.util.EventObject
         |
         +--org.osgi.framework.FrameworkEvent
```

All Implemented Interfaces: java.io.Serializable

Description
General framework event. The event class used when notifying listeners of general framework events. A type code is used to identify the event for future extendability.

OSGi reserves the right to extend the set of types in the future.

Member Summary

Fields

public static final ERROR
    An error has occurred.

public static final STARTED
    The framework has started.

Constructors

public FrameworkEvent(int, Bundle, Throwable)
    Construct a framework event with a related bundle and exception.

public FrameworkEvent(int, Object)
    Construct a framework event.

Member Summary

Methods

    `public Bundle getBundle()`
        Retrieve the bundle associated with the event.

  `public Throwable getThrowable()`
        Retrieve the exception associated with the event.

      `public int getType()`
        Retrieve the type of this event.

Fields

ERROR

    `public static final int ERROR`

    An error has occurred. There was an error associated with a bundle.

    The value of ERROR is 0x00000002.

STARTED

    `public static final int STARTED`

    The framework has started. This event is broadcast when the framework has started after all installed bundle that are marked to be started have been started.

    The value of STARTED is 0x00000001.

Constructors

FrameworkEvent(int, Bundle, Throwable)

```
public FrameworkEvent(int type, Bundle bundle,
        java.lang.Throwable throwable)
```

    Construct a framework event with a related bundle and exception. This constructor is used for framework events of type ERROR.

Parameters:
    type—The event type.

    bundle—The related bundle.

    throwable—The related exception.

FrameworkEvent(int, Object)

`public FrameworkEvent(int type, java.lang.Object source)`

Construct a framework event. This constructor is used for framework events of type STARTED.

Parameters:
    type—The event type.

    source—The event source object. (This may not be null.)

Methods

getBundle()

`public Bundle getBundle()`

Retrieve the bundle associated with the event. If the event type is ERROR, this returns the bundle related to the error. This bundle is also the source of the event.

Returns: A bundle if an ERROR event type or null.

getThrowable()

`public java.lang.Throwable getThrowable()`

Retrieve the exception associated with the event. If the event type is ERROR, this returns the exception related to the error.

Returns: An exception if an ERROR event type or null.

getType()

`public int getType()`

Retrieve the type of this event. The type values are STARTED, ERROR.

Returns: The type of bundle state change.

org.osgi.framework
FrameworkListener

Syntax
`public interface FrameworkListener extends java.util.EventListener`

All Superinterfaces: java.util.EventListener

Description
FrameworkEvent listener. FrameworkListener is an interface that may be implemented by a bundle programmer. A FrameworkListener is registered with the framework using the `BundleContext.addFrameworkListener(FrameworkListener)` method. FrameworkListeners are called with a FrameworkEvent when the framework starts and when asynchronous errors occur.

See Also: `FrameworkEvent`

Member Summary
Methods

`public void frameworkEvent(FrameworkEvent)`
Receive notification of a general framework event.

Methods

frameworkEvent(FrameworkEvent)

`public void frameworkEvent(FrameworkEvent event)`

Receive notification of a general framework event.

Parameters:
event—The FrameworkEvent.

org.osgi.framework
InvalidSyntaxException

Syntax
```
public class InvalidSyntaxException extends java.lang.Exception
```

```
java.lang.Object
   |
   +--java.lang.Throwable
         |
         +--java.lang.Exception
               |
               +--org.osgi.framework.InvalidSyntaxException
```

All Implemented Interfaces: java.io.Serializable

Description
Exception from the framework to indicate a filter string parameter has an invalid syntax and cannot be parsed.

Member Summary

Constructors

> public **InvalidSyntaxException**(String, String)
> > Create the exception with the given message and the filter string which generated the exception.

Methods

public String getFilter()
> Returns the filter string which generated the exception.

Constructors

InvalidSyntaxException(String, String)

```
public InvalidSyntaxException(java.lang.String msg,
        java.lang.String filter)
```

Create the exception with the given message and the filter string which generated the exception.

Parameters:
    msg—The message.

    filter—The invalid filter string.

Methods

getFilter()

public java.lang.String **getFilter**()

Returns the filter string which generated the exception.

Returns: The invalid filter string.

See Also: BundleContext.getServiceReferences(String, String), BundleContext.addServiceListener(ServiceListener, String)

org.osgi.framework
PackagePermission

Syntax
    public final class PackagePermission extends java.security.BasicPermission

    java.lang.Object
      |
      +--java.security.Permission
          |
          +--java.security.BasicPermission
              |
              +--**org.osgi.framework.PackagePermission**

All Implemented Interfaces: java.security.Guard, java.io.Serializable

Description
PackagePermission indicates a bundle's right to import or export a package. A package is a dot-separated string that defines a fully qualified Java package, e.g., org.osgi.service.http.

PackagePermission has two actions: "export" and "import." The export action also implies the import action.

Member Summary

Fields

    public static final EXPORT
                        The action string "export."
    public static final IMPORT
                        The action string "import."

Constructors

            public PackagePermission(String, String)
                        Define the permission to import and/or export a package.

Member Summary	
Methods	
public boolean	equals(Object)
	Checks two PackagePermission for equality.
public String	getActions()
	Return the canonical string representation of the actions.
public int	hashCode()
	Returns the hash code value for this object.
public boolean	implies(Permission)
	Checks if the specified permission is "implied" by this object.

Fields

EXPORT

    public static final java.lang.String **EXPORT**

    The action string "export."

IMPORT

    public static final java.lang.String **IMPORT**

    The action string "import."

Constructors

PackagePermission(String, String)

    public **PackagePermission**(java.lang.String name,
            java.lang.String actions)

Define the permission to import and/or export a package. The name is specified as a normal Java package name, with dots separating the parts. Wildcards may be used. For example,

        org.osgi.service.http
        javax.servlet.*
        *

Package Permissions are granted over all possible versions of a package. A bundle that wants to export a package must have the PackagePermission for "export" on that package. Similarly, a bundle that wants to import a package must have the PackagePermission for "import" on that package.

Access permission is granted for both classes and resources.

Parameters:
name—Package name.

actions—"export," "import" (canonical order)

Methods

equals(Object)

public boolean **equals**(java.lang.Object obj)

Checks two PackagePermission for equality. Checks that `obj` has the same package name and actions as this PackagePermission.

Overrides: java.security.BasicPermission.equals(java.lang.Object) in class java.security.BasicPermission

Parameters:
obj—the object to test for equality.

Returns: true if obj is a PackagePermission, and has the same package name and actions as this PackagePermission object. Otherwise, return false.

getActions()

public java.lang.String **getActions**()

Return the canonical string representation of the actions. Always returns present actions in the following order: export, import.

Overrides: java.security.BasicPermission.getActions() in class java.security.BasicPermission

Returns: The canonical string representation of the actions

hashCode()

public int **hashCode**()

Returns the hash code value for this object.

Overrides: java.security.BasicPermission.hashCode() in class java.security.BasicPermission

Returns: a hash code value for this object.

implies(Permission)

```
public boolean implies(java.security.Permission p)
```

Checks if the specified permission is "implied" by this object. This method checks that the package name of the target is implied by the package name of this object. The list of actions must either match or allow for the list for the target object to imply the target permission. The permission to export a package implies the permission to import the named package.

```
x.y.*,"export" -> x.y.z,"export"  is true
*,"import" -> x.y, "import"       is true
*,"export" -> x.y, "import"       is true
x.y,"export" -> x.y.z, "export"   is false
```

Overrides: java.security.BasicPermission.implies(java.security.Permission) in class java.security.BasicPermission

Parameters:
   p—the target permission to check.

Returns: true if the specified permission is implied by this object, false if not.

org.osgi.framework
ServiceEvent

Syntax
```
public class ServiceEvent extends java.util.EventObject

java.lang.Object
  |
  +--java.util.EventObject
        |
        +--org.osgi.framework.ServiceEvent
```

All Implemented Interfaces: java.io.Serializable

Description
Service life cycle change event. ServiceEvents are delivered to `ServiceListeners` when a change occurs in the service's life cycle. A type code is used to identify the event for future extendability.

OSGi reserves the right to extend the set of types in the future.

Member Summary

Fields

    public static final MODIFIED
        The properties of a registered service have been modified.

    public static final REGISTERED
        A service has been registered.

    public static final UNREGISTERING
        A service is in the process of being unregistered.

Constructors

    public ServiceEvent(int, ServiceReference)
        Construct a service event.

Member Summary

Methods

public ServiceReference getServiceReference()
: Retrieve a reference to the service who had a change occur in its life cycle.

public int getType()
: Retrieve the type of this event.

Fields

MODIFIED

public static final int MODIFIED

The properties of a registered service have been modified. This event is synchronously delivered AFTER the service properties have been modified.

The value of MODIFIED is 0x00000002.

See Also: ServiceRegistration.setProperties(Dictionary)

REGISTERED

public static final int REGISTERED

A service has been registered. This event is synchronously delivered AFTER the service has been registered.

The value of REGISTERED is 0x00000001.

See Also: BundleContext.registerService(String[], Object, Dictionary)

UNREGISTERING

public static final int UNREGISTERING

A service is in the process of being unregistered. This event is synchronously delivered BEFORE the service has completed unregistering.

If a bundle is using a service that is UNREGISTERING, the bundle should release its use of the service when it receives this event. If the bundle does not release its use of the service when it receives this event, the framework will automatically release the bundle's use of the service while completing unregistering the service.

The value of UNREGISTERING is 0x00000004.

See Also: `ServiceRegistration.unregister()`,
`BundleContext.ungetService(ServiceReference)`

Constructors

ServiceEvent(int, ServiceReference)

`public ServiceEvent(int type, ServiceReference reference)`

Construct a service event.

Parameters:
 type—The event type.

 reference—A ServiceReference to the service who had a change occur in its life cycle.

Methods

getServiceReference()

`public ServiceReference getServiceReference()`

Retrieve a reference to the service who had a change occur in its life cycle. This reference is the source of the event.

Returns: A reference to the service who had a change occur in its life cycle.

getType()

`public int getType()`

Retrieve the type of this event. The type values are REGISTERED, MODIFIED, UNREGISTERING.

Returns: The type of service life cycle change.

org.osgi.framework
ServiceFactory

Syntax
`public interface ServiceFactory`

Description
Service factories allow services to provide customized service objects. In order to gain control over the specific service object given to a bundle using the service, a bundle programmer can register a `ServiceFactory` object instead of a service object when registering a service.

When this is done, the `BundleContext.getService(ServiceReference)` method calls the service factory's `getService(Bundle, ServiceRegistration)` to create a service object specifically for the requesting bundle. The service object returned by the service factory is cached by the framework until the bundle releases its use of the service.

When the bundle's use count for the service drops to zero (including the bundle stopping or the service being unregistered), the service factory's `ungetService(Bundle, ServiceRegistration, Object)` method is called.

ServiceFactory objects are only used by the framework and are not made available to other bundles.

Member Summary

Methods

`public Object getService(Bundle, ServiceRegistration)`
    Create a service object.
`public void ungetService(Bundle, ServiceRegistration, Object)`
    Release a service object.

Methods

getService(Bundle, ServiceRegistration)

```
public java.lang.Object getService(Bundle bundle,
        ServiceRegistration registration)
```

Create a service object.

The framework invokes this method the first time a given bundle requests a service object using `BundleContext.getService(ServiceReference)`. The factory can return a specific service object for each bundle.

The framework caches the value returned (unless it is `null`), and will return the same service object on any future call to `BundleContext.getService(ServiceReference)` from the same bundle.

The framework will check the returned service object. If the service object is not an `instanceof` all the classes named when the service was registered, `null` is returned to the bundle.

Parameters:
    `bundle`—The bundle using the service.

    `registration`—The `ServiceRegistration` for the service.

Returns: A service object that **must** be an `instanceof` all the classes named when the service was registered,

See Also: `BundleContext.getService(ServiceReference)`

ungetService(Bundle, ServiceRegistration, Object)

```
public void ungetService(Bundle bundle,
        ServiceRegistration registration,
        java.lang.Object service)
```

Release a service object.

The framework invokes this method when a service has been released by a bundle. The service object may be destroyed at this time.

Parameters:
    `bundle`—The bundle releasing the service.

    `registration`—The `ServiceRegistration` for the service.

    `service`—The service object returned by a previous call to `getService(Bundle, ServiceRegistration)`.

See Also: `BundleContext.ungetService(ServiceReference)`

org.osgi.framework
ServiceListener

Syntax
```
public interface ServiceListener extends java.util.EventListener
```

All Superinterfaces: java.util.EventListener

Description
ServiceEvent listener. ServiceListener is an interface that may be implemented by a bundle programmer. A ServiceListener is registered with the framework using a `BundleContext.addServiceListener(ServiceListener, String)` method. ServiceListeners are called with a `ServiceEvent` when a service has been registered or modified, or when a service is in the process of unregistering.

`ServiceEvent` delivery to ServiceListeners are filtered by the filter specified when the listener was registered. If the Java runtime environment supports permissions, then additional filtering is done. `ServiceEvent`s are only delivered to the listener if the bundle which defines the listener object's class has the `ServicePermission` permission to "get" the service using at least one of the named classes the service was registered under.

See Also: `ServiceEvent`, `ServicePermission`

Member Summary
Methods
`public void serviceChanged(ServiceEvent)` Receive notification that a service has had a change occur in its life cycle.

Methods

serviceChanged(ServiceEvent)

```
public void serviceChanged(ServiceEvent event)
```

Receive notification that a service has had a change occur in its life cycle.

Parameters:
event—The ServiceEvent.

org.osgi.framework
ServicePermission

Syntax
```
public final class ServicePermission extends
    java.security.BasicPermission

java.lang.Object
  |
  +--java.security.Permission
       |
       +--java.security.BasicPermission
            |
            +--org.osgi.framework.ServicePermission
```

All Implemented Interfaces: java.security.Guard, java.io.Serializable

Description
ServicePermission indicates a bundle's right to register or get a service.

The "register" permission will allow the bundle to register a service on the specified names. The "get" permission allows a bundle to see a service and get it. Permission to get a service is required to see events regarding the service. Untrusted bundles should not be able to detect the presence of certain services unless they have authority to get the specific service.

Member Summary

Fields

`public static final GET`
    The action string "get."
`public static final REGISTER`
    The action string "register."

Constructors

`public ServicePermission(String, String)`
    Create a new permission for Service.

Member Summary

Methods

    `public boolean` `equals(Object)`
        Checks two ServicePermission for equality.

    `public String` `getActions()`
        Return the canonical string representation of the actions.

    `public int` `hashCode()`
        Returns the hash code value for this object.

    `public boolean` `implies(Permission)`
        Checks if this ServicePermission object "implies" the specified permission.

Fields

GET

`public static final java.lang.String` **GET**

The action string "get."

REGISTER

`public static final java.lang.String` **REGISTER**

The action string "register."

Constructors

ServicePermission(String, String)

`public` **ServicePermission**`(java.lang.String name,`
       `java.lang.String actions)`

Create a new permission for Service. The name of the service is specified as a fully qualified class name.

    `ClassName ::= <class name> | <class name ending in '*'>`

Examples:

```
org.osgi.service.http.HttpService
org.osgi.service.http.*
org.osgi.service.snmp.*
```

There are two possible actions: get and register. The get permission allows the owner of this permission to obtain a service with this name. The register permission allows the bundle to register a service under that name.

Parameters:
name—class name

actions—"get," "register" (canonical order)

Methods

equals(Object)

```
public boolean equals(java.lang.Object obj)
```

Checks two ServicePermission for equality. Checks that obj has the same class name and action as this ServicePermission.

Overrides: java.security.BasicPermission.equals(java.lang.Object) in class java.security.BasicPermission

Parameters:
obj—the object to test for equality.

Returns: true if obj is a ServicePermission, and has the same class name and actions as this ServicePermission object. Otherwise, return false.

getActions()

```
public java.lang.String getActions()
```

Return the canonical string representation of the actions. Always returns present actions in the following order: get, register.

Overrides: java.security.BasicPermission.getActions() in class java.security.BasicPermission

Returns: The canonical string representation of the actions

hashCode()

```
public int hashCode()
```

Returns the hash code value for this object.

Overrides: java.security.BasicPermission.hashCode() in class java.security.BasicPermission

Returns: a hash code value for this object.

implies(Permission)

```
public boolean implies(java.security.Permission p)
```

Checks if this ServicePermission object "implies" the specified permission.

Overrides: java.security.BasicPermission.implies(java.security.Permission) in class java.security.BasicPermission

Parameters:
p—the target permission to check.

Returns: true if the specified permission is implied by this object, false if not.

org.osgi.framework
ServiceReference

Syntax
`public interface ServiceReference`

Description
A reference to a service. The framework returns ServiceReference objects from the `BundleContext.getServiceReference(String)` and `BundleContext.getServiceReferences(String, String)` methods.

A ServiceReference may be shared between bundles and can be used to examine the properties of the service and to get the service object (See `BundleContext.getService(ServiceReference)`). Every registered service has a unique ServiceRegistration object and may have multiple, distinct ServiceReference objects referring to it. ServiceReferences to the same ServiceRegistration instance are considered equal (i.e., their `equals()` method will return `true` when compared) and have the same `hashCode`. If the same service object is registered multiple times, ServiceReferences to different ServiceRegistrations are considered different.

Member Summary

Methods

`public Bundle getBundle()`
    Return the bundle which registered the service.

`public Object getProperty(String)`
    Get the value of a service's property.

`public String getPropertyKeys()`
    Get the list of key names for the service's properties.

Methods

getBundle()

`public Bundle getBundle()`

Return the bundle which registered the service.

This method will always return `null` when the service has been unregistered. This can be used to determine if the service has been unregistered.

Returns: The bundle which registered the service.

See Also: `BundleContext.registerService(String[], Object, Dictionary)`

getProperty(String)

`public java.lang.Object getProperty(java.lang.String key)`

Get the value of a service's property.

This method will continue to return property values after the service has been unregistered. This is so that references to unregistered service can be interrogated. (For example: ServiceReference objects stored in the log.)

Parameters:
 key—Name of the property.

Returns: Value of the property or `null` if there is no property by that name.

getPropertyKeys()

`public java.lang.String[] getPropertyKeys()`

Get the list of key names for the service's properties.

This method will continue to return the keys after the service has been unregistered. This is so that references to unregistered service can be interrogated. (For example: ServiceReference objects stored in the log.)

Returns: The list of property key names.

org.osgi.framework
ServiceRegistration

Syntax
`public interface ServiceRegistration`

Description
A registered service. The framework returns a ServiceRegistration object when a `BundleContext.registerService(String[], Object, Dictionary)` method is successful. This object is for the private use of the registering bundle and should not be shared with other bundles.

The ServiceRegistration object may be used to update the properties for the service or to unregister the service.

If the ServiceRegistration is garbage collected the framework may remove the service. This implies that if a bundle wants to keep its service registered, it should keep the ServiceRegistration object referenced.

Member Summary

Methods

`public ServiceReference`	`getReference()` Returns a `ServiceReference` object for this registration.
`public void`	`setProperties(Dictionary)` Update the properties associated with this service.
`public void`	`unregister()` Unregister the service.

Methods

getReference()

```
public ServiceReference getReference()
        throws java.lang.IllegalStateException
```

Returns a `ServiceReference` object for this registration. The `ServiceReference` object may be shared with other bundles.

Returns: A `ServiceReference` object.

Throws:
java.lang.IllegalStateException—If this ServiceRegistration has already been unregistered.

setProperties(Dictionary)

```
public void setProperties(java.util.Dictionary properties)
        throws java.lang.IllegalStateException
```

Update the properties associated with this service.

The key "objectClass" cannot be modified by this method. Its value is set when the service is registered.

The following steps are followed to modify a service's properties:

1. The service's properties are replaced with the provided properties.
2. A `ServiceEvent` of type `ServiceEvent.MODIFIED` is synchronously sent.

Parameters:
properties—The properties for this service. Changes should not be made to this object after calling this method. To update the service's properties this method should be called again.

Throws:
java.lang.IllegalStateException—If this ServiceRegistration has already been unregistered.

unregister()

```
public void unregister()
        throws java.lang.IllegalStateException
```

Unregister the service. Remove a service registration from the framework's service registry. All `ServiceReference` objects for this registration can no longer be used to interact with the service.

The following steps are followed to unregister a service:

1. The service is removed from the framework's service registry so that it may no longer be used. `ServiceReference` s for the service may no longer be used to get a service object for the service.

2. A ServiceEvent of type ServiceEvent.UNREGISTERING is synchronously sent so that bundles using this service may release their use of the service.

3. For each bundle whose use count for this service is greater than zero:

4. The bundle's use count for this service is set to zero.

5. If the service was registered with a ServiceFactory, the ServiceFactory.ungetService(Bundle, ServiceRegistration, Object) method is called to release the service object for the bundle.

Throws:
 java.lang.IllegalStateException—If this ServiceRegistration has already been unregistered.

See Also: BundleContext.ungetService(ServiceReference)

Package
org.osgi.service.device

Description
The OSGi Device Access Specification.

The Device Manager service listens for new Device services and attaches drivers on top of devices.

Device manager
The device manager registers as service listener in the framework, detecting all newly installed Device services. For each new Device service, a list of driver bundles are located and installed. Then, all Driver services are located from framework and tested in a *bidding phase*, where each Driver may inspect the Device service. The highest bidding Driver gets *attached* to the device.

Device Manager Algorithm

- **Device detection** Listen for all new Device Services implementing `org.osgi.service.device.Device`
- For each new Device service:
- **Location phase** Use DriverLocators to locate additional drivers
- Get all DriverLocator services
- Query each DriverLocator for driver IDs by calling `locator.findDriver(Device)`
- Check which drivers are already present in Framework
- Load, install, and start new driver bundles by calling `locator.loadDriver(driver ID)` and `Framework.install(stream, driver id)`
- **Bidding phase** Let each driver bid on the device.
- Get all registered Driver services (implementing org.osgi.service.device.Driver) from Framework.
- For each Driver service:
- Call the Driver service's `match()` method with the Device as argument.

- Select the highest bidding Driver service
- **Attach phase** Attach highest bidder to device.
- Call the Driver service's `attach()` method.
- If `attach()` returns null, do nothing more.
- If `attach()` returns a new driver ID, repeat the location phase, but exclude the referring driver from the next match round.
- **Cleanup phase** Uninstall idle drivers.

Driver bundle ID

Each driver bundle is expected to have a universally unique string ID. This ID is used by the device manager to resolve driver revisions and is also used as framework location ID.

DriverLocator service

The Device Manager uses zero or more DriverLocator services to find new driver bundles to install. DriverLocators are typically implementation specific for a specific type of driver databases and network setups.

See Also: `DriverLocator`

Class Summary	
Interfaces	
`Device`	The Device interface should be implemented by services wishing to be discovered by the device manager.
`Driver`	A `Driver` service should be registered by each driver wishing to attach to device services provided by other drivers.
`DriverLocator`	A `DriverLocator` can find and load device driver bundles given a property set.

org.osgi.service.device
Device

Syntax
`public interface Device`

Description
The Device interface should be implemented by services wishing to be discovered by the device manager. Concrete devices subclass this interface adding methods appropriate to the device category.
If no drivers are interested in this device, the `noDriverFound()` method is called.

See Also: `Device`

Member Summary
Fields
`public static final MATCH_NONE`
Return value from `Driver.match(ServiceReference)` if the driver does not match the device.
Methods
`public void noDriverFound()`
Called by the device manager after it has failed to attach any driver to the device.

Fields

MATCH_NONE

`public static final int MATCH_NONE`

Return value from `Driver.match(ServiceReference)` if the driver does not match the device.

Methods

noDriverFound()

`public void noDriverFound()`

Called by the device manager after it has failed to attach any driver to the device.

If the device can be configured in alternate ways, the driver may respond by unregistering the device service and registering a different device service instead.

org.osgi.service.device
Driver

Syntax
`public interface Driver`

Description
A `Driver` service should be registered by each driver wishing to attach to device services provided by other drivers. For each newly discovered `Device`, the device manager enters a bidding phase. The `Driver` whose `match(ServiceReference)` method bids the highest for a particular device will be instructed by the device manager to attach to the device.

See Also: `Device`

Member Summary
Methods
`public String attach(ServiceReference)`
Attach this driver to the device represented by the given ServiceReference.
`public int match(ServiceReference)`
Check whether this driver can be attached to the device represented by the given ServiceReference, and return a value indicating how well this driver can support the given device, or `Device.MATCH_NONE` if it cannot support the given device at all.

Methods

attach(ServiceReference)

```
public java.lang.String attach(ServiceReference reference)
        throws java.lang.Exception
```

Attach this driver to the device represented by the given ServiceReference.

A return value of null indicates that this driver has successfully attached to the given device. If this driver is unable to attach to the given device, but knows of a more suitable driver, it must return the ID of that driver. This allows for the implementation of referring drivers whose only purpose is to refer to other drivers capable of handling a given device.

After having attached to the device, this driver is expected to register the device as a new service exposing driver-specific functionality.

This method is called by the device manager.

Parameters:
    reference—the ServiceReference of the device to attach to

Returns: null if this driver has successfully attached to the given device, or the ID of a more suitable driver

Throws:
    java.lang.Exception—the driver cannot attach to the given device and does not know of a more suitable driver

match(ServiceReference)

```
public int match(ServiceReference reference)
        throws java.lang.Exception
```

Check whether this driver can be attached to the device represented by the given ServiceReference, and return a value indicating how well this driver can support the given device, or Device.MATCH_NONE if it cannot support the given device at all.

The value returned must be one of the possible match values defined in the Device subinterface corresponding to the given device.

In order to make its decision, this driver may simply examine the properties associated with the given device or may get the referenced service object (representing the actual physical device) to talk to it, as long as it ungets the service and returns the physical device to a normal state before this method returns.

A driver should always return the same match code whenever it is presented with the same device.

The match function is called by the device manager during the matching process.

Parameters:
    reference—the ServiceReference of the device to match

Returns: value indicating how well this driver can support the given device, or Device.MATCH_NONE if it cannot support the device at all

Throws:

java.lang.Exception—the driver cannot examine the device

org.osgi.service.device
DriverLocator

Syntax
`public interface DriverLocator`

Description
A `DriverLocator` can find and load device driver bundles given a property set. Each driver is represented by a unique ID.

DriverLocator services provide the mechanism for dynamically downloading new device driver bundles into an OSGi device. They are supplied by OSGi providers and encapsulate all provider-specific details related to the location and acquisition of device driver bundles.

Member Summary

Methods

`public String` `findDrivers(Dictionary)`
Return an array of driver IDs of drivers capable of attaching to a device with the given properties.

`public InputStream` `loadDriver(String)`
Get an `InputStream` from which the driver bundle providing a driver with the giving ID can be installed.

Methods

findDrivers(Dictionary)

`public java.lang.String[]` `findDrivers(java.util.Dictionary props)`

Return an array of driver IDs of drivers capable of attaching to a device with the given properties.

Parameters:
  `props`—the properties of the device for which a driver is sought

Returns: the array of driver IDs of drivers capable of attaching to a device with the given properties, or `null` if this DriverLocator does not know of any such drivers

loadDriver(String)

```
public java.io.InputStream loadDriver(java.lang.String id)
        throws java.io.IOException
```

Get an `InputStream` from which the driver bundle providing a driver with the giving ID can be installed.

Parameters:
    `id`—the ID of the driver that needs to be installed.

Returns: the `InputStream` from which the driver bundle can be installed

Throws:
    `java.io.IOException`—the input stream for the bundle cannot be created

Package
org.osgi.service.http

Description
The OSGi HttpService Specification.

HttpService allows other bundles in the OSGi Framework to register resources and servlets to be accessed via Hypertext Transfer Protocol (HTTP). HttpService may implement either HTTP/1.0 (http://www.ietf.org/rfc/rfc1945.txt) or HTTP/1.1 (http://www.ietf.org/rfc/rfc2616.txt).

Two entity types can be registered with HttpService: servlets and resources. A servlet is an object which implements the Java Servlet API (http://java.sun.com/products/servlet/). Registering a servlet gives that servlet control over some part of the URI namespace. Registering resources allows HTML files, GIF files, class files, etc. to be made visible in the URI namespace by the requesting bundle.

Registering Servlets

Servlets which are registered using the same HttpContext object will share the same ServletContext. This is, HttpService provides a one-to-one mapping between ServletContexts and HttpContexts. Servlets can be registered using the `registerServlet` method.

For example:

```
HttpContext context = new HttpContext() {
    public boolean handleSecurity(
        HttpServletRequest request,
        HttpServletResponse response) throws IOException {
        return(true);
    }
    public URL getResource(String name) {
        return(getClass().getResource(name));
    }
    public String getMimeType(String name) {
        return(null);
    }
```

```
};
Hashtable initparams = new Hashtable();
initparams.put("some-key-name", "some-value-string");
Servlet myServlet = new MyServlet();
httpService.registerServlet("/servletAlias",
                            myServlet,
                            initparams,
                            context);
/* myServlet has been registered and its init method
   has been called */
...
httpService.unregister("/servletAlias");
/* myServlet has been unregistered and its destroy method
   has been called */
```

This would register the servlet "myServlet" at alias "/servletAlias." A request for `http://myserver:port/servletAlias` would map to the servlet myServlet and its `service` method will be called to process the request.

The context object in this example provides simple implementations of the HttpContext methods.

Registering Resources

Resources can be registered using the `registerResources` method. For example:

```
HttpContext context = new HttpContext() {
    public boolean handleSecurity(
        HttpServletRequest request,
        HttpServletResponse response) throws IOException {
        return(true);
    }
    public URL getResource(String name) {
        return(getClass().getResource(name));
    }
    public String getMimeType(String name) {
        return(null);
    }
};
httpService.registerResources("/files",
                              "/bundlefiles",
                              context);
```

```
...
httpService.unregister("/files");
```

The example registers the resource name "/bundlefiles" to the alias "/files." A request for `http://myserver:port/files/myfile.htm` would map to the name "/bundlefiles/myfile.htm." The context object will be called at the `getResource` method to maps the resource name "/bundlefiles/myfile.htm" to a URL. HttpService will then use the URL to read the read the resource and respond to the request.

The context object in this example provides simple implementations of the HttpContext methods. The implementation of `getResource` uses the bundle's class loader to return an URL for the resource. More sophisticated implementations could filter the input name restricting the resources that may be returned or map the input name onto the file system.

Mapping HTTP Requests to Servlet and Resource Registrations

HttpService's URI namespace may be "shared." For example, caller A registers alias "/a" and caller B registers alias "/a/b." A request URI of "/a/b" or request URIs that start with "/a/b/" will be mapped to B's registration. Other request URIs that start with "/a" will not be mapped to B's registration and may be mapped to A's registration. This implies that one registration can "hide" part of another registration. Registrations for identical aliases are not allowed. If caller A registers "/myAlias" and then caller B tries to register "/myAlias," caller B will receive a NamespaceException and its resource or servlet will not be registered. However, caller B can register "/myAlias/more" (if no other registration for this alias exists).

When an HTTP request comes in from a client, HttpService checks to see if the request URI matches any registered aliases. If it does, then we have a matching registration. If the registration corresponds to a servlet, then the servlet will be called at its `service` method to complete the HTTP request. If the registration corresponds to a resource, then a target resource name is constructed by substituting the alias name from the registration with the resource name from the registration. For example:

```
registrationName+requestURI.substring(registrationAlias.length())
```

The target resource name will be passed to the `getResource` method of the registration's `HttpContext` object. If the returned URL object is not `null`, then HttpService will return the contents of the URL to the client completing the HTTP request. If the returned URL object is `null`, then we continue as if there was no match.

If there is not a match, HttpService will attempt to match substrings of the requestURI to registered aliases. The substrings of the request URI are selected as follows: Remove the last '/' and everything to the right of it. HttpService will repeat this process until either a match is found or the substring is an empty string. If this happens, HttpService will return error Not Found(404) to the client.

For example, an HTTP request comes in with a request URI of "/a/b/foo.txt" and the only registered alias is "/a." The search for "/a/b/foo.txt" will not match an alias, therefore HttpService with search for aliases "/a/b" and then "/a." The search for alias "/a" will result in a match and its registration will be used.

Class Summary

Interfaces

HttpContext	HttpContext defines methods that HttpService may call to get information about a registration.
HttpService	HttpService allows other bundles in the OSGi Framework to dynamically register resources and servlets into the HttpService's URI namespace.

Exceptions

Namespace-Exception	A NamespaceException is thrown to indicate an error with the caller's request to register a servlet or resources into HttpService's URI namespace.

org.osgi.service.http
HttpContext

Syntax
`public interface HttpContext`

Description
HttpContext defines methods that HttpService may call to get information about a registration. Servlets and resources must be registered with a HttpContext object. Servlets which are registered using the same HttpContext object will share the same ServletContext.

This interface is implemented by users of HttpService.

Member Summary	
Methods	
`public String`	`getMimeType(String)` Map a name to a MIME type.
`public URL`	`getResource(String)` Map a resource name to a URL.
`public boolean`	`handleSecurity(HttpServletRequest, HttpServletResponse)` Handle security for a request.

Methods

getMimeType(String)

`public java.lang.String getMimeType(java.lang.String name)`

Map a name to a MIME type. Called by HttpService to determine the MIME type for the name. For servlet registrations, HttpService will call this method to support the `ServletContext` method `getMimeType`. For resource registrations, HttpService will call this method to determine the MIME type for the `Content-Type` header in the response.

Parameters:
>name—determine the MIME type for this name.

Returns: MIME type (e.g., `text/html`) of the name or `null` to indicate that HttpService should determine the MIME type.

getResource(String)

```
public java.net.URL getResource(java.lang.String name)
```

Map a resource name to a URL. Called by HttpService to map a resource name to a URL. For servlet registrations, HttpService will call this method to support the `ServletContext` methods `getResource` and `getResourceAsStream`. For resource registrations, HttpService will call this method to locate the named resource. The context can control from where resources come. For example, the resource can be mapped to a file in the bundle's persistent storage area via

```
bundleContext.getDataFile(name).toURL()
```

or to a resource in the context's bundle via

```
this.getClass().getResource(name)
```

Parameters:
>name—the name of the requested resource

Returns: URL that HttpService can use to read the resource or `null` if the resource does not exist.

handleSecurity(HttpServletRequest, HttpServletResponse)

```
public boolean handleSecurity(javax.servlet.http.HttpServletRequest
            request,
            javax.servlet.http.HttpServletResponse response)
     throws java.io.IOException
```

Handle security for a request. HttpService calls this method prior to servicing a request. This method controls whether a request is processed in the normal manner or an error is returned.

If a request requires authentication and the `Authorization` header in the request is missing or not acceptable, then this method should set the `WWW-Authenticate` header in the response object, set the status in the response object to Unauthorized(401) and return `false`. See also HTTP Authentication: Basic and Digest Access Authentication (http://www.ietf.org/rfc/rfc2617.txt).

If a request requires a secure connection and the `getScheme` method in the request does not return `https` or some other acceptable secure protocol, then this method should set the status in the response object to Forbidden(403) and return `false`.

When this method returns `false`, HttpService will send the response back to the client completing the request. When this method returns `true`, HttpService will proceed with servicing the request.

Parameters:
    `request`—the HTTP request

    `response`—the HTTP response

Returns: `true` if the request should be serviced, `false` if the request should not be serviced and HttpService will send the response back to the client.

Throws:
    `java.io.IOException`—may be thrown by this method. If this occurs HttpService will terminate the request and close the socket.

org.osgi.service.http
HttpService

Syntax
```
public interface HttpService
```

Description
HttpService allows other bundles in the OSGi Framework to dynamically register resources and servlets into the HttpService's URI namespace. A Bundle may later unregister its resources or servlets.

Member Summary
Methods
`public void` `registerResources(String, String, HttpContext)`   Register resources into the URI namespace.
`public void` `registerServlet(String, Servlet, Dictionary, HttpContext)`   Register a servlet into the URI namespace.
`public void` `unregister(String)`   Unregisters a previous registration done by registerServlet or register-Resources.

Methods

registerResources(String, String, HttpContext)

```
public void registerResources(java.lang.String alias,
        java.lang.String name, HttpContext context)
        throws NamespaceException, java.lang.IllegalArgumentEx
        ception
```

Register resources into the URI namespace. The alias is the name in the URI namespace of HttpService at which the registration will be mapped. An alias must begin with slash ('/') and must not end with slash ('/'). The name parameter must also not end with slash ('/'). See also *Mapping HTTP Requests to Servlet and Resource Registrations*.

For example, suppose the resource name /tmp is registered to the alias /files. A request for /files/foo.txt will map to the resource name /tmp/foo.txt.

```
httpservice.registerResources("/files",
                              "/tmp",
                              context);
```

HttpService will call the HttpContext parameter to map resource names to URLs and MIME types and to handle security for requests.

Parameters:
    alias—name in the URI namespace at which the resources are registered

    name—the base name of the resources that will be registered

    context—the HttpContext object for the registered resources

Throws:
    NamespaceException—if the registration fails because the alias is already in use.

    java.lang.IllegalArgumentException—if any of the parameters are invalid

registerServlet(String, Servlet, Dictionary, HttpContext)

```
public void registerServlet(java.lang.String alias,
           javax.servlet.Servlet servlet,
           java.util.Dictionary initparams, HttpContext context)
           throws NamespaceException, javax.servlet.ServletExcept
           ion, java.lang.IllegalArgumentException
```

Register a servlet into the URI namespace. The alias is the name in the URI namespace of HttpService at which the registration will be mapped. An alias must begin with slash ('/') and must not end with slash ('/'). See also *Mapping HTTP Requests to Servlet and Resource Registrations*. HttpService will call the init method of the servlet before returning.

```
 httpService.registerServlet("/myservlet",
                             servlet,
                             initparams,
                             context);
```

Servlets which are registered with the same HttpContext object will share the same ServletContext. HttpService will call the HttpContext parameter to support the `ServletContext` methods `getResource`, `getResourceAsStream` and `getMimeType` and to handle security for requests.

Parameters:
    `alias`—name in the URI namespace at which the servlet is registered

    `servlet`—the servlet object to register

    `initparams`—initialization parameters for the servlet or `null` if there are none. This parameter is used by the servlet's `ServletConfig` object.

    `context`—the HttpContext object for the registered servlet

Throws:
    `NamespaceException`—if the register fails because the alias is already in use.

    `javax.servlet.ServletException`—if the servlet's `init` method throws an exception

    `java.lang.IllegalArgumentException`—if any of the parameters are invalid

unregister(String)

```
public void unregister(java.lang.String alias)
        throws java.lang.IllegalArgumentException
```

Unregisters a previous registration done by registerServlet or registerResources. After this call, the registered alias in the URI namespace will no longer be available. If the registration was for a servlet, HttpService will call the `destroy` method of the servlet before returning.

If the bundle which performed the registration is stopped or otherwise "unget"s HttpService without calling `unregister(String)`, then HttpService will automatically unregister the registration. However, if the registration was for a servlet, the `destroy` method of the servlet will not be called in this case since the bundle may be stopped. `unregister(String)` must be explicitly called to cause the `destroy` method of the servlet to be called. This can be done in the `BundleActivator.stop` method of the bundle registering the servlet.

Parameters:
    `alias`—name in the URI namespace of the registration to unregister

Throws:
    `java.lang.IllegalArgumentException`—if there is no registration for the alias or the calling bundle was not the bundle which registered the alias.

org.osgi.service.http
NamespaceException

Syntax
```
public class NamespaceException extends java.lang.Exception
```

```
java.lang.Object
  |
  +--java.lang.Throwable
        |
        +--java.lang.Exception
              |
              +--org.osgi.service.http.NamespaceException
```

All Implemented Interfaces: java.io.Serializable

Description
A NamespaceException is thrown to indicate an error with the caller's request to register a servlet or resources into HttpService's URI namespace. This exception indicates that the requested alias is already registered.

Member Summary

Constructors

    public NamespaceException(String)
        Construct a NamespaceException with a detail message.

    public NamespaceException(String, Throwable)
        Construct a NamespaceException with a detail message and a nested exception.

Methods

public Throwable getException()
        Returns the nested exception.

Constructors

NamespaceException(String)

> `public `**`NamespaceException`**`(java.lang.String message)`
>
> Construct a NamespaceException with a detail message.
>
> **Parameters:**
> > message—the detail message

NamespaceException(String, Throwable)

> `public `**`NamespaceException`**`(java.lang.String message,`
> `            java.lang.Throwable exception)`
>
> Construct a NamespaceException with a detail message and a nested exception.
>
> **Parameters:**
> > message—the detail message
> >
> > exception—the nested exception

Methods

getException()

> `public java.lang.Throwable `**`getException`**`()`
>
> Returns the nested exception.
>
> **Returns:** the nested exception or `null` if there is no nested exception.

Package
org.osgi.service.log

Description
The OSGi LogService Specification.

The LogService takes log requests from bundles and the LogReaderService allows other bundles to read entries from the log. Although you can ask the LogService to log any message, it is primarily intended for reporting events and error conditions.
In general, the LogService interface provides the means for:

- Specifying the message and/or exception to be logged.
- Supplying a log level signifying severity of the message being logged.
- Specifying the service associated with the log requests.

The LogReaderService interface provides the means for:

- Getting recent past log entries.
- Getting notified of new log entries.

LogService

Making Log Requests

Callers make log requests through LogService after they get the Service object from the OSGi Framework. In the following example, the caller writes a message into the log:

```
logService.log(myServiceReference, LogService.LOG_INFO,
    "myService is up and running");
```

myServiceReference identifies the originator of the log request. The provided level LogService.LOG_INFO indicates that this is informational.
Following is another example that records error conditions:

```
try {
    FileInputStream fis = new FileInputStream("myFile");
    int b;
```

```
        while ((b = fis.read()) != -1) {
            ...
        }
        fis.close();
    } catch (IOException e) {
        logService.log(myServiceReference, LogService.LOG_ERROR,
            "Cannot access file", e);
    }
```

Note that in addition to the error message, the exception itself is also logged.

Methods for Logging

The LogService provides for the logging of different types of messages:

- Log a simple message at the given log level.
- Log a message with an exception at the given log level.

Although it is possible to call log methods without providing a service description, it is recommended that the caller supplies this parameter whenever appropriate.

Log Level and Error Severity

The LogService expects a level indicating error severity. This can be used to filter log messages according to the level of severity. The LogService interface defines the various severity levels.

Callers must supply log levels that they deem appropriate when making log requests.

Event Listening

The LogService also serves as an event listener for the OSGi Framework. There is no dedicated error handling service in the Framework. Because events are broadcast in the Framework, other interested listeners can still have the opportunity to receive the events. The LogService will log all Framework events at the LogService.LOG_INFO level, except for FrameworkErrorEvents which will be logged at the LogService.LOG_ERROR level.

LogReaderService

In addition to producing log entries a bundle programmer might also be interested in receiving log entries either as they happen or entries that have already occurred.

In secure implementations of the Framework, a bundle wishing to use the LogReaderService must have the appropriate permission.

Retrieving past log entries

Log entries from the past are obtained via the `getLog` method. This method returns an enumeration of LogEntries. The LogEntries will be ordered with the most recent entry first. It should be noted that the size of the log is implementation specific. Also, how far into the past the log goes will depend upon the size of the log. Finally, not all log entries will be recorded in the past log. Debug log entries, in particular, may not be recorded.

Subscribing to the LogReaderService

A bundle that is interested in the log entries will probably want to process log messages as they happen. Unlike the past log, all logging messages will be sent to a subscriber of the LogReaderService. A subscriber to the LogReaderService must implement the LogListener interface. The subscriber then subscribes to the LogReaderService using the `addLogListener` method. After starting the subscription, each time a message is logged, the `logged` method of the subscriber's LogListener will be called with a LogEntry object for the message that was logged.

Class Summary

Interfaces

`LogEntry`	The LogEntry interface provides the methods to access the information contained in an individual LogService log entry.
`LogListener`	The LogListener interface is used to subscribe to LogEntry objects from the LogReaderService.
`LogReaderService`	The LogReaderService provides methods to read LogEntry objects from the log.
`LogService`	The LogService provides methods for bundles to write messages to the log.

org.osgi.service.log
LogEntry

Syntax
```
public interface LogEntry
```

Description
The LogEntry interface provides the methods to access the information contained in an individual LogService log entry. A LogEntry may be acquired from the `LogReaderService.getLog()` method or by registering a `LogListener`.

Member Summary

Methods

public Bundle	`getBundle()` The bundle that created the LogEntry.
public Throwable	`getException()` The exception object associated with the LogEntry.
public int	`getLevel()` The severity level of the LogEntry.
public String	`getMessage()` The human readable message associated with the LogEntry.
public ServiceReference	`getServiceReference()` The ServiceReference for the service associated with the LogEntry.
public long	`getTime()` The value of `System.currentTimeMillis()` at the time the LogEntry was created.

Methods

getBundle()

```
public Bundle getBundle()
```

The bundle that created the LogEntry.

Returns: The bundle that created the LogEntry or `null` if no bundle is associated with the LogEntry.

getException()

```
public java.lang.Throwable getException()
```

The exception object associated with the LogEntry.

Returns: `Throwable` object of the exception associated with the LogEntry or `null` if no exception is associated.

getLevel()

```
public int getLevel()
```

The severity level of the LogEntry. This is one of the severity levels defined by `LogService`.

Returns: Severity level of the LogEntry.

See Also: `LogService.LOG_ERROR`, `LogService.LOG_WARNING`, `LogService.LOG_INFO`, `LogService.LOG_DEBUG`

getMessage()

```
public java.lang.String getMessage()
```

The human readable message associated with the LogEntry.

Returns: `String` containing the message associated with the LogEntry.

getServiceReference()

```
public ServiceReference getServiceReference()
```

The ServiceReference for the service associated with the LogEntry.

Returns: `ServiceReference` for the service associated with the LogEntry or `null` if no `ServiceReference` was provided.

getTime()

```
public long getTime()
```

The value of `System.currentTimeMillis()` at the time the LogEntry was created.

Returns: The system time in milliseconds when the LogEntry was created

org.osgi.service.log
LogListener

Syntax
`public interface LogListener extends java.util.EventListener`

All Superinterfaces:
java.util.EventListener

Description
The LogListener interface is used to subscribe to LogEntry objects from the LogReaderService. A LogListener object may be registered with the `LogReaderService` using the `LogReaderService.addLogListener(LogListener)` method. After the listener is registered, it will be called at the log method for each `LogEntry` created. The listener may be unregistered by calling the `LogReaderService.removeLogListener(LogListener)` method.

Member Summary

Methods

`public void logged(LogEntry)`
    Listener method called for each LogEntry created.

Methods

logged(LogEntry)

`public void logged(LogEntry entry)`

Listener method called for each LogEntry created. As with all event listeners, this method should return to its caller as soon as possible.

Parameters:
   entry—A `LogEntry` object containing log information.

See Also: `LogEntry`

org.osgi.service.log
LogReaderService

Syntax
`public interface LogReaderService`

Description
The LogReaderService provides methods to read LogEntry objects from the log. Two ways are provided to read `LogEntry` objects.

The primary way to receive LogEntry objects is to register a `LogListener` object which will be called at the `LogListener.logged(LogEntry)` method for each entry added to the log.

To receive past LogEntry objects, `getLog()` can be called which will return an Enumeration of all LogEntry objects in the log.

Member Summary

Methods

`public void`	`addLogListener(LogListener)`
	Subscribe to LogEntry objects.
`public Enumeration`	`getLog()`
	Returns an enumeration of all LogEntry objects in the log.
`public void`	`removeLogListener(LogListener)`
	Unsubscribe to LogEntry objects.

Methods

addLogListener(LogListener)

`public void addLogListener(LogListener listener)`

Subscribe to LogEntry objects. Registers a LogListener object with the LogReaderService. This object will be called at the `LogListener.logged(LogEntry)` method for each LogEntry placed into the log.

When a bundle which registers a LogListener is stopped or otherwise releases the LogReaderService, the LogReaderService must remove all the bundle's listeners.

Parameters:
> listener—A LogListener object to register to receive LogEntry object's.

getLog()

> public java.util.Enumeration **getLog**()

Returns an enumeration of all LogEntry objects in the log. Each element of the enumeration is a LogEntry object. The LogEntries will be ordered with the most recent entry first. Whether the enumeration is of all LogEntry objects since the LogService was started or some recent past is implementation specific. It is also implementation specific as to whether informational and debug LogEntry objects are included in the enumeration.

removeLogListener(LogListener)

> public void **removeLogListener**(LogListener listener)

Unsubscribe to LogEntry objects. Unregisters a LogListener object from the LogReaderService.

Parameters:
> listener—A LogListener object to unregister.

org.osgi.service.log
LogService

Syntax
`public interface LogService`

Description
The LogService provides methods for bundles to write messages to the log. Methods are provide to log messages with or without a ServiceDescription or an exception. Messages must be logged with a log level. The log levels have the following hierarchy:

1. `LOG_ERROR`
2. `LOG_WARNING`
3. `LOG_INFO`
4. `LOG_DEBUG`

Member Summary

Fields

`public static final LOG_DEBUG`
    A debugging message.

`public static final LOG_ERROR`
    An error message.

`public static final LOG_INFO`
    An informational message.

`public static final LOG_WARNING`
    A warning message.

Member Summary

Methods

    `public void log(int, String)`
        Log a message.

    `public void log(int, String, Throwable)`
        Log a message with an exception.

    `public void log(ServiceReference, int, String)`
        Log a message associated with a specific Service.

    `public void log(ServiceReference, int, String, Throwable)`
        Log a message with an exception associated with a specific Service.

Fields

LOG_DEBUG

`public static final int LOG_DEBUG`

A debugging message. Used for problem determination and may be meaningless to anyone but the developer.

LOG_ERROR

`public static final int LOG_ERROR`

An error message. The bundle or service may not be functional.

LOG_INFO

`public static final int LOG_INFO`

An informational message. This log entry may be the result of any change in the bundle or service and does not indicate a problem.

LOG_WARNING

`public static final int LOG_WARNING`

A warning message. The bundle or service is still functioning but may experience problems in the future because of the condition.

Methods

log(int, String)

```
public void log(int level, java.lang.String message)
```

Log a message. The ServiceDescription field and the Throwable field of the LogEntry will be set to null.

Parameters:
level—The severity of the message. (Should be one of the four predefined severities.)

message—Human readable string describing the condition.

log(int, String, Throwable)

```
public void log(int level, java.lang.String message,
        java.lang.Throwable exception)
```

Log a message with an exception. The ServiceDescription field of the LogEntry will be set to null.

Parameters:
level—The severity of the message. (Should be one of the four predefined severities.)

message—Human readable string describing the condition.

exception—The exception that reflects the condition.

log(ServiceReference, int, String)

```
public void log(ServiceReference sr, int level,
        java.lang.String message)
```

Log a message associated with a specific Service. The Throwable field of the LogEntry will be set to null.

Parameters:
sr—The ServiceReference of the service that this message is associated with.

level—The severity of the message. (Should be one of the four predefined severities.)

message—Human readable string describing the condition.

log(ServiceReference, int, String, Throwable)

```
public void log(ServiceReference sr, int level,
          java.lang.String message,
          java.lang.Throwable exception)
```

Log a message with an exception associated with a specific Service.

Parameters:

sr—The ServiceReference of the service that this message is associated with.

level—The severity of the message. (Should be one of the four predefined severities.)

message—Human readable string describing the condition.

exception—The exception that reflects the condition.

OSGi Service Gateway Specification
Copyright Information

Copyright © The Open Services Gateway Initiative (2000). All Rights Reserved. Implementation of certain elements of the Open Services Gateway Initiative (OSGI) Specification may be subject to third party intellectual property rights, including without limitation, patent rights (such a third party may or may not be a member of OSGi). OSGi is not responsible and shall not be held responsible in any manner for identifying or failing to identify any or all such third party intellectual property rights. This document and the information contained herein are provided on an "AS IS" basis and OSGI DISCLAIMS ALL WARRANTIES, EXPRESS OR IMPLIED, INCLUDING BUT NOT LIMITED TO ANY WARRANTY THAT THE USE OF THE INFORMATION HEREIN WILL NOT INFRINGE ANY RIGHTS AND ANY IMPLIED WARRANTIES OF MERCHANTABILITY OR FITNESS FOR A PARTICULAR PURPOSE. IN NO EVENT WILL OSGI BE LIABLE FOR ANY LOSS OF PROFITS, LOSS OF BUSINESS, LOSS OF USE OF DATA, INTERRUPTION OF BUSINESS, OR FOR DIRECT, INDIRECT, SPECIAL OR EXEMPLARY, INCIDENTAL, PUNITIVE OR CONSEQUENTIAL DAMAGES OF ANY KIND IN CONNECTION WITH THIS DOCUMENT OR THE INFORMATION CONTAINED HEREIN, EVEN IF ADVISED OF THE POSSIBILITY OF SUCH LOSS OR DAMAGE.

All Company, brand and product names may be trademarks that are the sole property of their respective owners. All rights reserved.

Permission to reprint the specification shall in no way imply any endorsement of this publication and its content by OSGi. Nor shall it imply any endorsement by OSGi of any vendors' implementation of the OSGi specification. OSGi encourages readers to visit its Web site, www.osgi.org, for updated versions of the specification.

Bibliography

[1] O'Driscoll, G. *The Essential Guide to Home Networking Technologies.* 2000. Englewood Cliffs, NJ: Prentice Hall PTR.

[2] Motorola Broadband Communications Sector. "Broadband Convergence." Search the product catalog for detailed specifications. Available at `http://www.gi.com/noflash/index.html`.

[3] Ericsson. "Ericsson Residential E-Services." 2000. Available at `http://www.ericsson.se/wireless/products/ebox/`.

[4] Gimein, M. "Sunspots: Excerpts from a Diary of a Networked Future." 1999. Salon.com. Available at `http://www.salon.com/tech/log/1999/11/18/sunspots`.

[5] Sun Microsystems, Inc. "PersonalJava™ Application Environment." 2000. Available at `http://java.sun.com/products/personaljava`.

[6] Sun Microsystems, Inc. "Connected Device Configuration (CDC) and the C Virtual Machine (CVM)." 2000. Available at `http://java.sun.com/products/cdc`.

[7] Sun Microsystems, Inc. "JSR-000046 J2ME Foundation Profile." 2000. Available at `http://java.sun.com/aboutJava/communityprocess/jsr/jsr_046_j2mefnd.html`.

[8] Sun Microsystems, Inc. "Java™ 2 Platform, Micro Edition (J2ME™ Platform)." 2001. Available at `http://java.sun.com/j2me`.

[9] Sun Microsystems, Inc. "Package Version Identification." 1998. Available at `http://java.sun.com/products/jdk/1.2/docs/guide/versioning/index.html`.

[10] Meyers, S. *Effective C++: 50 Specific Ways to Improve Your Programs and Designs, Second Edition.* 1998. Reading, MA: Addison-Wesley, p. 176.

[11] Bierce, A. *The Devil's Dictionary* (Albert and Charles Boni, Inc., 1911). Berkeley Digital Library SunSite. 1993. Available at `http://sunsite.berkeley.edu/Literature/Bierce/DevilsDictionary/`.

[12] Howes, T. "A String Representation of LDAP Search Filters." 1996. Available at `http://www.ietf.org/rfc/rfc1960.txt`.

[13] Borenstein, N. "A User Agent Configuration Mechanism for Multimedia Mail Format Information." 1993. Available at `http://www.ietf.org/rfc/rfc1524.txt`.

[14] Sun Microsystems, Inc. "JavaMail™ API." 2000. Available at `http://java.sun.com/products/javamail/index.html`.

[15] McLaughlin, L., et al. "Line Printer Daemon Protocol." 1990. Available at `http://www.ietf.org/rfc/rfc1179.txt`.

[16] Liang, S. *The Java™ Native Interface: Programmer's Guide and Specification*. 1999. Reading, MA: Addison-Wesley.

[17] Gosling, J., et al. *The Java™ Language Specification, Second Edition*. 2000. Boston, MA: Addison-Wesley. Available in HTML at `http://java.sun.com/docs/books/jls`.

[18] Freed, N., et al. "Multipurpose Internet Mail Extensions (MIME) Part One: Format of Internet Message Bodies." 1996. Available at `http://www.ietf.org/rfc/rfc2045.txt`.

[19] Freed, N., et al. "Multipurpose Internet Mail Extensions (MIME) Part Two: Media Types." 1996. Available at `http://www.ietf.org/rfc/rfc2046.txt`.

[20] Moore, K. "MIME (Multipurpose Internet Mail Extensions) Part Three: Message Header Extensions for Non-ASCII Text." 1996. Available at `http://www.ietf.org/rfc/rfc2047.txt`.

[21] Freed, N., et al. "Multipurpose Internet Mail Extensions (MIME) Part Four: Registration Procedures." 1996. Available at `http://www.ietf.org/rfc/rfc2048.txt`.

[22] Freed, N., et al. "Multipurpose Internet Mail Extensions (MIME) Part Five: Conformance Criteria and Samples." 1996. Available at `http://www.ietf.org/rfc/rfc2049.txt`.

[23] Franks, J., et al. "HTTP Authentication: Basic and Digest Access Authentication." 1999. Available at `http://www.ietf.org/rfc/rfc2617.txt`.

[24] Gong, L. *Inside Java™ 2 Platform Security: Architecture, API Design, and Implementation*. 1999. Reading, MA: Addison-Wesley

Index

Symbols
& (AND), 76, 77
* (asterisk), 77, 78
: (colon), 106
, (comma), 252
. (dot), 84, 88
! (NOT), 76, 77
/ (forward slash), 169
| (OR), 76, 77

Numbers
3Com, 25
10BaseT Ethernet, 4

A
accept method, 148, 150
AccessController class, 229
Actions, performing privileged, 238–245
Activator.java, 277–278, 283–284, 287, 296–297, 304, 309, 315–318
Activator(s). *See also* Bundle-Activator: header; BundleActivator interface
   basic description of, 31–32
   classes, 17–18, 109
   common mistakes related to, 105
   device access and, 201, 207–209
   nullifying references and, 156–157
   registering services in, 54–55
   service unregistration and, 120
   writing, 17
ACTIVE field, 337
ACTIVE state, 40, 262
addBundleListener method, 354
addFrameworkListener method, 355
addLogListener method, 432
addServiceListener method, 119, 355–356
Administration, permission-based. *See also* Administration, user
   APIs for, 261–264
   basic description of, 250–263
   code for, 297–319
   dynamic bundle resolution and, 251–252
Administration, user, 269. *See also* Administration, permission-based
admin.jar, 251, 253, 257
AdminPermission class, 227, 229, 237, 239, 331, 332–334
AdminPermission constructor, 333
AdminServlet.java, 305–309
ADSL (Asynchronous Digital Subscriber Line), 3
Algorithm(s)
   device management and, 404–405
   resolution, 258
   security and, 229, 241, 258
   sorting, 140
Alias(es)
   mapping, 169
   namespaces, 169–170
   parameters, 184
   registering, 171, 185
   syntax, 184–185

442 INDEX

Allied Business Intelligence, 2–3
AllPermission class, 234
American Standard Code for Information Interchange (ASCII). *See also* ASCII (American Standard Code for Information Interchange)
America Online (AOL), 25
ampersand (&), 77
APIs (application program interfaces). *See also* Interfaces
    Java Communications API, 187, 198–201, 205
    JavaMail API, 86–89, 137
    Java Servlet API, 170–171
    permissions required by, 230–231
Apple Computer, 195
Application(s)
    environment, new, 8–9
    logic, 120, 146
ASCII (American Standard Code for Information Interchange), 91
Assembly language, 189
Asterisk (*), 77, 78
Asynchronous Digital Subscriber Line (ADSL). *See also* ADSL (Asynchronous Digital Subscriber Line)
AT command, 213
attach method, 208, 212, 408–409
Auditing, 165
Authentication. *See also* Security
    basic, 178–184
    HTTP, 178–184
    performing, 181–184
    user administration and, 269
Authorization, 269. *See also* Authentication; Security

B

Base
    drivers, 193–194, 198–200
    URLs, 22
BasicPermission class, 229–231, 248
BasicSchemeHandler service, 178, 182–184
Bierce, Ambrose, 53
BlueTooth, 6, 7, 189
Browser(s)
    device access and, 218–220
    preferences, storing/retrieving, 268–269
    registering images and, 172–176
    security and, 238–245
Buffer size, 167
Bundle(s)
    basic description of, 16–18, 28–32, 325–326
    calling, 37, 61, 73
    commands for, 20–21, 22–23
    common mistakes related to, 105–106
    configuring, 269
    that contain native code, 96–105
    context, 33, 73
    cooperation among, 33–39, 107–129
    developing, 51–106, 271–278
    framework for, 32–33, 39–45
    help for, 20–21
    IDs, 19, 39, 262
    installing, 19–20, 39, 363–365
    JavaMail API and, 86–89
    life cycles of, 29–30, 32, 47, 146
    locations, 22, 44, 262
    the line printer daemon print service and, 89–95
    managing references among, 157–160
    multithread, 148–152
    permission-based administration and, 251–252
    phantom, 265–267
    removing, 265–267
    resolution of, 34, 251–252
    retrieving resources from within, 60–61
    running, 19–23
    service-providing, 37, 61, 66
    starting/stopping, 40, 45, 326, 343–345, 351
    state, 111
    transitive closure of, 251
    uninstalling, 45, 155, 158
    updating, 42–45
    writing, 51–56, 96–105
Bundle activator(s). *See also* Bundle-Activator: header; BundleActivator interface
    basic description of, 31–32
    classes, 17–18, 109
    common mistakes related to, 105
    device access and, 201, 207–209
    nullifying references and, 156–157
    registering services in, 54–55
    service unregistration and, 120
    writing, 17
Bundle-Activator: header, 105, 148, 326

INDEX 443

BundleActivator interface, 17, 41
  basic description of, 330, 350–351
  starting/stopping bundles and, 326
bundleChanged method, 375
Bundle-ClassPath: header, 84, 85, 88, 327
Bundle-ContactAddress: header, 261, 327
BundleContext interface, 40, 55, 62–63, 70, 73–80, 145, 218, 231, 263–264
  basic description of, 330, 352–358
  methods, 354–358
  service registry and, 143
Bundle-Description: header, 261, 327
Bundle-DocURL: header, 261, 327
BundleEvent event, 107, 128–129
BundleEvent class, 331, 369–372
BundleEvent constructor, 371
BundleException constructor, 374
BundleException interface, 373–374
BundleException exception, 331
Bundle interface, 231, 252, 261–263, 330, 335–349
BundleListener interface, 128–129, 330, 375
Bundle-Name: header, 261, 326
Bundle-NativeCode: header, 96, 97, 99, 329
bundles command, 20, 23, 56
Bundle-UpdatedLocation: header, 43, 327
Bundle-Vendor: header, 261, 326
Bundle-Version: header, 261, 326

C

C programming (high-level language), 10, 102, 105, 189
Cable modems. *See also* Modems
  data rates for, 6
  transforming, into residential gateways, 9
  usage statistics for, 2
Cable Television Laboratories, 6
cache directory, 21
Caching, 21, 69, 158
Cahners In-Stat, 2–3
Callback, 140–143, 159, 244
Cascading service registration, 123–125
CEBus, 2, 6, 7
Certificate(s). *See also* Security
  authorities, 226
  public keys in, 226
  self-signed, 243
CGI (Common Gateway Interface), 168

changeConfiguration method, 218
checkPermission method, 245, 246
Class(s). *See also* Classes (listed by name)
  compiling, 17–18
  encapsulation of, 228
  granting permissions to, 228
  inheritance, 228
  instantiation, 229
  loading issues, 64–65
  names, fully qualified, 64
  origin of, 226
  resolution, interbundle, 49
  signers of, 226
ClassCastException exception, 65
Classes (listed by name). *See also* Classes
  AccessController class, 229
  AdminPermission class, 227, 229, 237, 239, 331, 332–334
  AllPermission class, 234
  BasicPermission class, 248
  BasicPermissions class, 229–231
  BundleEvent class, 331, 369–372
  CodeSource class, 226, 228, 229
  Event class, 144–145
  FrameworkEvent class, 331
  HttpContext class, 416
  PackagePermission class, 227, 230, 331, 385–386
  ParameterServiceFactory class, 68
  ParameterStore class, 71, 128, 242–243
  Permission class, 226, 227
  Policy class, 227–228, 245
  PrintConnection class, 92–93
  Printer class, 93
  PrintService class, 93
  PrintServiceImpl class, 93
  ProtectionDomain class, 228, 229
  RealAudioPlayer class, 28
  SecureClassLoader class, 228, 229
  SerialServiceImpl class, 203
  ServerThread class, 149, 150–152
  ServiceEvent class, 331, 390
  ServicePermission class, 227, 229–230, 331, 396–397
  ServiceReference class, 40, 62, 78
  ServiceRegistration class, 55
  SweetHome class, 31
  Thread class, 152

Classes *(continued)*
    Vector class, 77
    WorkHourPermission class, 246–250
CLASSPATH environment variable, 17–18, 19, 30, 35, 49, 65, 82–83, 88, 132, 252, 256
clear method, 128–129
Clear To Send (CTS) pin, 202–203
Client bundles
    basic description of, 37, 61
    compiling, 65
    producing customized services for, 66–69
    security and, 236–237
CodeSource class, 226, 228, 229
Colon (:), 106
Comma (,), 252
Commands
    help for, 20–21
    summary of major, 22–23
Component-based design, 46–49, 133, 140
Configurable interface, 330, 376–377
Configuration
    of bundles, 269
    of devices, 191, 216–218
        management, 269
        of security, 232
        of services, 136
ContentTransformer, 142, 244–245
Content-Type: header, 178
Contracts, use of the term, 53
CPUs (central processing units), 4

D

DARPA (Defense Advanced Research Projects Agency), 1
Data types, 76
Debugging, 162. *See also* Errors
Defense Advanced Research Projects Agency (DARPA). *See also* DARPA (Defense Advanced Research Projects Agency)
Delegation, 140–143, 159
Dependency
    interbundle, 64–65
    package, 251–252
    resolution, 10
    service, 38–39, 41–42
    tree, for administrative bundles, 251–252
Design
    challenges facing, 132–133
    pitfalls and patterns, 131–160
    separating interfaces from implementation during, 131–140
    of services, 131–140
destroy method, 172
Device(s). *See also* Device access (DA); Device access services; Device managers
    detection, 191
    disconnecting, 214–216
    interfaces, data rates for, 6
    matching, confidence level for, 205
    reconfiguration, 191, 216–218
    refinement process, 190, 191
    security and, 260
Device access (DA). *See also* Device access services
    basic description of, 187–223
    code samples, 278–291
    driver locators and, 196
    driver services and, 193–195
    motivation for, 189–190
    software stack and, 187–189
    specification, 404–405
Device access services. *See also* Device access (DA)
    base drivers and, 198–200
    basic description of, 190–193
    device detection and, 200–205
    device refinement and, 205
    DriverLocator service and, 205–208
    Driver service and, 208–213
    disconnecting devices and, 214–216
    reconfiguring, 216–218
    writing, 198–218
DEVICE_CATEGORY property, 193, 203, 211
DEVICE_CLASS property, 193
Device interface, 191–193, 200–201, 405, 406–407
device.jar, 200, 222, 260
DEVICE_MAKE property, 193, 203
Device manager(s)
    algorithms, 404–405
    basic description of, 190, 196–197, 404
    downloading drivers with, 212
    driver locator services and, 211
    queries and, 195, 196–197
DEVICE_MODEL property, 193
DEVICE_REVISION property, 193

INDEX

DEVICE_SERIAL property, 193
DictionaryService interface, 56–60, 62–65
Digital cameras, 190. *See also* Devices
DigitalPlayer interface, 28
Digital Subscriber Line (DSL). *See also* DSL (Digital Subscriber Line)
Directories
  creating, 16
  docs directory, 17
  cache directory, 21
"Divide and conquer" strategy, 140
DLLs (Dynamic Linked Libraries), 104, 199
docs directory, 17
Documentation
  comments, 137–138
  importance of, 137–138
doGet method, 175, 176, 184
doPost method, 175
doPrivileged construct, 242–243, 245
dot (.), 84, 88
Driver(s). *See also* Devices
  base, 193–194
  basic description of, 193
  bundle IDs, 405
  IDs, 195, 196, 206–207, 211
  low-level, 189
  native, 189
  refinement, 194
  services, code samples for, 284–291
DriverImpl.java, 284–285
Driver interface, 405, 408–411
driver.jar, 208
DriverLocatorImpl.java, 281–282
DriverLocator interface, 196, 205–208, 405, 411–412
Driver service, 190, 195, 208–213
DSL (Digital Subscriber Line), 2
Dynamic Linked Libraries (DLLs). *See also* Dynamic Linked Libraries (DLLs)

E

Echelon, 2
Efficiency, increasing, 152
Einstein, Albert, 135
Energy companies, 13–14
equals method, 333–334, 386, 397
Ericsson, 3, 12
ERROR field, 379

Errors. *See also* Debugging
  asynchronous events and, 128–129
  authentication and, 178
  log services and, 162–163
Ethernet, 4, 5, 26, 189
Event(s)
  asynchronous, 112–113, 128–129
  cooperation with, 128–129
  handling, 107–111
  listeners, 107, 109–113, 117–119, 121, 128–129, 201–203
  framework, 107–113
  synchronous, 112–113
Event class, 144–145
EventListener interface, 144–145
Exceptions. *See also* Exceptions (listed by name)
  refusing services and, 127
  verifying services and, 114–115
Exceptions (listed by name). *See also* Exceptions
  BundleException exception, 331
  ClassCastException exception, 65
  getNestedException exception, 374
  InterruptedException exception, 152
  InvalidSyntaxException exception, 331, 382–383
  IOException exception, 127
  NamespaceException exception, 169, 416, 423–425
  NullPointerException exception, 114
  RuntimeException exception, 127
  SocketException exception, 150
Execution paths, branching, 121
EXPORT field, 385
Export-Package: header, 34, 36, 40, 49, 52, 55, 82–83, 132, 138, 262, 328
Export-Service: header, 261, 262, 328
exporting packages, 34–36, 230, 252. *See also* Export-Package: header

F

Facilitator code, 310–319
Facilitator.java, 310–315
FaxServiceFactory interface, 79
Fields
  ACTIVE field, 337
  ERROR field, 379
  EXPORT field, 385
  GET field, 396

446 INDEX

Fields *(continued)*
  IMPORT field, 385
  INSTALLED field, 337–338, 370
  LOG_DEBUG field, 162, 435
  LOG_ERROR field, 162, 435
  LOG_INFO field, 162, 435
  LOG_WARNING field, 162, 435
  MODIFIED field, 389
  REGISTERED field, 389
  REGISTER field, 396
  RESOLVED field, 338
  STARTED field, 370, 379
  STARTING field, 338
  STOPPED field, 370
  STOPPING field, 338
  UNINSTALLED field, 339, 371
  UNREGISTERING field, 389–390
  UPDATED field, 371
FilePermission, 241, 246
filesysinfo.dll, 96
File system services, 134–135
File Transfer Protocol (FTP), 136
Filter(s)
  arguments, 75–78
  parameters, 119
  service unregistration and, 119–120
findDrivers method, 196, 207, 211, 411–412
findExporters method, 256
FireWire, 6, 189
FontService, 123–126
Forward slash (/), 169
framework, the, 26
FrameworkEvent class, 331
FrameworkEvent event, 107–108, 128–129
FrameworkEvent interface, 378–380
FrameworkEvent constructor, 379–380
frameworkEvent method, 381
FrameworkListener interface, 330, 381
FTP (File Transfer Protocol), 136

G

Garbage collection, 156, 160
Gateway(s)
  hardware aspect of, 13–14
  operators, 14
getActions method, 386, 397
getAuthType method, 184
getBundleID method, 262, 339

getBundle method, 116, 263–264, 356–357, 371, 380, 399–400, 429–430
get command, 23
getConfigurationObject method, 376–377
getDataFile method, 70, 79–80, 357–358
getDefinition method, 59
GetDiskFreeSpace method, 103–104
getDiskOffset method, 134
getException method, 425, 430
GET field, 396
getFilter method, 383
getFreeSpace method, 100, 101
getHeaders method, 261–262, 339–340
getLevel method, 430
getLocation method, 262, 340–341
getLog method, 164–165, 433
getMessage method, 430
GET method, 175, 219
getMimeType method, 178–181, 417–418
getMissingPackages method, 253
getNestedException exception, 374
getNews method, 159, 244
getNewValue method, 203
getPort method, 200–201
getPropertyKeys method, 80, 400
getProperty method, 264, 358, 400
getReference method, 80–81, 401–402
getRegisteredServices method, 263, 341
getRemoteUser method, 184
getResourceAsStream method, 61
getResource method, 61, 179–181, 418
getResponse method, 184
getService method, 62, 65, 68–70, 78, 121, 157–158, 358–360, 391–392
getServiceReference method, 62–63, 75, 143, 360, 390, 430
getServiceReferences method, 75–78, 143, 360–363
getServicesInUse method, 263, 341–342
getState method, 262, 342
getStatus method, 93
getThread method, 155
getThrowable method, 380
getTime method, 430
getType method, 371–372, 380, 390
getUnsatisfiedBundles method, 253
GIF (Graphics Interchange Format) images, 61

H

handleSecurity method, 176, 178–181, 183–184, 243, 418–419
Hardware. *See also* Devices
hashCode method, 386–387, 398
Hash tables, 256
hasPermission method, 263, 342
HAVi (Home Audio Video Interoperability), 6, 7, 12, 218
Headers, 30–31, 55. *See also* Headers (listed by name)
    basic description of, 30–31, 326–329
    defining, 55
Headers (listed by name). *See also* Headers
    Bundle-Activator: header, 105, 148, 326
    Bundle-ClassPath: header, 84, 85, 88, 327
    Bundle-ContactAddress: header, 261, 327
    Bundle-Description: header, 261, 327
    Bundle-DocURL: header, 261, 327
    Bundle-Name: header, 261, 326
    Bundle-NativeCode: header, 96, 97, 99, 329
    Bundle-UpdatedLocation: header, 43, 327
    Bundle-Vendor: header, 261, 326
    Bundle-Version: header, 261, 326
    Content-Type: header, 178
    Export-Package: header, 34, 36, 40, 49, 52, 55, 82–83, 132, 138, 262, 328
    Export-Service: header, 261, 262, 328
    Import-Package: header, 34, 49, 62, 111, 139, 161–164, 252, 256, 259, 262, 328
    Import-Service: header, 261, 262
HelloServlet, 171, 175
help command, 22
Help, for bundles, 20–21
Home Audio Video Interoperability (HAVi). *See also* HAVi (Home Audio Video Interoperability)
home directory, 16
home.jar, 19, 44
Home Phoneline Network Alliance, 6
Home-Plug Powerline Alliance, 6
Home Radio Frequency Working Group, 6
HomeTheater service, 218
Host names, 184, 185
HTML (HyperText Markup Language), 28–29, 61
    device access and, 218, 219, 223
    embedding URLs in, 179

HttpService and, 169
news services and, 140
resource registration and, 172–176
servlet registration and, 172–176
HTTP (HyperText Transfer Protocol). *See also* HTTP services
    base URLs and, 22
    basic authentication, 178–184
    bundles, resolving, 251
    clients, 171, 172, 182, 184
    designing services and, 135–136
    device access and, 218, 222
    log services and, 165–168
    methods, 175
    request-response cycles, 176
    security and, 251, 260
HttpAdmin service, 185–186
HttpContext class, 416
HttpContext interface, 172–181, 243, 417–419
http.jar, 41–43, 222, 251, 257, 258
httppath.jar, 178
HTTPS, 178, 184, 185
HttpService interface, 40, 136–137, 168–176, 179, 416, 420–423
http.service package, 31, 35, 38, 41–45
HTTP services, 26, 168–170. *See also* HTTP (HyperText Transfer Protocol)
    alias namespace and, 169–170
    cooperating with, 33, 35
    HttpService API and, 168–171
HttpServletRequest, 184
HyperText Markup Language (HTML). *See also* HTML (HyperText Markup Language)
HyperText Transfer Protocol (HTTP). *See also* HTTP (HyperText Transfer Protocol)

I

IBM (International Business Machines), 12
IEEE (Institute of Electrical and Electronics Engineers), 4, 6, 195
iLink, 6
Images
    fetching, with HTTP clients, 172
    registering, 172–176
    resources, 172
IMAP, 136
implies method, 249, 250, 334, 387, 398

448 INDEX

IMPORT field, 385
Importing. *See also* Import-Package: header
    packages, 34–36, 40–41, 204, 230
    servlets, 170–171
Import-Package: header, 34, 49, 62, 111, 139, 161–164, 252, 256, 259, 262, 328
Import-Service: header, 261, 262
index.html, 179
Infrared Data Association, 6
init method, 118, 119
InputStream object, 160
Inside Java 2 Platform Security, 225
install command, 19, 22
installation
    of bundles, 19–20, 39, 363–365
    Java Embedded Server software, 15–16
installBundle method, 363–365
INSTALLED field, 337–338, 370
INSTALLED state, 39, 43, 262
Integer objects, 144
Interfaces. *See also* Interfaces (listed by name)
    designing, 131–140
    discussion of, among design teams, 139
    documenting, importance of, 137–138
    recommended approaches to, 133–139
    saving, as "spare parts," 132
    separating, from implementation, 131–140
Interfaces (listed by name). *See also* Interfaces
    BundleActivator interface, 17, 41, 326, 330, 350–351
    BundleContext interface, 40, 55, 62–63, 70, 73–80, 143, 145, 218, 231, 263–264, 330, 352–358
    BundleException interface, 373–374
    Bundle interface, 231, 252, 261–263, 330, 335–349
    BundleListener interface, 128–129, 330, 375
    Configurable interface, 330, 376–377
    Device interface, 191–193, 200–201, 405, 406–407
    DictionaryService interface, 56–60, 62–65
    DigitalPlayer interface, 28
    Driver interface, 405, 408–411
    DriverLocator interface, 196, 205–208, 405, 411–412
    EventListener interface, 144–145
    FaxServiceFactory interface, 79
    FrameworkEvent interface, 378–380
    FrameworkListener interface, 330, 381
    HttpContext interface, 172–181, 243, 417–419
    HttpService interface, 40, 136–137, 168–176, 179, 416, 420–423
    LogEntry interface, 164, 428, 429–430
    LogListener interface, 165, 428, 431–432
    LogReaderService interface, 161, 168, 234, 427–428, 432–433
    LogService interface, 136, 161–168, 428, 434–437
    PackagePermission interface, 384–387
    ParameterService interface, 66–69, 72, 129, 234–250
    PrintService interface, 74, 89–95, 119, 123–127, 138
    PrivilegedExceptionAction interface, 243
    SerialService interface, 200–209, 212–218, 278–284
    ServiceEvent interface, 116–117, 119, 127, 129, 388–390
    ServiceFactory interface, 68, 72, 330, 391–392
    ServiceListener interface, 121–123, 231, 330
    ServicePermission interface, 395–398
    ServiceReference interface, 38, 80–81, 209, 330, 399–400
    ServiceRegistration interface, 55, 72, 80–81, 330, 401–403
interrupt method, 152
InterruptedException exception, 152
InvalidSyntaxException constructor, 382–383
InvalidSyntaxException exception, 331, 382–383
IOException exception, 127
IP (Internet Protocol), 5, 184
isFromClasspath method, 256
ISPs (Internet Service Providers), 12, 13–14

J

JAAS (Java Authentication and Authorization Service), 269
JAF (Java Beans Activation Framework), 86, 88
JAR (Java archive) files. *See also* JAR files (listed by name)
    basic description of, 16
    bundles as, 28–29
    common mistakes related to, 106
    creating, 18, 58
    creating bundles and, 56

library bundles and, 83–84
naming, 58
nested, 84
signing/verification of, 243
JAR files (listed by name). *See also* JAR (Java archive) files
   admin.jar, 251, 253, 257
   device.jar, 200, 222, 260
   driver.jar, 208
   home.jar, 19, 44
   http.jar, 41–43, 222, 251, 257, 258
   httpath.jar, 178
   log.jar, 222
   mp3.jar, 40–45
   newdictionary.jar, 58–59
   param.jar, 251, 257
   serial.jar, 204, 211, 222
   servlet.jar, 170, 222, 257, 258
   thesaurus.jar, 84–85
jarsigner, 243
JavaBeans, 48
Java Communications API, 187, 198–201, 205
Java Development Kit (JDK), 15, 104–105
   dynamic permissions and, 267
   event handling and, 107
   security and, 232, 259, 267
javadoc, 137–138
Java Expert Group. *See also* OSGi Core Platform Expert Group
.java files
   Activator.java, 277–278, 283–284, 287, 296–297, 304, 309, 315–318
   AdminServlet.java, 305–309
   DriverImpl.java, 284–285
   DriverLocatorImpl.java, 281–282
   Facilitator.java, 310–315
   ModemService.java, 287–289
   ModemServiceImpl.java, 289–290
   ParameterAdminImpl.java, 300–301
   ParameterAdmin.java, 298
   ParameterServiceFactory.java, 299–300
   ParameterServiceImpl.java, 298–299
   ParameterStore.java, 301–304
   ParamService.java, 297–298
   PrintConnection.java, 274–277
   Printer.java, 272–273
   PrintServiceImpl.java, 273–274
   PrintService.java, 271–272
   SerialListener.java, 280–281
   SerialServiceImpl.java, 279–280
   SerialService.java, 278–279
   SerialServlet.java, 291–296
   SweetHome.java, 17
java_home, 232
java.io, 70, 135
java.lang, 74, 138, 155
Java Language Specification, 138
JavaMail API, 86–89, 137
Java Native Interface (JNI), 105, 187
Java Runtime Environment, 104
Java Servlet API, 170–171
java.util, 77
Java Virtual Machine, 9, 155, 160
   dynamic permissions and, 267
   security and, 226, 227–228, 267
   shutting down, 226
javax.comm package, 187
jes_policy, 232, 233, 234
Jini technology, 7, 189
JPEG (Joint Photographic Experts Group) images, 61. *See also* Images
Just-in-time delivery, 10
JVM (Java Virtual Machine). *See also* Java Virtual Machine

K

keytool, 243

L

LANs (local-area networks), 5
Laptop computers, 190
LDAP (Local Directory Access Protocol), 75–76, 119, 145
LD_LIBRARY_PATH environment variable, 105, 199
Library-based models, 46–48
Library bundles
   basic description of, 37
   constructing, 82–85
   designing, 139–140
Life cycle, of bundles, 29–30, 32, 47, 146
Line(s)
   adding extra new, at the end of the manifest, 106
   empty, 167
   length limits, 106

INDEX

Linux, 98. *See also* Platforms
loadDrivers method, 412
load method, 71
Log(s)
    entries, retrieving past, 428
    errors and, 427
    getting snapshots of, 164–165
    monitoring, 165
    phantom bundles and, 267
    requests, making, 326–448
    security and, 233–234, 239–245, 260
LOG_DEBUG field, 162, 435
LogEntry interface, 164, 428, 429–430
LOG_ERROR field, 162, 435
logged method, 431
LOG_INFO field, 162, 435
Login names, 162
log.jar, 222
LogListener interface, 165, 428, 431–432
log method, 163, 436–437
LogReaderService interface, 161, 168, 234, 427–428, 432–433
Log service, 26, 161–168. *See also* LogService interface
LogService interface, 136, 161–168, 428, 434–437
LOG_WARNING field, 162, 435
LonWorks (Echelon), 3, 6, 7

M

Macro management, 250
manifest command, 23
Manifest file. *See also* Manifest headers
    basic description of, 30–31
    code samples, 289, 284, 291, 297, 305, 309, 319
    common mistakes related to, 105
    defining, 16–17
Manifest headers, 30–31, 55. *See also* Manifest headers (listed by name)
    basic description of, 30–31, 326–329
    defining, 55
Manifest headers (listed by name). *See also* Manifest headers
    Bundle-Activator: header, 105, 148, 326
    Bundle-ClassPath: header, 84, 85, 88, 327
    Bundle-ContactAddress: header, 261, 327
    Bundle-Description: header, 261, 327
    Bundle-DocURL: header, 261, 327
    Bundle-Name: header, 261, 326
    Bundle-NativeCode: header, 96, 97, 99, 329
    Bundle-UpdatedLocation: header, 43, 327
    Bundle-Vendor: header, 261, 326
    Bundle-Version: header, 261, 326
    Content-Type: header, 178
    Export-Package: header, 34, 36, 40, 49, 52, 55, 82–83, 132, 138, 262, 328
    Export-Service: header, 261, 262, 328
    Import-Package: header, 34, 49, 62, 111, 139, 161–164, 252, 256, 259, 262, 328
    Import-Service: header, 261, 262
Marshalling protocols, 167
match method, 212, 409–410
MATCH_NONE, 209, 212, 406
MATCH_OK, 209, 212
Memory. *See also* RAM (random-access memory)
    buffer size, 167
    caching, 21, 69, 158
    cards, 190
    as a component of native platforms, 4
    flash, 4, 190
    log services and, 165, 167
    service objects and, 158
MemoServiceImpl, 120
Methods
    accept method, 148, 150
    addBundleListener method, 354
    addFrameworkListener method, 355
    addLogListener method, 432
    addServiceListener method, 119, 355–356
    attach method, 208, 212, 408–409
    bundleChanged method, 375
    changeConfiguration method, 218
    checkPermission method, 245, 246
    clear method, 128–129
    destroy method, 172
    doGet method, 175, 176, 184
    doPost method, 175
    equals method, 333–334, 386, 397
    findDrivers method, 196, 207, 211, 411–412
    findExporters method, 256
    frameworkEvent method, 381
    getActions method, 386, 397
    getAuthType method, 184
    getBundleID method, 262, 339

INDEX

getBundle method, 116, 263–264, 356–357, 371, 380, 399–400, 429–430
getConfigurationObject method, 376–377
getDataFile method, 70, 79–80, 357–358
getDefinition method, 59
GetDiskFreeSpace method, 103–104
getDiskOffset method, 134
getException method, 425, 430
getFilter method, 383
getFreeSpace method, 100, 101
getHeaders method, 261–262, 339–340
getLevel method, 430
getLocation method, 262, 340–341
getLog method, 164–165, 433
getMessage method, 430
GET method, 175, 219
getMimeType method, 178–181, 417–418
getMissingPackages method, 253
getNew method, 159
getNews method, 244
getNewValue method, 203
getPort method, 200–201
getPropertyKeys method, 80, 400
getProperty method, 264, 358, 400
getReference method, 80–81, 401–402
getRegisteredServices method, 263, 341
getRemoteUser method, 184
getResourceAsStream method, 61
getResource method, 61, 179–181, 418
getResponse method, 184
getService method, 62, 65, 68–70, 78, 121, 157–158, 358–360, 391–392
getServiceReference method, 62–63, 75, 143, 360, 390, 430
getServiceReferences method, 75–78, 143, 360–363
getServicesInUse method, 263, 341–342
getState method, 262, 342
getStatus method, 93
getThread method, 155
getThrowable method, 380
getTime method, 430
getType method, 371–372, 380, 390
getUnsatisfiedBundles method, 253
handleSecurity method, 176, 178–181, 183–184, 243, 418–419
hashCode method, 386–387, 398
hasPermission method, 263, 342
implies method, 249, 250, 334, 387, 398

init method, 118, 119
installBundle method, 363–365
interrupt method, 152
isFromClasspath method, 256
loadDrivers method, 412
load method, 71
logged method, 431
log method, 163, 436–437
match method, 212, 409–410
modemAccessed method, 214
newPermissionCollection method, 246, 249, 334
noDriverFound method, 218, 407
onPrinter method, 90
POST method, 175, 219
print method, 93
readFile method, 134
registerService method, 143, 231, 365–366
registerServlet method, 171, 421–422
removeBundleListener method, 366–367
removeFrameworkListener method, 367
removeLogListener method, 433
removeServiceListener method, 367
resolve method, 256
serialEvent method, 203
serviceChanged method, 120, 393–394
ServiceListener method, 393–394
setAttribute method, 184
setProperties method, 81, 402
start method, 17, 19, 37, 40, 54–55, 62, 146–148, 152, 157, 343–344, 351
stop method, 20, 27, 42, 147–148, 152, 157, 202, 344–345, 351
terminate method, 150
ungetService method, 63, 65, 70, 72, 78–79, 158, 159, 368, 392
uninstall method, 345–346
unregister method, 81, 172, 402–403, 422–423
update method, 347–349
Micro management, 250
MIME (Multipurpose Internet Mail Extension), 137, 176, 178, 181
modemAccessed method, 214
Modems, 193, 195. *See also* Cable modems; Devices
NULL, 198, 200–205, 214, 211
writing DA services and, 198–218
ModemService, 209–215, 284–291

452 INDEX

Methods *(continued)*
   ModemService.java, 287–289
   ModemServiceImpl, 211, 289–290
   ModemServiceImpl.java, 289–290
   MODIFIED field, 389
   Motivation, 25–26, 189–190
   Motorola, 4
MP3 files, 28–29, 33–34, 40–45
mp3.jar, 40–45
MSN (Microsoft Network), 25
Multihome machines, 184, 185

N

NamespaceException constructor, 425
NamespaceException exception, 169, 416, 423–425
newdictionary.jar, 58–59
newPermissionCollection method, 246, 249, 334
News services, 140–143, 159–160, 244
NewsService, 140–143, 159–160, 244
NICs (network interface card), 184
noDriverFound method, 218, 407
NULL modems, 198, 200–205, 214, 211
NullPointerException exception, 114
Null values, 114, 123, 155, 156, 159, 256.

O

Object(s)
   allocation, managing, 155–160
   references, managing, among bundles, 157–160
   references, nullifying, after use, 156–157
objectClass property, 77
Operating systems. *See also* Platforms
OR (|), 77
org.osgi.framework (OSGi Services Framework)
   basic description of, 73–81, 323–331
   concepts, 324
   conformance statement, 330
   event handling and, 107–111
   goals of, 323–324
   services, 325
   starting/stopping, 329–330
org.osgi.service.device (OSGi Device Access Specification), 404–405

org.osgi.service.http package (OSGi HttpService Specification), 413–416
org.osgi.service.log (OSGi LogService Specification), 426–428
OSGi (Open Services Gateway) consortium, 11–13, 193
OSGi Core Platform Expert Group, 265
OSGi Java Expert Group, 12–13

P

Package(s)
   dependency, 38–39, 251–252
   exporting, 34–36, 230, 252, 258, 260
   importing, 34–36, 230
   names, obtaining, 252
   phantom bundles and, 265–267
PackagePermission class, 227, 230, 331, 385–386
PackagePermission constructor, 385–386
PackagePermission interface, 384–387
Parallel ports, 6, 187, 190
ParallelService, 190–195
param.jar, 251, 257
ParameterAdminImpl.java, 300–301
ParameterAdmin.java, 298
ParameterAdmin service, 235–245
ParameterServiceFactory class, 68
ParameterServiceFactory.java, 299–300
ParameterServiceImpl.java, 298–299
ParameterService interface, 66–69, 72, 129, 234–250
ParameterStore class, 71, 128, 242–243
ParameterStore.java, 301–304
ParamService.java, 297–298
Parks Associates, 2–3
Parsing, 176, 178, 182, 252
Passwords, 178, 181–184. *See also* Security
PATH environment variable, 199
Performance analysis, 165
Permission-based administration. *See also* Permissions
   APIs for, 261–264
   basic description of, 250–263
   code for, 297–319
Permission-based security. *See also* Permissions
   basic description of, 225–231
   checking permissions, 235–238
   code for, 226, 297–319

creating your own permission types, 245–250
performing privileged actions and, 238–245
using permissions in services, 234–250
Permission class, 226, 227
PermissionCollection, 245
Permissions. *See also* Permission-based administration; Permission-based security
basic description of, 226–227
checking, 235–238
classes and, 226–227
dynamic, 267
granting, to classes, 228
required by framework APIs, 230–231
types of, creating your own, 245–250
using, in services, 234–250
PINs (personal identification numbers), 227
Platform(s). *See also specific platforms*
independence, 12
Linux, 98
Solaris, 9, 96–97, 100, 102, 105, 199
UNIX, 90, 105, 199
Windows, 9, 96–97, 102–105, 189
writing bundles and, 96–97
Plug-and-play, 189.
Policies. *See also* Security
basic description of, 227
enabling security and, 232–234
dynamic permissions and, 267
setting up, 232
use of the term, 227
Policy class, 227–228, 245
Policy object, 228, 267
POST method, 175, 219
Post-PC era, 2
Power lines, 6
PowerPacket, 6
Preferences, storing/retrieving, 268–269
PrintConnection class, 92–93
PrintConnection.java, 274–277
Printer class, 93
Printer.java, 272–273
Printer object, 90
Print services, 89–95, 116–127, 138, 163
cascading service registration and, 123–125
designing, 135, 138, 145
refusing service and, 125–127
PrintService class, 93

PrintService interface, 74, 89–95, 119, 123–127, 138
PrintServiceImpl class, 93
PrintServiceImpl.java, 273–274
PrintService.java, 271–272
Private
keys, 226, 243
modifiers, 157
PrivilegedExceptionAction interface, 243
Properties
contentTransformType property, 141
DEVICE_CATEGORY property, 193, 203, 211
DEVICE_CLASS property, 193
DEVICE_MAKE property, 193, 203
DEVICE_MODEL property, 193
DEVICE_REVISION property, 193
DEVICE_SERIAL property, 193
objectClass property, 77
PropertyPermission, 234
ProtectionDomain class, 228, 229
Public keys, 226, 243

R

Radio frequencies, 6
RAM (random-access memory). *See also* Memory
as a component of native platforms, 4
device access and, 190
flash, 4, 190
RealAudioPlayer class, 28
Recursion, 252
Refinement drivers, 194, 196
Refusal of service, 125–127
REGISTERED field, 389
REGISTER field, 396
registerService method, 143, 231, 365–366
registerServlet method, 171, 421–422
Relational operators, 76, 78
removeBundleListener method, 366–367
removeFrameworkListener method, 367
removeLogListener method, 433
removeServiceListener method, 367
Resolution algorithms, 258
RESOLVED field, 338
RESOLVED state, 40, 45, 262
resolve method, 256

INDEX

Resources, registering, 171–176, 178, 179–181, 414–416, 420–421
Revision numbers, 195
RMI (Remote Method Invocation), 7
Robustness, increasing, 152
Runnable object, 155
RuntimeException exception, 127

S

Salon.com, 8
SCSI (Small Computer Systems Interface), 6, 190
SDK (Software Development Kit), 15, 106, 227, 269
SecureClassLoader class, 228, 229
Security. *See also* Permissions; Policies
    configuration files, 232
    enabled, running the Java Embedded Server software with, 231–234
    enabling, 232–234
    logs and, 233–234, 239–245, 260
    managers, 29, 245
    passwords, 178, 181–184
    URLs and, 226, 239, 243, 256, 259
SecurityExtension, 229, 237, 244
sendChallenge, 184
serialEvent method, 203
serial.jar, 204, 211, 222
SerialListener, 203, 214–216
SerialListener.java, 280–281
SerialPort API, 201–202
SerialPortEventListener, 211
Serial ports, 187, 198–200, 211–214, 219
    data rates for, 6
    code for, 291–297
    Web interface to, 291–297
SerialService interface, 200–209, 212–218, 278–284
SerialServiceImpl class, 203
SerialServiceImpl.java, 279–280
SerialService.java, 278–279
SerialServlet.java, 291–296
Server(s)
    LogListener and, 165–168
    multithreaded, 148–152
    service bundles and, 116
    upgrades, 116
ServerSocket, 148–149
ServerThread class, 149, 150–152

Service(s). *See also* Service bundles; Services (listed by type)
    aggregators, 14
    basic description of, 2–5, 26, 27–28
    caches, 69
    carrying on without, 116–121
    cooperation among, 33–39
    customizing, 66–72
    designing, 131–140
    discovery, 10, 115–116
    implementing, 53–54
    objects, getting references to, 115–116
    obtaining, 37–38, 40–41, 61–65, 70
    picking alternative, 121–123
    publishing, 37
    refusing, 125–127
    registered, calling, 61–65
    registering, 37–38, 54–55, 111, 123–125
    registry, leveraging, 143–146
    releasing, 70
    resolution of, 40
    stale, 115–116
    standard, 161–186
    starting without, avoiding, 114–115
    unregistration, 114–127
    updates, 10
    use count, 65
    using permissions in, 234–250
    withdrawn, 38
Service bundles
    cooperation among, 107–129
    writing, 51–56
serviceChanged method, 120, 393–394
ServiceEvent class, 331, 390
ServiceEvent constructor, 390
ServiceEvent event, 108
ServiceEvent interface, 116–117, 119, 127, 129, 388–390
ServiceEventListener, 120–121
Service factories
    asynchronous events and, 128–129
    creating services with, 158–159
    instantiating, 158
ServiceFactory interface, 68, 72, 330, 391–392
Service interfaces
    designing, 52–53, 132–133
    implementations of, 56–60, 131–140
ServiceListener interface, 121–123, 231, 330

ServiceListener method, 393–394
ServiceMonitors, 117–118
ServicePermission class, 227, 229–230, 331, 396–397
ServicePermission interface, 395–398
ServiceReference class, 40, 62, 78
ServiceReference interface, 38, 80–81, 209, 330, 399–400
ServiceRegistration class, 55
ServiceRegistration interface, 55, 72, 80–81, 330, 401–403
Services (listed by type). *See also* Print services; Services
   BasicSchemeHandler service, 178, 182–184
   Driver service, 190, 195, 208–213
   file system services, 134–135
   FontService, 123–126
   HomeTheater service, 218
   HttpAdmin service, 185–186
   HTTP services, 26, 33, 35, 168–171, 184
   Log service, 26, 161–168
   ModemService, 209–215, 284–291
   NewsService, 140–143, 159–160, 244
   ParallelService, 190–195
   ParameterAdmin service, 235–245
   ZipDiskService, 190–195
services command, 23, 56, 59, 204
ServiceSpace architecture, 13
Servlet(s)
   HttpService API and, 168, 169
   importing, 170–171
   mapping HTTP requests to, 415
   parameter configuration, 305–310
   registering, 171–176, 179, 413–414, 421–422
ServletContext, 177–178
servlet.jar, 170, 222, 257, 258
Session object, 86
setAttribute method, 184
set command, 23, 148
setProperties method, 81, 402
Social aspect, of interface design, 139
SocketException exception, 150
Software stack, 187–189
Solaris, 9, 96–97, 100, 102, 105, 199. *See also* Platforms
Sony, 195
SSL (secure socket layer), 178
start command, 22

STARTED field, 370, 379
STARTING field, 338
STARTING state, 40, 262
start method, 17, 19, 37, 40, 54–55, 62, 146–148, 152, 157, 343–344, 351
statvfs call, 100
stop command, 22
stop method, 20, 27, 42, 147–148, 152, 157, 202, 344–345, 351
STOPPED field, 370
STOPPING field, 338
STOPPING state, 45, 262
SunOS, 96–97. *See also* Platforms
SweetHome class, 31
SweetHome.java, 17

T

T1 connections, 5
Tab character, 106
TCP/IP (Transmission Control Protocol/Internet Protocol), 90, 136, 148
   security and, 178, 256
   servers, writing, 148–149
Telephone lines, 6
telnet command, 257
terminate method, 150
thesaurus.jar, 84–85
Thread(s). *See also* Threading
   pools, using, 152–155
   preventing runaway, 146–148
Thread class, 152
Threading. *See also* Threads
   basic description of, 146–155
   security and, 241
   using thread pools, 152–155
   writing multithread server bundles, 148–152
throw_exception function, 102
TiVo service, 3
Transitive closure, 251

U

UDP (User Datagram Protocol), 135
ungetService method, 63, 65, 70, 72, 78–79, 158, 159, 368, 392
uninstall command, 22
UNINSTALLED field, 339, 371
UNINSTALLED state, 45
uninstall method, 345–346

unique IDs, 129
University of Cambridge, 1
UNIX, 90, 105, 199. *See also* Platforms
UNREGISTERING field, 389–390
unregister method, 81, 172, 402–403, 422–423. *See also* unregistration, of services
unregistration, of services, 114–127. *See also* unregister method
update command, 22
UPDATED field, 371
update method, 347–349
UPnP (Universal Plug and Play), 6, 7, 12, 189
URLs (Uniform Resource Locators), 59, 179–180
    accessing servlets with, 175
    backup, 167–168
    base, 22
    device access and, 207, 212
    embedding, in HTML, 179
    HttpService and, 169, 171
    logs and, 136, 167–168
    pointing to resources, 61
    print services and, 90, 135
    security and, 226, 239, 243, 256, 259
USB (Universal Serial Bus), 4, 26
    data rates for, 6
    device access and, 189, 190, 193
User administration, 269
Usernames, 178, 181–184
utils.h header file, 102

V

Vendor independence, 12
verifyMedia API, 135
Version specifications, 138–139
Visual C++ (Microsoft), 104

W

Web browser(s)
    device access and, 218–220
    registering images and, 172–176
    security and, 243
White board approach, 144
White space, 106
Wildcard characters, 77
win32com.dll, 199
Windows (Microsoft), 9, 96–97, 102–105, 189. *See also* Platforms
WorkHourPermission class, 246–250
Wrappers, 187

X

X10, 2
XCoffee, 1, 3
XML (eXtensible Markup Language), 7

Z

ZIP disks, 16, 190–195
ZipDiskService, 190–195

The Java™ Series

The Java™ Programming Language, Third Edition — Ken Arnold, James Gosling, David Holmes
ISBN 0-201-70433-1

Effective Java™ Programming Language Guide — Joshua Bloch
ISBN 0-201-31005-8

The Real-Time Specification for Java™ — Bollella, Gosling, Brosgol, Dibble, Furr, Hardin, Turnbull
ISBN 0-201-70323-8

The Java™ Tutorial, Third Edition: A Short Course on the Basics — Mary Campione, Kathy Walrath, Alison Huml
ISBN 0-201-70393-9

J2EE™ Technology in Practice: Building Business Applications with the Java™ 2 Platform, Enterprise Edition — Rick Cattell, Jim Inscore, Enterprise Partners
ISBN 0-201-74622-0

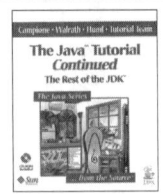

The Java™ Tutorial Continued: The Rest of the JDK™ — Campione, Walrath, Huml, Tutorial Team
ISBN 0-201-48558-3

The Java™ Developers Almanac 2000 — Patrick Chan
ISBN 0-201-43299-4

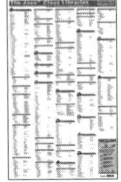

ISBN 0-201-75282-4

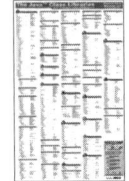

ISBN 0-201-75484-3

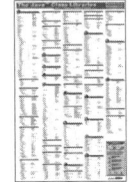

ISBN 0-201-71623-2

The Java™ Class Libraries, Second Edition, Volume 1: java.io, java.lang, java.math, java.net, java.text, java.util — Patrick Chan, Rosanna Lee, Douglas Kramer
ISBN 0-201-31002-3

The Java™ Class Libraries, Second Edition, Volume 2: java.applet, java.awt, java.beans — Patrick Chan, Rosanna Lee
ISBN 0-201-31003-1

The Java™ Class Libraries Second Edition, Volume 1: Supplement for the Java™ 2 Platform, Standard Edition, v1.2 — Patrick Chan, Rosanna Lee, Douglas Kramer
ISBN 0-201-48552-4

Programming Open Service Gateways with Java™ Embedded Server™ Technology — Kirk Chen, Li Gong
ISBN 0-201-71102-8

Java Card™ Technology for Smart Cards: Architecture and Programmer's Guide — Zhiqun Chen
ISBN 0-201-70329-7

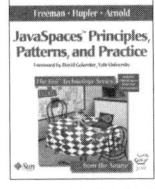

JavaSpaces™ Principles, Patterns, and Practice — Freeman, Hupfer, Arnold
ISBN 0-201-30955-6

Inside Java™ 2 Platform Security: Architecture, API Design, and Implementation — Li Gong
ISBN 0-201-31000-7

The Java™ Language Specification, Second Edition — James Gosling, Bill Joy, Guy Steele, Gilad Bracha
ISBN 0-201-31008-2

The Java™ FAQ — Jonni Kanerva
ISBN 0-201-63456-2

Designing Enterprise Applications with the Java™ 2 Platform, Enterprise Edition — Nicholas Kassem, Enterprise Team
ISBN 0-201-70277-0

Concurrent Programming in Java™, Second Edition: Design Principles and Patterns — Doug Lea
ISBN 0-201-31009-0

JNDI API Tutorial and Reference: Building Directory-Enabled Java™ Applications — Rosanna Lee, Scott Seligman
ISBN 0-201-70502-8

The Java™ Native Interface Programmer's Guide and Specification — Sheng Liang
ISBN 0-201-32577-2

The Java™ Virtual Machine Specification, Second Edition — Tim Lindholm, Frank Yellin
ISBN 0-201-43294-3

Applying Enterprise JavaBeans™: Component-Based Development for the J2EE™ Platform — Vlada Matena, Beth Stearns
ISBN 0-201-70267-3

Programming Wireless Devices with the Java™ 2 Platform, Micro Edition — Roger Riggs, Antero Taivalsaari, Mark VandenBrink
ISBN 0-201-74627-1

Java™ 2 Platform, Enterprise Edition: Platform and Component Specifications — Shannon, Hapner, Matena, Archbold, Freire, Stearns
ISBN 0-201-70456-0

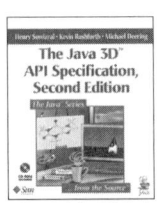

The Java 3D™ API Specification, Second Edition — Henry Sowizral, Kevin Rushforth, Michael Deering
ISBN 0-201-71041-2

The JFC Swing Tutorial: A Guide to Constructing GUIs — Kathy Walrath, Mary Campione
ISBN 0-201-43321-4

JDBC™ API Tutorial and Reference, Second Edition: Universal Data Access for the Java™ 2 Platform — White, Fisher, Cattell, Hamilton, Hapner
ISBN 0-201-43328-1

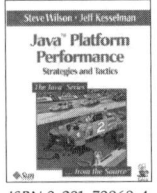

Java™ Platform Performance: Strategies and Tactics — Steve Wilson, Jeff Kesselman
ISBN 0-201-70969-4

The Jini™ Specifications, Second Edition — Edited by Ken Arnold
ISBN 0-201-72617-3

Please see our web site (http://www.awl.com/cseng/javaseries) for more information on these titles.

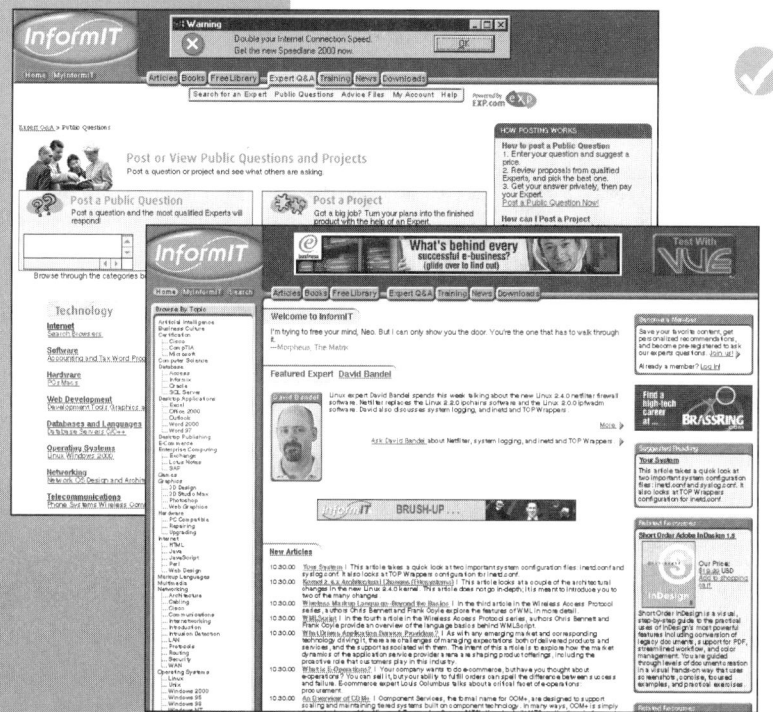

Register Your Book

at www.aw.com/cseng/register

You may be eligible to receive:
- Advance notice of forthcoming editions of the book
- Related book recommendations
- Chapter excerpts and supplements of forthcoming titles
- Information about special contests and promotions throughout the year
- Notices and reminders about author appearances, tradeshows, and online chats with special guests

Contact us

If you are interested in writing a book or reviewing manuscripts prior to publication, please write to us at:

Editorial Department
Addison-Wesley Professional
75 Arlington Street, Suite 300
Boston, MA 02116 USA
Email: AWPro@aw.com

Addison-Wesley

Visit us on the Web: http://www.aw.com/cseng